Nurture and Neglect

Nurture and Neglect: Childhood in Sixteenth-Century Northern England addresses a number of anomalies in the existing historiography surrounding the experience of children in urban and rural communities in sixteenth-century northern England. In contrast to much recent scholarship, which has focused on affective parent–child relationships, this study directly engages with the question of what sixteenth-century society actually constituted as nurture and neglect. Whilst many modern historians consider affection and love essential for nurture, contemporary ideas of good nurture were consistently framed in terms designed to instil obedience and deference to authority in the child, with the best environment in which to do this being the authoritative, patriarchal household.

Using ecclesiastical and secular legal records, hitherto an untapped resource for children's voices, to form its basis, this book tackles important omissions in the historiography, including the regional imbalance, which has largely ignored the north of England and generalised about the experiences of the whole of the country using only sources from the south, and the adult-centred nature of the debate, in which historians have typically portrayed the child as having little or no say in their own care and upbringing. *Nurture and Neglect* will be of particular interest to scholars studying the history of childhood and the social history of England in the sixteenth century.

Loretta Dolan is an honorary research fellow in the School of Humanities at the University of Western Australia (UWA). She recently completed a Ph.D. at UWA under the supervision of the late Professor Philippa Maddern and Dr Stephanie Tarbin, researching children and childrearing practices in the north of England, *c.* 1450–1603. She is the author of 'Child Marriage in Sixteenth-Century Northern England: The Emotional Undertones in the Legal Narratives', *Limina: A Journal of Historical and Cultural Studies*, 20.3 (2015) and the forthcoming 'Poverty, Pilfering and Pleadings: The Microeconomics of Parental Deprivation in Northern England c. 1485–1603'.

Nurture and Neglect
Childhood in Sixteenth-Century Northern England

Loretta Dolan

Routledge
Taylor & Francis Group

LONDON AND NEW YORK

First published 2017
by Routledge
2 Park Square, Milton Park, Abingdon, Oxon OX14 4RN

and by Routledge
605 Third Avenue, New York, NY 10017

First issued in paperback 2022

Routledge is an imprint of the Taylor & Francis Group, an informa business

Publisher's Note
The publisher has gone to great lengths to ensure the quality of this reprint but points out that some imperfections in the original copies may be apparent.

British Library Cataloguing in Publication Data
A catalogue record for this book is available from the British Library

Library of Congress Cataloging in Publication Data
Names: Dolan, Loretta, author.
Title: Nurture and neglect : childhood in sixteenth-century Northern England / Loretta Dolan.
Description: Abingdon, Oxon ; New York, NY : Routledge, 2017. | Includes bibliographical references and index.
Identifiers: LCCN 2016009868| ISBN 9781472470188 (hardback : alk. paper) | ISBN 9781315535692 (ebook)
Subjects: LCSH: Children--England--Social conditions--16th century. | Children--England--History--16th century. | Families--England--History--16th century.
Classification: LCC HQ792.G7 D65 2017 | DDC 305.23094209/031--dc23
LC record available at https://lccn.loc.gov/2016009868

ISBN: 978-1-03-240241-3 (pbk)
ISBN: 978-1-4724-7018-8 (hbk)
ISBN: 978-1-315-53569-2 (ebk)

DOI: 10.4324/9781315535692

Typeset in Times New Roman
by Taylor & Francis Books

Dedication: For my parents, James and Anna Alexander. In memory of Philippa Maddern, a truly inspirational teacher and supervisor.

Contents

Tables

Preface

This book started life as a Ph.D. thesis in 2010 under the supervision of Professor Philippa (Pip) Maddern and Dr Stephanie Tarbin at the University of Western Australia (UWA). To both supervisors, I am indebted not only for their expertise, enthusiasm and encouragement, but also their friendship. Sadly, Pip died before my thesis was returned from the examiners but I am always reminded of her cheerful countenance and willingness to debate aspects of sixteenth-century childhood with me as I read the pages in this book. Stephanie Tarbin remains a good friend and I am indebted to her for her ongoing advice in relation to the preparation of this book. In addition to Pip's and Stephanie's work, I have drawn on the works of many historians of childhood, as my footnotes indicate, and I have benefitted greatly from their insights.

The idea of studying children in late medieval and early modern northern England was in part due to my experience as a history undergraduate at the University of Chester and exposure to the wonderful archives that survive in the county and diocese repository in the city. My decision to expand the geographical area from Chester northwards and eastwards means that I am indebted to the hard-working staff at a number of archives – too many to mention – who provided much-needed assistance on my research trips to the UK. Those same research trips would not have been possible if it had not been for financial assistance from the School of Humanities at UWA, and the many, generous family and friends who considerately looked after me when I was in England. Thanks must also go to *Limina: A Journal of Historical and Cultural Studies*, where parts of Chapter 6 have previously been published.

Finally, I must acknowledge my family. I am grateful for the wholehearted support of my husband, Chris, and my children, Alasdair, Eloise and Georgina, who have embraced sixteenth-century childhood over the last four or five years, despite the disruption it has occasionally caused in their own household. And to my parents, James and Anna Alexander, both sadly deceased, I am forever indebted for my own nurturing childhood in twentieth-century northern England.

Loretta A. Dolan
Perth, Australia

Abbreviations

Ariès, *Centuries*	Ariès, Philippe, *Centuries of Childhood* (London: Jonathan Cape, 1962)
BIA	Borthwick Institute for Archives
CALSS	Cheshire Archives and Local Studies Services
CROK	Cumbria Record Office, Kendal
DCA	Durham Cathedral Archives
DNB	*Dictionary of National Biography* (Oxford, 2004), available online at www.oxforddnb.com
DUSC	Durham University Special Collections
EYLA	Explore York Libraries and Archives
LRO	Lancashire Record Office
LVRO	Liverpool Record Office
TNA	Kew, The National Archives

Introduction

> Yet the common sort of parents think that they have done their duty toward
> their children abundantly, if they keep them from fire and water, and from other
> dangers; if they cleanly apparel them; if they give them meat and drink
> enough.[1]

This book analyses childhood and childrearing practices and their effects on
children's life experiences in northern England, c. 1450–1603. The quote,
above, from Protestant reformer Thomas Becon, states that sixteenth-century
parents thought that they had exercised their duty to their children if they
protected them from danger, kept them clean and well-clothed and gave them
enough to eat and drink. Providing children with 'meate drinke clothe and
other necessities',[2] was not the sum of necessarily good nurture. Rather it was
the minimum expectation and, according to the Bible, those who did not
provide for their own families were 'worse than an infidel'.[3] While the Bible
stipulated that parents must provide for their children, Becon was concerned
that adults who had the care of children were content with the bare minimum
of support and were ignoring their spiritual and moral well-being. This contemporary view raises the question of exactly how notions of nurture and
neglect were conceptualised by adults during the period in question, and in
what ways these notions influenced childhood experiences of child marriage,
education, apprenticeship and parental deprivation.

Modern historical debate on childhood and childrearing has been in the
main precipitated by Philippe Ariès's seminal text, *Centuries of Childhood* and
his conclusion that 'there is no place for childhood in the medieval world'.[4]
Using paintings as part of his evidence, Ariès argued that they did not contain
any images of children, just of men painted on a smaller scale than adults.
This he says was not due to 'incompetence or incapacity' but reflected the
view that medieval painters had little interest in children and that childhood
was an ephemeral period unlikely to be remembered once it had passed.[5] Ariès
did use other evidence, including printed sources, but it was his use of pictorial
evidence that has attracted the greatest attention among historians. Adrian
Wilson's criticism of Ariès's methods was the assumption that art was a
mirror image of behaviour at a certain point in history, which, Wilson argues,

ignores the subjective nature of the artist's interpretation.[6] Barbara Hanawalt
regards Ariès's treatment of the sources as 'cavalier', unlike the historians of
earlier centuries who had been extremely diligent with their interpretations.[7]
But it is perhaps historians' misinterpretation of Ariès's findings that has
stimulated most debate. For Ariès, this lack of a concept of childhood did not
mean that children were neglected, or that any notion of childhood should be
confused with affection for them. Rather, it was the awareness of a notion of
childhood that Ariès said was lacking, not the affection in medieval society.[8]
The legacy of Ariès's research has formed itself into two overarching questions in
regards to childhood: was there a concept of childhood in the medieval period
and what were the emotional relationships between parents and children?

The existence of a concept of children in pre-industrial times has been rigor-
ously defended amongst historians. There are those like Colin Heywood who
argue that the concept of childhood was not absent but difficult to locate,
being 'loosely defined and sometimes disdained'.[9] Clearly there were biological
markers that defined a child as different to an adult, which, as Barbara
Hanawalt comments, cannot be bypassed by children from any social order.[10]
Thus, Shulamith Shahar demonstrates that there were thought to be separate
and very distinct stages of childhood, in relation to both the physical and
mental limitations of the child.[11] Parents were aware of these distinct stages of
development of children through their reading of literary material, medical
and scientific texts and, as Hanawalt indicates, 'ages of man' literature, commonly available as illustrations on church walls, in books and in stained glass
windows.[12] All the life stages were clearly illuminated with childhood and
adolescence visibly defined. Even those adults who had no access to texts or
to an aptly decorated church could observe markers of life-stages in their
community customs, laws and practices. This, as Jerome Kroll notes, could
have been through the community's relationship with the Church and the law:
the Church through the reference to children in chronicles and monastic rules,
and also in canon law on the valid ages of marriage; and the law through its
recognition of minority status and its attempts to protect the well-being and
property of children.[13] Childhood, however, is not an automatic, biological
state but is created through a number of interacting factors.

In addition to biological markers, childhood is brought into being by the
actions of society, which in late medieval and early modern England would
have been dictated by social and cultural conditions that differed across geographical locations.[14] In respect of all of these considerations, Nicholas
Orme's observation that childhood was a 'concept' both as a unique period of
life and as one divided into its individual stages[15] has implications for how we
go about analysing childrearing practices and their effects on children's
experiences. For although we can establish that parents were aware of a concept of childhood during the period under discussion in this study, there is, as
Hanawalt suggests, a paucity of sources that can establish how medieval (and
we can add early modern) parents regarded this concept in relation to the
responsibility they had towards their children.[16] The absence of such sources

in part suggests a lack of research into what parents and others thought was appropriate nurture of children. So it is with some apprehension that we must approach the second question generated by Ariès's thesis – what were the emotional relationships between parents and children?

The issue of emotional parenting in the scholarship has particular resonance for this study in regards to the notions of nurture and neglect. Historians' interest in emotional parenting is by and large invested in the parent–child relationship, with interpretations of these relationships usually falling into two distinct factions: 'domination or affection'.[17] Those that subscribe to the domination theory consider neglect of children in pre-modern times the usual method of childrearing. Children in pre-industrial society in this account were considered to be 'not terribly important'[18] or 'not uncommonly looked upon as a real burden' who often called forth resentment and hostility.[19] Certain historians are more vocal in their condemnation of the parenting skills of adults in past times. Lawrence Stone thought children in sixteenth-century England 'were neglected, brutally treated and even killed',[20] while Edward Shorter compares uncaring mothers of old to the caring ones of modernity, claiming that 'good mothering is an invention of modernization'.[21] Children are still neglected and badly treated today, just as neglectful mothers are not hard to locate in the national press, so it is not surprising that it happened in the past. The only difference is that in Stone's present-centred viewpoint neglect and abuse were the normative method of childrearing, whereas today they would be exceptional. This in turn imposes anachronistic notions of neglect on the period. For example, Lloyd DeMause is of the opinion that a great many children disciplined by their parents would be classified as 'battered children' today.[22] DeMause's argument fails to differentiate between the types of disciplining, the contexts in which the discipline was used and the pre-modern parent's motives for using them; nor does he consider the possibility that pre-modern adults may have distinguished between allowable and excessive beatings. Finally, he does not deliberate on how the use of such punishment may have been read by the children themselves. Pre-modern children could arguably have internalised their parents' notions of suitable correction, so that even if they did not like it, they would not have considered or understood it as abuse. As Richard Gelles notes, there is no 'universal standard' for the best way to raise a child and as values alter across culture and time the divisions between good and neglectful parenting become obscured.[23] Furthermore, the problem of positively identifying neglectful or abusive practices is extremely difficult because definitions that diagnose such behaviour almost without exception rely on value judgements.[24] The same argument can be applied to affection.

Ariès's work has precipitated an exceptional response to the issue of affective parenting. Historians including Barbara Hanawalt, Ralph Houlbrooke, Linda Pollock and Shulamith Shahar have maintained that, contrary to the domination theory, parents did genuinely care about their children in pre-modern England.[25] Claims have been made that new research in the decades following Ariès's work has established that parents held sentimental attachments to their children. Old research has been revisited that reinterprets practices that may appear detrimental to the child by modern standards as being believed best for the child at that time.[26] There is also the matter of the choice of groups studied in regards to Ariès's and his supporters' claims. Houlbrooke repudiates the notion that affective parent–child relationships only developed in later centuries as 'suspect', except in relation to certain small and overly studied groups.[27] Families, Houlbrooke concludes, were emotional, nurturing entities no matter what the century.[28] Houlbrooke's comments are revealing because they uncover the assumption that he regards affection and nurture as one and the same. Yet this imposes anachronistic notions of nurture during the period, just as those historians who subscribe to the domination theory impose anachronistic notions of neglect onto it. The moral here is for historians to be extremely careful not to make judgements on what constituted nurture or neglect based on their own set of values. The question raised for this study is, how did pre-modern adults understand and assess what was good nurture and bad nurture? This in turn raises questions about children's experiences.

The focus on parent–child relationships in the scholarship in recent years has concentrated very much on adults' perspectives and left little room for the experiences of children.[29] This may be because the main problem with assessing children's experiences, and even children's agency in their own upbringing, is that much of the literature is focused not on these experiences but on adult attitudes towards childhood. Adult attitudes are important but, as John Sommerville rightly states, it takes much refinement and conjecture to extract the experiences of children from adult opinion.[30] The reliance by historians on adult opinion is understandable. Goldberg comments that as children did not own land, pay taxes or bring court cases this has made them 'comparatively invisible' in the available historical records.[31] There are, of course, those who consider that it is difficult to say anything meaningful about the experiences of children because their pasts can only be derived from the discourse of adults,[32] but this is not the opinion shared in this book.

As a result of the adult-centred stance, children's experiences have been unduly neglected in history. True, there has been some groundbreaking work like that of Hanawalt, whose analysis of inquisitions post-mortem has identified the activity of children within households, but much of this scholarship is centred upon children outside England.[33] Karin Calvert's study of wealthy children in early modern America considers the experiences of children under seven in relation to the objects specifically designed for their use.[34] In more recent research specifically on England, Anthony Fletcher has explored the experiences of childhood in wealthy families in England from 1600 to 1914.[35] The child diaries that Fletcher bases part of his analysis upon are revealing in noting the power structures within households, the gendered upbringing of the children within them, and the relationships between the child, their parents and siblings. But whether these same interactions would have been replicated in all families regardless of status is open to question. The diaries reveal little about children's experiences before 1750, but the entries are unique as they record exceptional and emotional events in the children's lives.

Authors such as Orme and Keith Thomas, who, like Fletcher, have attempted to uncover the culture of childhood, have in the main revealed the experiences of adolescent boys.[36] Their findings do to some extent reflect the different ways in which children were socialised within society. Predominately male childhood experiences like schooling and apprenticeship were formal in nature and have left behind evidence of those experiences. Conversely, the socialisation processes for girls were much more informal and less likely to be remarked upon and thus not recorded. It is therefore essential that we not only uncover what pre-modern adults' notions of good and bad nurture were, but also ask what the effect of these notions was on both girls' and boys' experiences. For only then can we understand children's experiences in relation to the culture of the times.

Another problematic feature of the parent–child debate has been the concentration of scholarship on the nuclear family. Peter Laslett's work has identified that the typical Western family was nuclear in its composition, consisting of parents and their dependent children living in the same household.[37] Much of the scholarship on children then has been subsumed within research on the nuclear family. So, while studies like Heywood's are useful for providing a framework for how children should be looked after by parents within a single household, they are not so constructive for the experience of nurture of the individual child beyond the household because of their focus on parent–child relations.[38] Diverse households were common in England and the relationships formed by children with the wider kin group as well as other members of the household, like servants, were significant in children's lives. Sandra Cavallo has highlighted how wet nurses became nursemaids to the children they fed, and so became inextricably linked to the memory of the early years of childhood and the care children received.[39]

There has been some recent research that details the experiences of the child outside the nuclear family. Philippa Maddern has established that there was a vast assortment of household types in late medieval England through which children moved freely and where adults other than parents were the caregivers.[40] Maddern's research excepted, much of the recent scholarship on non-nuclear families does not deal with England or is on a later period. Bianca Premo's study of childhood in seventeenth-century Lima found that many of the city's children were reared and trained by diverse adults, but this was not necessarily within strictly nuclear, patriarchal families. Premo observed that this reflected a 'diverse urban universe of childrearing'.[41] Both Maddern's and Premo's findings offer different assumptions on childrearing than has been evident in previous scholarship and therefore it is incumbent on this study to ask: what sort of family and household contexts were responsible for raising children?

The final examination of the existing scholarship must concentrate on the continuity or change in childcare over the period of the Reformation, which occurred in the middle of the timescale under consideration in this study. To date, there has been a tendency for authors to write about the medieval or the post-1500 periods without examining the possible continuities and changes between the two. Houlbrooke's study is an exception noting both the continuity of parental attitudes towards children and the greater variety of models of upbringing in the sixteenth century, but his analysis is limited as his work focuses on the family and not solely on children.[42] For other historians who have considered the continuity and change between the two periods, the pre-Reformation period in their study has been comparatively short. Pollock, for example, stresses the continuity in childcare from 1500 to 1900, despite the massive technological and social developments.[43] In summing up her findings, she ponders why parental care is 'so curiously resistant to change'.[44] This is not a surprising outcome from a historian who assumes that parents always love and care for their children. Additionally, Pollock did not really employ much evidence from before 1600 so her study is not useful for detecting change over the course of the sixteenth century.

Underlying reasons are apparent for this lack of comparison between the pre- and post-Reformation periods. There is an acceptance by most historians that the Reformation changed European people in some way,[45] and that the religious changes impacted upon the family and thence on childhood.[46] Most notably, it resulted in an increase of Protestant groups committing their thoughts and beliefs on children to print. Stone thought that the Puritans had a 'compelling anxiety' to do this and the result was an increase in didactic literature pertaining to children and their upbringing.[47] This may explain, in part, Sommerville's view that the general interest in children in England began with the Puritans.[48] This fact in itself has raised the possibility of comparison with pre-Reformation practices. Margo Todd has noted striking similarities between didactic texts on children produced before the Reformation by humanists and advice offered by Puritan writers after the Reformation.[49] Further investigation is therefore required and this question must be asked: did notions and practices of nurture and neglect change over the period of the Reformation? This is important because culture determines how children are brought up. If cultural attitudes towards children change, so will the children's experiences.[50]

Trying to determine the experiences of children (or any subordinate group for that matter) is always going to be challenging, as sources relating to them are famously scarce. They rarely appear in autograph sources such as letters and diaries, written by adults or by children themselves, during the dates of this study, but there are extant sources that offer us sightings of children within their pages. It has been necessary for this study to locate documents where children appear as third parties and in which details of their everyday lives can be discerned. Most people in sixteenth-century England did not leave a written account of their experiences, but they did use both the ecclesiastical and secular courts to resolve many disputes encountered in day-to-day lives. People young enough to be considered children were sometimes called to depose, or provide testimony in court, which can provide us with a sense of what their worlds and experiences were. Maud Preece, for instance, was probably not much beyond the age of twelve when she was examined by a magistrate in Chester in 1599, and gave details of how she survived in the city by herself.[51] As a consequence, the narratives of childhood, parent–child relationships and the day-to-day experiences of children expressed by the adults – and in a few cases the children themselves – in legal records can be used to build a picture of children's experiences in their homes and places of instruction.[52]

Evidence for this book has been gathered using both ecclesiastical and secular court records: ecclesiastical depositions, Act Books, Chancery petitions, Quarter Session Records, House Books, Indexes of apprentice indentures, wills and didactic literature. Although complex in their nature, these sources permit access to unintentional information given by witnesses surrounding the legal causes, allowing us to construct an image of how children were cared for, and of their experiences. Moreover, they are not just descriptive in nature but convey the ways in which adults thought about children. As to how best to approach these sources, there is a great deal of capacity for interpreting the same source in entirely different ways in order to be relevant to a particular historical framework.[53] Charles Donahue believes that a quantitative approach must be taken when analysing sources like depositions to help historians 'avoid the fascination of the "interesting" case'.[54] Yet it is precisely these 'interesting cases' that this study is actively seeking. A quantitative methodology, however, will identify how many cases of a particular cause appear in the records and state what is normal within these cases by alerting the historian to the frequency of descriptions and phrases. This, of course, is the appeal for many historians who use this approach. Pat Hudson believes that quantitative data is invaluable for accessing information on ordinary people, particularly where the documentation relates to a large proportion of the populace.[55] But history underpinned by statistics makes for very dry reading. There is no understanding of the actual lived experiences of the children, which hitherto has depersonalised and thus devalued the lives of those involved. Furthermore, statistics can be misleading as they deal only with what has been recorded in official records. For example, if we consider that a large proportion of court cases did not progress beyond the citation to appear and thereby left no record in the legal system,[56] then divorces resulting from child marriage represent only a small fraction of the actual child marriages that took place. A quantitative studies analysis of the divorces from child marriage then will not greatly inform us about the child marriage as a whole. It is more productive, therefore, for this study to look at qualitative indicators in relation to what they meant to the experiences of the children involved, precisely because the detailed information, opinions and sentiments relating to the life of a child that are contained within narratives can never be conveniently reduced to a quantitative measurement.

Even allowing for the personal nature of narrative sources, we can still identify how bigger cultural themes present themselves in individual cases. As

Clifford Geertz considers, it is possible to locate wider arguments in confined spaces and it is through the intensive, qualitative research in such contexts that bigger themes emerge.[57] This has proved invaluable for this study in understanding such things as accepted levels of supervision for children or community responses to child marriage.[58] For unless we appreciate the cultural and societal norms of the communities we are studying we can never understand the significance of the recorded events in the lives of the children within those communities.

What we mean by 'children' requires careful definition, as many characterisations exist within sixteenth-century sources. The Church, in relation to ages of marriage, considered childhood to end with the onset of puberty, at definite ages of twelve for girls and fourteen for boys. Parents had differing ideas with some considering childhood to last until marriage and independence from the family.[59] Therefore, childhood in the historical sources extends beyond the earliest years.[60] The ages of children in this study (where it has been possible to establish an age) range from birth to teenage years and thus conform to the definition of childhood represented by the medieval authors of medical manuals and advice literature. The common scheme divided childhood into three stages: birth to seven years (*infantia*), early childhood – seven to twelve for girls, seven to fourteen for boys – (*pueritia*), and twelve or fourteen to adulthood.[61] There were other wide-ranging indicators of stages of life in the late medieval and early modern periods, as Maddern and Stephanie Tarbin argue. These could be observed in a number of contexts, using a variety of measures, including infancy and weaning; age of acquiring reason; age at entering the world of work; and age of transition to adulthood.[62] Recognition of these stages by adults was reflected in the testimony of people in relation to children. William Thakerary told Church officials that his niece, Isabella, was so young when she was married to John Wright in Yorkshire in 1532, that 'he hath byn oft tymes left in the housse to kepe her', thus assuming that the need for supervision could be taken as a measure of young childhood.[63] Similarly, Margaret Watmoughe was identified as being under the age of seven at her marriage to Richard Waterhouse in Halifax, Yorkshire in *c*. 1543 on the basis of speech development: she could not speak the words of matrimony.[64]

There were normative expectations of children in each age group but age in the sixteenth century was not necessarily definitive in structuring children's experiences. It was never the primary factor for children's participation in any activity and can never be separated from other factors that interacted with age, particularly wealth, status and gender. The children discussed in this study are not defined as one social class, but as part of the whole community that participated in everyday life in sixteenth-century northern English towns and villages. Inevitably, though, status (and indeed gender) would preclude some children from involvement in certain activities, while dictating their involvement in others. Childhood in this study is thus defined through the actual experiences of the child and also with regards to age, gender or status.

As the dates of this study (1450–1603) span two defined historical periods, late medieval and early modern, I have chosen to refer to this period as the sixteenth century. It is rather a 'long' sixteenth century, but referring to it as such is convenient shorthand for the longer period. Additionally, the time-frame for this book has been deliberately chosen to address one of the main questions of this study: did notions and practices of nurture and neglect change over the period of the Reformation? In this respect, it allows us to carry out a continuous analysis of childrearing practices without presuming the question of change at the Reformation.

The scholarship on childhood has so far largely ignored the north of England, concentrating instead mainly on the south. For this reason, the geographical area of this study has been chosen to allow for a representative sample of childhood experiences across sixteenth-century northern England, parts of which have been described at the time as being geographically remote, economically backward and thereby resistant to change.[65] The dioceses of Chester, Durham and York provide the ecclesiastical sources, which along with Carlisle and Sodor and Man constituted the archbishopric of York, the smaller and less densely populated northern half of the ecclesiastical domain of the Church in England. Although Chester did not become a diocese until 1541, belonging before this date to the diocese of Litchfield, consistory court records survive for the archdeaconry of Chester from 1529 and the judicial records were continuous.[66] The jurisdiction of the three dioceses has enabled this study to examine childhood experiences within a considerable expanse of the area corresponding to the modern-day counties of Cheshire, County Durham, Cumbria, Denbighshire, Lancashire, Merseyside, Yorkshire and Northumberland. Secular records originate, where available, from municipal record offices located in the major city within each diocese. Additional material has been obtained from the Lancashire Record Office, Liverpool Record Office, Court of Chancery for the counties of Cheshire, Durham and York and the occasional entry for Cheshire's neighbouring county Shropshire. Such an expanse of the region is required as there is a real need to study the widest possible range of northern sources due to the concentration of research on the south of England. As Clifford Geertz has concluded, you cannot locate national trends by just studying one small town.[67] It would therefore be unwise to generalise about the experiences of sixteenth-century children over the whole of England by only using sources from the south. However, what is found in the archives, as well as what is not found, indicates the individuality of the regions. Areas of England applied both the ecclesiastical and the secular law very differently within each jurisdiction, and this includes variations in what they did and did not record. Consequently, certain records can be plentiful in some areas and sparse in others.

The book begins by examining the ecclesiastical and secular legal records which form the basis for this study. Chapter 1 considers the language of the legal records, exploring the methods by which the sources can be read for children and the community norms towards the nurture of children. The second chapter discusses the normative discourses about childrearing with an emphasis on how sixteenth-century parents and adults represented notions of 'good nurture' in oral narratives and written texts. How did parents gain the knowledge to nurture their children? How were children defined within the community? Chapter 3 explores the under-researched issue of child marriage. Particular emphasis has been placed on the nurture the child received once married and the implications of underage marriage for the governance of the child once the marriage had taken place. The motivation of the family for marrying their children under age and the emotional responses and reactions of the child to the marriage will also be considered. Chapters 4 and 5 take an holistic view of the educational provisions in later childhood. Chapter 4 establishes the variety of accessible learning contexts: were these available for children from all social groups and gender? What was the availability of formal schooling and who were its intended participants? Chapter 5 outlines the system of apprenticeship from a child-centred perspective, articulating the expectations of the child in relation to nurturing and adequate instruction. The relationship between the apprentice and master is discussed in regards to concepts of social order and authority, and the effects of these concepts upon the child if the relationship deteriorated. Chapter 6 provides a framework for the main causes and common experiences of parental deprivation. It deliberates on such issues as, in the absence of parents, who was responsible for the nurture of the child? What were the costs involved in raising parentally deprived children? What expedients did both carers and children adopt to address these costs?

Significant gaps in the historiography to date have demonstrated there is a need for research into the care children received in sixteenth-century northern England, especially how notions of 'good nurture' impacted upon the experiences of the child. The contexts in which children were nurtured and by whom are equally important considerations because these may have affected the care the child received. Common discourse and practices of childrearing can be located in the legal records of both Church and state, social policy, and didactic texts of the sixteenth century, thus highlighting static and shifting attitudes towards children at the time. The relationship between adults and children, fundamental to any ordered society, can be observed within these mediums. So, although this book is primarily about the experiences of the child, the part that adults, Church and state played in these experiences is paramount to the type of nurture the child received.

Notes

1 Thomas Becon, *The Catechism of Thomas Becon, S. T. P. Chaplain to Archbishop Cranmer, Prebendary of Canterbury, &c. With Other Pieces Written by Him in the Reign of King Edward the Sixth* (ed.) John Ayre, vol. ii (Cambridge: Cambridge University Press, 1844), pp. 351–2.
2 BIA, Cause Papers, HC.CP.ND/2.

3 1 Timothy 5:8, *King James Bible*, available online at www.kingjamesbibleonline. org/1-Timothy-5. Accessed on 3 March 2014.

4 Ariès, *Centuries*, p. 33.

5 Ariès, *Centuries*, pp. 33–4.

6 Adrian Wilson, 'The History of the History of Childhood: An Appraisal of Philippe Ariès', *History and Theory*, 19 (1980), 132–54 (p. 140).

7 Barbara Hanawalt, 'Medievalists and the Study of Childhood', *Speculum*, 77 (2002), 440–60 (p. 441).

8 Ariès, *Centuries*, p. 128.

9 Colin Heywood, *History of Childhood: Children and Childhood in the West from Medieval to Modern Times* (Cambridge: Polity, 2001), p. 17.

10 Barbara Hanawalt, *The Ties That Bound: Peasant Families in Medieval England* (Oxford and New York: Oxford University Press, 1986), p. 187.

11 Shulamith Shahar, *Childhood in the Middle Ages* (London: Routledge, 1992), pp. 21–31.

12 Hanawalt, 'Study of Childhood', p. 443.

13 Jerome Kroll, 'The Concept of Childhood in the Middle Ages', *Journal of the History of Behavioural Sciences*, 13 (1977), 394–93.

14 Heywood, *History of Childhood*, p. 9.

15 Nicholas Orme, *Medieval Children* (New Haven, CT: Yale University Press, 2001), p. 7.

16 Hanawalt, *Ties That Bound*, p. 185.

17 Ilana Krausman Ben-Amos, 'Reciprocal Bonding: Parents and Their Offspring in Early Modern England', *Journal of Family History*, 25 (2000), 291–312 (p. 291).

18 M. J. Tucker, 'The Child as the Beginning and End: Fifteenth and Sixteenth Century English Childhood', in Lloyd DeMause (ed.), *History of Childhood* (New York: Harper & Row, 1975), pp. 229–57 (p. 229).

19 William L. Langer, 'Foreword', in DeMause (ed.), *History of Childhood*, pp. vii–viii (p. viii).

20 Lawrence Stone, *The Family, Sex and Marriage in England 1500–1800* (London: Weidenfeld and Nicolson, 1977), p. 99.

21 Edward Shorter, *Making of the Modern Family* (New York: Basic Books, 1975), pp. 168–204.

22 Lloyd DeMause, *Foundations of Psychohistory* (New York: Creative Roots, 1982), p. 46.

23 Richard J. Gelles, 'What to Learn from Cross-Cultural and Historical Research on Child Abuse and Neglect: an Overview', in Richard J. Gelles and Jane B. Lancaster (eds), *Child Abuse and Neglect: Biosocial Dimensions* (New York: Aldine de Gruyter, 1987), pp. 15–55 (p. 20).

24 Gelles, 'What to Learn', p. 20.

25 Barbara Hanawalt, 'Childrearing among the Lower Classes of Late Medieval England', *Journal of Interdisciplinary History*, 8 (1977), 1–22; Ralph Houlbrooke, *The English Family 1450–1700* (London and New York: Longman, 1984), pp. 127–56; Linda A. Pollock, *Forgotten Children: Parent-Child Relations from 1500 to 1900* (Cambridge, Cambridge University Press, 1983); Shahar, *Childhood in the Middle Ages*.

26 Hanawalt, 'Study of Childhood', p. 441; Heywood, *History of Childhood*, p. 42.

27 Houlbrooke, *English Family*, p. 254.

28 Houlbrooke, *English Family*, p. 254.

29 P. J. P. Goldberg, 'Childhood and Gender in Later Medieval England', *Viator*, 39 (2008), 249–62 (p. 249).

30 C. John Sommerville, *The Discovery of Childhood in Puritan England* (Athens: University of Georgia Press, 1992), p. 3.

31 Goldberg, 'Childhood and Gender', p. 249.

32 Ludmilla Jordanova, 'Children in History: Concepts of Nature and Society', in G. Scarre (ed.), *Children, Parents and Politics* (Cambridge: Cambridge University Press, 1989), pp. 3–24 (p. 6).
33 See Hanawalt, 'Childrearing among the Lower Classes'.
34 Karin Calvert, *Children in the House: The Material Culture of Early Childhood, 1600–1900* (Boston: Northeastern University Press, 1992).
35 Anthony Fletcher, *Growing Up In England: The Experience of Childhood 1600–1914* (New Haven, CT: Yale University Press, 2008).
36 Nicholas Orme, 'The Culture of Children in Medieval England', *Past & Present*, 148 (1995), 48–88; Keith Thomas, 'Children in Early Modern England', in G. Avery and J. Briggs (eds), *Children and their Books* (Oxford: Clarendon Press, 1989), pp. 35–77.
37 Peter Laslett, *Family Life and Illicit Love in Earlier Generations* (Cambridge: Cambridge University Press, 1983), p. 13.
38 See Heywood, *History of Childhood*.
39 Sandra Cavallo, 'Family Relationships', in Sandra Cavallo and Silvia Evangelisti (eds), *A Cultural History of Childhood and Family in the Early Modern Age* (Oxford and New York: Berg, 2010), pp. 15–32 (p. 30).
40 Philippa Maddern, 'Between Households: Children in Blended and Transitional Households in Late-Medieval England', *Journal of History of Childhood and Youth*, 3 (2010), 65–86.
41 Bianca Premo, *Children of the Father King: Youth, Authority, and Legal Minority in Colonial Lima* (Chapel Hill: University of North Carolina Press, 2005), p. 58.
42 Houlbrooke, *English Family*, pp. 155–6.
43 Pollock, *Forgotten Children*, pp. 267–8.
44 Pollock, *Forgotten Children*, p. 271.
45 Lyndal Roper, *Oedipus and the Devil: Witchcraft, Sexuality and Religion in Early Modern Europe* (London and New York: Routledge, 1994), p. 145.
46 Sandra Cavallo and Silvia Evangelisti, 'Introduction', in Cavallo and Evangelisti (eds), *Cultural History of Childhood and Family*, pp. 1–14 (p. 1).
47 Stone, *Family, Sex and Marriage*, p. 13.
48 Sommerville, *Discovery of Childhood*, p. 4.
49 Margo Todd, 'Humanists, Puritans and the Spiritualized Households', *Church History*, 49 (1980), 18–34.
50 Hanawalt, 'Study of Childhood', p. 458.
51 CALSS, Quarter Session Examinations, QSE 5/123. For further discussion on Maude Preece, see Chapter 6, pp. 204–5.
52 Premo, *Children of the Father King*, pp. 5–6.
53 Mary Fulbrook, *Historical Theory* (London and New York: Routledge, 2002), p. 98.
54 Donahue, 'Female Plaintiffs', p. 185.
55 Pat Hudson, *History by Numbers: An Introduction to Quantitative Approaches* (London: Arnold, 2000), pp. 6–7.
56 Houlbrooke, *Church Courts*, p. 40.
57 Clifford Geertz, *The Interpretations of Cultures: Selected Essays* (London: Fontana, 1993), pp. 22–3.
58 See Chapters 2 and 3 for discussion on these points.
59 Sommerville, *Discovery of Childhood*, p. 15.
60 Sommerville, *Discovery of Childhood*, p. 15.
61 Shahar, *Childhood in the Middle Ages*, pp. 21–31.
62 Philippa Maddern and Stephanie Tarbin, 'Life Cycle', in Cavallo and Evangelisti (eds), *Cultural History of Childhood and Family*, pp. 113–33.
63 BIA, Cause Papers, CP.G. 294.
64 BIA, CP.G. 619.

65 Christopher Haigh, *Reformation and Resistance in Tudor Lancashire* (Cambridge: Cambridge University Press, 1975).

66 C. Donahue (ed.), *The Records of the Medieval Ecclesiastical Courts: Reports of the Working Group on Church Court Records II: England* (Berlin: Dunker & Humblot, 1994).

67 Geertz, *Interpretations of Cultures*, pp. 21–2.

1 Interpreting the sources

> The history of a nation is not limited to the record of its public transactions, to its wars by sea and land, its battles and sieges, its treaties and alliances, its dynasties and revolutions ... the private and domestic life of the people pursues its steady course.[1]

Jeremy Black and Donald MacRaild have observed that many of the subjects historians would like to study most are the least well documented.[2] The subject of children in sixteenth-century England certainly confirms Black and MacRaild's observation due to their infrequent appearances in contemporary autograph sources such as letters and diaries. It is true that parents and others may have documented the lived experiences of some children,[3] but on the whole the majority of the country's minors are conspicuously absent from such records. As a consequence, historians have turned to records, in particular legal records, where children feature as 'other parties'. Few people in the sixteenth century left behind narratives of their lives, but there were a considerable number who used the ecclesiastical and secular courts to resolve many disputes arising from day-to-day living.

Historians have on the whole concluded that the history of children is always mediated through the voices of adults. Keith Thomas, for example, refers to the notion of children being a 'muted group' in history, a sentiment echoed by Willem Frijhoff, who asserts that 'adults speak for children'.[4] Ludmilla Jordanova develops this point of view further by claiming that there can never be a history of children separate from that of adults because 'there is no autonomous, separate voice of children in which a separate history could be rooted: their testimony is inevitably bound in with the world of adults, through which they learn their languages, mental habits, and patterns of behaviour'.[5] Admittedly, it is very rare to uncover a source individuals wrote by themselves when still a child but that does not mean that we do not hear the sound of children's voices. The historian just has to work harder at teasing out children's voices from those that mediate children's pasts, a process little different from writing the history of many other groups in society. There would be an insignificant historiography on the poor and illiterate if the only sources historians had at their disposal were those written by the subjects themselves. And, as is the case in all histories of civilisation, you will hear the voices of some children louder than others due to the nature of how the sources were recorded.

Turning our attention to what extant sources are available for this study, it should be observed that sixteenth-century English society was heavily influenced by the written and printed word regardless of class.[6] The expansion of record keeping in the fifteenth and sixteenth centuries by governments and civic bodies, aligned with the increase in printing, resulted in the plentiful survival of written records.[7] The skill of writing was generally associated with professional scribes and trained clerics, whose sphere of activity concerned business matters. Artisans and merchants would also have been literate enough to keep accounts, as indicated by an extract from the Brewers of London's First Book, which states in 1422 that henceforth all records were to be kept in English as 'many of our craft of Brewers have the knowledge of writing and reading in the said English idiom, but ... the Latin and French ... they do not in anywise understand'.[8] Even those who could not read the written word were privy to ideas and news through oral culture and tradition, giving them a degree of functional literacy. It is with this breadth of diversity in mind that I have approached the sample group of children for this book, defining them not by social class but as part of the whole community that participated in everyday life in sixteenth-century northern English towns and villages.

People in the sixteenth century would not have referred to themselves in the class divisions historians do today, but rather by the occupations of their neighbours, or the lands and tenements that they held.[9] Such practice is reflected, almost without exception, in all the sources used in this book. This is an important consideration as it allows us to perceive how ordinary people made sense of their worlds and how they compared themselves to their neighbours. Moreover, it enables us to avoid using anachronistic analysis of the sources by realising that people in the past did not think as we do today.[10] But how can we best discern the lived experience of children from legal records while avoiding the anachronistic pitfalls of interpreting children's history? It is imperative that this study is guided by the sources as to how childhood was defined in sixteenth-century northern England and the first step we must take is to appreciate the kinds of cases in which children appear, as well as the roles they occupied in the testimony. Such an appreciation will naturally shape the nature of the appearances of children the evidence offers us, and will influence how we assess the evidence.

Children regularly appeared in a number of legal sources but in the main these were limited to four distinct types of proceedings: suits relating to underage marriage (church courts); disputes over inheritance and wardships (Court of Chancery); disagreements over service contracts (Court of Chancery and Quarter Sessions); and maintenance in relation to illegitimate children (church courts and Quarter Sessions). They were also cited in items in Town or Mayors' Books. However, children were rarely called as witnesses in sixteenth-century court cases. Certainly, under canon law it was forbidden for a child below the age of puberty (twelve for girls, fourteen for boys) to act as a witness.[11] Additionally, in no circumstance could a child testify on behalf of one of their parents. The reasoning behind this decision reflected the belief not only that children did not have the discretion or reason to give testimony that would protect adult interests but also that allowing a child to speak in the courtroom would weaken adult authority.[12] The children included in this book did not appear as witnesses when children but did appear as litigants or witnesses when they were old enough to give legal testimony and thereby gave retrospective accounts of their childhood.[13] In addition, children appear as underage subjects of parental or adult concern and protection, and also as third parties casually mentioned in adult testimony.

It is important to remember when dealing with legal documents that the 'grammar of the law' is crucial to understanding the cultural implications of how the trial process operated.[14] Who was legally allowed to appear as witness and what was acceptable testimony, as well as the rules governing the creation of court documents all conspired to shape the narratives produced in the depositions. It is in acknowledgement of these considerations that the questions for this chapter have been developed. How did the legal process work and how was the evidence recorded? Was there a particular social composition to those who used the courts and was it different from that of the whole of society? How can we read the sources for evidence of the lived experiences of children? What can we deduce from the records about community norms in relation to children?

The use of legal documents is not a new phenomenon for historical research. F. W. Maitland, the English legal historian, observed that they were 'the best, often the only, evidence we have for social and economic history'.[15] Maitland may have been referring to the secular courts but, as Christopher Haigh has noted, the observation applies equally to records of the ecclesiastical court, whose influence over the behaviour of people during the period in question was equal to that of their temporal counterparts, if not greater.[16] As Ronald Marchant has indicated, the function church courts performed within sixteenth-century English society reflected the Bible's view of conflict resolution. Matthew 18:15–17 states that if the person who has sinned against you will not listen to reason from you or from others, then you must 'tell it to the church'.[17]

With such advice it is little wonder then that the church courts regulated the lives of parishioners in sixteenth-century England, and none more so, according to Ralph Houlbrooke, than that of the relations between men and women.[18] These relationships inevitably include sightings of children within the testimony. Houlbrooke's study of the church courts at Norwich and Winchester cautions us to not think of the matrimonial and sexual incontinence cases – which form a large proportion of the ecclesiastical sources used in this book – passing through the court as just statistics, because behind these statistics 'lies the sharp reality of misery'.[19] As to the documents produced from the church courts, there is a consensus among historians that the records are difficult to use,[20] yet Dorothy Owen states that the depositions which provide much of the evidence for this book are 'the most obviously attractive and accessible' of the church court records, useful for uncovering social customs and attitudes.[21] This is an essential element in regards to how children were treated within society.

Secular courts present their own problems of interpretation due to the diversity of the offences they investigated.[22] Esther Moir points out that offences presented at the Quarter Session court could include arson, rape, robbery, diverting a watercourse, killing a dog and forestalling.[23] As the institution moved into the sixteenth century and the administrative work of the Justice of the Peace increased, many of the records used in this book began to be produced, and thereby we can understand how these records reflect the prevailing orthodoxy towards children in the sixteenth century. Bertram Osborne outlines the Tudor schemes of control, whereby the varying statutes empowered the Justice of the Peace to bind poor children as apprentices without the consent of their parents.[24] Changing orthodoxies towards children are also present in municipal records where the jurisdiction of the Justice of the Peace overlapped with that of the Mayor. Lorraine Attreed has observed that Town Books (referred to as Mayor's Books or House Books in some cities) demonstrate how the law was implemented locally and the values society held at a certain point in history.[25] Unlike depositions or Chancery petitions, Town Books are records of the activities and responsibilities of the civic officials, the voice of authority and not the people. These records define how the local authorities looked upon the children within their jurisdiction.

W. J. Jones has produced one of the major works on the most important equity court of the sixteenth century, that of the Court of Chancery, whose records are used extensively throughout this thesis.[26] Along with the work of Timothy Haskett, Jones has elucidated on not only the process of the court, but also the way in which the petitions were written and by whom, which is crucial to the understanding of any information given about children, who were usually peripheral to the dispute.[27] Cordelia Beattie has taken the analysis of the procedure of the Court of Chancery further by synthesising the process with that of a case from the end of the fifteenth century.[28] Beattie at least had both the petition and the opponent's answer for her analysis. This study has only petitions to draw upon, but, as Beattie comments, the written documents were crucial in the dispute as appearing before the Chancellor, if it actually happened, was towards the end of the process.[29]

When it comes to interpreting legal sources, historians agree that evidence in such documents, derived from the word of litigants or witnesses, were narratives designed to tell a credible story to the court. Natalie Zemon Davis believes it is the way in which the narratives were shaped and created using certain words that form the centre of analysis for historical research.[30] According to Davis, we must consider how sixteenth-century people told stories, and especially how rules for certain documents would interact with the rules of explanation and description.[31] For, as Keith Thomas underlines, any contemporary narrative, regardless of its function, will have been 'structured and shaped' by the storytelling principles of the day.[32] This was certainly true for legal documents, whose purpose was defined by the courts. The witnesses would create narratives that they thought the court wanted to hear. Davis argues that these narratives would have been shaped as much by the prescriptions of the law as by cultural considerations.[33]

The narratives in these statements were also a reflection of what events were important to contemporaries; 'what events stuck in their minds'.[34] These, according to John Bedell, uncover a great deal of information on everyday life.[35] Bedell argues that it is the things that appear the most frequently in the statements that are important reference points in people's lives, commonly the births, deaths and marriages of their own family, in which children undoubtedly feature.[36] Regardless of the fact that the testimonies presented in court cases are essentially 'narratives of dispute', Laura Gowing believes them to have their own significance outside the courtroom as they demonstrate both the morals and judgements of the day and the rules of gender.[37] Furthermore, as will be discussed below, they reveal assumptions and community norms that speakers were probably quite unconscious of conveying. It is important to note, though, that the documents produced by the different courts influenced the type of information we can deduce about children's lived experiences and therefore it is essential to understand the legal process of each court.

Legal process

How did the legal process work and how was the evidence recorded? The answer to this question is divided into two parts: first for the ecclesiastical courts and second for the secular courts.

Ecclesiastical courts

The church courts were made up of a number of competing jurisdictions, with the diocese being the central unit of administration.[38] The bishop of each diocese had a paternalistic role towards his congregation and had two functions as far as the law was concerned: to correct those who had transgressed against the moral law (*ex officio* causes – which included illegitimacy) and to resolve disputes between parties by either making them come to an agreement or deciding in favour of one or the other (*instance* causes – which included child marriages). Every diocese had a consistory court officiated over by a judge, the bishop's official. The Consistory functioned as a court of appeal from the archdeaconries in the diocese as well as being courts of first instance. The issue of appeals is very relevant as some of the cause papers at York were assembled as part of an appeal process and as such are unusually full, complete and well-written sets of papers. Below the Consistory court, each archdeacon had a court, as did rural deans and minor clerics. Church courts of varying importance were also to be found in some monasteries.[39] The majority of the ecclesiastical evidence used in this study comes from the Consistory court, with a few from the Archdeaconry of Chester (pre-1541), one or two from the Court of High Commission and Dean and Chapter respectively.[40] Appeals from these lower courts would be directed to the bishop's court of audience. From there, appeals went to the archbishop's court, which for this study is the Provincial Court at York. The next and last court of appeal (up until the Reformation) was the Papal court at Rome.

The type of cause dictated the process of the court hearings and the documentation they produced. *Ex officio* causes came about as a result of a bishop's visitation or from being reported by a neighbour or court official and were initiated by the court itself not by the litigants. These included investigations of sexual immorality, which could include paternity and maintenance disputes. A citation was issued for the accused to appear before the judge. He or she may at that time produce evidence to counter the claim and, if accepted by the judge, be discharged. Alternatively, they could admit their guilt and were given penance accordingly. If on the other hand the accused contested the charge, they would be able to call upon the oaths of four, six or eight compurgators who were of similar age, sex and social standing as themselves.[41] *Ex officio* causes followed a summary procedure and a large number of them could be dealt with relatively quickly. The records they produced were mainly in the form of Act Books, recording the barest details of the cases and their progress. Conversely, *instance* causes followed a plenary procedure and were therefore more time-consuming and costly, but also rewarding for the historian in the number of documents produced by the process.

Like *ex officio* causes, *instance* causes began with a citation, only in such cases the citation was initiated by a request from the plaintiff to the registrar of the court for the defendant to answer the charges. The libel for the plaintiff – the written declaration of the dispute – was then produced, read in court and to it the defendant could make exceptions. The judge then decided if the cause could move forward and if so, the plaintiff's case was again set forth, whereupon the defendant denied its points. After this stage came the oaths of both parties before the libel was read once more, the witnesses named, cited, sworn and examined.[42]

The witnesses gave their evidence in response to the articles in the libel, which determined the questions asked of deponents and consequently the nature of the evidence recorded by the court with the witnesses' narrative was heavily structured by the libel. This process has significant ramifications for the reliability of witness statements recalling events – like child marriages – that happened some time in the past. It was not uncommon for these cases to take in excess of ten years to come before the ecclesiastical courts.[43] In theory, only two witnesses were required to settle most causes in ecclesiastical cases, but in reality more than two were produced to allow for all the articles of the libel to be addressed.[44] The deputy registrar recorded the depositions verbatim. Referred to as 'foul drafts', depositions were copied out before being read to the court and then signed by the witness and the registrar.[45] It should be noted that the language of the church courts was Latin and even evidence given *in vulgari* (English) was translated into Latin for the official record.[46] Although English started to be used regularly in depositions from about 1520, the legal forms were still recorded in Latin.

The witnesses could also be required to give answers to questions or inter-rogatories set by the opposing party's proctor and agreed upon by the judge. These questions were designed to elicit details that would have been of interest to the opposing party and to ascertain how the witness acquired the knowl-edge they were deposing.[47] Many of the depositions therefore repeat the same information and did not encourage superfluous information irrelevant to the questions. However, on occasion the first five questions were germane to all witnesses but the next three were only to be put to particular witnesses.[48] Regardless of the substance of the questions, all had to be relevant to the cause or matter.[49] Whilst the questions themselves provided the framework in which stories were elaborated, the witnesses and litigants created a narrative credible enough for the court to find in either the plaintiff's or the defendant's favour.

Ecclesiastical law, unlike common law, had the power to require certain actions to be taken by guilty parties, and for the diocese administration to receive confirmation that it had been done.[50] In addition to the depositions, these records provide evidence of who was providing nurture for children in disputed paternity and maintenance cases. Robert Wilson of Frosterley, County Durham, had been ruled to be the father of an illegitimate child and was ordered to take the child by the Archdeacon of Durham, John Pilikington. In a letter to the archdeacon in 1573, his sureties were keen that 'your worshippe shall vnderstande the truthe what his desertes hath bene towards the child' and to inform the archdeacon that 'he did take the child according vnto your comanndeements'.[51] This function of ecclesiastical law was never replicated within secular law, although some records generated by secular courts do allow us to access the living arrangements of children included in this study.

Secular courts

Secular justice operated on an urban, county and national level and, within each level, the responsibilities of the courts were clearly defined. In the geo-graphical area of this study, an additional stratum of jurisdiction existed in the form of the Palatinates of Chester, Lancaster and Durham but this did not affect the jurisdiction of the courts at a local level. Although the most abundant source of records concerning children generated by the secular courts comes from the Quarter Session records, it is worth mentioning the urban courts that were presided over by the mayor of each town. These courts would have dealt with presentments normally found in the Quarter Sessions before their estab-lishment. For example, the Chester Quarter Session court was not established until 1506. Recordings of these courts can be found in House Books, Mayor's Books or their equivalent.

Quarter Session court

Since the fourteenth century, Quarter Session courts were held in each county four times a year, at Easter (April), Midsummer (July), Michaelmas (October) and Epiphany (January). It was at these sessions that the most important routine duties of the Justices of the Peace were carried out.[52] In larger counties, the court did not always meet in the principal town of the county but moved around a progression of market towns. The Lancashire Quarter Sessions court moved around the major centres of Lancaster, Manchester, Preston, Ormskirk and Wigan within the month of the court meeting, whilst the sessions for the West Riding of Yorkshire sat in nine different towns.[53] The Justices were accompanied at each session by the High Sheriff or his deputy, coroner, high and petty constables, juries, witnesses and the accused.[54]

The purpose of the Quarter Sessions was not only to prosecute those who committed ordinary crimes; they also had the remit of correcting public nuisances. Landlords like Thomas Smith, whose house in the Linen Market in Chester was in danger of falling down 'to the danger of the lives of those which shall be vnder it', found themselves before the Justices alongside those who had stolen goods.[55] As the sixteenth century progressed, administrative duties resulting from various acts and statutes came to take up more of the Justices' time and precipitated many of the documents used in this book such as maintenance cases and apprentice disputes. Trial by jury was the main *modus operandi* for cases in the Quarter Session court, although in certain cases, where statutes indicated, specific authority was given to the Justices to hear cases without the jury.[56]

The records generated by Quarter Sessions varied in nature. Session roles or files were created for each session, which were strips of miscellaneous jottings strung together on parchment or a piece of string. Within this file lay many of the documents featured in this study: presentments – informal charges usually relating to 'nuisances' such as neglecting to repair roads or bridges, keeping disorderly alehouses and being absent from church; examinations of defendants or of witnesses (akin to depositions in ecclesiastical courts); recognisances – bonds to secure the appearance of the defendant or witnesses at the next session or to keep the peace; petitions, complaints, certificates and testimonial from individuals or by collective members of a parish.[57] Thus the Quarter Session records offer a valuable insight into grievances that affected the treatment of children including abandoned children, the necessity of families to petition for poor relief, disputed paternity and masters not teaching their apprentices a trade. Yet Quarter Session records also provide evidence of positive practices. On 3 May 1603, Chester Quarter Session recorded that a 'yearlie collection and allowance of the sum of 20s' was made for the education of a boy.[58]

Chancery courts

Chancery courts by mode of their execution were secular courts, although they provided a unique function within the legal system. The Court of Chancery was the court of the Lord Chancellor of England. The Lord Chancellor also held the office of archbishop or bishop, although it was in his secular capacity, and not through his ecclesiastical office, that he exercised power. Decisions made in the court were subject to natural justice in cases for which the common law either could not or would not provide an adequate outcome, or where the operations of the common law would have been unfair to one of the parties.[59] In order to petition Chancery, therefore, the petitioner had to conform to one or more of three prerequisites: they would not receive justice in a common law court due to the nature of their cause, they were too poor to pay for legal advice or their opponent was so well connected that the trial would be biased.[60] The court was one of equity and was based on a system of conscience as opposed to the inflexible rules of common law. Conscience, which is subjective and thereby fluid, contradicts the premise of law, which is to have determined rules.

Suits in the Court of Chancery required a written submission consisting of a statement of the circumstances upon which complainants based their claims, known as Chancery petitions, in addition to written evidence, which took the form of depositions much like those of the ecclesiastical courts. The petitions were formal in their nature and were not the verbatim words recorded in the ecclesiastical depositions. But, as with the depositions, they conformed to certain rules or 'a distinct canon of form'.[61] Yet, within the canon of form of the Chancery petition, the vernacular of the locality where the pleading originated may be identified.[62] It is for this reason that Timothy Haskett argues that scribes outside the Chancery composed Chancery petitions, with memoranda being written on the front of the document when brought in by the petitioner.[63] These pleadings provide the Court of Chancery evidence for this study, allowing for an alternative picture of adult behaviour towards children than that displayed in the ecclesiastical depositions. In addition, they elucidate the circumstances that brought the case before the court and the child's involvement in the same, thereby not concentrating on one particular event in a child's life.

Using the Chancery petitions is not without difficulty. The petitions are not directly dated, being addressed to the Chancellor but identified by the bishopric held by him and hence could have originated at any time during the tenure. Additionally, very few depositions or writs survive alongside the petitions, and, particularly for the early petitions, the defendant's answer or the plaintiff's replication rarely exist. All these, where they survive, tend to expand the stories considerably. Unfortunately, as it stands, the historian is prohibited from following the suit through its subsequent stages. It also means that we only hear one of the respective voices concerned in the dispute.[64] Nonetheless, the petitions draw attention to adult practices towards children in addition to lived experiences of the children and place them into a defined chronological period.

The workings of all courts provide a great number of documents for the historian, which reflect the expectations of its users, the social and cultural norms communicated through their narratives and, above all, the descriptions of lived experiences of children in their evidence. For it is through these qualities of the court records that we can at least start to catch glimpses of the lives of sixteenth-century children in northern England who appear in the disputes.

Social status of court users

Was there a distinct social composition to those who used the courts and was it different from that of the whole of society? This is an important question to answer at the beginning of this book, as social status tended to influence the childrearing practices parents employed. If we can ascertain the general social standing of the clientele of the courts, then we can infer the social status of the children in cases where explicit markers of status are absent.

The social structure of England was not consistently legally or fiscally defined in the sixteenth century, except the peerage and the knighthood at one end of the spectrum and those who received organised (and thus recorded) poor relief at the other.[65] For the majority of the population, social identity consisted of a number of factors and combinations, related to wealth, status, occupation, religion, educational opportunities, household composition and consumption, and was fluid in nature. Status could also be defined more by profession than by wealth. For example, it was probably common for a merchant to earn more money than a gentleman, but the position of his birth meant he would not have been regarded as gentle. Similarly, a poor curate may have earned little more than a labourer yet was considered socially closer to a gentleman.[66] To study the lives of children in the sixteenth century it is important to understand the contemporary ranking criteria of people. This is because children's experiences were influenced not only by their age but also by their status and gender. In order to obtain a more balanced expression of children's lives during the period, we must be conscious of both the commonalities and the divergences of their experiences and this will be reflected in the types of legal documents in which they appear.

Sharpe believes that it is extremely difficult to discern the social status of users of any court solely by referring to isolated legal documents.[67] Yet it becomes apparent when examining the data gathered for this study that people involved in the cases from the Quarter Sessions and Court of Chancery fall into two distinct social classes. Quarter Sessions record the maintenance battles and disputes of the poorest members of the community, like those relating to the parentally deprived children discussed in Chapter 6. The Court of Chancery, despite in theory being an avenue of justice for those who were unable to afford legal counsel, mainly provided redress for those disagreements involving land and money and, thereby, members of the community who were decidedly better placed socially than users of the Quarter Sessions. When we consider the ecclesiastical courts, however, there appears to be no such clearly defined demarcation.

The social status of people using the church courts varied. Although Helmholz has argued that the lowest and the highest strata of society would not have used the courts,[68] ecclesiastical justice was egalitarian in its nature. Scriptures prescribe the Christian duty to protect the poor from exploitation by the rich and one facet of this was the poor person's right to bring a case in the courts to defend themselves from such oppression by means of gratis legal advice and representation.[69] Depending upon how much the plaintiff was worth – a sum that was unique to each court – they could be admitted *in forma pauperis* and pay nothing for the legal service.[70] In reality, there was a limit to the number of cases each lawyer could take, and, due to the paucity of available documents citing that the church court paid the fees of poor people, we can never know how prevalent this practice was. What is clear is that a number of people of lowly status did bring suits in the church courts, particularly for defamation and sexual slander, and one must ask whether lawyers subsidised fees but did not record these actions.[71] This argument may be borne out by examples from the archives.

Jane Pringle brought a case against Ralph Bilborough, a fellow servant in the house of Henry Sawgeld and the putative father of her illegitimate child, at the church court at York in 1578. Sawgeld described Jane as 'a verie poore woman' and he stated that she had to sell all her clothing to pay for her child.[72] This was a woman who struggled financially to keep her child let alone pay legal fees. It could be possible that Jane considered taking out a citation for Ralph to appear in court would be enough to persuade him to pay maintenance for the child and thereby avoid the cost of a trial. Houlbrooke argues that a third or more of the suits introduced into the church courts in the sixteenth century progressed no further than the citation.[73] But, as this did not happen in Jane's case, someone who had a strong belief that ecclesiastical law would work in Jane's favour and therefore provide nurture for her child must have absorbed the costs. While it is apparent that poor people did make use of the church courts, were these cases more the exception than the norm?

In a study of the church court at York in the fourteenth century, Frederik Pedersen argues that people who used it were unrepresentative of the population of the northern province.[74] The greater the distance from York, the wealthier the litigant would be. In this aspect, Pedersen concurs with the findings of Charles Donahue.[75] In addition, Pedersen argues that only those poorer people who lived closer to York and near to decent roads feature in these archives. It would appear, however, that Pedersen has overlooked certain considerations, which Jeremy Goldberg believes would influence analysis of these cases.[76] York was a court of appeal for those cases that had already been heard in other parts of the province and, as Goldberg argues, one cannot expect a regular procession of cases to York from these regions as they had already been heard in the consistories or archdeaconries of their own diocese.[77] Further, Goldberg argues that it is precisely the fact that the people using the courts at York and their cases were so incongruent that illuminates the trends of broader society.[78] Thus, the people using the church courts in the fourteenth-century north of England came from various social levels and were representative of the majority of the population, with many using York on a local basis and only those close to York or appealing a case going directly to the higher court. The same could be argued for later centuries. Sharpe concludes that the people involved in defamation cases at York in the sixteenth century were of the 'rural middling sort', such as yeoman, artisans and shopkeepers, while witnesses were typically butchers, labourers or husbandmen.[79] Despite Sharpe's specific identification of the occupations of witnesses, Helmholz notes that in ecclesiastical law every person was deemed a suitable witness except for those of servile status unless proved otherwise.[80]

While it may be argued that specific courts had distinct clients ecclesiastical courts were the most inclusive in relation to their users. However, taken together, the litigation from all courts provides evidence from a broad section of society, albeit in relation to different causes. Correspondingly, despite the diversity in the records, there are some common approaches that can be taken to enable us to read the sources for children.

Reading the sources for children

How can we read the sources for evidence of the lived experiences of children? None of the sources used in this book, like most sources, were ever created with a view to them being used by future historians. Rather, they have emanated from the often-turbulent lives of individuals and communities.[81] Bearing this in mind alongside the disparate nature of the sources to be used, how should we begin to interpret the information in the extant records to give us the best possible chance of identifying the depictions of experiences of the children?

One important concept when it comes to narrative sources like depositions or Chancery petitions is that, essentially, they record collective memories of the events that brought the case to court. More importantly, they not only recount what has passed but contain implicit hopes for the future of the people concerned[82] and this has a particular resonance for children. They are also a valuable source of what people thought was acceptable behaviour of and towards children. The scholarship of Barbara Hanawalt has highlighted the normative supervision of children using coroners' rolls.[83] The rolls contain the events that led to the deaths of children, giving an indication of the level of supervision provided by the parents or babysitter in addition to the types of activities undertaken by the child. Although there are historians who doubt that such broad assumptions can be drawn from the small number of inquests that survive,[84] Hanawalt's research has highlighted the benefit of studying sources for reasons other than their original purpose. Witnesses told stories that they thought were normal: who was caring for the child and how they were being treated. Much of this information was unintentional either because the narrators were unaware of what messages they were conveying or because such detail was so obvious to them there was no need to hide it. This information was quite different to the evidence the witnesses knew the court wanted to hear and contained both offhand and throwaway remarks.

Offhand remarks about the places and confines in which events occurred can help the historian build a picture of the lifestyles and expectations of childhood. For example, many of the children discussed in the depositions in this study were sent away from their own home to that of a wet nurse, and their first experience of nurture came not from their own parents but from unrelated adults. John Somerforth of Astbury, Cheshire, was sent to stay with Elizabeth Parkinson and her husband John soon after his birth around 1548 and remained there for the first year of his life.[85] At times, we learn that this separation of mother and child did not take place immediately after the birth of the child but was brought about by a crisis in the family. Elizabeth Whyte of Clifton, York, was sent to John Cartwright's wife six months after her birth about 1550, two weeks after the death of her father.[86] But offhand comments can also show that not all parents who feature in the same type of documents employed the same practices such as wet-nursing their children. Robert West of High Hoyland, Yorkshire, born around 1542, was seen by his neighbour William Wordsworth to 'suke vpon his motheres brest'.[87]

Taking Robert West as an example, we can build upon the above remark to construct a picture of Robert's life by combining further offhand comments from the narratives with information the witness knew the court expected to hear. Thomas Crossley, another neighbour of Robert West's, stated that he had observed Robert at about one month old 'in a wenches armes', meaning that although Robert's mother fed him herself she was wealthy enough to pay for someone to help look after him. William Wordsworth had seen him 'lie in his cradle', and in that respect Robert was no different to other babies featuring in the depositions. Margaret Dickson, born in 1539 near Halifax, was seen 'lienge in the credle' by her neighbour.[88] Robert lived for the first two years of his life in the house next to William Wordsworth, in Penistone, Yorkshire, and then moved to High Hoyland. He was married at age seven to Elizabeth Beaumont, who came to live in his father's house, although his father sent Robert away to school. By the time he was sixteen, he was petitioning for divorce in the consistory court at York.[89] Using offhand remarks to fill in gaps not addressed by the official testimony from the witnesses can, in some cases, give an interesting account of a life of a child.

Throwaway remarks, on the other hand, give us an insight into values and attitudes so common that they are barely discussed elsewhere. These common assumptions can be just as informative about the lives of children as ones that directly reference childhood experience. So, when John Dawson testified to the church court in 1587 at Durham to the behaviour of the curate of Billingham church, he told them that he gave no warning to the church that he was bringing his child to be baptised. However, John was unhappy because the curate was absent and, along with the rest of the party, he had to wait from 8 a.m. until 2 p.m. before the curate turned up to baptise the child, despite it being a Sunday. Hence, we can deduce that not only was baptism an *ad hoc* affair, but there was an expectation that sixteenth-century parents would be able to have their child baptised whenever they pleased. As a side note, John Dawson had complained that the curate 'taried so long' he 'was forced to seke one new godfather'.[90] While baptism was an important ritual in a child's life, god-parents it seems, were dispensable and new ones could be found at short notice. This suggests that it was availability rather than particularity that at times informed parents' choices of suitable candidates.

As has been stated above, with a qualitative approach historians can map out bigger cultural themes by using individual narratives and one example of this is the mobility of children in the sixteenth century. Depositions in child marriage cases reveal not only the mobility after the wedding of the children married under age but also the composition of the family they lived in before they were married. Often, the children were living with grandparents, siblings and guardians or sometimes even with unrelated adults. Ten-year-old John Stackhouse of Slaidburn, Yorkshire, was living with James Rudde, a shoemaker, three months before his marriage to Isabel Swinglehurst in 1567 or 1568.[91] John's father had died when he was five or six but there is no indication that John had been apprenticed to James Rudde, as John went to live with Isabella's mother after the wedding. Nor does it appear that he was tabled with James Rudde in order to attend school as James described himself as a neighbour of John's father and mother.

What we have to ask is how John came to be living in James Rudde's household? The answer lies in the fact that much of the information we need to fully understand the depositions was implied as background knowledge.[92] It was obviously not important to James Rudde's story where John had lived between his father's death and going to live with Rudde, and this shaped the unintentional information he gave to the court. In some cases, however, we learn of a child's mobility precisely because the changing procession of nurturers was central to the litigation. A case in point was that of John Delavale, whose wardship was bought by Thomas Hopton of York from Henry VII in the latter part of his reign.[93] A petition to establish rightful custody of John Delavale highlighted that in the space of six years or less five people had been responsible for John's care and nurturing: his father, the king, Thomas Hopton, Thomas's widow, Anne, and Philip Dacre, whom Anne had married after Thomas's death. As the matter was in the Chancery court it would seem likely that the number of people involved in John's care would increase.

Narratives emanating from depositions and petitions are useful for locating local customs and practices as well as the social and cultural norms that related to communities in the sixteenth century.[94] For children may not have been the focal point of many of the court records, but the records are still a valuable source of information of children's lived experiences. The uninten-tional information given by witnesses as they describe the events surrounding the court cases construct an image of how children were fed, their sleeping arrangements, who looked after them and even how many households they may have lived in. But, importantly, the records reveal much more than just the descriptive elements of lives of children in the past. They convey the way people thought about the children within their community.

Community norms reflected in the sources

What can we deduce from the records about community norms in relation to children? Whilst court documents were not always reliable as factual descriptions of actual events, they were credible accounts of what happened. In this respect they were believed by their contemporaries and as such had their own significance both inside and outside the courtroom.[95] On occasion, witnesses presented hearsay as vital evidence,[96] which would be repeated in testimonies despite the possibility that the rumour might not be true. What is important here is not that people gave different versions of the same set of events, depending upon their motives and purposes of recounting the facts, but that their stories often converged despite the variations.[97]

John Browne of Prestbury, Lancashire, reported a story he had heard from one Margery Barlow to the ecclesiastical court at Chester in 1546. Margery had informed John Browne that she had had 'words' with Richard Falowes concerning the illegitimate child of Joan Astroft. Richard had wanted Margery to go to Joan's house and give her 6s. 8d. and tell Joan that she must father her child upon himself and not John Watson as John had 'goten ij bastardes afore'. If John's father found out about the baby, he would have been so displeased that he would have taken away John's tenement. However, despite Richard volunteering to be named the father, Margery was to inform Joan that, 'as sone [soon] as the noise was slaked', John would marry her.[98]

John Browne may have been repeating the words verbatim he heard from Margery Barlow, but there is nothing in his deposition to say whether he believed those words. Moreover, it is observable that the truth of who was the real father was camouflaged in the charade recounted inside the courtroom. Did it matter if John Browne thought that Margery Barlow was lying? The significance of his statement is that John communicated to the court – and anyone else who would read his statement – what he thought was best for the child. Rationally speaking, Joan would not have had to be bribed to name Richard as the father of her child if he really had been the father. However, the deposition gives no clue as to the status of Richard and how wealthy he may have been. John Watson, on the other hand, had a tenement, which translated into a regular income and therefore security for Joan and her baby. The child's future would have been all the more settled if, as Richard was reported as saying, John had married Joan once all the controversy over her pregnancy had died down. How Richard was going to extricate himself from the situation to allow the wedding to take place is almost unfathomable and this question presents itself as one of many flaws in the story. What is important in the telling of these events is not who the real father may have been, but the community sense of what was in the best interests of the child.

With so many people implicated in this narrative, there existed a tacit assumption that it was the community's responsibility to find long-term support for the child and that the responsibility of looking after the child did not stop with the parents. A letter (*c.* 1490) from William Whitaker, a neighbour of Sir Robert Plumpton, the head of the Yorkshire gentry family, reveals just such assumptions. William's female servant had become pregnant by one of Sir Robert's servants and according to William she had nurtured it for as long as she could despite the fact that 'she hath not a cloth to hir back'. William had kept the child 'of my owne proper cost' but was desirous of financial assistance from Sir Robert, for as it was his servant who was the father he had a responsibility to ensure the child was looked after.[99] If the father of the child could not pay for it, then the next authoritative male was culpable, even in the interim of establishing who was responsible long-term for the costs.

False accusations of fatherhood within the community surfaced regularly in the depositions. Beatrice Tailyer of Durham had been encouraged by her friends to name Rauff Appleby as the father of her illegitimate child to the archdeacon in 1575, although there were two other men who could have been the father.[100] Rauff implicated another man, Edward Hall, who failed compurgation and was motioned to take the child despite Beatrice denying that Edward had ever had carnal relations with her. Edward was not keen to take the child as it was 'great with wrongs', an indication that he was acutely aware of the level of nurture this child required. It was not clear who the father was but it was the responsibility of the court and the community to ensure that the child was looked after, and all the more so in this case as the child had obvious disabilities. It is possible that the compurgators manipulated their evidence by constructing their narratives to reflect what they thought would benefit the child.

Witnesses for Dionisia Wheldrake of Helmsley, Yorkshire, in her case against Richard Dobson at York in 1570, all testified to the fact that she was poor and without means. Richard, they told the court, had failed at his purgation to clear his name of being the father of Dionisia's child and yet he still would not admit openly to being the father. John Stocke, with whom Richard had stayed when he was apprenticed, said that Dionisia had come to his house to ask Richard to pay for her board, telling him that he was the father of the child with whom she was now pregnant. Richard answered by informing Dionisia that if she could prove that he was the father he would 'do as a man ought to do' but, if not, he would 'vtterlie denye' that he was the father.[101] John Stocke added that he had heard that Richard was 'well able to lyve', implying that he had plenty of money to support the child, which was in contrast to Dionisia's poverty. Not only did John indicate to the court there was a possibility that Richard may be the father, but also that he was more than able to pay for the child.

It is interesting that in his comments John Stocke implied that, although trying to extricate himself from the responsibilities of fatherhood, Richard was aware of what the community expected him to do in relation to the child. What 'a man ought to do', although an offhand remark, assumes that the father of an illegitimate child was normatively expected to take financial responsibility for the nurturing of the child. This belief was enshrined in legislation six years after this case by the statute 18 Elizabeth I, c 3, which established regulations for maintaining illegitimate children.[102]

It was not just the welfare of children in the community that can be detected in the sources but also the expectations of how those children were supposed to behave. At Easter 1520, the civic authorities in York stated that no parents living in the city and the suburbs should 'suffrer ther children to go with clappers vppon shere thursday and good friday'.[103] If parents did not stop their children from running with the clappers, then they had to forfeit to the chamber of the mayor. As it was only the under-clerk or the chief clerk who was permitted to carry out the operation to summon people to Mass, the children were trespassing on the prerogatives of the city officials. It would be fair to assume that it was not the act of the children using the clappers per se to which the authorities objected, but the great noise they made in the process that parents encouraged by allowing them to do it. Children were to be seen and not heard.

Sources establish the fact that communities in sixteenth-century northern England had commonly held notions in relation to children: who should take responsibility for them, what care they were entitled to and who should control their behaviour. In this respect, the welfare of the child was as much a concern of the community as it was of the parents. In the case of illegitimate children, the community was concerned to produce the best outcome for the both the mother and, the child without disrupting any hierarchal structure. If the father could not pay for his child, then the community was prepared for the next authoritative male in the family or household in which the mother or father lived to meet that cost.

Conclusion

When reconstructing children's lives in sixteenth-century northern England using legal sources there are a number of salient points to note. Unquestionably, the use of documents produced for an entirely different purpose is not without its difficulties. The historian must understand the reasons behind the creation of those sources and all factors that influenced the information given, regardless of its honesty.[104] Any evidence given to the court would have been carefully rehearsed and, in some cases, the evidence masked or written in a particular way to achieve a number of objectives.

One must also bear in mind that witnesses can only recount what they have seen or been told, ignoring large parts of the story.[105] But this does not mean that we cannot build upon the narratives they give along with any unintentional information, to observe *in situ* the social and cultural customs and mores to create an image of the contexts in which children lived. Correspondingly, the information can be used to identify common assumptions about childhood and the responsibilities of adults in relation to children. Such meaningful insights are of particular significance if they are not restricted to one single group of children within the community. It is fortunate, therefore, that the sources in this study are not limited to any distinctive social class. Especially in relation to ecclesiastical jurisdiction, the sources are representative of broader society covering the majority of the dealings of everyday life. The plaintiffs, defendants and witnesses who attended the church courts all reflect the social make-up of a broader community and thus their testimonies refer to children from across all social classes.

While the extant records available to this book are a fertile source for exploring the parent–child relationship, what the records ultimately show about childrearing is that there existed a wider responsibility for the child. The narratives recited in court reveal the nurture children received from their parents and carers, who was caring for the children and what forms the nurture took. Also couched within these narratives are examples of community and civic responsibility for the children resident within their boundaries. Witnesses were not against standing up in court and giving or repeating information that might not have been totally accurate to ensure the best outcome for the child. Community norms of how parents and adults should act towards children were concealed within casual remarks given in the narratives of witnesses, while civic authorities lectured parents on the expected level of behaviour of their children.

Even if these narratives are only part of the bigger picture of childhood, it is by synthesising information from a wide range of documents that we can form a clearer picture of children in the past. In addition, it is in the legal system and its documents that shifting attitudes towards children and changing childrearing practices can be located even if the law remained static.[106] For it is by uncovering the attitudes towards children and approaches to childrearing in sixteenth-century northern England that we can translate them into the lived experiences of the child. True, that 'child' remains muted to some extent but we can in part relive their childhood and uncover their voices through retrospective accounts in witness statements, examinations and all the other documents that provide a social, economic and political commentary on children's lives.

Notes

1 K. R. Burns, *The Administrative System of the Ecclesiastical Courts in the Diocese and Province of York: The Medieval Courts* (York: Leverhulme Research Scheme, 1952), Preface.

2 Jeremy Black and Donald D. MacRaild, *Studying History* (Houndmills, Basingstoke: Palgrave, 2000), p. 13.

3 See Ralph Houlbrooke (ed.), *English Family Life, 1576–1716: An Anthology from Diaries* (Oxford: Basil Blackwell, 1988).

4 Keith Thomas, 'Children in Early Modern England', in G. Avery and J. Briggs (eds), *Children and their Books* (Oxford: Clarendon Press, 1989), pp. 35–77 (p. 47); Willem Frijhoff, 'Historian's Discovery of Childhood', *Paedagogica Historica: International Journal of the History of Education*, 48 (2012), 11–29 (p. 12).

5 Ludmilla Jordanova, 'New Worlds for Children in the Eighteenth Century: Problems of Historical Interpretation', *History of the Human Sciences*, 3 (1990), 69–83 (pp. 78–79).

6   Adam Fox, *Oral Literate Culture in England 1500–1700* (Oxford: Oxford University Press, 2000), p. 5.

7   John Tosh, *The Pursuit of History: Aims, Methods and New Directions in the Study of Modern History*, 5th edn (Harlow and New York: Longman, 2010), p. 90.

8   Extract from the Brewers' First Book, in R. W. Chambers and M. Daunt (eds), *A Book of London English 1384–1425* (Oxford: Clarendon Press, 1931), p. 139.

9   K. Wrightson, 'Sorts of People in Tudor and Stuart England', in Barry and Brooks (eds), *The Middling Sort*, pp. 28–51 (p. 30). Wrightson is discussing Richard Gough, *The History of Myddle*, (ed.) D. Hey (Harmondsworth: Penguin, 1981).

10 Robert Darnton, *The Great Cat Massacre and Other Episodes in French Cultural History* (New York: Vintage, 1985), p. 4.

11 R. H. Helmholz, *Marriage Litigation in Medieval England* (Cambridge: Cambridge University Press, 1974), p. 155.

12 Elizabeth Foyster, 'Children and the Breakdown of Domestic and Social Order in Early Modern England', in A. Fletcher and S. Hussey (eds), *Childhood in Question: Children, Parents and the State* (Manchester: Manchester University Press, 1990), pp. 57–73 (p. 64–5).

13 Even though considered adults by the Church, girls and boys could be as young as twelve and fourteen respectively when giving evidence.

14 Cynthia Herrup, *A House in Gross Disorder: Sex, Law and the 2nd Earl of Castlehaven* (New York and Oxford: Oxford University Press, 1999), p. 8.

15 F. W. Maitland, Inaugural Lecture Cambridge University (1889), cited in Christopher Haigh, 'Slander and the Church Courts in the Sixteenth Century', *Transactions of the Lancashire and Cheshire Antiquarian Society*, 78 (1975), 1–13 (p. 1).

16 Christopher Haigh, 'Slander and the Church Courts in the Sixteenth Century', *Transactions of the Lancashire and Cheshire Antiquarian Society*, 78 (1975), 1–13. (p. 1).

17 Ronald Marchant, *The Puritans and the Church Courts in the Diocese of York 1560–1642* (London: Longmans, 1960), p. 1.

18 Ralph Houlbrooke, *Church Courts and the People During the English Reformation 1520–1570* (Oxford: Oxford University Press, 1979), p. 55.

19 Houlbrooke, *Church Courts*, p. 55.

20 See Eric Kemp, Review of Arthur J. Willis (ed.), *Winchester Consistory Court Depositions, 1561–1602* (1960), *Journal of Ecclesiastical History*, 14 (1965), p. 266. Kemp refers to church court records as 'the most intractable and forbidding of historical sources'.

21 J. S. Purvis, *An Introduction to Ecclesiastical Records* (London: St Anthony's Press, 1953), p. 10; Owen, Dorothy, 'Ecclesiastical Jurisdiction in England 1300–1550: The Records and their Interpretation', in Derek Baker (ed.), *The Material Sources and Methods of Ecclesiastical History: Papers Read at the Twelfth Summer Meeting and the Thirteenth Winter Meeting of the Ecclesiastical Society* (Oxford: Basil Blackwell, 1975), pp. 199–221 (pp. 213–4).

22 For the origins and workings of the secular courts see Baker, J. H., 'Introduction', in J. H. Baker (ed.), *Legal Records and the Historian: Paper Presented to the Cambridge Legal History Conference, 7–10 July 1975, and in Lincoln's Inn Old Hall on 3 July 1974* (London: Royal Historical Society, 1978), pp. 1–6; F. G. Emmison and Irvine Gray, *County Records (Quarter Sessions, Petty Sessions, Clerk of the Peace and Lieutenancy)* (London: Historical Association, 1961); Bertram Osborne, *Justices of the Peace 1361–1848: A History of the Justices of the Peace for the Counties of England* (Shaftesbury: Sedgehill, 1960).

23 Esther Moir, *The Justice of the Peace* (Harmondsworth: Penguin, 1969), pp. 22–4.

24 Osborne, Bertram, *Justice of the Peace 1361–1848: A History of the Justices of the Peace for the Counties of England* (Shaftesbury: Sedgehill, 1960).

25 Lorraine C. Attreed, *York House Books, 1461–1490, vol. 1* (Phoenix Mill: Alan Sutton, 1991), p. xi.

26 W. J. Jones, *The Elizabethan Court of Chancery* (Oxford: Clarendon Press, 1967).

27 Timothy S. Haskett, 'The Presentation of Cases in Medieval Chancery Bills', in W. M. Gordon and T. D. Fergus (eds), *Legal History in the Making: Proceedings of the Ninth British Legal History Conference Glasgow 1989* (London: Hambledon, 1991), pp. 11–21.

28 Cordelia Beattie, 'Single Women, Work, and Family: The Chancery Dispute of Jane Wynde and Margaret Clerk', in Michael Goodich (ed.), *Voices from the Bench: The Narratives of Lesser Folk in Medieval Trials* (New York and Basingstoke: Palgrave Macmillan, 2006), pp. 177–202 (pp. 179–82).

29 Beattie, 'Single Women', p. 181.

30 Natalie Zemon Davis, *Fiction in the Archives: Pardon Tales and their Tellers in Sixteenth-Century France* (Stanford: Stanford University Press, 1987), p. 3.

31 Davis, *Fiction in the Archives*, p. 4.

32 Keith Thomas, *History and Literature* (Swansea: University College of Swansea, 1988), p. 10.

33 Davis, *Fiction in the Archives*, p. 4.

34 R. H. Hilton, Review of *Calendar of Inquisitions Post Mortem, XV, 1–7 Richard II* (1970), *English Historical Review*, 88 (1973), 170–1.

35 John Bedell, 'Memory and Proof of Age in England 1272–1327', *Past & Present*, 162 (1999), 3–27 (pp. 12–13).

36 Bedell, 'Memory and Proof of Age', p. 5.

37 Laura Gowing, *Domestic Dangers: Women, Words, and Sex in Early Modern London* (Oxford: Clarendon Press, 1996), pp. 232–3.

38 Martin Ingram, *Church Courts, Sex and Marriage in England, 1570–1640* (Cambridge: Cambridge University Press, 1987), p. 35.

39 See M. Lynch (ed.), *Life, Love and Death in North-East Lancashire: A Translation of the Act Book of the Ecclesiastical Court of Whalley* (London: Chetham Society, 2006).

40 The Court of High Commission was created by Elizabeth I to enforce the rules of the Reformation. It was in regular use from the 1580s until its abolition in 1641 and is associated with *ex officio* causes. The Court of Dean and Chapter exercised jurisdiction during periods where there was no archbishop.

41 Owen, 'Ecclesiastical Jurisdiction', p. 206.

42 Owen, 'Ecclesiastical Jurisdiction', p. 209.

43 CALSS, Consistory Court Deposition Books, EDC 2/7/79–80. Ellen Dampart and John Andrew were married thirteen years before their case came before the ecclesiastical courts.

44 Houlbrooke, *Church Courts*, pp. 40–41.

45 Tarver, *Church Court Records*, p. 18.

46 Purvis, *Ecclesiastical Records*, p. 12.

47 Ritchie, *Ecclesiastical Courts*, p. 140.

48 Purvis, *Ecclesiastical Records*, p. 91.

49 See Ritchie, *Ecclesiastical Courts*, p. 140.

50 Christopher Hill, *Society and Puritanism in Pre-Revolutionary England* (London: Secker & Warburg, 1964), p. 306.

51 DUSC, Archdeaconry Act Book, DCD/D/SJA/1, fol. 133.

52 Moir, *Justice of the Peace*, p. 35.

53 Osborne, *Justices of the Peace*, p. 58.

54 Moir, *Justice of the Peace*, p. 36.

55 CALSS, Quarter Session Files, QSF/48.

56 Osborne, *Justices of the Peace*, p. 26.

57   Emmison and Gray, *County Records*, pp. 5–7. Some of the documents may have been filed separately due to the rolls becoming too bulky. This appears to have been the case at Chester.

58   J. H. E. Benet and J. C. Dewhurst (eds), *Quarter Session Records of County Palatinate of Chester 1550–1760* (Record Society of Lancashire and Cheshire, 1940), p. 51. Education here means nurture and not schooling.

59   See the definition of 'equity' provided in the glossary to the TNA's Equity Pleadings Database, available online at http://www.nationalarchives.gov.uk/help/equity/glossary.htm#etoh. Accessed 18 November 2015.

60   Beattie, 'Single Women', p. 179.

61   Haskett, 'Presentation of Cases', p. 11.

62   Timothy S. Haskett, 'Country Lawyers? The Composers of English Chancery Bills', in P. Birks (ed.), *The Life of the Law: Proceedings of the Tenth British Legal History Conference Oxford 1991* (London: Hambledon, 1993), pp. 9–23 (p. 12).

63   Haskett, 'Country Lawyers?' pp. 11–13.

64   Beattie, 'Single Women', p. 182.

65   J. Barry, 'Introduction', in J. Barry and C. Brooks (eds), *The Middling Sort of People: Culture, Society and Politics in England 1550–1800* (New York: St Martin's Press, 1994), pp. 1–27 (p. 12).

66   Barry, 'Introduction', p. 17.

67   Sharpe, *Defamation and Sexual Slander*, p. 17.

68   Helmholz, *Marriage Litigation in Medieval England*, p. 161.

69   J. A. Brundage, 'Legal Aid for the Poor and the Professionalization of the Law in the Middle Ages',*Journal of Legal History*, 9 (1988), 169–79 (p. 170).

70   Houlbrooke, *Church Courts*, p. 51.

71   Brundage, 'Legal Aid for the Poor', p. 174.

72   BIA, DC.CP.1578/4. See Chapter 6, p. 308 for a more detailed account of this case.

73   Houlbrooke, *Church Courts*, p. 40.

74   F. Pedersen, 'Demography in the Archives: Social and Geographical Factors in Fourteenth-Century York Cause Paper Marriage Litigation', *Continuity and Change*, 10 (1995), 405–36.

75   Charles Donahue, Jr, 'Female Plaintiffs in Marriage Cases on the Court of York in the Later Middle Ages: What Can we Learn From the Numbers?', in S. Sheridan Walker (ed.), *Wife and Widow in Medieval England* (Ann Arbor: University of Michigan Press, 1993), pp. 183–213 (p. 185).

76   P. J. P. Goldberg, 'Fiction in the Archives: The York Cause Papers as a Source for Later Medieval Social History', *Continuity and Change*, 12 (1997), 425–45.

77   Goldberg, 'Fiction in the Archives', p. 429.

78   Goldberg, 'Fiction in the Archives', p. 425.

79   Sharpe, *Defamation and Sexual Slander*, p. 17.

80   Helmholz, *Marriage Litigation in Medieval England*, p. 161.

81   Ludmilla Jordanova, *History in Practice* (London: Arnold, 2000), p. 30.

82   James Fentress and Chris Wickham, *Social Memory* (Oxford: Blackwell, 1992), pp. 25–6.

83   See Barbara Hanawalt, *Of Good and Ill Repute: Gender and Social Control in Medieval England* (Oxford: Oxford University Press, 1998); Barbara Hanawalt, 'Childrearing among the Lower Classes of Late Medieval England', *Journal of Interdisciplinary History*, 8 (1977), 1–22.

84   C. Smith, 'Medieval Coroners' Rolls: Legal Fiction or Historical Fact', in Diana E. S. Dunn (ed.), *Courts, Counties and the Capital in the Later Middle Ages* (New York: St Martin's Press, 1996), pp. 93–115.

85   CALSS, EDC 2/7, fols 165–165^{v}.

86 BIA, CP.G.1167.
87 BIA, CP.G.735.
88 BIA, CP.G.575.
89 BIA, CP.G.735.
90 DUSC, DDR/EJ/CCD/1, fol. 2^v.
91 BIA, CP.G.2096.
92 Clifford Geertz, *The Interpretations of Cultures: Selected Essays* (London: Fontana, 1993), p. 9.
93 TNA, C1/325/14.
94 Davis, *Fiction in the Archives*, p. 3.
95 Gowing, *Domestic Dangers*, p. 232.
96 Donahue, 'Proof by Witness', p. 148.
97 Barbara Herrnstein Smith, 'Narrative Versions, Narrative Theories', in W. J. T. Mitchell (ed.), *On Narrative* (Chicago: University of Chicago Press, 1981), pp. 209–32 (p. 213).
98 CALSS, EDC 2/3/112.
99 Joan Kirby (ed.), *The Plumpton Letters and Papers* (London: Cambridge University Press for the Royal Historical Society, 1996), pp. 103–04.
100 DUSC, DDR/EJ/CCD/1/4, fols 96–96^v.
101 BIA, CP.G.1524.
102 R. H. Tawney and Eileen Power (eds), *Tudor Economic Documents, Being Select Documents Illustrating the Economic and Social History of Tudor England*, 3 vols (London: Longman, 1924), II, 331.
103 EYLA, B 10, fol. 5. Clappers were rattles used to summon people to mass in Holy Week.
104 Smith, 'Medieval Coroners' Rolls', p. 115.
105 Davis, *Fiction in the Archives*, p. 5.
106 Bianca Premo, *Children of the Father King: Youth, Authority, and Legal Minority in Colonial Lima* (Chapel Hill: University of North Carolina Press, 2005), p. 8.

2 Notions of nurture and neglect in adult–child relationships

'... by wantyng the continuall care and diligence, that is necessarie for them, [children] are seen to lacke their naturall force and vertue, and finallie become wilde'.[1]

The words of Thomas Salter above demonstrate that people in the sixteenth century had a definite understanding of what constituted nurture and neglect in regards to children. According to Salter, they had to be diligently and continually nurtured and, if they were not, over time they would become wild. But it was not only in the written texts that we can find evidence of what people considered notions of nurture and neglect to be. Witnesses in ecclesiastical and secular courts gave clear indications of how they thought children should be cared for. The libel for a maintenance case at York in 1571, involving a baby who had been put to foster carers by its father, asked witnesses to consider if the child 'was verye pitifully arrayed by evell keeping', and if the baby had any 'cotes saving some beggerlie couerlet ragges'.[2] This was the representation of a child that was neglected by its carers and not clothed to commonly acceptable standards. The use of the term 'beggerlie' by itself connoted the social status of the carers and therefore the consideration of appropriate nurture given by them to the child. Moreover, the wording of the libel indicated the requirement to keep a child warm, with 'couerlet ragges' being woefully inadequate.

The aim of this chapter is to identify the notions of nurture and neglect that are identifiable in the extant sources, notions that will subsequently underpin the rest of the book. However, we must be careful to avoid anachronistic comparisons here with modern-day assumptions about both nurture and neglect. What may be viewed as neglect – or even abuse – today, was not regarded in the same light in the sixteenth century. Conversely, what sixteenth-century parents regarded as nurture could be taken as neglect today. One father, quoted in an instructional text printed in 1581, says that for his children not to grow up as if they belonged to the most barbarous of nations 'I chide, I threaten, yea and sometimes I strike them'.[3] Clearly, this father considered his actions as nurturing and by taking them he was caring for and encouraging the development of his child. The historically defined notions of nurture and neglect, therefore, are fluid and open to interpretation.

It is with the fluid interpretations of nurture and neglect in mind that we should approach any historiography on the subject. Discussion of these concepts by historians is in the main subsumed within an argument on childhood and in particular parent–child relationships as discussed in the general introduction of this book. It is therefore only necessary to reiterate the salient points of the historiographical debate as it affects our understanding of this chapter. Much of the discussion has been in reply to Philippe Ariès's argument concerning the state of childhood before the early modern period. His thesis has been largely misinterpreted and historians have directed their efforts towards disproving his supposed conclusion that parents did not love their children even though this is not what Ariès actually said. What he did assert was that affection for children did not constitute childhood. Rather, it was people's awareness of certain characteristics that differentiated the child from the adult and so it was the awareness that Ariès said was lacking, not the affection in medieval society.[4] What the revisionists' reaction amounts to is the tendency of historians to judge entirely by modern standards. Ivy Pinchbeck and Margaret Hewitt illustrate this point by decrying the lack of importance attached to childhood in Tudor times, in contrast to their perceived centrality of the child in twentieth-century society.[5] This is a dangerous practice for the historian to undertake because our understanding of children in the present does not necessarily generate questions that can be asked of children in the past.

It is much better to ask questions of the sources that lead the historian to an understanding of how sixteenth-century parents and other adults represented notions of 'good nurture'. Through what kinds of sources were the notions of nurture and neglect communicated to parents and other adults in the sixteenth century? For what audiences were these sources intended and did they have limited resonance for particular groups? For what aspects of a child's upbringing were parents and other adults held to be responsible, and was the advice gender specific for both adults and children? How was nurture defined or depicted within the sources? How was neglect defined or depicted within the sources? What criteria were used to distinguish nurturing discipline from cruel abuse? Was there a community understanding of what constituted nurture and neglect within the parishes and towns of sixteenth-century northern England?

The chapter is organised into two main sections. First, infants and young children up to seven years of age will be discussed, followed by children aged seven to adolescence. This demarcation is necessary because the contemporary writers of conduct literature considered seven to be the age at which learning should begin and the majority of the conduct literature is directed at children from seven years upwards. The question – in what kinds of sources were the notions of nurture and neglect communicated – will be discussed in relation to both groups as will the last two questions – the intended audience for advice and the community understanding of what constituted nurture and neglect – to avoid repetition. The remainder of the questions will then be considered in relation to each age group where appropriate.

Forms of communication

Through what kinds of sources were the notions of nurture and neglect communicated to parents and other adults in the sixteenth century? There were two main avenues through which formal advice was given in relation to childrearing in the sixteenth century: the Church and advice literature. The vast majority of advice literature was directed towards the rearing of children from the age of seven to adolescence, although manuals written specifically for the care of young babies were available, particularly on the continent. All forms of advice literature will be discussed below.

Turning our attention to the Church, we can see that their counsel formed the main part of advice to parents of children up to seven years of age (commonly referred to as infants). It was delivered through the intermediary of the local parish priest and, as most of the community was directly exposed to the influence and teachings of the Church through attendance at services every Sunday, it was a perfect medium for educating parishioners in the accepted way to nurture their children.

The Church had a paternalistic function towards all parishioners. It was the parish priest's duty to instruct his flock, just as it was a father's duty to instruct his household. Important messages regarding the well-being of parishioners' children were incorporated into and implicit in literature intended for the masses and disseminated through the medium of the sermon or homily. Edwin Sandys, who became the Archbishop of York in 1577, thought sermons to be essential for the particular calling of all parishioners. They showed 'the superior how to govern, the inferior how to obey; the minister what to teach, the people what to learn'.[6] Particularly after the Reformation, sermons were created for use in each parish and were to be read on successive Sundays so that every parishioner in England received the same message. Their use continued throughout the year, expanding upon topics thought, by the Church and ecclesiastical writers, to be significant, and they were supported by scripture and rhetoric.[7] Parish priests were not expected to create their own sermons and bishops or theologians usually prepared them. As early as the thirteenth century, canon law decreed that every priest would have at his disposal a book of homilies for Sundays and holy days.[8]

The nurturing of children, whether through direct instruction or the diffusion of advice to their parents by means of these sermons, serves to illustrate the extensive involvement of the Church in the lives of ordinary people. More importantly, sermons can be significant in understanding the norms that prevailed in regards to the treatment of children as well as childhood itself,[9] although much of the advice appears to be constant throughout the centuries and not specific to the fifteenth or sixteenth centuries. *Libri poenitentiales* (penitential books), which contained the penances for the most confessed sins and acted as a valuable part of the education of priests, point to a similar understanding of the punishments required for specific crimes involving children across the centuries. For instance, the penance for overlaying a child was a constant three years regardless of the origin of the penitentials.[10] Although considered to have been obsolete by the thirteenth century, the penitentials play an important part in the history of theology and canon law as they were integrated in the codification of penitential canons of later centuries. Many of the canonical penances inherited from the early Middle Ages were viewed as 'authentic' by later periods and therefore fitting for the sin.[11]

The power of the sermon was not the only way that religion could spawn avenues of advice to the community. Mystery Plays, which were a selection of biblical stories performed as a kind of carnival by amateur actors connected to the craft guilds, took their message to the streets of many northern towns including Chester and York and were staged well into the sixteenth century.[12] The material for the plays came from a number of sources, demonstrating the authority of the Bible while exploiting its contents to press home a desired message to the people of the town. In the story of Abraham and Isaac, God tells Abraham that he will send him a son and that he should, as all good fathers should, have his son circumcised, because if a man is not circumcised: 'Then unobedient that man is.'[13] The narrator tells the crowd that after the coming of Christ circumcision was replaced by baptism. From this message we can infer that for all good fathers (and mothers) the first duty to their children is to have them baptised so they may be obedient to God and to cleanse them of original sin. As one of the seven sacraments, baptism was a visible form of obedience to God. It was essential that babies were baptised as soon as possible after birth so that if they died 'their soules goe straight to heauen'.[14] The story of Abraham and Isaac also places a great stress upon the child's and the parent's obedience to God, a message that is heavily underlined in the conduct literature.

Printed advice literature on childrearing, also referred to as didactic texts, instructional texts or conduct books, became increasingly available in England during the sixteenth century due to the introduction of the printing press into England by William Caxton in 1476. The manuals, which were printed in the vernacular and produced for those parents, children and masters 'ignorant of the Latine tongue',[15] placed heavy emphasis on the household and the management of it by adults. Advice literature written in the vernacular was available in England before the introduction of printing and these were subsequently printed as individual volumes or included in books, after the introduction of the printing press. Hugh Rhodes's *Boke of Nurture*, published a number of times from 1554, contained John Lydgate's *Stans puer ad mensam*, which had been posthumously published *c.* 1460.[16] Lydgate's work was itself a translation of a poem of the same name by Robert Grosseteste, a thirteenth-century theologian and Bishop of Lincoln who was noted for his attention to courtesy and into whose household the nobility sent their sons to be educated.[17] Therefore, the advice offered by Grosseteste in the poem and Lydgate in his translation of it had resonance with communities far beyond the audience for which it was intended. Some of the advice discussed in this book will have come from texts produced before 1450 but publishers considered it relevant and worth printing and reprinting. The text would undoubtedly have gone through some transformations between editions and translations from Latin to the vernacular, but it was the increased availability of these texts and not a post-Reformation shift in attitudes that led to a heightened interest in this genre in the sixteenth century.[18]

Advice concerning infants was available to English parents through translations of continental paediatric works, such as Thomas Phayer's *Boke of Children*, or from domestic offerings like John Jones's *The Arte and Science of preserving Bodie and Soule*.[19] These texts were intended for a wide-ranging audience, of whom parents were just one of many groups targeted by the authors.[20] For older children, advice was dispensed under the auspices of the government of the household, which included the upbringing and education of children and servants.[21] By the sixteenth century, the availability of printed conduct literature had steadily increased, with a shift of accent towards the 'godly training up of children'.[22] Children were accountable to God first, parents second and lastly to schoolmasters and teachers.[23] Underpinning the counsel was the New Testament and the Ten Commandments, with advice for the treatment of children inextricably linked to the Fifth Commandment: honour thy father and thy mother. Rules set down by parents were to be obeyed by children to ensure the smooth running of the household. Training in obedience was an essential aspect of a child's upbringing and the prime responsibility of the parents. The stress on obedience, however, was not an initiative new to the sixteenth century, as the example of *Dives and Pauper*, mentioned below, reinforces.

Birth to seven years of age

Responsibility of adults in regards to children

For what aspects of a child's upbringing were parents and other adults held to be responsible, and was the advice gender specific for both adults and children? The responsibility of nurturing and educating a child was in theory divided between both parents but in practice, the care and education of a child up to the age of seven was almost always the responsibility of the mother. In available advice manuals she assumed the biological role of the caregiver, ensuring the child's well-being and ultimately its survival.[24] Thomas Becon, the Protestant reformer and chaplain to Archbishop Cranmer, wrote that children should be watched carefully day and night to ensure no harm should come to them, which he thought should be the 'office of the mother, which ought principally to attend upon the young ones in their infancy'.[25] Within this role, the mother was responsible for requirements such as feeding, bathing and swaddling that would fulfil the basic needs of the child.

Ecclesiastical guidance about childrearing was not gender specific in regards to the child, but there was an acknowledgement that the mother was the primary caregiver, reflecting the biological role postulated by the childrearing manuals. It was not as prescriptive in reference to the basic tasks of feeding, clothing and caring for a child as the manuals were, and arguably this was because these tasks were taken to be innate to all women and therefore did not need to be mentioned. What was contained within the advice of the Church was what *not* to do to the child.

Women were 'monished' to nourish their children 'warely' by the *Provinciales*, the ancient Canons of the Church.[26] Produced by William Lynwood, the fifteenth-century ecclesiastical lawyer and bishop of St David's between 1422 and 1434, the *Provinciales* stated the general law of the Church while also raising points of contention.[27] It directed women on the supervision required to safeguard their children and it was with the mother that the blame would rest if any harm came to the child due to the mother's neglect in ensuring its safety. Bartholomew of Exeter, the twelfth-century theologian and canon lawyer, placed the blame for the death of a child firmly with the mother. For if she placed her baby near the fire and her husband then decided to boil a pot of water on the fire which overflowed and scalded the baby to death, it was the fault of the mother for negligently leaving her child in a location where it could come to harm and she alone had to do penance.[28] Neglect therefore was regarded as predominantly a female trait by the ecclesiastical authors.

Where written advice did exist for the caring of infants, it was recommended for the mother to feed her own baby and not send it to a wet nurse. Juan Luis Vives believed it best to let women feed their children 'as other living things do',[29] as this would foster the spiritual development of the child.[30] Bartholomew Batty was keen for mothers to nourish their own children as the practice had 'brought suche great effect, rewarde and merite with our elders'.[31] Sixteenth-century writers differed little from their earlier counterparts or the Church in this respect, thinking breastfeeding best for the child for both emotional and physical health.[32]

Writers thought it important for children to 'have the same person as mother, nurse, and teacher', because the maternal bond created by the feeding and nurturing would bolster any early moral training given to the child.[33] This contemporary advice rather contradicts the arguments of DeMause and Shorter, who propound that the pre-modern period did not foster empathy between mother and children.[34] If a mother were not able to feed her child herself then 'vnto whom the bringing vp of suche children apperteineth'[35] must select wise nurses with good characters for, according to Vives, 'he who was nurtured with the milk of a sow had rolled in the mire'.[36] The moral character of the nurse was very important because, Batty believed, parents must choose a nurse who 'can well frame her tongue' unless they wanted their children to display 'corrupt maners, & vnseemely words' caused by drinking milk from 'lewed nurses'.[37] Thomas Elyot was also clear that the choice of wet nurse was of great importance and they should have no notable vices for the child will 'often time … soukethe the vice of his nouryse'.[38] Thus, many of the contemporary writers believed that the traits of a nurse would be passed on to her charge through her milk.[39]

As children learn by imitating others, no 'wanton or vnclene' words are to be spoken in the nursery and, to ensure that could not happen, all men except the doctor were to be kept out.[40] Elyot is evidently suggesting that at this stage the nurture of a child should be firmly in the hands of a woman and only those who use clean and polite English. As well as the character, the manner in which the nurse was to care for the child was of paramount importance to Batty for he tells the parents not to let the nurse sing 'euerie trifling tale' and nonsense songs to their charges, 'lest from their Cradle it shall fortune, that they be nouseled in folly, and fraught with corrupt conditions'.[41] The personality of the child therefore would reflect that of the nurse.

Paediatric manuals guided the mother on how to feed her child. According to John Jones a sixteenth-century physician, a baby should be allowed to suck at the breast until 'his former teeth be bredde'.[42] The timescale mentioned by Jones is anywhere from seven to past twelve months, although teeth can appear earlier. At least two of the children of the sixteenth-century mathematician and astronomer John Dee were weaned at thirteen months, suggesting that it was probably age rather than the appearance of teeth that initiated weaning.[43] Jones also offered advice about what to feed the child once weaned, washing the child on waking in the morning in breast milk 'if there be plentie' and putting a child to sleep in a cradle.[44] This last piece of advice was not only so that the child could be rocked to sleep, but also to protect the child from any hurt that may occur 'as by hauing it in bedde often hapneth'.[45] Overlaying a child had been a consistent concern for medieval writers and the Church, and this did not alter throughout the time period of this study, as the discussion below will show.

Although targeted at the mother, advice contained within the manuals was rarely gender specific, but weaning was the exception. In explaining the length of time that a child should be breastfed, Jones thought that the male should feed longer than the female, although he does not give a specific reason for this.[46] Continental advice on this practice was more forthcoming. Michele Savonarola, a fifteenth-century professor of medicine at Padua, said that girls should be weaned three to twelve months earlier than boys because men live longer than women, while Bernard de Gordon wrote at the end of the thirteenth century that it was because women required less strength than men.[47] Laurence Joubert, the French physician, considered the weaning of girls earlier than boys was due to their mothers believing them to be 'moist'.[48] Joubert, however, recommended that girls be nursed longer to maintain this moisture, which was he said, necessary for them 'to be fecund and to have beautiful children'.[49]

It is evident that both the Church and the advice manuals considered the mother to be the primary carer for all children under the age of seven. As Elyot suggested, the nursery was not a place for a man and the nurture of infants was most definitely women's work. If any harm came to a child when under her care, regardless of the part the father may have played in that harm, the Church held the woman responsible. The guidance offered by neither medium was gender specific, except when it came to weaning with mothers being advised to feed boys longer than girls. Feeding aside, children were to be nurtured in the same manner until they reached the age of seven, when the polarisation of care of the different sexes emerged and the father began to take the mantle of nurturer of his sons from their mother.

Notions of nurture and neglect

How were the notions of nurture defined within the sources? We need look no further than the works of sixteenth-century writers to confirm that contemporary parents did love their children. John Foxe wrote that 'among all the affections of nature, there is none that is so deeply graved in a father's mind as the love and tender affection towards his children'.[50] The sixteenth-century astrologer and medical practitioner Simon Forman recalled how his father loved him the best of all his siblings and 'for the affection he had to him, wold always have hym ly at his bedes feete in a lyttle bed'.[51] Mothers too have left testimony to the affection they felt for their children. Ellen Tailour of Skelton, Yorkshire, declined to work as a wet nurse for Ellen de Rouclif, saying that 'she loved her son just as much as Ellen loved hers' and she would not put his life at risk by weaning him so that she could feed Ellen's son John.[52] Such sources have been pivotal to the debate by revisionist historians, who have concentrated on the issue of parents and their love for their children. But loving a child is not the same as nurturing them. Children could be brought up in a number of diverse households where the adults caring for them could not be said to 'love' the child or be emotionally attached to them. The debate, therefore, requires reorienting to be able to examine what was understood to be good and bad nurture in the sixteenth century. This can only be done by investigating how it was defined within the sources.

The Church, as the universal channel of guidance for parents and adults, presented advice on nurture by publicising practices the Church thought harmful to children and thus good nurture in the canonical literature manifested itself only through definitions of its opposite. Notions of neglect were readily observed through the *Provinciales*. Advice contained within the Canons was incorporated into the homilies given in church on Sundays. Explicitly, the *Provinciales* advised parents against such practices as taking a baby into bed with them, to prevent the overlaying and possible suffocation of the child. Women should 'lay not the younglings nigh to them in the night lest they oppress them'.[53] Such advice was to be 'shewed them every Sunday'[54] and to ignore this advice was regarded as neglect and therefore a sin. The *Provinciales* directed parents' actions towards their children that they may not leave them in their houses where is fire, or nighhand to the water, alone without a keeper'.[55] Good nurture consisted of supervision in regards to the dangers of fire and water.

Consequences for ignoring the advice of the Church were great, as Christopher and Isabella Wryght from Northallerton in Yorkshire experienced. In 1497, the couple appeared before the Prior's Court at Durham accused of leaving their child unattended and allowing him to be burned to death in his cradle.[56] The chancellor of the prior of Durham, Thomas Swalwell, imposed upon them the penance of being whipped at the mother church of Allerton and the chapel of

Brompton and immediately afterwards walking barefoot dressed only in shifts and carrying candles which they were to offer after the offertory at the High Mass in each church or chapel. They were also commanded to fast on the next four consecutive Fridays on bread and water. Visible punishments such as these were not only a method to punish individuals for the neglect of their child, but also acted as an indication to the community of the stance of canon law in regards to neglect of children.

Christopher and Isabella's actions were neglect in the eyes of the Church, but the burning of children in their cradles was the most common accident for babies of both sexes in late medieval and early modern England.[57] After being nursed, the baby would be left in its cradle next to the fire, being the warmest place in the house, where there was always the possibility of burning embers landing upon the child. Babies were commonly swaddled in linen or wool, and the smell of the burning material would alert the parents if they were in the house. The nurturing action of trying to keep a baby warm was also a source of possible neglect when the baby was left unattended. Church authorities did consider this predicament when investigating infant deaths in the community. Priests were to carefully examine the death and, if it were found to be by the hands of the parents, then they would take into account certain considerations and could reduce the traditional penance.[58] The Church therefore, had strict guidelines on what they deemed neglect by parents but would also consider mitigating circumstances.

There was recognition by the Church of a correlation between poverty and neglect of a child, sometimes leading to infanticide. The penitential of Bede drew a distinction between a woman who had killed her child because she could not afford to maintain it and one who killed in order to hide the fact that she had had an illegitimate child.[59] Thus the Church understood the burdens placed upon poor parents, especially mothers, in relation to caring for a child and this was incorporated into their treatment of any cases of neglect that came before their courts. Christopher and Isabella's penance was remarkably light in comparison to the sentence for killing an adult or indeed those set out in penitentials for infanticide. For overlaying a child, the penitential of Saint Columban favoured a penance of one year on bread and water and then a further two years without flesh or wine.[60] Both parents expressed extreme remorse over the death of their child and this no doubt persuaded the ecclesiastical authorities at Durham that Christopher and Isabella acted in what they thought to be the best interests of their child by placing the cradle near the fire.

Some of the advice from the Church was directed 'for them that have slain their children',[61] which raises the question of why the Church was only giving advice after children had suffered from neglect at the hands of a parent or adult. The explanation here is not one of retrospective advice but related to the jurisdiction of the church courts. Church courts were responsible for investigating the deaths of infants, while the secular courts dealt with the deaths or mistreatment of older children. On having the death of an infant reported to them, the church courts had a duty to investigate if the death were really an accident or whether the parents, or another person, through insufficient care, had caused it. The *Provinciales* were actually of more use to the investigators of the courts by providing questions to be asked of the parents of the dead child, than as a source of advice to the actual parents themselves as its original purpose was as a resource for canon lawyers. Notwithstanding, the public penances of the parents fulfilled an educative function by clearly setting out the expectations of the Church in relation to caring for infants.

The advice of the Church appears to have been fixated on a limited number of tribulations that could have befallen small children, particularly overlaying. John Mirk was concerned that the influence of evil forces including the Devil precipitated overlaying, stating that Lucifer and his angels '[th]ay make wymen to ouerlye hor children'.[62] It is not surprising then that in his *Instructions for Parish Priests* he warns not just parents who take a child into bed with them and 'so by-twene you they chylde I-slayn', but also offers advice to godparents in relation to this matter. He tells them: 'By hem also they schele not slepe' and 'Tyl [th]ey con hem self wel kepe'.[63] By addressing the godparents directly, canonical literature was acknowledging that not just parents were responsible for the nurturing of young children. Nicholas Orme notes that 'Sarum' service-books used in the south of England issued godparents a charge to ensure that the parents of their godchild keep it safe from fire, water and other dangers up until the age of seven.[64] Hence the nurture of the child was to be shared by both the parents and the godparents, and all were to heed the warnings of the Church as all were culpable should anything happen to the child.

Despite this fascination with the overlaying of infants, where coroners' records detail the deaths of young children the cause was invariably death by drowning or fire.[65] Miracle texts heavily influenced by the Church, such as *The Miracles of Henry VI*, tended to report accidents that happened within or around the home or workplace, giving evidence of the prevalence of deaths other than overlaying.[66] An argument can thereby be made that canon law texts did not adequately represent the real conditions in which children lived and, more importantly, the actual practices of the parents. Continual supervision of children would not have been possible, especially for parents in rural areas where the industry of both parents was required to work the land. In a study of child death by unintentional injury in Sussex between 1485 and 1688, Elizabeth and John Towner found that almost 70 per cent of deaths occurred between March and August (and predominately between the hours of 1 p.m. and 5 p.m.), when the women would have been working in the fields sowing, weeding or harvesting the crops.[67]

The Church did not appear to consider that parents needed to be warned against dangers other than drowning, overlaying and burning that would threaten their children. No warning was given concerning being accosted by strangers, accidents in the street and around the home, or about accidents involving animals, despite evidence suggesting children did encounter these kinds of dangers. The narratives contained within *The Miracles of Henry VI* confirm this situation to be true. The stories convey a catalogue of hazards children encountered in their everyday lives: three-year-old children playing under a large stack of firewood which collapsed on one of them; a two-year-old left unsupervised in a house in which a sharp knife had been left lying and the child fell upon it; and a five-year-old girl kicked in the head by a horse; all testify to the dangers that prevailed at the time and yet no warning was issued by the ecclesiastical authorities.[68] The common theme of these accidents was the lack of supervision of the child by the parents, but the Church did not enforce the necessity of adequately supervising children when they were playing. One reported miracle concerned an infant of about one year old that had been allowed to wander in the street by herself at 11 p.m. and was subsequently hit by a cart. Not only did the chronicler blame the driver of the cart for the accident and not the parents for allowing the child to wander alone, but, once the child recovered, she was cheerfully reported by the chronicler to be back playing in the open street.[69]

Nurture, according to the Church in late medieval and early modern England, hinged upon avoiding those practices they considered to be neglectful. Yet, the sermons and ecclesiastical writers only promulgated certain categories of neglect: those that could be interpreted as possible infanticide. Not supervising your child when it was in the house or playing outside was not as important for the Church as, if the child came to harm, it was not through the deliberate intervention of the parents. Conversely, overlaying and burning in cradles were due to the direct actions of the parents and this could be interpreted as intentional harm. There were also unlikely to be any witnesses. Bearing in mind that ecclesiastical writers had established a link between poverty and infanticide, it is probable that the advice of the Church was intended for poor parents. Medical texts and advice literature on the other hand were intended for families from wealthier backgrounds and offered proactive advice on how parents should nurture their children. Breastfeeding, weaning and the choice of nurse were discussed alongside what the child should be taught. In this genre of literature, there was an acknowledgement that a number of adults would be responsible for the nurture of a child including parents, godparents and nurses. This represented a noticeable collective responsibility for the nurture of the child.

Seven years to adolescence

Responsibility of adults in regards to children

For what aspects of a child's upbringing were parents and other adults held responsible, and was the advice gender specific for both adults and children? Advice literature was intended to inform, instruct and educate parents in the right ways to bring up their children, with the underlying theme being moral instruction for children in middle childhood: approximately seven to twelve years of age for girls, and seven to fourteen for boys.[70] This kind of moral education, with its emphasis on religion, obedience, manners and discipline, was thought to be both appropriate and necessary to care for one's child. According to John Jones, the sixteenth-century paediatrician, 'the custome must be such as wil make [the] mind godly, maners ciuil, & [the] body te[m]perate'.[71] Jones's advice was perhaps intended to prepare children for the subsequent phase of life, adolescence, which was thought by writers to be an age of indiscipline and carelessness.[72]

Within the advice, there was a distinct emphasis on the family unit and household with the father at the head,[73] detailing what the parents should do in order to nurture their child. In this respect, the principle envelops the Roman family law principle of *patria potestas*, whereby the father exercised control over all of his children and those brought into the household such as servants or apprentices. William Gouge stated that 'children vnder the gouernment of their parents, and seruants in a familie, their whole calling is to be obedient to their parents and masters'.[74] Reflected in this arrangement was the notion of the family as a miniature commonwealth of both Church and state, with its governance mirroring that of both institutions.[75] The family also served as a hothouse for both Church and state, training the children to serve each body when they became older, especially boys. Mothers, whom didactic writers had decreed should rear their sons up until the age of seven, now relinquished their instruction to their fathers or another patriarchal figure.[76]

There is an argument that this link between governance and parenting was more pronounced after the Reformation as these principles resonated with the ideals of Protestantism.[77] By curtailing the authority of the priest, the Reformation could be said to have increased the authority of the father or head of household, who in turn acted as mediator between the members of the household and Church and state. However, this correlation between governance and parenting was not unique to the post-Reformation period and can be taken to be part of a continuum of childcare precepts to be found in the Bible. *Diues et Pauper*, a didactic tract centred upon the framework of the Ten Commandments and originally produced around 1405, states that 'we arn tau[gh]t to worchepyn fader & moodir, [th]at arn our begynnyng nest aftir God'.[78] God had decreed that parents had a duty to nurture their children and a child's obedience to their parents was a sign of obedience towards God. Furthermore, teaching children to fear God and to 'bringe them vp in the nurtoure and informacion of the lord' would have taken on greater significance in this stage of child development.[79]

Parents were seen to be the primary carers in the advice literature, but other adults were then constructed as pseudo-parents.[80] For the purposes of instruction, the term 'parents' in the literature referred to anyone under whose governance a child might live, including 'Magistrates, Pastors, Teachers, Tutors, Maisters'.[81] This was a necessary caveat due to the make-up of the family unit in sixteenth-century England. Instruction for non-related children, such as servants and apprentices resident in households, was the responsibility of the head of each family. Hugh Rhodes dedicated his book to 'men,

seruaunts, and children' as a 'Schoole of good maners'.[82] Rhodes's acknowledgement of a household where children from the family and young servants
would live side by side provided the head of the household with the practical
knowledge required to govern another man's children.

As the nurture of a child was not the sole responsibility of the parents, it
was vitally important that parents chose carefully the adults who would
instruct their child. Advice literature is unambiguous in its message as to who
should be allowed to be *in loco parentis*, regarding these foster carers as
'spirituall Parents' who 'beget and bring forth in thee vertues and all
Godliness'.[83] For children placed outside the natal home, Rhodes advises: 'see
that their maysters be such as feare God, and lyue vertuouslye, such as can
punishe sharpely with pacience, and not with rygour', as those who punish
with rigour would make the child rebel and run away.[84] If you did not choose
wisely the person who attended upon your child, there was a danger that such
children would become 'intached with barbourous speche and depryued
maners', and then 'embrace of them some vicious disposicion'.[85] For, as
Rhodes advised parents, children (and here he was referring to older children)
'sheweth the disposytions and conditions of their parentes or masters, vnder
whome they haue beene gouerned'. If the master is evil, then the child will be
evil.[86] Advice about how to select masters appears similar to that of choosing
a wet nurse, with the emphasis being on the tendency of the child to imitate
the traits of its carers. The anonymous author of *A glasse for housholders* used
the analogy of a cockerel to stress this point: 'the younge cocke croweth like
as he heareth the olde.'[87]

The father inherited the mantle of educator to the sons of the family from
the mother once they reached the age of seven. However, it was the view of
the authors of such literature that both mother and father had equal responsibility for bringing up children and that they required instruction on how to
be good parents.[88] The authors of the more theoretical advice literature were
male while women authors of practical guides were conspicuously absent in
this genre, although it is possible that female authorship was behind anonymous literature of the time.[89] Guidance was aimed primarily towards boys and
mainly intended for use by the father. A good father must teach his children to
fear God, administer correction to sons, daughters and servants alike and above
all 'bee a faithful father & a gouerner of houshold'.[90] Despite the dominant
patriarchal instruction, the role of the mother in socialising the child was
highly regarded.[91]

Sixteenth-century writers had definite ideas about the mother's role in the
care of children. Vives counselled the mother to consider her children 'all her
treasure' and in the nurturing of these treasures 'no effort should be spared'.[92]
He believed women were an important source of knowledge, because children
'ask her advice about everything ... whatever she answers they believe, admire,
and consider as the gospel truth'.[93] But Vives was writing from a male viewpoint and ignored the female perspective. Correspondingly, there were few
texts written by, and intended to be used by, women in the period of this

study. Dorothy Leigh, whose written advice to her young sons was published as *The Mothers Blessing* (*c.* 1616), sometime after her death, is unique in that she cites her motivation for writing as both 'motherly affection' and 'to move women to be careful of their children'.[94] She thought her advice to be particularly useful for 'children ... by reason of their young years, stand most in need of instruction'.[95] The use of the word 'motherly' accentuates the female perspective on nurturing and is one that was used by other mothers in the extant sources. Jane Umfrey told the court at York in 1571 that she was moved by 'motherly pittye' when confronted with the sight of her neglected child who had been put to foster parents by its father.[96] This strongly suggests that emotional attachment between mothers and children was still evident despite the child being cared for by someone else. But while the mother was responsible for the nurturing of small children of both sexes, she was particularly important in the social and moral education of girls.

Goldberg argues that the socialisation process and upbringing of pre-pubescent girls is problematic to recreate.[97] The meagre advice literature directed solely towards women suggests that they had the primary responsibility for the education of their daughters. *How the Goodwife Taught her Daughter* is one of only a few didactic texts intended solely for women that survive from the medieval period.[98] Despite its title, Felicity Riddy believes that the poem was not a literal address from mothers to daughters but related more to the family the daughter may have moved into during service. It was, in fact, a text by which the mistress of a household could socialise the non-kin girls living within the family. Riddy notes that the father (or the master) is conspicuous by his absence in the text, which she says is to represent a 'female domestic zone'.[99] We know from the sources that this was a realistic depiction of training and domestic arrangements for girls living in a non-natal household who were instructed by the mistress of the house.[100] Despite this apparent female autonomy, Riddy believes that the text had male origins, appearing first in a friar's handbook around 1350.[101]

It is clear that advice literature was gender specific in relation to the audiences of the texts. Women were directed to advice for children under the age of seven and for girls from seven to adolescence. Men were considered the best educators for boys from age seven and men wrote the majority of the texts, for use by men entirely for this purpose. Even those texts supposedly written by women were not without male intervention, as Riddy has observed. Regardless, the notions of nurture contained within the advice genuinely written by women are consistent with those notions present in the legal sources, reflecting a more accurate depiction of sixteenth-century childcare than that given by the male writers.

Notions of nurture and neglect for the older child

How was nurture defined or depicted within the sources? According to the conduct literature, merely providing your child, or the children within your household, with meat, drink and clothes was not adequate to nurture them properly. For as Robert Cleaver had commented 'Papists, Atheists, yea, Turkes and Infidels, doe yield this dutie' as well as any Christian, indicating that adequate feeding and clothing of your children were considered only basic nurturing.[102] For the purpose of instructing mothers and fathers in the actions that were considered to go beyond this basic nurturing, the conduct literature drew upon the Bible for inspiration and motivation. Christian parents were to model themselves upon Mary and Joseph, who could move parents to 'be carefull in [the] studie of godlinesse & willingly to obey publick ministratio [n]'.[103] Jesus was held up as perfect example of a compliant child who always obeyed his mother and Joseph 'euen in verie small thinges', such as fetching water.[104] Using the exemplar of the Holy Family seems fitting as parents were not bringing up and instructing their own children, but God's children whom God had created for himself.[105] It was to God that children owed their primary duty, with parents relegated to second place.[106]

Teaching a child to know its place in the sixteenth-century household was an important part of nurturing, yet sources indicate that adults had differing conceptions of exactly where that place might be. In a divorce case brought before the ecclesiastical courts at York in 1447, Peter Benson was accused by Agnes Helagh, his wife's mother, of unacceptable behaviour towards his stepson. He had ordered the boy to stand back from the table at mealtimes in addition to giving him little or nothing to eat.[107] To deny the child access to the table would directly affect the nurturing of the boy. Apart from the obvious lack of food that the boy would experience, the table was important in the fifteenth and sixteenth century for teaching a child its proper place in society, as it was an environment for regular and controlled instruction. It was at the table that children learnt in both explicit and implicit ways to be respectful to their parents and other adults present, to be patient and to exercise self-control.[108] The very public and observable nature of mealtimes in households meant it was an arena in which the behaviour of the child could be seen in relation to the others at the table.[109] Such was the importance of what was learnt there that Desiderius Erasmus dedicated over twenty pages to table etiquette,[110] and *Stans Puer ad Mensum*, a text produced exclusively for boys,[111] was reprinted and incorporated within texts throughout the sixteenth century. The ability of the child to stand at the table was important to both socialise the child and to inculcate the need for the child to place the good of the family and household above that of their own desires.[112] Moreover, the injunction to stand when the master addressed them or make sure they did not let their gaze wander as if they were 'voyde of curtesye'[113] when speaking to the head of the household demonstrated that age- and status-related training was a vital factor in the nurture children received. Obedience learnt when young would lead to a life free from vice when older.[114]

Part of the socialisation and nurturing of the child was regular discipline and this was stressed in the literature. Nevertheless, discipline would not be successful unless the child were open to reason and, according to medieval theologians, this did not occur until they reached the age of seven or there-abouts. From this age, the child was thought responsible for its own actions. In the *Christian's Man's Closet*, Bartholomew Batty's epistle on childrearing, the wise Theodidactus advocates the use of the rod to correct a child: 'For if thou smirest him with the rodde, he shal not die therof: thou smirest him with the rodde, but thou shal deliver his soul from hell'[115] and 'Who so spareth the rodde, marreth his childe'.[116] From the terminology used by Batty, he is talking about the disciplining of boys here and such correction would be particularly applicable at this life stage. Once a youth was passed the age of sixteen, however, beatings were considered ineffective.

The use of physical punishment as a means of nurturing one's child was sanctioned by the Church and advised by Christian writers in their publications. Thomas Becon considered correction was as important to the nurturing of children as 'meat and drink'.[117] Even exiled Roman Catholic priests like Laurence Vaux thought it appropriate to remind parents of the duty they held towards their children and the necessary practices they should employ. He believed that by correcting children with the rod 'fathers & mothers may deliuer the Childre[n]s soules fro[m] hel', adding that it was 'better to be vndone then vntaught'.[118] Vaux did stipulate that the use of the rod should be 'ruled by reason'. Similar advice is given by Theodidactus in Batty's epistle, who raises a note of caution for parents when chastising their children. Parents should correct their children 'fatherly, not tyrannously' and they should not be too extreme in their corrections but 'obserue and keepe the Golden meane'. Excessive disciplining would 'discourage them with their two sharpe and bitter reproaches: or with their rigour and creuelitie to kill and murder them'.[119] Although addressing both parents, Batty's use of the word 'fatherly' emphasises he considered the disciplining of male children to be a father's role.

This penchant for the contemporary writers to advise parents and carers to use reason when disciplining their child may suggest that heavy-handiness towards children in matters of correction was the acceptable norm, and that they had to be instructed to be moderate. At the same time, the writers are clear in their instructions that there is an acceptable use of force in disciplining a child, but there is also a continuum upon which this force is measured and parents must ensure that they do not overstep the mark. Certain commentators, for example Richard Whitford, placed the responsibility for beatings on the children themselves. In his book, *A werke for housholders*, he includes a remorseful verse that parents should have their child, or any child that may happen to be in their company, recite on a daily basis

Yf I lye/backbyte/or stele
Yf I curse/scorne/mocke/or swere
Yf I chyde/fyght/stryue/or threete
Than am I worthy to be bête
Good mother or maystres myne
Yf any of these nyne

I trespace to your knowynge
With a newe rodde and a fine
Erly naked before I dyne
Amende me with a scourgynge.[120]

Whitford follows up this verse by advising parents to 'perfourme theyr peticyon & request & thynke it not cruelly / but mercy fully done', which reinforces the fact that discipline will only work when the child accepts responsibility for its actions and that it was essential for the nurture of the child.[121]

Like Batty, Whitford was an advocate for the use of the rod in disciplining the child and parents who did not employ this method of control 'hateth the childe'.[122] It is interesting that Whitford directs the child's plea for correction towards the mother as the chastisement of the family was a male-dominated role. This could have been because mothers were thought to be too lenient towards their children and were thus reluctant to beat them, although there are examples of mothers only too willing to perform that task. In 1589, John Dee's wife gave their eight-year-old daughter Katherine 'a blow on the eare' that made her 'bled at the nose very much',[123] confirming Whitford's belief that mothers were commonly disciplinarians,[124] although probably only for their daughters and female servants. Regardless of who did the correcting, whether in 'lasshes/ or in wordes', Whitford advises that it should be done 'with the charitie of our Lord/and with a milde and soft spirite'.[125]

Discipline, when carried out rationally, was required to nurture a child, whether it was administered by parents or by those *in loco parentis*. It was necessary, not just to instil fear into the child but also to inculcate love for their parents and carers, thus underlining punishment as an important part of parenting. Rhodes reinforces this point by telling the reader 'And yee that are friends or Kynne shall labour how to make them loue and dreade you, as well for loue as for feare'.[126] These actions were important as obedience and deference to parents were necessary components in the construction of social order and the parent–child relationship was the first of many hierarchies that existed during this period.[127] It is also interesting to note that the similarity of advice from authors from such diverse religious backgrounds – Whitford a Bridgettine monk, Vaux a Catholic priest and Batty a Puritan – indicates a consistency in childrearing techniques that transcends the Reformation, a point made by Margo Todd in relation to the supposed spiritualisation of the household by the Reformation.[128] The belief that to discipline a child was to nurture a child was one not altered by religious reform.

Neglect of the older child

How was neglect defined or depicted within the sources? Apart from the over-zealous disciplining of a child, the conduct literature's stance towards neglect was articulated through its promulgation of the practices contained within its pages. Not to follow this advice was neglect in itself. For, as the proverb stated, it was 'better children weep than old men cry', meaning that to ignore the moral instruction of your child would only bring misery to the father – figuratively the family – later on.[129]

The advice of Plutarch, the first-century philosopher whose guidance was available to sixteenth-century parents courtesy of Thomas Elyot's translation, concentrates on the inconveniences that happen from the negligence of fathers. He directs his advice towards fathers of youths because he believes that 'more hede oughte to be taken of them, than whan they were chyldren'.[130] Despite the fact that children may have been virtuously trained during their childhood they soon abandon the manners and ways they have learnt, once they 'entre into mannes age'.[131] The distractions of the adolescent years, which include 'riottous lyuynge, consumynge substance & inheritance, inordinate & chargeable gaminge' and 'defloracion of mayde[n]s', Plutarch believed, were more harmful to children than the negligence of tutors and lack of obedience.[132] This advice has great significance for the apprentices discussed in Chapter 5 who were routinely warned about refraining from such vices in their indentures.[133]

The major fault of parents in the sixteenth century according to the literature was that of overindulgence of their offspring, especially among wealthier families. John Jones dedicates part of a chapter on 'the abuse of sundry parentes' to explaining that 'unreasonable parentes are rightly compared of Lawne to Apes, who with ouer-diere embracing their yong ones, doe strangle them'.[134] There is perhaps an analogy to be made with the stifling actions of these parents and the freedom children evidently had before the accidents discussed earlier in the chapter. Jones obviously felt that children needed to be responsible, self-reliant and resilient in the sixteenth century and this would not happen if given too much attention by their parents. Parents' lack of supervision of their offspring could in fact be considered nurturing. Notwithstanding this point, Jones's comparison of parents to apes reduces their 'negligent' actions to that of animals who are without the reasoning and godliness of human beings.

There was, however, no acknowledgement of what today may be termed abuse or cruelty within the advice literature and, as Orme points out, physical abuse in the household warranted little interest or intervention.[135] Arguably this was because it was a father's prerogative how he treated his child within the confines of his own home. It was easier to detect abuse outside the home, in situations where another adult was responsible for the welfare of the child, and perhaps this was why the literature warned parents to be careful about whom they chose to look after their children. There would appear to be a double standard in regards to abuse: parents were not censured in regards to their own children but would be judged in regards to non-related children for whose nurture they were responsible. But when and how did neglect become apparent in these situations and by what means was it articulated in the sources?

Nurturing discipline or cruel abuse?

What criteria were used to distinguish nurturing discipline from cruel abuse? Despite the endorsement of discipline towards children, there was a dichotomy between discipline per se and what could be termed as neglect or abuse, and this was inextricably linked to the amount of force used in the process. It is apparent from the sources that sixteenth-century parents clearly articulated when they thought a child was being abused. John Atkinson of Newcastle overstepped this mark in 1563 with his correction of his apprentice, whose surname was Hewbank (no Christian name is given). Hewbank's mother confronted Atkinson about the force he used on her child, telling him 'shew not your crewellty vpon the boy as ye vse to your wife'.[136] Atkinson was evidently not the sort of master who would nurture and care for his charges. Possibly the most telling detail of this incident is the fact that there was an acknowledgement of wife-beating – although possibly not condoned – the like of which would not be tolerated in regards to children.

The mother believed the beating of her son to be excessive but her words betray the fact that she found John Atkinson's treatment of his wife to be equally unreasonable. Thus she measured the force Atkinson used towards her son by publicly accusing him of unreasonable behaviour towards both his wife and his apprentice. What we have here transcends the boundaries of neglect and manifests itself as abuse. For Atkinson had not neglected to nurture his apprentice; he had physically abused him and this was not acceptable to the boy's mother or to a witness to the altercation, John Whitfield, who stated that Atkinson beat the boy 'unmercifullye'.[137]

The terms used by Hewbank's mother and John Whitfield are in themselves problematic when attempting to construct notions of neglect from the extant records, for rarely has any attempt been made in the literature to positively define the limits of acceptable correction.[138] So, although the motive of John Atkinson in correcting his apprentice was important, and it was expected that apprentices had to be disciplined 'with lawfull castigacion as occasion shall require',[139] if it were done with 'crewellty' or 'unmercifullye' then it was wrong. Both the mother and John Whitfield, though not questioning the motivation for the beating, identified that it went well beyond the limits of acceptable punishment, and therefore transgressed the commonly accepted notion of moderation in the manner necessary to correct the child as a sign of good nurture.

Bartholomew Batty was keen to emphasise that the rod was a wiser alternative to parents' fists or cudgels when disciplining a child because these could render children 'deaf lumpishe, ignorant and foolishe'.[140] Batty's thoughts on the use of force in correcting a child demonstrate a ritualised approach to discipline. If a parent used their fists or cudgels then this would more than likely to have been precipitated by anger and would not be nurturing beating, rather spontaneous reaction. If, however, the parents used a particular instrument, especially made for the job of disciplining like the rod, then it showed that the parents were sure of their motives in using it. Therefore it was much better to deliberately use the rod than rashly use the fists in order that children become 'wise and worthie'.[141]

Detectable in depositions from sixteenth-century court records from northern England is the fact that people concurred with the advice offered by Batty and his fellow writers, although perhaps more through commonly held notions than reading conduct literature. Thomas Lincolne was treated so badly by his master, one Fonyby of York, that after serving only three years of his eight-year apprenticeship he did not wish to be apprenticed to Fonyby any longer.[142] A petition in the Court of Chancery told of how Thomas was beaten by his master with 'tonges off iron and such oder vnresonable wepons', that he was in fear of his life.[143] Had Fonby used reasonable weapons like the rod, then, it is likely that the boy would have accepted his punishment as being justified even if he probably did not like it. At the very least, this case shows that petitioners in court cases were aware that use of 'reasonable' weapons were the defining factor in appropriate beatings.

Cases of such overt cruelty appear only twice in all the sources I have gathered, and both concerned children who were not blood relations to the person administering the beatings, but these findings reinforce Orme's view that abuse was easier to spot when the child was cared for by adults other than their parents.[144] Nevertheless, the lack of records should not be taken as a sign that abuse of children was minimal in sixteenth-century northern England. Cases of abuse did not always make it as far as the courtroom but there were reports of children being chastised physically in the sources. Thomas Pek slapped Elizabeth Savell in the face hard enough to make her cry when she refused to marry John Clay at Wakefield, Yorkshire in 1509.[145] The use of the word 'unreasonable' in the court records informs us that there was a universally held notion of what was acceptable punishment for children and anything that went beyond this mark was abuse of the child.

Intended audience of advice for both age groups

For what audiences were the sources of advice intended and did they have limited resonance for particular groups? The use of sermons, and other literature derived from canon law like that of the *Provinciales*, provided a conduit through which prescribed childrearing practices could percolate down to ordinary people.[146] It was recognised by the writers of sermons that it was the parents who were the intended audience as children under seven were unlikely to benefit from the preaching.[147] At any Sunday service there was a cross-section of the community present and every church was expected to have had seats and pews fitting for all social classes.[148] All present at a service would be exposed to the advice on offer, but the terminology used in the sermon was perhaps more pertinent to certain social classes within the congregation. Parents wealthy enough to employ a nurse to look after their infants escaped the censure of the Church for they had afforded the safety of their children by providing an adult to watch over them and making sure they would never be left alone. Poorer parents, on the other hand – who ironically were probably at church without their children[149] – could neither afford to pay someone to look after their offspring nor stay with them continually because of having to work both in and outside the home. These parents were the intended recipients of the advocacy of the Church.[150]

Many of the parents who appeared in the depositions in the underage marriage cases discussed in this book arguably would not have been the intended audience for this type of advice. Several of the witness statements discuss the supervision the child experienced in addition to that of their own parents. Constance Good, who was married aged six in 1537 in Bolton Percy, Yorkshire, had both a wet nurse and a governess during her childhood. Margaret Whitehouse told the church court at York that she had the governance and ordering of Constance on her wedding day because she 'was not of discretion to rule her self'.[151] Bearing in mind the Church's recognition of the connection between poverty and neglect of children, their advice would have had more resonance for those parents who appeared in the Quarter Session records and ecclesiastical records in relation to illegitimate children. Women like Elizabeth Kyrke, who was accused of infanticide at Chester Quarter Sessions in 1566 by means of burying her newborn baby in the sands by the River Dee, was a prime example of the audience for whom the advice was intended.[152] Thus the Church attempted to safeguard the lives of children where the poverty of their parents directly influenced the nurture they received. This was not the intention of advice literature.

Charles Briggs argues that establishing the audience for any medieval text (or early modern one for that matter) is problematic.[153] Texts could have been read in a number of ways, for a variety of reasons and by a diverse number of people.[154] To work out who was reading them and how often, you have to have knowledge of ownership of the books, how often they were produced, in addition to who was actually reading them.[155] So it is with caution that we should accept Linda Pollock's insistence that advice literature remains the main source of evidence for recreating childhood in past centuries, linking, as she says, both the theories relating to childrearing and the actual practice of the time.[156] Finding empirical evidence that suggests this argument to be true is challenging and we should not commit to printed sources as the only avenue of establishing sixteenth-century accepted childrearing practices, particularly as they exclude a large proportion of the population. Jay Mechling refers to this practice as a 'problem of *sampling*', whereby access to printed child-rearing advice was dependent upon socioeconomic status.[157] It is within the advice literature itself, however, that the conundrum of the intended audience can be solved.

Merridee Bailey has identified that by the sixteenth century it was the middling-status families who were the intended audience for advice books concerned with socialising the child.[158] Both Hugh Rhodes and Francis Seagar refer to young people as servants in households in their texts, while Seagar even refers to children serving their own parents, which seems to signify the middling-status of the intended audiences of his text.[159] A few writers did consider parents from poorer households or, as Batty phrased them, 'poor, base destitute parents who are not of quick wit',[160] but in reality it would have been extremely unlikely that they would have access to these writings. With little money to support their families, poorer parents would not have been concerned with socialising their children using texts; rather, they would use methods passed down through the generations. But, as we know little about sources of childrearing information for the poorer classes except from the Church, we must conclude that the idea of tradition as a basis of advice was exactly that – an idea.

Existing relationships within the family, especially the parent–child relationship, were considered to be the conduit by which these socialising lessons were best absorbed, especially in households where the family lived in close proximity to one another,[161] and thus typified the types of families who employed the literature. In larger households, particularly after the Reformation, communal reading would take place in the hall, where children, servants and visitors gathered to hear the master of the house read, but the parlour and the kitchen were the rooms of choice in smaller residences.[162] These venues were at the centre of everyday life and offered opportunities for impromptu reading sessions interwoven with the activities of the family.[163]

While these texts projected the desired behaviour of the children as well as the duties of their parents in regards to instruction, we cannot assume that this was a genuine reflection of how households operated. Nevertheless, the message taken from them is clear; the parents were responsible for the behaviour of their children and other young people in their care. Unfortunately, historians often concede that there is no way to measure the response to advice literature and that there were 'huge variations' between the advice and the reaction.[164] This is not surprising considering that the literature was not intended for a sizeable proportion of the sixteenth-century population. More importantly, as contemporary writers were trying in many cases to modify behaviour, they could have endorsed approaches that went against accepted practice of the time.[165] Interestingly, twentieth-century studies in the United Kingdom found that baby-care manuals did not provide a true reflection of how children were raised in homes.[166] If modern parents ignore prescriptive advice, then as historians we can only surmise that sixteenth-century parents may have treated advice literature in much the same way. But we should not dismiss their value as informative historical documents. The discussion of legal evidence above indicates congruity between theories of good nurture and people's behaviour and attitudes (against excessive beating, for example), even if we cannot measure the 'take-up' of these theories exactly.

Trying to establish the audience for any source of advice is not without its problems. Notwithstanding, the advice offered by the Church was consistent over a long period of time and suggests a widespread dissemination of the theories propagated by it. The Reformation did not challenge this authority as the central elements of ecclesiastical jurisdiction did not alter[167] and therefore advice to parents from the Church remained unchanged throughout the dates of this study. Historians have concluded that attitudes towards marriage and the family have remained constant in church court records and folk customs over the centuries,[168] suggesting that the Church's teaching was not adjusted during that time. In contrast, advice literature was revised and adapted over time to suit different audiences, all with a degree of prosperity. Yet, even if we can narrow down the types of families that would have been exposed to advice literature, we can never be certain that the advice was put into practice however committed the writers were to their ideals. Considering both sources together, there is an indication that there were general doctrines of advice aimed at specific groups at particular times in history.

Community ideals of nurture and neglect

Was there a community understanding of what constituted nurture and neglect within the parishes and towns of sixteenth-century northern England? Trying to assess community understanding of what was thought to constitute nurture and neglect is difficult. Nonetheless, there are subtle indications that commonly held beliefs about the care of children existed, especially in regards to supervision and maintenance, although the former is a questionable subject in relation to sixteenth-century parenting no matter the age of the child. Certainly ecclesiastical writers like John Alcock, Henry VII's first Chancellor, understood the perils of leaving children alone. He preached that a man without laws was 'as a childe hauynge noo nouryce nor guyder deputed to hym may as well renne in to the fyre or water', a reference to the dangers of children being left unsupervised.[169]

Jerominus Roberts was only seven years old when he drowned in 1592 whilst bathing in the River Dee in Chester.[170] The fact that an inquest was held signifies that the authorities thought his death to be worthy of investigation and Barbara Hanawalt has argued that inquests into the deaths of children displayed a 'community fascination with childhood'.[171] People generally knew the names and ages of the children in the locale and coroners' inquests demonstrate that both parents and the community took the death of a child seriously. Conversely, the lack of coroners' inquests on children – and I located only two in my study – does cast doubt on this supposed 'fascination'. It could be argued that the paucity of coroners' records in relation to child deaths indicates an acceptance by the community of the hazards children might encounter in their day-to-day activities and the fact that parents were not always able to supervise their children's activities. This scenario was not neglect by itself but was rather the realities of life, where neglect created by time-poor, working parents who could not supervise their children adequately meant that their children were not in a safe environment at all times.

Although the inquest gives little evidence of the circumstances surrounding Jerominus's death, it would not be unreasonable to assume that his parents or other adults were not immediately present and consequently there was no one to restrain him from diving into a potentially dangerous situation. It would appear that by the time children reached the age of seven they had considerable freedom. The chronicler of Henry VI's miracles spoke of one seven-year-old girl who drowned in a neighbour's fishpond as having the 'liberty such children have to play where they will'.[172] The inquest does, however, state that Jerominus was suddenly and accidentally drowned, 'subitor et casualiter submerses', so even if an adult had been present it would be unlikely that they could have saved him as it is doubtful that they knew how to swim. The ability to swim in the sixteenth century was not a skill the ordinary people of England possessed and was generally confined to the aristocracy,[173] nor was it seen as a problem that needed addressing. When parents frequently lost infants to disease but rarely lost older children to drowning, then teaching children to swim was not a necessary part of nurture.

The inquest into Jerominus's death does not detail the outcome of the inquest, but the use of the word *casualiter* does confirm that in the view of his contemporaries he was accidentally drowned and therefore no one could be held responsible for the death. Inquests were meant to determine the cause of death and whether this was accidental or the fault of somebody – usually through assault rather than by neglect – and they would have been very thorough in their investigations. Juries regularly visited riverbanks and sites of accidents in order to ascertain if the death had been unintentional or premeditated.[174] Hence, what juries classified as murder or accident gives us a more detailed impression of what actual community ideals of neglect or acceptable behaviour of parents towards their children might have been. Allowing a seven-year-old who could not swim to bathe unsupervised in a river may appear to be neglectful to modern-day parents, but it is evident that sixteenth-century jurors – and thereby the community – did not believe this to be a problem.

There does appear to be a fine line between acceptance and disapproval in regards to supervision. The failure of parents to supervise their children, resulting in injury or death, was not always tolerated by the authorities or the communities. Displeasure at parents who left children with inadequate care was apparent,[175] as the case of Christopher and Isabella Wryght mentioned above demonstrates. It was, though, a distinction based on age. Babies were supposed to be kept from dangerous situations but the responsibility did not last longer than infancy, as the case of Jerominus Roberts demonstrates. Further evidence of censure of not supervising infants can be located in documents that detail accidents to children within a community. In a pre-amble to the telling of a miracle attributed to Henry VI, the chronicler reserved strong words for parents who failed to supervise their children. A fifteen-month-old baby named John Hargrave had been left unattended in the house while his parents were at church and subsequently burned his head. The chronicler warned the reader that those who 'nurse the young or have charge of boys' education' should listen to this cautionary tale, noting 'how many dangers and hurts to which infants are exposed by the carelessness of their parents'.[176]

Such censure does not appear to be consistent. The chronicler does not comment on why parents would leave a young girl alone in a house where she managed to hang herself on a leather strap that secured a cellar door, even going as far as to blame the girl for being 'careless and mischievous as children will be'.[177] Reading on through the list of miracles concerning children, it becomes apparent that lack of supervision was the norm and often parents were only alerted to the accidents of their children by the screams of their playmates.[178] Correspondingly, Martin Ingram has noted that young children were vulnerable to sexual abuse because of these deficiencies of supervision, both in the household and when they were in the streets or the fields.[179] Accordingly, we may accept that the author of the miracles was heavily influenced by canon law; warning parents about the danger of leaving children by fire was normal, warning them against leaving them unsupervised in other circumstances was not.

It is evident that the community had an understanding of what was considered to be nurture or neglect in relation to children, one that was reinforced by the courts. Despite being before the dates of this study, it is worth citing a late thirteenth-century court case from Wiltshire to exemplify this fact. A woman had brought her one-year-old son to his father to be looked after but the father refused to take the child. The woman then left the child in the street and it subsequently died from exposure during the night. Although the jury did not find the parents guilty of murder, the justices fined both parents and the whole village, holding them responsible for causing the boy's death through their negligence.[180] In a similar manner, the justices in sixteenth-century northern England underlined that both parents and community were responsible for the nurturing of a child, demonstrated through maintenance awards for illegitimate children. Robert Spencer of Huyton, Lancashire, was ordered to pay 13s. 4d. per annum in 1603 for his illegitimate daughter Ellen, but the parishioners were also to contribute, paying 26s. 8d.[181] Thus the nurture of a child was at times not the sole responsibility of the parents but became the collective responsibility of the community.

Conclusion

When formulating the notions of nurture and neglect for this chapter, it has been important to locate the beliefs and norms that sixteenth-century parents and other adults held in regards to children. To do this, it has been necessary to study canon law and conduct literature to ascertain what parents' behaviour towards their children should have been according to contemporary schools of thought but it is perhaps the actions and reactions of the parents apparent in the extant sources that best reveal what these notions actually were. What these channels of advice do, however, is highlight what was thought to be good and bad in regards to childrearing by those with either power or influence at the time.

For parents of children from birth to seven years, their education in relation to correct childrearing practices came courtesy of Church law incorporated into sermons and writings, although there was available literature on the care of infants. How to nurture a child was demonstrated through warnings against negative practices such as taking a baby into bed or leaving a child alone close to water. Yet when we reflect on the practices sixteenth-century parents thought to be good for children, the beliefs and norms of what was considered as nurturing are at times completely opposite to that of modern-day parents, in particular the condoning of lack of supervision and oversight in potentially dangerous situations. Evidence of the censure of parents who failed to supervise their children is sparse despite the resultant unintentional injuries and, in some cases, deaths. This was not, however, neglect in the sense of indifference to the development of the child but should be seen in light of the fact that it was normal and desirable for small children to play freely. Jones openly criticised parents who stifled children with too much attention, as it was detrimental to their development, a practice Ariès refers to as 'coddling'.[182] If we couple this with parents' reactions to difficult circumstances, such as trying to keep an infant warm or having to leave a child alone in order to work, it shows that parents did what they thought best to care for small children.

Older children's nurture was primarily addressed through conduct literature. The prominent message in this form of instruction was one of moral instruction, with its emphasis on religion, obedience, manners and discipline. The literature focused on physical care, socialisation and education towards the child becoming a good Christian, and to children obeying God and their parents. Obedience and deference were necessary to the construction of social order and the parent–child relationship was the first in many hierarchies that a child would encounter throughout its life. Disciplining and chastising children were also seen as part of this process and as essential nurturing, for 'he who loves his children corrects them well'.[183] The use of the rod to discipline children normalised the process, bringing with it a ritualised approach that placed the task into accepted practice. To use fists or cudgels could only have been the result of irrational thinking. And this is where the advice literature was invaluable to avoid an act of nurture progressing into one of neglect or abuse. The writers were keen to emphasise that the use of the rod should be 'ruled with reason', acknowledging that tyrannous disciplining could be an act of cruelty and neglect of the child.

Conduct books can be of scant value as social documents, revealing little of adults' genuine actions towards their children, but they do signal an ideal of what family relationships and, therefore, parents' behaviour towards children should have been according to contemporary writers.[184] Indeed, the existence of advice literature was perhaps necessary precisely because practice was contrary to the recommended counsel.[185] John Davyson, a York tailor, was a prime example of a parent whose behaviour towards his children did not match the advice in the literature. He left one of his children in the castle, in order that the child would commit a 'trispas' against the gaoler.[186] This was not the obedient behaviour advanced by the conduct books, although it appears that the child was obedient to Davyson, raising the question whether advice literature is evidence of childrearing values, or 'childrearing manual-writing values'.[187]

While we cannot measure the response to advice given by the Church and conduct literature, analysis of the extant sources reveals that there were community-held notions of what constituted nurture or neglect in sixteenth-century northern England. Whether through the terminology used by witnesses in court cases or analysing a jury's actions in a child's death, we are able to identify those notions of nurture or neglect which must direct the understanding of the actions of parents and adults in relation to the children discussed in this book. For example, the cases discussed above show there is a noticeable agreement that most pre-modern adults, whether they learnt it through texts or elsewhere, thought that beating children was an acceptable part of nurture. Even in cases of objections to excessive beatings, apparent community norms of reasonable force and acceptable motives for child beating are present. Another key assumption of community norms is that adults other than the parents would have authority over children and responsibility for their care at some stage, both directly and indirectly. So, whether or not people had actually read the conduct literature, the literature itself seems to reflect, and more importantly reinforce, some community norms. We may conclude then that the available advice reflected to some degree the actions and beliefs of the parents and community in regards to children, although this could change depending upon the situation and the socioeconomic status of the child.

Notes

1   Thomas Salter, *A mirrhor mete for all mothers, matrons, and maidens, intituled the Mirrhor of Modestie no lesse profitable and pleasant, then necessarie to bee read and practiced* (London, 1579), Preface. Salter uses the analogy of a plant to advocate the need for good instruction of children.

2   BIA, CP.G.1521.

3   Bartholomew Batty, *The Christian's Man's Closet* (trans.) William Lowth (London, 1581), p. 2.

4   Ariès, *Centuries*, p. 128.

5   Ivy Pinchbeck and Margaret Hewitt, *Children in English Society*, 2 vols (London: Routledge & Kegan Paul, 1969–73), I (1969), 4.

6   Edwin Sandys, *The Sermons of Edwin Sandys, D.D., to which are added some miscellaneous pieces by the same author*, (ed.) John Ayre (Cambridge: Cambridge University Press, 1842), p. 3.

7   Ronald B. Bond (ed.), *Certain Sermons or Homilies (1547) and a Homily against Wilful Rebellion (1570): A Critical Edition* (Toronto: University of Toronto Press, 1987), pp. 3–4.

8   D. W. Robertson, 'Frequency of Preaching in Thirteenth-Century England', *Speculum*, 24 (1949), 376–88 (p. 376).

9   Jenny Swanson, 'Childhood and Childrearing in *ad status* Sermons by Later Thirteenth-Century Friars', *Journal of Medieval History*, 16 (1990), 309–31 (p. 309).

10   John T. McNeill and Helena M. Gamer (eds and trans), *Medieval Handbooks of Penance: A Translation of the Principal 'libri poenitentiales' and Selections from*

Related Documents (New York: Columbia University Press, 1938; 1990). The earliest recorded penitential in the book is for Finnian of Clonard, a distinguished sixth-century Irish monastic founder and teacher.

11 R. Emmet McLaughlin, 'Truth, Tradition and History: The Historiography of High/Late Medieval and Early Modern Penance', in Abigail Firey, (ed), *A New History of Penance* (Leiden, Boston: Brill, 2008), pp. 19–71 (p. 19).

12 Edward Burns, *The Chester Mystery Cycle: A New Staging Text* (Liverpool: Liverpool University Press, 1987), p. viii. The final production of the Chester plays was presented in 1575, after which, pressures from Elizabeth I's government brought the cycle to an end. Originally performed at the Feast of Corpus Christi before moving to Whitsuntide in the early years of the sixteenth century, these plays were performed on moveable stages, such as carts and wagons that stopped at various places around the towns and repeated the plays.

13 Burns, *Chester Mystery Cycle*, pp. 31–2.

14 Laurence Vaux, *A Catechisme of Christian Doctrine for Children and ignorante people, briefly compiled by Laurence Vaux, Bacheler of Diuinite: with an other later addition of instruction of the laudable Ceremonies vsed in the Catholicke Churche* (Rouen: George L'Oyselet, 1583), chap. 4.

15 Batty, *Christian Man's Closet*, p. 2.

16 Hugh Rhodes, *The boke of nurture, or Schoole of good maners for men, Seruants, and children, with Stans puer ad mensam* (London, 1577).

17 R. W. Southern, 'Grosseteste, Robert (*c.* 1170–1253)', *DNB*.

18 Kathleen M. Davies, 'The Sacred Condition of Equality: How Original Were Puritan Doctrines of Marriage?' *Social History*, 2 (1977), 563–80 (p. 564).

19 Thomas Phayer, *The Regiment of life, whervnto is added a treatyse of the pestilence, with the booke of children newly corrected and enlarged* (London, 1545); John Jones, *The Arte and Science of preseruing Bodie and Soule in al Health, Wisedome, and Catholike Religion: Phisically, Philosopically, and Diuinely deuised* (London, 1579).

20 Jones's book was directed at princes, rulers, nobles, bishops, preachers, parents and members of Parliament.

21 C. L. Powell, *English Domestic Relations 1487–1653: A Study of Matrimony and Family Life in Theory and Practice as Revealed by the Literature, Law, and History of the Period* (New York: Russell & Russell, 1917), pp. 101–02.

22 Batty, *Christian Man's Closet*, title page.

23 William Phiston, *The Schoole of good manners. Or, A new Schole of Vertue; teaching children & youth how they ought to behave themselues in all companies, times, and places* (London, 1595), sig. B1^v.

24 Shulamith Shahar, *Childhood in the Middle Ages* (London: Routledge, 1992), p. 115.

25 Thomas Becon, *The Catechism of Thomas Becon, S. T. P. Chaplain to Archbishop Cranmer, Prebendary of Canterbury, &c. With Other Pieces Written By Him in the Reign of Edward the Sixth* (Cambridge: Cambridge University Press, 1844), p. 348.

26 *Lyndwood's Provinciale: The text of the canons therein contained, reprinted from the translation made in 1534*, (eds) J. V. Bullard and H. Chalmer Bell (London: Faith Press, 1929) (hereafter *Lyndwood's Provinciale*), p. 133.

27 R. H. Helmholz, 'Lyndwood, William (*c.* 1375–1446)', *DNB*.

28 Adrian Morey, *Bartholomew of Exeter Bishop and Canonist: A Study in the Twelfth Century* (Cambridge: Cambridge University Press, 1937), p. 224: 'pro negligentia mater peniteat et ille homo securus sit.'

29 Juan Luis Vives, *The Education of a Christian Woman: A Sixteenth-Century Manual* (ed. and trans.) Charles Fantazzi (Chicago: University of Chicago Press, 2000), p. 269.

30 Margo Todd, 'Humanists, Puritans and the Spiritualized Household', *Church History*, 49 (1980), 18–34 (p. 27).

31 Batty, *Christian's Man's Closet*, p. 53^v.

32   Shahar, *Childhood in the Middle Ages*, p. 55.
33   Vives, *Education of a Christian Woman*, p. 270; Todd, 'Humanists, Puritans', p. 27.
34   Lloyd deMause, 'The Evolution of Childhood', in Lloyd deMause (ed.), *The History of Childhood* (New York: Harper & Row, 1975), pp.; Edward Shorter, *Making of the Modern Family* (New York: Basic Books, 1975), pp. 168–204.
35   This was usually the father. Sir Thomas Elyot, *The Boke Named the Governour* (1531; Menston: Scolar Press, 1970), fol. 16^v.
36   Vives, *Education of a Christian Woman*, p. 54.
37   Batty, *Christian Man's Closet*, p. 54.
38   Elyot, *The Boke Named the Governour*, fol. 16^v.
39   Shahar, *Childhood in the Middle Ages*, p. 56.
40   Elyot, *The Boke Named the Governour*, fol. 16^v.
41   Batty, *Christian Man's Closet*, p. 54.
42   Jones, *Arte and Science*, p. 39.
43   James Orchard Halliwell (ed.), *The Private Diary of John Dee, and The Catalogue of his Library of Manuscripts, from the original manuscripts* (New York: Johnson Reprint, 1842). Both Arthur and Frances Dee were weaned at thirteen months old.
44   Jones, *Arte and Science*, p. 51; p. 50; p. 49.
45   Jones, *Arte and Science*, p. 47.
46   Jones, *Arte and Science*, p. 43.
47   Luigi Belloni (ed.), *Il trattato ginecological-pediatro in volgare* (Milan, 1952), p. 154; Bernard de Gordon, *Regimen Sanitatis*, cited in Luke Demaitre, 'The Idea of Childhood and Child Care in Medical Writings of the Middle Ages', *Journal of Psychohistory*, 4 (1977), 461–90 (p. 474).
48   Laurent Joubert, *Popular Errors*, (trans. and annotated) Gregory David De Rocher (Tuscaloosa: University of Alabama Press, 1989), p. 242.
49   Joubert, *Popular Errors*, p. 242.
50   John Foxe, *The Acts and Monuments of John Foxe* (ed.) Josiah Pratt (London: Religious Tract Society, 1877), p. 722.
51   James Orchard Halliwell (ed.), *The Autobiography and Personal Diary of Dr Simon Forman, 1552–1602* (London, 1849), p. 3.
52   P. J. P. Goldberg (trans. and ed.), *Women in England c. 1275–1525: Documentary Sources* (Manchester: Manchester University Press, 1995), p. 73.
53   *Lyndwood's Provinciale*, p. 133.
54   *Lyndwood's Provinciale*, p. 133.
55   *Lyndwood's Provinciale*, p. 116.
56   DCA, Court Book of the Prior's Official DCD off. Bk, fol. 119^v.
57   Barbara Hanawalt, 'Childrearing Among the Lower Classes of Late Medieval England', *Journal of Interdisciplinary History*, 8 (1977), 1–22 (pp. 14–15).
58   Thomas of Chobham, *Summa Confessorum* (ed.) Frederick Broomfield (Paris: Beatrice-Nauwelaerts, 1968), p. 466: 'sed diligenter debent investigare sacerdotes si multa vel parva fuerit negligentia, et secundum hoc penitentiam aggravare vel mitigare.'
59   McNeill and Gamer (eds), *Medieval Handbooks*, p. 225.
60   McNeill and Gamer (eds), *Medieval Handbooks*, p. 254.
61   *Lyndwood's Provinciale*, p. 133.
62   John Mirk, *Mirk's Festial: A Collection of Homilies, Part I*, (ed.) Theodor Erbe (London: Kegan Paul, 1905), p. 150.
63   John Myrc, *Instructions For Parish Priests*, (ed.) Edward Peacock (New York: Kraus Reprint, 1975), p. 42; p. 5.
64   Nicholas Orme, *Medieval Children* (New Haven, CT: Yale University Press, 2001), p. 202.
65   Barbara Kellum, 'Infanticide in England in the Later Middle Ages', *History of Childhood Quarterly*, 1 (1974), 367–88 (p. 371); Hanawalt, 'Childrearing', pp. 14–15.

66 Shane Leslie and Ronald A. Knox (eds), *The Miracles of King Henry VI: Being an Account and Translation of Twenty-three Miracles taken from the Manuscript in the British Museum (Royal 13c. viii)* (Cambridge: Cambridge University Press, 1923). Cases are dated between 1481 and 1500.

67 Elizabeth Towner and John Towner, 'Developing the History of unintentional Injury: The Use of Coronors' Records In Early Modern England', *Injury Prevention*, (2000) 6, pp. 102–5 (p. 103).

68 Leslie and Knox (eds), *Miracles of King Henry VI*, pp. 51, 63, 141.

69 Leslie and Knox (eds), *Miracles of King Henry VI*, pp. 159–62.

70 Merridee L. Bailey, 'In Service and at Home: Didactic Texts for Children and Young People, c. 1400–1600', *Parergon*, 24 (2007), 23–46 (p. 23).

71 Jones, *Arte and Science*, p. 57.

72 Danièle Alexandre-Bidon and Didier Lerr, *Children in the Middle Ages* (trans.) Jody Gladding (Notre Dame, IN: University of Notre Dame Press, 1999), p. 23.

73 Bailey, 'In Service', p. 31.

74 William Gouge, *Of Domesticall Duties Eight Treatises* (London, 1622), p. 19.

75 Christopher Hill, *Society and Puritanism in Pre-Revolutionary England* (London: Secker & Warburg, 1964), pp. 443–81.

76 Shahar, *Childhood in the Middle Ages*, p. 209.

77 Hill, *Society and Puritanism*, pp. 446–8.

78 Priscilla Heath Barnum (ed.), *Dives and Pauper* (London: Oxford University Press for the Early English Text Society, 1976), p. 304.

79 William Tyndale, *The Obedience of a Christian Man* (1528; Menston: Scolar Press, 1970), fol. xlviii^v.

80 Merridee L. Bailey, *Socialising the Child in Late Medieval England c. 1400–1600* (York: York Medieval Press, 2012), p. 129.

81 Batty, *Christian Man's Closet*, p. 62.

82 Rhodes,*The boke of nurture*, Title page.

83 Phiston, *Schoole of good manners*, sig. B2.

84 Rhodes,*The boke of nuture*, sigs Aii^v–Aiii.

85 Plutarch, *The education or bringinge vp of children* (trans.) Thomas Elyot (London, 1532), sig. Biii.

86 Rhodes,*The boke of nuture*, sigs Aii–Aii^v.

87 Anon., *A glasse for housholders, wherin that they may se, both howe to rule them selfes & ordre their housholde verye Godly and frutfull* (London: in Officina Richard Graftoni, 1542), sig. Ei^v.

88 Batty, *Christian Man's Closet*, p. 4.

89 Suzanne W. Hull, *Chaste Silent and Obedient: English Books for Women 1475–1640* (San Marino: Huntingdon Library, 1982), pp. 34–5.

90 Batty, *Christian Man's Closet*, p. 16.

91 Davies, 'Sacred Condition', p. 570.

92 Vives, *Education of a Christian Woman*, p. 269.

93 Vives, *Education of a Christian Woman*, p. 272.

94 Cited in Kate Aughterson (ed.), *Renaissance Woman: A Sourcebook. Constructions of Femininity in England* (London and New York: Routledge, 1995), pp. 98–101.

95 See Aughterson (ed.), *Renaissance Woman*, p. 98.

96 BIA, CP.G.1521.

97 Goldberg (ed.), *Women in England*, p. 5.

98 Felicity Riddy, 'Mother Knows Best: Reading Social Change in a Courtesy Text', *Speculum*, 71 (1996), 66–86 (p. 69).

99 Riddy, 'Mother Knows Best', p. 72.

100 See the discussion on female apprentices, Chapter 5, pp. 268–72.

101 Riddy, 'Mother Knows Best', p. 70.

102   Robert Cleaver, *A Godly Forme of Hovsholde Governement: For The Ordering of Private Families, according to the direction of Gods word* (London, 1614), sig. A3.

103   Batty, *Christian Man's Closet*, p. 8.

104   Batty, *Christian Man's Closet*, p. 69.

105   Batty, *Christian Man's Closet*, p. 16.

106   Phiston, *Schoole of good manners*, sig. B2.

107   BIA, CP.F. 235.

108   Steven Ozment, *When Fathers Ruled: Family Life in Reformation Europe* (Cambridge, MA: Harvard University Press, 1983), pp. 140–41.

109   Bailey, *Socialising the Child*, p. 145.

110   Desiderius Erasmus,*The ciuilitie of childehode with the discipline and instruction of children distributed in small and compe[n]dious chapters* (trans.) Thomas Paynell (London, 1560), sigs Ciii–D.

111   Orme, *Medieval Children*, pp. 279–80.

112   Ozment, *When Fathers Ruled*, p. 141.

113   Rhodes, *Boke of nurture*, sig. Biiii.

114   Rhodes, *Boke of nurture*, sig. B^v.

115   Batty, *Christian Man's Closet*, p. 21.

116   Batty, *Christian Man's Closet*, p. 26.

117   Becon, *Catechism*, p. 353.

118   Vaux, *A Catechisme of Christian Doctrine*, chap. 3.

119   Batty, *Christian Man's Closet*, pp. 24–5.

120   Richard Whitford, *A werke for housholders/or for them [that] have the gydynge or gouernaunce of any company* (London, 1533), sig. Dii.

121   Whitford, *A werke for housholders*, sig. Dii.

122   Whitford, *A werke for housholders*, sig. Dii.

123   Halliwell, *Private Diary of John Dee*, pp. 30–1.

124   Whitford, *A werke for housholders*, sig. Dii^v.

125   Whitford, *A werke for housholders*, sig. Dii^v.

126   Rhodes, *Booke of Nurture*, sig. Aiii.

127   Michael J. Braddick and John Walter, 'Introduction. Grids of Power: Order, Hierarchy and Subordination in Early Modern Society', in Braddick and Walter (eds), *Negotiating Power in Early Modern Society: Order, Hierarchy and Subordination in Britain and Ireland* (Cambridge: Cambridge University Press, 2001), pp. 1–42 (p. 1).

128   Todd, 'Humanists, Puritans', pp. 18–19.

129   Morris P. Tilley (ed.), *A Dictionary of the Proverbs of England in the Sixteenth and Seventeenth Centuries: A Collection of the Proverbs Found in English Literature and the Dictionaries of the Period* (Ann Arbor: University of Michigan Press, 1950), p. 98, C326.

130   Plutarch, *Bringinge vp*, sig. F.

131   Plutarch, *Bringinge vp*, sig. F.

132   Plutarch, *Bringinge vp*, sig. F^v.

133   See also Chapter 5, p. 280–1.

134   Jones, *Arte and Science*, pp. 59–60.

135   Orme, *Medieval Children*, p. 101.

136   DUSC, Northumberland Act Book, DDR/EJ/CCA/3/2. This incident is also discussed in Chapter 5, p. 156.

137   DUSC, DDR/EJ/CCA/3/2.

138   Paul Griffiths, *Youth and Authority: Formative Experiences in England 1560–1640* (Oxford: Clarendon Press, 1996), p. 315.

139   LVRO, Liverpool Town Books 352, MIN/COU, Book 1, fol. 130.

140   Batty, *Christian Man's Closet*, p. 26.

141 Batty, *Christian Man's Closet*, p. 26.
142 See also Chapter 5, pp. 258–59.
143 TNA, C1/324/12. Petition made between 1500–1515.
144 Orme, *Medieval Children*, p. 101.
145 BIA, CP.G.102. This case is discussed in more detail in Chapter 3, pp. 142–3.
146 Swanson, 'Childhood and Childrearing', p. 311.
147 Swanson, 'Childhood and Childrearing', p. 317.
148 Julia Merritt, 'The Social Context of the Church in Early Modern Westminster', *Urban History*, 18 (1991), 20–31 (p. 21).
149 Leslie and Knox (eds), *Miracles of King Henry VI*, p. 130. In the case of fifteen-month-old John Hargreaves discussed below who was burnt, the accident was said to have happened when his parents were at church.
150 Leslie and Knox (eds), *Miracles of King Henry VI*, pp. 114–18. See the case of Joan Walran, whose parents were said to both be out on household business when she accidently hanged herself.
151 BIA, CP.G.347. This case is discussed in more detail in Chapter 3, pp. 98–99.
152 CALSS, OSF/24, fol. 3.
153 Charles F. Briggs, *Giles of Rome's 'de regime principum': Reading and Writing Politics at Court and University, c. 1275–c. 1525* (Cambridge: Cambridge University Press, 1999), p. 6.
154 Briggs, *Giles of Rome*, p. 2.
155 Juanita Feros Ruys, 'Introduction: Approaches to Didactic Literature – Meaning, Intent, Audience, Social Effect', in Juanita Feros Ruys (ed.), *What Nature Does not Teach: Didactic Literature in the Medieval and Early-Modern Periods* (Turnhout: Brepols, 2008), pp. 1–38 (p. 8).
156 Linda A. Pollock, *Forgotten Children: Parent–Child Relations from 1500–1900* (Cambridge: Cambridge University Press, 1983), p. 43.
157 Jay Mechling, 'Advice to Historians on Advice to Mothers', *Journal of Social History*, 9 (1975), 44–63 (p. 47). Emphasis in original.
158 Bailey, *Socialising the Child*, p. 128.
159 Bailey, *Socialising the Child*, p. 141.
160 Batty, *Christian Man's Closet*, p. 73.
161 Bailey, *Socialising the Child*, p. 128.
162 Andrew Cambers, *Godly Reading: Print, Manuscript and Puritanism in England, 1580–1720* (Cambridge: Cambridge University Press, 2011), pp. 87–110.
163 Cambers, *Godly Reading*, p. 93.
164 Natasha Glaisyer and Sara Pennell, 'Introduction', in Natasha Glaisyer and Sara Pennell (eds), *Didactic Literature in England 1500–1800: Expertise Constructed* (Aldershot: Ashgate, 2003), pp. 1–18 (p. 14).
165 Pollock, *Forgotten Children*, p. 44.
166 See Mechling, 'Advice to Historians', p. 45
167 Helmholz, 'Lyndwood', *DNB*.
168 See Davies, 'Sacred Condition', p. 563, n. 2.
169 John Alcock, 'Sermon for a Boy Bishop, *c.* 1489–91', in Mary C. Erler (ed.), *Records of Early English Drama: Ecclesiastical London* (London: British Library; Toronto: University of Toronto Press, 2008), p. 242.
170 CALSS, Coroners' Inquests, QCI/6/12.
171 Barbara Hanawalt, *Of Good and Ill Repute: Gender and Social Control in Medieval England* (Oxford: Oxford University Press, 1998), p. 162.
172 Leslie and Knox (eds), *Miracles of King Henry VI*, p. 138.
173 Nicholas Orme, *Early British Swimming 55BC–AD1719: With the First Swimming Treatise in English, 1595* (Exeter: University of Exeter Press, 1983), pp. 62–5.
174 Carol Loar, 'Medical Knowledge and the Early Modern English Coroner's Inquest', *Social History of Medicine*, 23 (2010), 475–91 (p. 477).

175 Hanawalt, *Of Good and Ill Repute*, p. 163.
176 Leslie and Knox (eds), *Miracles of King Henry VI*, p. 130.
177 Leslie and Knox (eds), *Miracles of King Henry VI*, pp. 114–5.
178 Leslie and Knox (eds), *Miracles of King Henry VI*, p. 51.
179 Martin Ingram, 'Child Sexual Abuse in Early Modern England', in Braddick and Walter (eds), *Negotiating Power*, pp. 63–84 (p. 83).
180 Cited in Naomi D. Hurnard, *The King's Pardon for Homicide before 1307 A.D.* (Oxford: Clarendon Press, 1969), p. 107.
181 LRO, QSR 6/34d.
182 Ariès, *Centuries*, p. 130.
183 Tilley (ed.), *A Dictionary of the Proverbs*, p. 99, C342.
184 Patrick Collinson, *The Birthpangs of Protestant England: Religious and Cultural Change in the Sixteenth and Seventeenth Centuries* (Basingstoke: MacMillan, 1988), p. 90.
185 Hugh Cunningham, *Children and Childhood in Western Society since 1500* (London and New York: Longman, 1995), p. 43.
186 EYLA, B 2, 3, 4, fol. 12.
187 Mechling, 'Advice to Historians', p. 53.

3   Child marriage

Where there is no consent there is no marriage; and so those who give girls to boys in their cradles achieve nothing (*nichil faciunt*) – unless both the children give consent after they have come to the age of discretion.[1]

On 9 March 1885, a letter appeared in *The Manchester Guardian*, which brought to light 'a very curious phase of the bygone social life of this district' during the sixteenth century.[2] The 'curious phase' referred to in the letter was that of child marriage, or *infra annos nubiles* to give its Latin term, a phenomenon traditionally associated with royalty and the elite of late medieval and early modern England. Distinction must be made between child marriage referred to in this letter and the forced child marriage we associate with less economically developed economies today. In countries such as India and Yemen, children are on occasions married at an early age and expected to conform to all aspects of an adult marriage including sex and childbirth. The evils of the latter state of child marriage may be assessed through works such as Eleanor Rathbone's *Child Marriage: The Indian Minotaur* or more recent accounts, some from the children themselves.[3] As you will read below, the children in sixteenth-century child marriages in the north of England were not expected to conform to the expectations of adult marriage in anything other than marital status.

The purpose of this chapter is to give a clearer understanding of how the practice of child marriage affected the nurture of the child. By analysing the emotional responses and reactions of children to their marriages, we are able to appreciate the practice from the perspective of the child. This gives children a voice through which we can observe conflicts with authority and how children attempted to exercise agency in relation to their marriages. Ecclesiastical depositions form the basis for this chapter with the evidence given by the witnesses in matrimonial court cases providing social detail as well as the circumstances surrounding the marriage.[4] As discussed in Chapter 1, depositions also allow for a considerable range of social class situations to be analysed. Reputation and honour was of paramount concern to people who used the services of the church courts, and all were eager to defend their reputations.[5]

In total, 137 marriage cases have been analysed from the dioceses of Chester and York. Durham, as is noted below, is an anomaly in regards to underage marriage and I have identified only three cases of underage marriage which occur during the dates of this study. Of the marriages from Chester and York, the earliest union discussed in this chapter took place in 1497 and the latest in 1593. Whilst the chronological distribution of the marriages does not cover the dates of this study in its entirety, they do include the last decade of the fifteenth century and span every decade of the sixteenth century. The cases are interesting in their geographical distribution across the dioceses. For those cases heard at Chester, many came from the central and northern parts of Lancashire, including places in the Ribble Valley such as Colne, which is over 50 miles from Chester, with only a few from the urban centres of Chester or Liverpool. Cases from York followed this pattern of rural location with the majority of cases coming not from the urban areas, but from the clothing regions of the West Riding of Yorkshire with many locations a considerable distance from York. For example, six cases originated from the areas around Halifax, which is over 35 miles from York.

There are two possibilities for this spatial arrangement of the cases. One, argued by Jeremy Goldberg and discussed in Chapter 1, is that, at least for York, the cases being heard before the consistory court were appeal cases, which had already been heard at a church court local to the litigants. The other could be that this distribution signalled difference within the North as a region in relation to certain childrearing practices, with child marriage far less frequent in urban areas than rural ones, where land and estates were required to be protected and retained within families. As Wrigley and Schofield have argued, minor trends in marriage patterns at a national level may not be observed at a local level. Any peculiarity, therefore, can lie within the parish.[6] This may be the case with child marriage, but it also highlights differences within the region.

Authors on marriage litigation like Richard Helmholz and Kathryn Taglia have highlighted that child marriage did occur by the very fact canon law legislated on the matter.[7] Historically, however, child marriage remains subordinated to the family and parent–child relations and where there is some discussion the topic is subsumed within studies of childhood. To date, there remains no single secondary source on child marriage. Many general works have chosen to ignore the practice of child marriage altogether, while some like Nicholas Orme's *Medieval Children* have considered the practice in brief, but only in relation to marriages of the elites.[8] Where discussion is generated on the subject, it invariably draws on one source of information: Frederick Furnivall's transcription of the depositions from the diocese of Chester, 1561–1566.[9] As an edited volume of primary sources it only covers a seven-year period and as such does not contribute widely to the scholarship, but it has become the foundation of debate for those few authors who have written about child marriage in the early modern period.

Ivy Pinchbeck and Margaret Hewitt dedicate a whole chapter to the topic of child marriage using cases from Furnivall.[10] There is, however, little of substance on actual child marriage excepting those cases cited by Furnivall, while their inquiry offers little in the way of explanation of the practice. Gary Gibbs's assessment of Furnivall's cases provides a certain amount of interpretation, with his motivation for re-examining the Chester annulments remaining similar to the Early English Text Society's for whom Furnivall undertook the project: children were younger than he had anticipated, annulment documented in an age of supposedly unbreakable marriage and the cases offer a window onto the social interactions in Elizabethan families.[11] Arguing that child marriages were not 'simply random phenomena' he highlights the fact that not all children were from elite or wealthy families.[12]

Geographically, child marriage in the sixteenth century has been dismissed by Eric Carlson as being 'peculiar to the north',[13] but without a comprehensive study of all the available ecclesiastical sources in England this claim cannot be substantiated. The probability of such a study being undertaken in the near future appears unlikely. Nevertheless, Carlson's claim weakens when we consider available data from the rest of the country. Of a sample of twenty-five child marriages that occurred in England in the period 1345–1510, over half (thirteen) of these came from other parts of England – two each from Essex and Kent, one each from Cornwall, Lincoln, Northampton, Somerset and possibly London, and four from Devon.[14] The evidence of child marriage being a northern phenomenon in the preceding centuries to this study is therefore weak and as such the situation was unlikely to have changed by the start date of this study. Nor is the evidence conclusive on child marriage being a gentry phenomenon.

Christopher Haigh discusses the practice in relation to the gentry of Lancashire whose early age at marriage, he believes, led to unstable marriages.[15] Like Carlson, he considers child marriage to be something of a northern phenomenon, although he only considers Lancashire in his study. No acknowledgement is given by Haigh that child marriage was other than a pursuit of the upper classes. Correspondingly, Peter Laslett states the marriages recorded by Furnivall cannot be held as common practice among those without land or property, a view held by Pinchbeck and Hewitt.[16] On the contrary, depositions, as we shall see, show child marriages were arranged by some families whose landholdings were far from extensive and who could not, by any stretch of terminology, be termed 'wealthy'. Andrew Haworth and Constance Entwisell were married because Andrew's father had obtained the goodwill of the landlord who owned the tenement where Constance's father lived.[17] So, although property was involved, it was sometimes only a small amount.

According to Laslett, the cases outlined by Furnivall were less than 1 per cent of all the annulment proceedings heard at Chester during those years, but they were still a significant number – thirty in total – highlighting frequency of practice. Add to this number the 107 underage marriages presented in the ecclesiastical courts of the north of England identified by this study[18] and it is puzzling that such a major factor in annulment cases should have been so consistently ignored by historians, even by those whose concern was marriage during the period under discussion. Alan Macfarlane, Conor McCarthy,

Frederick Pedersen and Lawrence Stone are strangely quiet on the subject, although Pedersen does comment on two marriages of underage wards in relation to marital affection.[19] Carlson devotes just over two pages to child marriages, referring to a few of Furnivall's cases, one early Chancery petition and two cases from Yorkshire.[20] Like Shannon McSheffrey's volume on marriage in late medieval London, these studies are useful for understanding the complexities of marriages in the period, much of which would apply to child marriage.[21] What we can deduce from the scholarship is that the examples of child marriage from the diocese of Chester, published by the Early English Text Society in 1897 and a good deal of assumption, are the basis of the historiography that has been produced in the subsequent 118 years. But why the apparent neglect of a subject that was clearly affecting the lives of children in the sixteenth century?

The disregard of child marriage by historians may in part be due to the acceptance of the view of marriage formation in Europe proposed by John Hajnal in the 1960s.[22] Hajnal argued that young people delayed marrying until their mid to late twenties and that there was a high percentage of people who did not marry at all.[23] E. A. Wrigley and R. S. Schofield have reinforced Hajnal's conclusions, stating that young people in England did not marry until they had established an independent household and for both men and women this tended to not be until they had reached their mid to late twenties.[24] This observation has remained unchallenged while leaving child marriage as an irregularity in the history books. This study does not wish to disprove this theory, as late marriage was the usual option to the large number of young people who entered into service or took up an apprenticeship.[25] Rather, it aims to demonstrate that child marriage was an accepted childrearing practice in sixteenth-century northern England.

This study also acknowledges that what is required for the subject of child marriage is a thorough study of ecclesiastical sources and references to child marriages in a range of legal sources (including Chancery petitions) from other parts of England. Until this has been completed, historians cannot make the assumption that child marriage was a northern, gentry phenomenon and we can only infer from those sources that have survived what the trend may have been. If such a survey were undertaken, then we can establish if the practice was as widespread in the south of England as historians believe it was in the north.

The lack of scholarship on this particular subject means that many questions are unanswered. As a consequence I am not able to place my own findings within an established framework of historical inquiry. A number of questions, therefore, must be considered to establish such a framework: what were the legal definitions of child marriage in the sixteenth century as outlined by canon law? Was the practice of child marriage consistent across all three of the ecclesiastical dioceses examined in this book? What motivated parents, guardians and families to marry their children and wards below the age of canonical consent? What role did family and friends play in the making of child marriages? What was the community response to child marriages? Was the practice of child marriage exclusive to the children of wealthy parents and benefactors? What can we learn from the sources about the lived experiences of children who were married under age? What were the emotional responses and reactions of the children to their marriages?

Legal definitions of child marriage

What were the legal definitions of child marriage in the sixteenth century as outlined by canon law? Canon law decreed that no child under the age of seven could legally contract a marriage,[26] although, as this chapter demonstrates, not all parents adhered to this directive. Contemporary commentators expressed their opinion vis-à-vis this stipulation: Henry Swinburne, a judge of the Prerogative Court in York, clearly stated that children under the age of seven could not contract marriage as 'these young Infants want Reason and Judgement to judge these Affairs'.[27] Above the age of seven, the contract could be made but the marriage would not be valid unless ratified by both parties when they came to the age of consent. Canon law created a legal definition of puberty as twelve for girls and fourteen for boys.[28] Ecclesiastical authorities in Durham regarded even these ages as being too low, for the bishop's visitation of 1577 required all priests to inform their parishioners that 'no yonge man haithe power to contracte matrimony before he be fully xvj yeres of age nor any woman before she be fully xiiij yeres of aige'. Anyone going against these directives was to be 'sharplie and severely' punished.[29] It was possible for children to reach natural puberty earlier than these ages, and in some cases sexual maturity led to the marriage being consummated while the parties were still under the age of consent. In such cases, the act of consummation rather than the legal age thresholds could be deemed sufficient to make a marriage legal.[30] Additional confusion arose from the fact that, although children could be legally betrothed from the age of seven, they had to wait until reaching puberty before a marriage could be annulled. To achieve an annulment, it had to be proven that the parties did not consent to the marriage either vocally or by cohabitation and consummation. Force and fear would also be a good reason for annulment and many depositions reference that children were forced into the marriage.[31] Hence, the legal age of discretion as stipulated by the Church along with consent was the fulcrum on which child marriage would become legal.

In reality, these child marriages were contracted by *verba de futuro* (words of future consent). Both parties would have to agree to ratify the marriage when they came to the legal age for it to be legally binding, unlike *verba de presenti* (words of present consent), where the Church ruled that an indissoluble bond had been created. Cohabitation and consummation past the age of consent was accepted as ratification of the union, although a few cases of legal ratification do appear in the records. John Dutton came before the consistory court in Chester in 1552 'without compulsion constreynt and cohirtion' to ratify his marriage to Elenore Calveley.[32] Tentatively, any disagreement was to be made in the ecclesiastical courts, although this was not legally necessary and could be made before witnesses.[33] Many child marriages could arguably have ended this way, but there are no records to prove this. Only when there was disagreement between the parties and each side felt they had valid grounds for an annulment did the suit come before the courts.[34]

For an annulment to occur, the ecclesiastical courts had to be certain that the couple were married under age. People petitioning and those deposing in the courts were invariably aware of this prerequisite to an annulment. Without exception, the libel required the witness to state the age of the parties at the time of marriage. Often witnesses would recount an event from around the time that the child was born to prove that they knew their age at marriage. This could be the birth of his or her own child, the taking of a lease from the father of the child or recalling when a particular mayor was in office. A number of witnesses in the case of Elizabeth Waite and William Bransby, heard before the consistory at York between 1561 and 1564, knew the age of Elizabeth at the time of her marriage because William Lewes was then lord mayor.[35]

As the requirement to register baptisms, marriages and deaths was introduced only in 1538, and the keeping of these registers was erratic across the parishes, people could not always accurately tell the ages of the children involved and therefore they estimated them. Katherine Dutton, from Ince in Lancashire, who in 1548 was attempting to gain an annulment from her husband, Robert Bushell, was described by one witness at the time of the marriage as being 'of a greatt stature and able to lie with any man'.[36] Implicit in the words of this witness was the fact that Katherine had obviously reached puberty and was therefore passed the age of consent when she married and consequently the marriage was legal. Her mother, who had forced Katherine to marry Robert, insisted that she had been on or just below the legal age of twelve. Conversely, Elizabeth Studley was presumed to be under twelve years of age at her marriage to Robert Woodhead at Bardsey, Yorkshire, in 1565, 'by reason she was of very litle stature and childishe countennce and not likely to be any older'.[37] It was not until the directives of the Reformation took hold in the north of England that the age of the children could be correctly identified by the use of the register. Witnesses were able to inform the courts that they had 'sawe and redd in the register booke' when one of the parties had been baptised.[38] Frances Stephenson was able to establish that her husband John Wright was under age when they married around 1593 because she went with her brother to the church where John was baptised and checked the baptismal register.[39]

Familiarity with canon law was just as much a consideration to parents and guardians when contracting an underage marriage as were the details of the marriage settlement. Edmund Trafford of Trafford and John Booth of Barton, both in Lancashire, had a marriage agreement drawn up for their children Edmund and Margaret in 1569. Not only did it specify the transaction of lands and money between the two fathers, but stipulated what was to happen in the case of marital breakdown, taking into consideration whether carnal copulation had taken place or not.[40] No age is stated for the children but the inclusion of a clause in relation to consummation of marriage suggests that they were both minors and that the fathers understood the implications of the law in regards to a binding marriage.

Some parents and relatives were more explicit in their understanding of canon law. When Katherine Tatlock and Edmund Mollinuex were married by the rector of Sefton, Lancashire (whose surname was also Mollineux), in 1538, he suggested that 'she shuld have hym for the space of ij years and then iff theye cold agre to gether itt were well. iif not he promised hir that she shuld be Divorsed agayne'.[41] Similarly, Christian Hope informed her son Peter, who had married Alice Ellis in 1547, that if he and Alice could not agree to the marriage by the time they reached lawful age 'the said Peter shuld be at Libertye and the Matrimony shuld be void'.[42] But the children themselves were aware of the protocol for a lawful marriage and their agency in respect to this can be observed in actions they took in order to achieve an annulment. Margaret Wall, who married John Venables in Great Budworth, Cheshire, in 1562, would not even take her husband a drink after she came to lawful age in case people thought that she liked him.[43] Children had to be seen by potential witnesses to dissent from the marriage in order to have any success at securing an annulment once past the age of consent.

In addition to legal age and consent, another requirement of canon law concerning marriages was the publication of banns. This constituted a public intention to marry and was a system by which parishioners could inform the priest if there were any impediment to the marriage that would render it unlawful.[44] This practice then involved the community at large in enforcing canon law relating to matrimony and displayed social control over intended unions.[45] It is doubtful whether banns were actually read for child marriages and thus the requirement was circumvented. Ellen Morris and John Ramsbottom were married in a chamber of Ellen's father's house in Clitheroe, Lancashire, around 1569, although witnesses at the annulment case said that they had not heard any banns read.[46] Evidence suggests at times banns were read after the marriage had taken place, as happened at the wedding of eleven-year-old Anne Goodshawe and William Stephenson in 1569, also at Clitheroe.[47] It appears priests did not always adhere to the rule of the Church in relation to banns, as the case of James and Anne Ballard illustrates. They were married at 10 p.m. in the parish church of Colne, Lancashire, in 1560 by Sir Roger Blakley despite no banns being read.[48] Nonetheless, failure to publish banns did not make the marriage invalid and parents and guardians were able to flout ecclesiastical rules to secure a desirable match for their children.

The Church and not parents laid down the basis of a lawful marriage.[49] However, parents were aware of canonical law and were adept at circumventing that law to arrange marriages for their children. Priests, it seems, chose to bend or ignore the law to allow these marriages to take place. If the rules of the Church were so readily flouted by parents and clerics alike, was the practice of child marriage consistent across all three dioceses?

Consistency of practice across the dioceses

Was the practice of child marriage consistent across all three of the ecclesiastical dioceses examined in this book? Child marriage was a common enough practice in Chester and York, as examination of the records from those dioceses in the sixteenth century demonstrates. Durham, on the other hand, appears to be an anomaly, with only three cases appearing in the extant records that I could locate: the marriage of Richard Laton and Elizabeth Berker, which came before officials at Durham, *c.* 1490; that of Richard Hogg and Anne Kristop *c.* 1597; and that of Mary Darcy and William Lord Eure, 1541.[50] Of these only the second appears in the depositions, while the first appears in the Court Prior's Book and the latter is included in a Bishop's Register and Act Book. If, as Christopher Haigh has argued, the social hierarchy and geographical isolation of Lancashire encouraged child marriages,[51] then one must presume that these factors would be more concentrated the further north one progressed and child marriage would be as much in evidence in Durham as it was in Lancashire.

There could be a number of explanations why this discrepancy should exist. Arguably the reason does not lie in the fact that the inhabitants of the diocese of Durham had extremely obedient children who did not wish to disobey the wishes of their parents and guardians by refusing to ratify their underage marriages. Rather, the explanation may be located in the concerns of the consistory courts at Durham, whose focus at the time appears to have been recording instances of adultery and illegitimacy. In the cases of disputed marriages, those that appear in the depositions are where agreements had been broken or marriages which were invalid due to prior contracts. This explains why the marriage of Richard Hogg and Anne Kristop appears in the depositions. Richard brought it before the courts, not to petition for annulment but to enforce their contract of marriage. Richard and Anne had been married some years earlier when Richard was only eight years old. Anne was then successively married to James Hogg in 1601, the year before the petition, without divorcing Richard and Richard had decided to sue to resume his marriage to Anne. Richard's wish to enforce the marriage had forced Anne and James into the courtroom.

We can reasonably deduce that the differences in the figures between the three jurisdictions may be due to diverse court practices in each diocese. In which case, we remain uninformed about the incidence of child marriage in the diocese of Durham. Even so, we may infer that circumstances surrounding child marriages and the experiences of the children involved in the diocese of Durham were not dissimilar to those of the children in the other two dioceses despite not having any tangible evidence.

Motivations for child marriage

What motivated parents, guardians and families to marry their children and wards below the age of canonical consent? The practical nature of marriages during the period of this study reflected the reciprocal duty of parents and children: parents to make a good marriage for their children and children to accept their parents' choice of marriage partner. It was, as Peter Rushton described, the 'lynchpin of the family system', around which the family elders of both parties placed vested interests.[52] Nevertheless, a good match was not necessarily arranged with the happiness of the bride and groom in mind but more with safeguarding or advancing fortunes, protecting land and forging connections.[53] Parental power had not diminished in early modern England where minors were concerned: they could be forced into profitable matches.[54] This was unsurprising considering some of the children were extremely young when they were married. Constance Good told the consistory court in York that when she married John Bickerton in Bolton Percy, Yorkshire, in 1537 she was 'vere young and with ought discretion and knowe not what she did abought suche businis'.[55]

Few depositions cite any detail as to the circumstances of child marriage and it is unclear whether the witnesses themselves were aware of the reasoning behind the marriages. Several mention that the marriage was 'made rather by thinstigacion and information' of parents, or that a child was 'forced' by one parent or another.[56] Common opinion during the sixteenth century was that marriages were only for the benefit of the parents. Philip Stubbes enunciated this understanding in 1583 by writing that 'little Infants in swaddling Cloutes, are often married by their ambitious Parentes and friendes, when they know neither good or euill'.[57] Pinchbeck and Hewitt question whether this observation could be a reliable benchmark for the poorer classes. They argue that Stubbes's observations were intended only for those marriages where the wealth of the parents and children were the intended outcome.[58] From my research, it is clear that child marriage was linked to social and economic factors which influenced a parent's choice of partner for their child, as well as when the marriage would take place.[59] Reasons for why child marriages had occurred can be identified in the depositions and all hinge on agreements between parents and other adults. None identifies the agency of the child in choosing their own marriage partner. Evident are negotiations concerning debts, identification of one of the parties as being a 'good bargain', the marriage of stepchildren due to the union of their parents, marriage of wards, coercion of the child by adults other than their parents and, lastly, compulsion of family and friends. All were considered valid motives for the marriages to take place.

By far the most frequently mentioned reason in the depositions for the occurrence of child marriages was formal or verbal agreements between parents or guardians involving land or money. The witnesses rarely referred to formal, witnessed agreements, like that between the fathers of Edmund Trafford and Margaret Booth, although some do mention covenants. The marriage of William Stopford and Anne Longley in 1523 was recorded in covenants between William's father Robert and Thomas Longley. Robert Stopford told the Chester consistory that 'the copie wher off be remayneing hire in the registrs'.[60] Similarly, Nicolas Stokes and Anne Irlande were married 'bie certon

indentures off covenites made betwixt William Stokes father to the said
Nicolas and the father of Anne Irlande'.[61] There is no indication to the terms
and conditions of the marriage contained within the covenants, but the age of
the children was stated in them. Verbal (or at least not formally recorded)
agreements, where money was the overriding factor in making the marriages,
were more revealing about the motives of the parents.

The children themselves were often aware that money had been the motivation for their marriage. Alice Carter believed that her marriage to Thomas
Barrowe was made by the mediation of Thomas's father only to obtain money
from her own father.[62] Nor was Alice unique in her reasoning on child marriage.
Emma Talbot, who was married to Gilbert Gerrard aged six, stated that she
had been 'sold' to James Gerrad, Gilbert's father.[63] And, while the circumstances
surrounding this marriage are not known, implicit in Emma's statement is the
hostility and resentment she felt towards her father, sentiments felt by other
children. Richard Waterhouse was determined he would not take Margaret
Watmoughe as his wife because 'Robert Crosseley his uncle toik money for
him'.[64] But it would appear that marrying your child under age was a *bona
fide* method of raising family revenue, as a witness at the annulment case of
Richard Mason and Elizabeth Lock testified at Chester in 1567. Hugo Rathbone
told the court the marriage was arranged by Richard's father 'to get a piece of
money toward the taking of his house'.[65] However, for some parents, accepting
or offering money for the marriage of their children was a measure of desperation and, although still a monetary bargain, was one brought about by
great need.

Marriages of underage children were sometimes arranged at short notice.
The wedding of thirteen-year-old Peter Hope and nine-year-old Alice Ellis took
place in Chester in 1547, but none of the deponents could testify as to the
reason for the marriage at their annulment hearing in 1563.[66] More detail is
to be found in a will made by Alice's father, Matthew, in the same year of the
marriage. Matthew Ellis had paid Christian Hope, Peter's mother, £23 for
the match.[67] This money was in addition to Alice's child's portion of £33.
Peter must have been a desirable partner because if Alice were to die before the
marriage took place Peter was to marry her sister. Matthew Ellis was ensuring
his daughter would be married and settled despite him not being alive to
negotiate the terms of a contract of marriage. He was not the only father to
do so. William Monckton and Elizabeth Robert of Kingston upon Hull in
Yorkshire were married in 1581 precisely because William's father was very
sick and not likely to live long, while Agnes Kippax's father had left money
(and no doubt instructions) in his will for her to be married to William
Ellend, the marriage occurring in 1537.[68] The death of a father placed the
mother in a vulnerable position in relation to family finances, which in some
instances forced her to contract a marriage for her children despite them
being below age. Joan Stevenson accepted £20 for her son John to marry
Elizabeth Orme in 1565 after her husband died. Joan stated that 'with having
to pay the lands lorde for and income' she accepted the offer to marry her

son to Elizabeth, rather than lose the house she lived in.[69] Witnesses reported that John and Elizabeth married in haste and, taking into consideration the circumstances of how the marriage was arranged, John had never shown any sign of good will or good deed towards his wife.

Property and acquisition of land were attractive incentives when marrying children under age. Ellen Dampart and John Andrew were married *c.* 1553 because Ellen, an illegitimate daughter of her father, was heir to John Smith, who owned one half of the tenement and John's father who lived in the other half.[70] Often, money had been lent to a father by way of a bond to purchase land with the caveat of marriage between the two men's children if the money were not repaid by a certain date. This was certainly the case for John Bridge, whose grandfather borrowed money from Elizabeth Ramsbottom's father to purchase some land, and in so doing made a bargain of marriage between the two children.[71] On the death of his grandfather in 1558, thirteen-year-old John was married to Elizabeth at Bury, Lancashire, to save his father from paying back the bond. As John himself describes his situation 'yf he had not gone to the Churche and there have spoken the wordes after the priest his father had bene vndone'.[72] The security of his family was dependent upon John acquiescing to his father's wishes.

Across the Pennines, the practice of borrowing money with a surety of a contract of marriage with a child was also in evidence. In Ilkley, Yorkshire, eleven-year-old Isabel Wadsworth's grandfather James Thakery was bound by the bond of £40 to Richard Wright.[73] The terms of the bond stated that Isabel would be married before she was twelve or James would have to repay the bond and she was subsequently married to Richard *c.* 1532 at the age of eleven.[74] Of course, once Isabel reached the age of twelve, she would have had to consent to the marriage, which in all likelihood she would not do. Making a guarantee of marriage with underage children on lending money to an acquaintance was an assured way of gaining access to someone's lands through inheritance. What the transaction of bonds implies is that there was at least an understanding that the money could have been repaid before the deadline and the marriages avoided. But this was not the situation with every exchange of money. Thomas Fletcher was reportedly married *c.* 1554 by his father to Anne Whitfield 'for a piece of mony for discharge of his said debts' with no pretence of actually paying back the money.[75] Yet the desperation of parents concerning either the exchange of money or relating to the safeguarding of it can be detected in the depositions. In 1569, John Goodshawe married his eleven-year-old daughter Anne to a man eleven or twelve years older than her.[76] Little is mentioned about the groom, William Stephenson. His parent's names are absent from the depositions, but indications are that he was a business partner of Anne's father or at least someone in whose affairs he had invested money. John tried to persuade Anne to marry William 'bie all devises He cold' as William was keen to have her but also because John Goodshawe 'had spent much monie in his afairs'.[77] Marrying his daughter to William Stephenson was a measure to protect the family finances.

Not all parents regarded child marriage as a conduit through which to raise required capital. For the most part, parents were concerned about ensuring their children were well provided for in adult life. Child marriage was a means of achieving this despite the prospective bride and groom being of a young age. Elizabeth Hulse was married to George Hulse when she was four years of age and he seven in 1547 'biecause her frendes thought she shuld have had a lyvinge bie hym'.[78] Unfortunately, the good living envisioned by Elizabeth's family and friends was not to be. George somehow lost his inheritance and had to bind himself to a shoemaker in Congleton, Cheshire, and once he had finished his apprenticeship became a journeyman. Even before she came to the age of consent, Elizabeth had decided that George was not what she wanted for a husband, especially as he was not able to maintain her. George, who would have still taken Elizabeth for his wife, deposed to the church court at Chester that because he had lost his living he had become 'a poore wastes man' and that Elizabeth 'depisethe hym & dothe set little bie hym'.[79]

Inheritance did not involve parents alone but could encompass a diverse group of family and friends.[80] The fragility of any inheritance in the sixteenth century and the powerful relationship between those who held property and those who inherited, shown in the case of Elizabeth and George, was not unique. Thomas Bentham's marriage to Elena Bolton in 1552 at Beetham in West Yorkshire was arranged because Elena's grandfather was very wealthy and it was hoped he would 'bestowid somme good ferme upon her'.[81] Unfortunately for Thomas, Elena 'plaid manie light points', bearing three illegitimate children to two different men, which so displeased the grandfather that he left her nothing in his will.[82] Whether it was the lack of inheritance or Elena's behaviour that prompted Thomas to sue for annulment of the marriage we can never know, but even when inheritance was assured it did not make for successful child marriage. Joan Leyland was married to Rafe Whittall because Rafe had 40s. a year in land and that 'she shold have had bie hym a pretty bargane yf they cold have lovid on the other'.[83] In the same manner, Alice Clerk was married when she was seven to twelve-year-old Richard Cropper in 1566 because his father had left him certain goods when he had died. Alice's father, 'thinkinge that the said Richard was a good bargaine', negotiated a contract of marriage with Hugo Billinge, Richard's guardian.[84] Unfortunately, Richard could not 'love or fansie' Alice and the marriage was never ratified.

If the prospect of a good living from a decent inheritance was an attractive motive for parents to marry their children under age, then the opportunity for the interested parent to access that inheritance must have been even greater. This may explain the marriages of stepchildren due to the union of their parents. Although not as prevalent as other motives, the marriage of stepchildren appears enough times – four in total – in the records to warrant discussion. In only one of those cases did the parents articulate why they thought it a good idea to marry their children to each other. Elene Venables's eleven-year-old daughter Margaret was married to the five-year-old son of her husband George Venables on the same day in 1562 at Great Budworth church, Cheshire, that she married George. The reasoning was that 'it wold be thought a better quietnes and occasion of perpetuall agreement betwixt this deponent and her husband and for the house and living sake the parentes tought good to joyne their children … together'.[85] The marriage of the children further consolidated both the assets and the unity of the family.

Marrying off a child to the son or daughter of a new spouse did not always make for harmony in the household. Robert Mason of Preston was married in 1555 at the age of eleven to Margaret Dugdale because her father had married his mother. Not only did Robert dislike his bride, but also her father because 'he kept the mother of the said Roberte to paramour afore he maried her, & consumed the said Robertes goodes'.[86] Robert was so unhappy with the situation he found himself in, that less than a year after the marriage he left his father-in-law's house and went to stay with friends and according to his uncle, 'neuer came in house with the said Margaret to dwell sins that tyme'.[87] Undoubtedly, Robert's reaction reflects a child's eye view of the economics of marriage. Similarly, in Birstall, Yorkshire, ten-year-old Thomas Smith married his stepsister, Anne Goodale, in 1526. So miserable was Thomas with the arrangements, that when he reached fourteen he left his father's house for two years. On his return, John Smith, Thomas's father, was required to send Anne out of the house to stay with friends because of Thomas's dislike of her. When John tried to bring Anne back into the house eighteen months later, Thomas's objections forced John to send Thomas to school in Wakefield. As John Smith's servant Edward Craven described the relationship between Thomas and Anne, 'if she had gone to the church he wold agon to the chapell and she had gon to the chapell he wold agone to the church'.[88] Thomas may have gone through with the ceremony, but he exercised his agency to ensure that the marriage was not ratified.

Depositions concerning the last couple to be married in this way, Henry Accars and Jane Kenrike of Prescott, Lancashire, reveal nothing of the reasoning for the marriage or the relations within the household after it had taken place *c.* 1538,[89] yet by the very fact that the two were petitioning for annulment, one can assume that everyday life would have been just as discordant in their household as in the other three. The parents may have been oblivious to the possibility of such unrest within their blended family when they decided to consolidate lands and goods. But they would have known that it was a forbidden union according to canon law. The rule of consanguinity, whereby people could not marry another person they were related to either by blood or marriage was disregarded by the parents to protect their interests as a family, so the marriage would have been illegal regardless of whether the children had been past the age of consent.

On a few occasions, adults other than their parents and guardians and without their consent or knowledge coerced children into marriage. Thirteen-year-old William Parre of Prescott, Lancashire, was married to Jane Stanley of Barwick-in-Elmet, Yorkshire, without the knowledge of his father in 1553. Although not stated in the depositions, it was probable that William had been sent as a servant to Jane Stanley's father. The Stanleys' ancestral seat was in Lancashire as the Earls of Derby, although at certain times in the sixteenth century members of the Stanley family were responsible for the defence of England's northern border, which may have placed them in Yorkshire. As an esquire, William's father would have been socially conversant with such a family. The first that Thomas Parre knew of his son's marriage was when William returned home and told him he had been married to Jane. On enquiring why Thomas had not been made aware of the marriage, William had replied that he had been told it was his father's will that he should marry Jane and 'that you and your ffrendes wolde be at the mariage'.[90] Thomas's first reaction was that William would just have to accept the marriage, telling his son 'well as ye haue brued so drynke'.[91] William then fell to his knees and pleaded with his father to help him obtain an annulment. Thomas's reaction does not appear to be one of disappointment at not being informed about the marriage, so maybe there was an understanding between the fathers that this marriage was a possibility. Nonetheless, the speed with which the case came before the ecclesiastical courts – two years or less after the marriage – shows that Thomas was concerned for his son's future happiness. The situation is also indicative of the vulnerability of children placed in another's household and governance.

No doubt Jane Stanley's father had a good reason for marrying his daughter to William, although the reason will remain elusive to the historian. Yet, other children appeared to have been coerced into marriage on the whim of others not responsible for their upbringing. Grace Boyes was in the guardianship of her grandfather in 1558 when the wife of Robert Talbot's half-brother John desired Grace to come to her house 'to make mery'.[92] While she was there, Grace was married to Robert 'against the consent and will of the said Grace'.[93] Conversely, James Ballard, aged ten, went willingly to the church of Colne, Lancashire, in 1560 to marry Anne Holden after being 'intised … with two Apples'.[94] His two uncles, with whom he lived, knew nothing of the wedding until James was brought back to their house in Wooler, parish of Colne, at midnight by two 'fellowes' whom his uncle had supposed were witnesses at the wedding.[95] Anne was not known to either uncle. They 'neuer sawe the said Anne in the Towne nor neuer knewe of her beinge there'[96] but she was described by a witness as 'a bigge damsel & mariageable'.[97] What we can infer from the report of this marriage is that James appears to have had an extraordinary amount of freedom for an eleven-year-old boy. He was allowed to wander through the streets of Colne until midnight and, as the wedding took place at Christmastime, it would have been dark from around 5 p.m. We can also question why the priest who married them, Sir Roger Blakley, who in all probability knew James and his uncles, did not question why James stood before him with a stranger to the parish and was asking to be married in his church at 10 p.m.? The curate was subsequently punished for the transgression of 'marieng at inconvenient tymes and vnlawfull persons'.[98]

Children without parents were at the mercy of those who had guardianship of them. Yet, from as early as the thirteenth century in cities such as London and Bristol, borough orphans were entitled to the protection of the courts in defending the interests of deceased parents by protecting the monies and property left to their children.[99] Legislation similar to that of London was not established until 1574 in Chester.[100] As to marriage of wards, in London guardians were fined and threatened with imprisonment if they allowed their wards to marry without the mayor's approval but the same punishments were not in evidence in the rest of the country.

Wardships were valuable commodities and the forced marriage of wards was not uncommon. The annulment case of Barbara Wentworth and Anthony Norman reveals little of the circumstances around their marriage in Ardwick, Lancashire, in 1530, when Anthony was seven and Barbara six years of age.[101] On further investigation, a petition lodged in the Chancery court just after the wedding discloses that Anthony was a ward of Thomas Norman and Miles Nelvton, gentlemen of York, who were bequeathed the custody of Anthony and the use of his lands by Anthony's father, John Norman. Roger Wentworth, Barbara's father, is alleged to have forcibly removed Anthony from their custody and married him to his daughter.[102] The Chancery petition apparently failed as Anthony remained married to Barbara for nineteen years until the petition for annulment of the marriage was filed at York. Ordinarily, the annulment petition should have been heard at Chester because Ardwick was within that diocese, but it appears in the papers at York, a deviation that was questioned by one of Roger Wentworth's servants, suggesting that this case had not been previously heard at a court closer to Wentworth's home. One would have to wonder if this change of venue for petitioning for annulment of marriage had anything to do with the fact that Barbara went on to become the wife of Robert Holgate, Archbishop of York, after the annulment was granted.

The motivations of guardians sometimes differed to those of parents in regards to the underage marriage of wards. The marriages could generate large profits for the guardians and many were made purely for the rewards of the union without the intention that the children should live together. Isabelle Orrell, married to Henry Lathom in 1568, was taken away immediately after the wedding by the Earl of Derby, Henry's guardian.[103] Guardians, like parents, were not to be disobeyed once they had arranged a marriage, despite objections from family and friends. Robert Randle's marriage to Margaret Randle in Bangor, north Wales, in 1559 went ahead, despite the objections of two of Robert's uncles, after it was arranged by another uncle and guardian, Robert ap Richard.[104] Humphrey Winstanley, who was married to Alice Worsley in the same year as Robert, had been the ward of Sir Thomas Gerrard since the death of his father due to 'a bargen'.[105] His uncle by marriage said that he was married 'by the constreynt of Sir Thomas'.[106] The interpolations of both Robert's and Humphrey's uncles reveal that family and close friends took an interest in the marriages of children close to them but what role, if any, did family and friends play in the making of child marriages?

Role of family and friends

What role did family and friends play in the making of child marriages? The involvement of family and friends in the process of child marriage exposes that it was not an isolated act of irrational parents or guardians. Conversely, the collective involvement and organisation of these friends and family amounts to what M. G. Smith terms a 'corporation' and this is evident from the actions of the adults involved.[107] The term 'friends', Randolph Trumbach argues, relates to kin and those to whom an individual was associated by sponsorship or affection.[108] It could also serve as a distinction between close relations such as parents or grandparents and more distant relations.[109] 'Friends' is a term used frequently in the depositions of annulment cases and therefore many of the historical studies of the term have been undertaken in these contexts.[110] Nonetheless, consideration should be given to the relationship these friends had with the children and thus their motivations for taking part in the proceedings.[111] Undoubtedly, friends were an integral group who provided significant support for both the children involved and their parents. As Rushton has observed, no references appear that indicate friends acted in an antagonistic manner if their advice were not taken,[112] so we may assume that their role was more pastoral than powerful.

In most instances, family and friends were noted as taking an interested part in the contracting of marriage, the ceremony itself, and supporting the children after their marriage. Witnesses noted that many of the weddings were arranged by the mediation of family and friends and the children were either persuaded or compelled to accept the match by these same family and friends. William Deavon, a friend of the father of Alice Clapham, told Alice that she must 'be of good cher for ther ys no remedy but ye must be maried with Francys Procter' before her wedding, *c.* 1565, despite Alice's initial refusal to agree to the marriage. After the wedding, Alice told William that she would never have married Francis 'but by threatening of my father & my frendes'.[113] Implicit in these arrangements was that the family and friends were in agreement that the marriage would be beneficial to one or both parties. The involvement of the wider family and friends provided certain checks and balances to ensure that parents had considered their actions. Eight-year-old Elizabeth Tilston was not afforded this protection by her sister Agnes or by the father of her groom, Richard Pole, when they persuaded her to marry eleven-year-old William Pole at Marbury, Cheshire. The only people present at the wedding were the parties, Agnes, Richard and the priest who married them. Elizabeth's friends did not know for three years that she had been married.[114] Agnes and Richard Pole obviously had reasons for not wanting the friends to know, and went as far as marrying the children before sunrise 'with the torche light and candall light' to prevent them from finding out.[115]

Family and friends involved in wedding celebrations took an active role especially where the children were of a particularly young age. Gilbert Gerrard, who was around five years old at his wedding to Emma Talbot sometime before 1532, was held up from the ground by his uncle Rauff Gerrard, who also 'spake the words off matrimonie Befor the childes parte'.[116] The carrying of children to the church by family and friends to be married is repeated in a number of depositions. Robert Parre, married at three years old in 1539 to Elizabeth Rogerson, was carried to the church by his uncle Edward Bunburie who, like Rauff Gerrard, spoke the words of matrimony for his nephew because 'att wich tyme the said Robert colde scace speke'.[117] Robert did not go willingly, as the court at Chester was told in 1548. His uncle had to bribe him to go to the church, with one witness observing that Robert 'was hired for an aple by his vncle to goe to the church'.[118] Three-year-old John Somerforth was held for the entire ceremony by a relative who spoke the words at his marriage *c.* 1552 due to his 'younge age', while John's two-year-old bride, Jane Brerton, was carried by James Holford, who spoke the words of matrimony for her.[119] The marriages took place regardless of the youth of the parties.

These same family and friends that partook in the ceremonies became a support for the children after the marriage. John Mason, the uncle to Robert Mason married to his stepsister in 1555, became a confidant for Robert. Robert disclosed to John details about the state of his marriage, with John telling the court at Chester that he 'hath bene privye to all his doinges in that behalf'.[120] Besides confiding in family and friends, children entreated them to become intermediaries between themselves and their parents. Thomas Smith had implored his godfather, Gilbert Ottes, to speak to his father so that he might be released from his marriage to Anne Goodale but his father would not agree to part them.[121] Gilbert, at least, was prepared to mediate on behalf of Thomas.

Friends also provided a refuge for children from marriages when the post-nuptial living arrangements became untenable. Ellen Mynstor was married in 1537 to John Mynstor when both were under twelve. After the marriage they lived in John's father's house for a year or so and then when John's father died Ellen went to live with friends while John remained with his mother.[122] But family and friends were not always accepting that the marriage was not going to work, or that the children were unhappy in their domestic circumstances. Isabelle Harford, married age 4 or 5 *c.* 1525, was forced to stay at the house of her husband Thomas Haes's father because when she complained to her friends, 'they wold not let hir gowe awaye from hym and she tarried ther agenst hir will ij or iij yeres after'.[123] Andrew Haworth and Constance Entwisell, who had been married by the persuasion of Andrew's parents and their friends *c.* 1552, were 'kept so longe together' for the duration of twelve years by the compulsion of their friends despite never consenting to the marriage.[124] Evidence shows that while trying to keep the parties in the same house, family and friends were negotiating with the young people in an effort to persuade them to consent to the marriage. Attempts by the priest Thomas Gerrard at inducing William and Alice Gerrard to take each other as man and wife failed,[125] as did the intermediation of another Thomas Gerrard, knight, with Henry Accars and Jane Kenrike. Despite the persuasion of 'other gentlemen' in addition to that of Sir Thomas Gerrard, the parties would not consent.[126]

Cases emerge in the records that challenge Rushton's notion, previously discussed, of unity and goodwill between friends and family and the children involved. The marriage of John Clay and Elizabeth Savell took place in the parish church of Wakefield, Yorkshire, in about 1509.[127] The marriage appears to have been arranged by Thomas Pek, a kinsman of Elizabeth Savell, who was rector at Thornlie, a village near Wakefield. A witness, John Savell, reported seeing Elizabeth in the house of Thomas Pek sometime before the marriage, where she did not want to consent to the marriage. Another witness, Hugh Stancefield, said he was present in the house of John Closse, a Wakefield cobbler, with John Savell and others, and heard these people contracting marriage *verba de presenti* between Elizabeth and John. Further, he said that Thomas Pek, at that time related to Elizabeth, took her by the arm after she had refused to consent to the marriage, calling her a 'false wenche' and saying 'wilust thow be handfast with hym and I have had so moche besines for the' and immediately slapped her in the face with his hand, 'et incontinenti dedit manu sua alapam in facie'. Unsurprisingly, Elizabeth began to cry but, after the recitation of the marriage vows by Thomas Pek, she said the words of matrimony, as did John Clay. The detachment with which the witnesses recall the events surrounding the marriage of the children discussed here hint at an ambiguous reaction towards child marriage. In part, they reflect Pinchbeck and Hewitt's view that the customary image of marriage – to a greater degree for those performed under age – in Tudor England was 'practical rather than romantic'.[128] It is, however, possible to measure the community response to such unions from the sources.

Community response to child marriage

What was the community response to child marriages? The responses of witnesses to the libel and interrogatories indicate an acceptance of the practice by the community as a whole. In only one deposition studied as part of this chapter did an adult challenge the decision to contract an underage marriage. Alice Jonson, the godmother of twelve-year-old Thomas Pendleton of Prescott, Lancashire, questioned Thomas's father at the marriage of Thomas to Elena Mistis *c.* 1538, saying that she would never have believed he could marry off his son 'beying but a boye of xij yere old'.[129] In relation to some of the other marriages discussed above and below, Thomas Pendleton was one of the older children. Members of the community did however recognise that the parties in these marriages were just children. Reference was often made to the bride and groom 'beying then children', 'beying but a child off age' or 'a little child of thage of foure yeres or not so much'.[130] Other admissions to the youthful nature of the parties concerned their inability to speak the words of matrimony such as the case of four-year-old Richard Elston, who was carried to the church in someone's arms in 1557 to wed Elizabeth Orrell. His mother spoke the words for him or counselled Richard to speak them after her.[131] The children at one wedding at Brereton, Cheshire, in 1552 were so small that John Holford described them as 'beinge then both infantes' and that 'it was the youngest marriage that ever he was at'.[132] None of the witnesses raised concerns over the ages of the children, commenting only on them in relation to the process of the court to establish the children's inability to consent to the marriage due to being in their minority. The community's complaisance at the time of the marriages suggests that they thought the whole process was perfectly normative. It is arguably the issue of age where the explanation of this complaisance may lie.

Analysis of the records gives a clear indication of the age of children married below consent. If we look more closely at the records and in particular those where the ages of the children can be positively identified, the majority were married between the ages of seven and thirteen (see Table 3.1). So, although examples of children being married as young as two can be found in the depositions, these can be taken to be the exception rather than the rule. What analysis of the cause papers suggests is that parents waited until the children were past the age of seven, when, according to canon law, it was legal to contract marriage for a child. In fact, there would appear to be a suspicious clustering of the cases when the children were aged around eight or nine years old, as if the parents were waiting for them to reach the due age. Indubitably, parents were aware of the requirements of canon law when they arranged child marriages – as was the community – and did so within the confines of it. This replicates the argument of Michael Sheehan, who found that, in Ely in the fourteenth century, people clearly understood the law on marriage and applied it to suit their own needs.[133] There was, however, acknowledgement by the community that these unions once made were not a marriage in the adult sense. Henry Crosse, a witness in the case of Nicolas Stokes and Anne Irlande in Chester in 1552, said that the children did not lie together 'for want of age', while the marriage of Robert Parre and Elizabeth Rogerson was never consummated 'for cause off the yowthe off the said Robert'.[134]

Regardless of the community's recognition of this particular life-stage, child marriages were celebrated in the same manner as those performed above the age of consent. Many members of the community attended the church service and witnesses were able to recall the names of those present in addition to the total number of guests. There were twenty-four people present at the marriage of Margaret Dickson and Michael Waterhouse in Halifax in 1543, while the curate who married Eleine Ball and Thomas Wicksted at Marbury, Cheshire, in 1556 commented that they were married 'in the presence of a great multitude of people'.[135] Within this multitude of people were the local

Table 3.1 Ages of Children Married Under Age at Chester and York

Age of children at time of marriage	2	3	4	5	6	7	8	9	10	11	12	13	14
Number of children married at this age	2	5	10	10	8	21	14	25	33	28	18	13	4

Source: BIA Cause Papers and CALSS Ecclesiastical Deposition Books EDC2/2–9.

gentry and pillars of the community. At the wedding of Barbara Lutton and Miles Belton at Menston, Yorkshire, in 1563, the assembled guests included 'many more gentlemen and other honeste men of the parishe of Menston'.[136] Child marriages were viewed as a community celebration regardless of the age of the bride and groom.

Witnesses recall that the marriages were sometimes celebrated in the body of the church and performed with 'all service and other seremonyes done which was then vsed at the solempnisacion of mariage'.[137] For those marriages performed after the Reformation, reference is made to the Book of Common Prayer being used to perform the marriage. Sir Thomas Barthelote admitted to marrying seven-year-old Robert West to sixteen-year-old Elizabeth Beaumont at High Hoyland, near Barnsley, Yorkshire, in 1549 using the Book of Common Prayer. As his parish did not own a copy he had to send to Cawthorne to borrow their book.[138] While the priest's actions undoubtedly show the progression of the Reformation in the north of England, it also indicates that he did not consider the procedure of marrying underage children to be anything but routine. Some parish priests, therefore, blatantly ignored the canonical directives in relation to marriageable age despite warnings issued through bishops' visitations such as that from Durham, cited above, and a number of other contemporary texts. John Myrc warned that priests should, 'Loke also they make non odde weddynges, lest alle ben cured in that doynage'.[139] This advice was not heeded if the number of priests giving evidence in the annulment causes is considered, for all testify to the ages of the children but none raise any concerns about the matches.

The celebrations did not end at the church door. Wedding feasts were common, with witnesses either dining or serving at them.[140] A marriage dinner was provided for guests in Hopwood Hall, Lancashire after the marriage of Anne Bellfield and Richard Leigh in 1562 while the parsonage at Badsworth, Yorkshire, was the location for the wedding dinner for William Parre and Jane Stanley in 1553.[141] The manner in which the witnesses discussed the child marriages they attended suggests that the community identified the marriage as no different to marriages performed after the age of consent. Child marriage was normalised for the community, in part through their understanding and manipulation of canon law, and therefore an acceptable practice in which to involve children from within the community. As the following discussion demonstrates, the practice of child marriage was not exclusive to the children of wealthy parents and benefactors.

Social class of children married under age

Was the practice of child marriage exclusive to the children of wealthy parents and benefactors? There are some signposts in the depositions that not all children who were married in their minority came from wealthy homes or from households with a high social status. Occupations of the fathers or stepfathers of the parties, where mentioned, give a good indication of social class.

High-status occupations that were frequently cited included gentleman, esquire and knight. Further down the social scale came yeomen and husbandmen, who may or may not have owned the land that they worked. Yet nestled in the depositions are occupations that would question the practice of child marriage as being the preserve of the wealthy or at least those families with land. William Watmoughe, who married his daughter Margaret to Richard Waterhouse in 1544, described himself as a shoemaker at the annulment proceedings twelve years later. Similarly, Robert Woodhead's step father, Thomas Heyle, is listed as an innkeeper in the annulment proceedings between Robert and Elizabeth Studley in 1575.[142] Aside from occupations, clues about the social standing of the parents and parties may be gleaned from the statements themselves.

Ecclesiastical courts were naturally suspicious about the motives for suing for annulment, particularly if there was a long period of time between the marriage and the annulment petition. The father of Joan Leyland, who had brought a suit against her husband Rafe Whittall in 1562, long after they both came to the age of consent, deposed that Joan had not done so earlier because 'she was poor and had no money and nowe she hath gotten somewhat in Service and nowe spendes hit in trial of the Lawe'.[143] Going into service emerges as a practical way for the children from less-wealthy parents to survive when their marriages failed. Alveall Flemyng was a servant to a Mr Ward in Middlesex at the time of his annulment from Frances Rawson in 1558, which would attest to him having no money or inheritance of his own. These cases may be the exception but, aligned with the evidence of bargains over inconsiderable amounts of land,[144] they show that child marriage was not an unacceptable practice to the lower orders in sixteenth-century northern England. Clearly, the impact of the failure of such a marriage would have been felt more keenly by these children than by children from wealthy homes.

Even if the witness statements do not yield any information concerning the status of the people who married their children and wards below the age of consent, they can still be a valuable source of empirical evidence for the same. One way to obtain this is by analysis of the records in relation to the occupations of witnesses giving evidence for each litigant. Of the forty-two cases of child marriage from York included in this study, only two witnesses are listed as servants while twenty-one are listed as being gentlemen and twenty-one as husbandmen (see Table 3.2). Other professions of some standing are represented, including armiger, esquire and merchant. Interestingly, at York nineteen witnesses are described as being 'free' while one is described as a pauper. Unfree people and paupers were not regarded as reliable witnesses, although 'free' is likely to mean working-class in this context. It originally distinguished the free peasant from the serf, who was not supposed to testify on the grounds that their servile status might make them vulnerable to pressure from the manorial lord.

These findings support the argument that the children involved usually (but not always) came from families with money and sometimes property. Taking into consideration the cost of litigation alone would indicate that such families were not of the lowest orders, although they would not have been the elite.

Table 3.2 Occupations of Witnesses Appearing in Child Marriage Cases at York

Occupation of witnesses	Number of witnesses in each occupation
Armiger	2
Carpenter	1
Clerk	15
Collier	1
Clothier/cloth maker	21
Esquire	1
Farmer	2
Free	19
Husbandman	21
Innkeeper	2
Labourer	5
Merchant	1
Milner	1
Motley maker	1
Pauper	1
Scholar	2
Servant	2
Sherman	2
Tanner	1
Weaver/webster	3
Widow	4
Wright	2
Yeoman	23

Source: BIA Cause Papers.

For, as argued by Helmholz, the very rich would have had direct access to the bishop and so rarely appear in the court documents, while the very poor would have been precluded by the cost of the action.[145] Caution must be exercised with these findings for they are not conclusive and simply suggest the status of the families involved in petitioning for the annulment of a marriage contracted under age. As the evidence suggests, it is quite possible that a proportion of the children in these marriages did not come from wealthy households. The statistics offered above merely display the cases of child marriages that were legitimately dissolved (or not) in the church courts and ignore ones where litigation was not an option because of cost. Just because the lowest social groups are absent in the extant sources, we cannot take this as conclusive evidence that they did not subscribe to a specific childrearing practice such as child marriage.

Lived experiences of children

What can we learn from the sources about the lived experiences of children who were married under age? For many of the children married under age, their living arrangements remained unchanged as they returned home with their parents or friends after the ceremony. Analysis of the marriages in this chapter where the living arrangements of the children immediately after the marriage can be ascertained show that, in 33 per cent of the cases, children remained with their parents or guardians (see Table 3.4). John Smyth and Margaret Sonders, who were married as ten-year-olds in Farnworth, Lancashire, in 1536, did not live together after the marriage, with both fathers taking their children home on the night of the wedding. John remained with his father, as did Margaret, moving to her brother's house when her father died.[146] The same situation prevailed for Elenore Hoggton and Thomas Townley from Brindley, Cheshire, who lived with their respective fathers after their 1532 wedding, although Thomas did go to visit his wife at her father's house 'nowe and then'.[147]

For the rest of the marriages, the decision as to which of the children left the natal home was not necessarily decided by gender. A breakdown of the total number of marriages where one of the children has been identified as moving out of the natal home revealed that 56 per cent were girls and 44 per cent were boys (see Table 3.3). What did sway the parents and guardians was the age of the children. Only 20 per cent of the children that left their parents or guardians were the younger of the two children (see Table 3.3). This percentage does increase to 27 per cent when you discount the marriages where the children were the same age or a precise age is not given. Taking this last fact into consideration, the percentages of girls and boys that remained would vary over time depending upon the ages of the bride and groom. It should also be noted that at times the older child that moved to the household of his or her father-in-law was not much older than the child that remained with their parents. George Spurstow, at six, was only one year older than his wife, Brigitte Dutton, when he moved in with her family in 1556.[148]

Children involved in child marriages did, in some instances, leave home at an early age. According to one witness, John Somerforth was just three when he went to live with Jane Brerton's father after their wedding in 1552 at Brereton, Cheshire. However, this case should not be taken as conclusive evidence that parents in sixteenth-century England were happy to remove their children to foreign households at a tender age. On the contrary, the majority of the children leaving home on account of child marriage were nine, ten or eleven years old, and past the legal age for contracting a marriage (see Table 3.4).

Practical considerations dictated where children would live after marriage. Thomas Bentham never lived with Elena Bolton after they married in 1552

Table 3.3 Number and Gender of Children Leaving their Natal or Guardian Homes Immediately after Marriage

	Percentage of total	Percentage of total number of marriages where one of the parties left	Percentage of total number of marriages where one of the parties left and the children are of different ages
Total number of marriages where living arrangements of children immediately after marriage can be validated	79		
Number of marriages where both the girl and the boy remained in their natal/guardian household	29	37%	
Total number of marriages where one of the children left the natal/guardian home immediately after marriage	50	63%	
Number of girls remaining in the natal/guardian household after marriage	28	35%	56%
Number of boys remaining in the natal/guardian household	22	28%	44%
Number of children where the youngest child of the marriage remained at home	27	34%	54%	73%
Number of children where the youngest child of the marriage left the natal/guardian home	10	13%	20%	27%

Source: BIA Cause Papers and CALSS Ecclesiastical Deposition Books EDC2/2–9.

NB: there is a discrepancy between the total number of marriages where one of the children left the natal household and the total number of marriages where either the youngest child stayed/left. This is due to the fact that in a number of marriages the children were described as being the same age as each other, under age or the age of one of the parties is not given.

Table 3.4 Ages of Children at Leaving Natal or Guardian Home Immediately after Marriage

Age of children at time of marriage	Number of children leaving the natal/guardian house at this age
2	0
3	1
4	2
5	1
6	2
7*	3
8	4
9	7
10	5
11	7
12	4
13	1
14	4
15	0
16	1
Underage	2

Source: BIA, Cause Papers and CALSS, Deposition Books, EDC2/2–9.

NB: the inclusion of ages past the age of consent – i.e., fourteen–sixteen is warranted because the spouses of these young people remained in the natal home and were all below the age of consent.

* The age at which a contract of marriage could be lawfully drawn up.

because he was constantly in service with either Richard Bentham, his grandfather, or Thomas Walmesley. Service and sending boys away to school emerge as the most commonly mentioned reasons for the separation of children after their marriages. During his marriage to Anne Dutton, William Stanley had 'bene at Lathum at schole there sins the said mariage and in Service with thele of Derby'.[149] School also separated William Westby and his bride Anne Sothworth as William was sent away to school or was taught by a tutor at his father's house.[150]

Even if one of the parties moved to the other's house, schooling was a means of ensuring that the children were separated from each other. Robert West was sent to school by his father after his marriage to Elizabeth Beaumont at High Hoyland, Yorkshire, in 1549 so that he was hardly ever at his father's house when Elizabeth was there.[151] Furthermore, separating the children through schooling could have been used as a form of mediation where the children disagreed. Thomas Smith of Halifax, West Yorkshire, was prepared to borrow a noble (6s. 8d.) from friends to enable him to board with a Doctor Savell in the south of Yorkshire rather than stay in his father's house while his wife Anne Goodale was living there. His father persuaded his son to 'tarie' and then promptly sent him to school.[152]

Parting the children through schooling may well have been a conscious decision by the parents to separate them until they came to lawful age. John Orrell told the Chester consistory court in 1570 that he sent his son-in-law, Richard Elston, to school when he was seven and thereby kept him infre-quentlyin the house with his daughter Elizabeth 'biecause he wold have hym to be furth for learning sake'.[153] These examples establish that marriage in the sixteenth century was not necessarily a move towards adult life and that the children involved were not expected to follow the conventions of a married couple. Rather, they were to continue the activities children of their social status would undertake until they reached an age where they were ready to assume the formalities of marriage. For children married under age, matrimony did not signal a break from parental control and an end to childhood.

We must not discount other, more complicated reasons as to why children lived apart after they were married. Margery Vernon and Randle More, who were married at Haslington, Cheshire, in 1551, were kept apart after the ceremony, living in their respective family homes. Margery did go to stay at Randle's house at times of 'merriment' and Randle would visit Margery's house for dinner but would not stay the night. A witness reported that Randle was 'very sickly and hath somme gret Impedimente apon hym', which caused Margery to petition for an annulment. It may have been unrealistic for Randle's and Margery's parents to think that the children could have a normal marriage as Robert Short commented that, as far as consummating the marriage, Randle had 'yet small mynd of such matters'.[154] Nevertheless, it does prove that infirmity of either the body or the mind did not preclude children from being deemed as suitable marriage partners. The overriding importance of family and perhaps the inheritance of property are apparent here. Despite the fact that Randle could never be a husband in the biological sense, his family were described as living at the 'Hall of the Heath' and as such would have been quite wealthy and a desirable family to marry into. Marriage was an opportunity to secure the futures of children through the transmission of property from both sides of the family and to look after the interests of the same.[155]

A number of depositions mention that the children lived together for only short periods of time after they were married. This could have been a symbolic move by parents indicating that it was never their intention that the children should remain out of the natal home when they were so young. Seven-year-old John Spencer lived with his bride, Elizabeth Holland, in her father's house for less than twelve weeks after his marriage in 1536 before returning to live with his father.[156] Edward Ramsbottom lived for only six months in his father-in-law's house before moving back home after his marriage to Elizabeth Hand near Stockport, Lancashire, in 1546.[157] Often the periods of time spent together in one house were even shorter than this. Rafe Whittall lived in Joan Leyland's house for about one month, going next to live with his mother, and then returning to live at Joan's father's house when he was fifteen or sixteen.[158] By this age, Rafe was past the age of consent and no doubt it was hoped he could be persuaded to ratify the marriage.

It was not uncommon for those children who remained in their father-in-law's house to leave when either or both parties reached lawful age. Isabel Camponet was twelve when her husband, Richard Wright, left her father's house, while John Stokely of Holt in north Wales moved out of Joan Medow's father's house when he came of age.[159] John moved in with John Pickering and never visited Joan's house again. The impetus for the move at this particular age was linked directly to canon law and the desire of the parties and sometimes their parents to secure an annulment. If the children had stayed in the same house then it would be harder to prove that they had not lived together as man and wife.

It is not the length of time that these children stayed in the houses of their in-laws but the fact that they moved out of their family home before they reached the age of adolescence that is significant. By doing so, it makes this particular group of children one of the most mobile in sixteenth-century northern England. Philippa Maddern has identified child marriage as one of a range of situations that led to children moving between households or spending large amounts of time in households other than their birth ones.[160] The statements of the witnesses in the annulment cases testify that some children lived in three or more households during their childhood. John Somerforth, mentioned above, lived from birth until the age of twelve months with a wet nurse, Elizabeth Parkinson, and her family at Astbury, near Congleton, Cheshire, before returning to his father's house. When he was between three and four years old he was married to Jane Brerton and moved to her father's house at Brereton, Cheshire, where he stayed for the next ten years before moving again at the age of twelve or thirteen.[161] In spite of this, John McLaughlin's contention that the placing of these children into another's home was 'nothing more than a transfer of a child from one nursery to another'[162] is far too simplistic a view of what was a complex and, at times, emotionally charged experience for those concerned.

One of the most frequently discussed issues of the marriage in the depositions is the sleeping arrangements of the children. This was an area of great importance in the annulment petitions of child marriages and the libel more often than not contained an item relating to *carnali copula* (sexual intercourse), requiring the witnesses to establish for the court whether the marriage had been consummated or not. The picture that emerges from the witnesses' evidence describes children being placed in bed together on the night of their wedding alongside other children or servants. As with leaving children in their respective in-laws' houses for a short period of time, placing children in bed with one another on their wedding night may have been a symbolic gesture by the parents at legitimising the marriage. This was true for William Stead and Joan Firth of Claverley, Yorkshire. After they were married in 1543, they lay together on the first night but one Dionysis Hill lay with them.[163] For John Andrew of Winsford, Cheshire, it was two of the sisters of his bride, Ellen Dampart, who slept between them after their marriage in 1548.[164] Correspondingly, people other than their spouse became bed fellows to one or other of the children during their marriage. Alexander Holme testified that he knew the 1549 marriage between Anna Arderne and his ten-year-old brother James had not been consummated because all the time that Anna lived in his father's house James slept with him and another brother.[165] By the same token, Humphrey Winstanley, who was sent away to school after his marriage to Alice Worsley in 1559 when he was aged ten, shared a bed with his uncle when he came home from school.[166]

On occasions children were advised against sleeping in the same bed as their spouses. Katherine Tatlock, who, as mentioned above, had been advised by a member of the Mollineaux family that if her marriage to Edmund Mollineux did not work out after two years she would be divorced, was told by the same person 'thou art yonge and shall not lye with hym off a yere or ij and iff you can not agree then in that space I shall fynde a meanys for you' to be divorced.[167] This not only demonstrates the knowledge of canon law that people had – a marriage would never be annulled if it had been consummated regardless of the age of the children at marriage – but also the power that family had in these marriages. The exercise of power by family members at important times in the life-cycle was a necessary feature of kinship structure.[168]

Despite being married and having to live in the same house as their spouses, the sleeping arrangements demonstrate that those concerned were just children and reacted to their new-acquired spouses as children were wont to do. Nine-year-old Robert Randle from Bangor, north Wales, said that he did not ever lie with his wife Margaret after their marriage *c.* 1559, but in the way of sport and play 'he did leape from one bed to an other bed of which bedes she the Margaret did lye with an other maide'.[169] What we could take from Robert's reaction was that he considered Margaret as just another child in his house. This was not an unusual response to child marriage by the children themselves. Children were often brought up alongside each other as though part of the same family. Anthony Norman and Barbara Wentworth, who were seven and six respectively when they married in 1530, would call each other by their Christian names, like good friends or siblings.[170] There was often affection in these relationships but it was platonic rather than intimate, as illustrated by Richard Lacey admitting to kissing his wife Elizabeth Southall 'as one frende to a nother' after their marriage *c.* 1540.[171]

It was not easy for the children to progress from considering each other friends or family to becoming husband and wife. The expectation that the marriage had to be consummated proved to be a difficult hurdle for many of the couples. Elyis Broughton, who was said to have been between ten and thirteen years old when he married Joan Broughton at Holt, north Wales, in 1551, was encouraged by his father, Rauffe, to lie with Joan. However, at night Elyis would bar or make fast the door of the chamber against Joan 'lest she should have come to bed to him'.[172] Other husbands mentioned in the depositions had the opposite problem and tried various means to persuade their wives to submit to their sexual advances. William Bayley, a labourer, stated that thirteen-year-old Thomas Smith had told him that if his wife, Anne, who was sick at the time of the conversation, died, he would never marry again and in fact, would become a priest. In the next breath, Thomas was giving William a penny 'to buy apples with for to hire Anne Goodale with to come to bed to the said Thomas Smith'.[173] Alexander Woodward encountered a similar problem with his wife, Cecilie, after he married her at the parish church of Wigan in 1541 when he was seven. As he became older he resorted to bribing the maid who slept with Cecilie 'with pynnes and powntis', so that the she would rise from the bed and Alexander would 'come and lie in hyr place'.[174] The responses of Elyis, Thomas and Alexander highlight some of the emotional pressures that the children of these marriages experienced and it is perhaps only by examining the children's emotional responses to their marriages that we can discover the child's eye view of their experiences of child marriage.

Emotional responses and reactions

What were the emotional responses and reactions of the children to their marriages? Before we discuss the children's emotional response to their marriages, it is worth raising a note of caution in relation to the use of depositions to locate a child's emotional state. Finding evidence of a child's emotional state in ecclesiastical court documents is not an easy task. Their function in marital cases was to recount the events surrounding the marriages, some of which took place a significant amount of time before the court case. Undoubtedly, the witnesses may not have even considered emotions when giving their evidence and thus their language was not emotive. They merely intended to create a credible narrative that would stand up in a court of law and prove the case for whichever party they were testifying for. The inclusion of any references to emotions may purely have been coincidental, for in reality the witness must have observed the emotion in order to relate this to the court in the hope of securing an annulment.

Consider the case of Elizabeth Rogerson, who at nine was five years older than her husband, Robert Parre, when they married in 1539, and would 'lepe forth off the beed' every time that Robert entered her chamber.[175] This was observed by a servant who shared her bed and in whom she confided that she 'wisshed diverse tymes that she had parte off her moneye ageyne so that She was ridd from hym'.[176] Leaping off the bed could appear as genuine fear of a sexual encounter on Elizabeth's part, but it could also be interpreted as a deliberate ploy by her to arm the servant with the evidence required to achieve her annulment. Hence we can argue that there always had to be an object to an emotion in relation to depositions and that it produced some sort of effect.[177]

We can also interpret the antics of Elyis Broughton, Thomas Smith and Alexander Woodward in the same light. All the witnesses testifying for Elyis make a clear case for annulment while the witnesses for Alexander Woodward reveal that he tried to ratify the marriage by attempting to sleep with his wife. However, previous witness statements contradict the servant's statement, saying that the marriage was never consummated because Alexander and Cecilie, his wife, were too young.[178] The witness statement concerning Thomas Smith uncovers the fact that Thomas had expected his marriage to work even to the point of trying to bribe Anne, his wife, to lie with him. If Anne had taken the enticement of the apples, present-day historians would never have known that the marriage had taken place at all.

The biggest problem with assessing people's emotional states in past times is the placing of our own values into the interpretation.[179] It is therefore imperative that, as historians, we recognise the empathy that existed between the witness and the court.[180] I refer back to Elizabeth Rogerseon and her bed-leaping antics. The witness understood that she had to outline a plausible story of fear and aversion to the court, while the court had a duty to process that information in regards to how it interacted with the notion of consent that made for a valid marriage. So to effectively assess the emotions of the children in this study who were married under age, taking into consideration their categorisations of emotions as well as our own, there is a need to refer to both a modern psychological and medieval theological theories at the same time.[181] Sometimes these are not all that different.

For a modern-day example, we could use the emotions wheel proposed by Robert Plutchik, who argues that the eight basic emotions – fear, anger, joy, sadness, acceptance, disgust, anticipation and surprise, together with their synonyms – produce all the emotions we would expect to find expressed in our society.[182] It is evident that a number of sixteenth-century theories of emotions, or passions as they were more generally referred to, had evolved with the majority accessible through theological treatises. Thomas Aquinas, for example, considered emotions to be voluntary and as such liable to be judged morally good or bad.[183] He classified them into eleven basic passions – love, hate, desire, aversion, pleasure, sadness, hope, despair, fear, courage and anger – and this categorisation continued to be used in later centuries.[184] Aquinas arranged passions into corresponding pairs, much like Plutick, emphasising their bipolar nature.[185] His pairing of confidence and fear is akin to that of Plutchik's acceptance and disgust, and both emotions are symbiotically evident in the depositions.

Constance Good was only about six years old at the time of her marriage to John Bickerton at Bolton Percy, Yorkshire, in 1537. John's personal statement to the court shows that at times Constance had accepted the marriage and was once content to 'taking and accepting hym alwaye for her lawfull husband', as likewise John did take her for his lawful wife.[186] Constance, however, emphasises the fact that although she accepted tokens from John, she never received them in corroboration of marriage or 'with any glad hirt or good will she bare towards' her husband. She had previously deposed that 'she never called the said Bykerton husband nor accepted hym as her husbond'. Witnesses report that Constance and John had often been seen treating each other in a 'familiiar and loving fashion' and yet at other times Constance could be heard calling John a 'drocken knave and foole'. Constance's father, John, said that his daughter refused to have John as her husband and believed him to 'bee but a fole and a givan lyer'.

Constance's vacillating attitude towards her husband is difficult to understand from the depositions and yet they do give the historian an insight into why she responded to John in this manner. A year or so before the case was heard by the court, John had asked Constance 'to goo to bed with hym and she denied so to doo'. The next morning John removed himself to Cottingham and was still living there at the time of the court case. Her fear of a sexual encounter is elucidated by Alice Thompson, who said that Constance would never have John as her husband and 'that noman shuld mak hyr to lye with hym'. Constance would 'wepe full sore' when she spoke these words. Alice said that although Constance rebuked John she 'dyd nowe the said Constance of tymes to love the said Bykerton and said that he was a good gentleman'. Constance was still young when she gave her evidence to the court. The marriage had taken place nine years before the petition for annulment in 1546, making Constance at most fifteen years old at the time she gave her evidence and it exposes her emotional response to marrying so young. John Duns Scotus, a fourteenth-century theologian who saw emotions as cognitive acts of will, would explain Constance's distress as a direct result of being married against her will even though she displayed acceptance of her parent's wishes.[187] This was not surprising as Constance was so young and would have complied unwittingly. She had to be looked after by Margaret Whitehouse on the day of the wedding because she was 'not of discretion to rule herself'.

Almost without exception, all the people appearing in the court for annulment of an underage marriage did not consent and were forced or intimidated into saying their marriage vows by parents or kin. Witnesses for both Katherine Dutton and Elizabeth Savell, mentioned above, agree that their vows were extracted from them in this manner.[188] Eleven-year-old Alice Clapham was forced to consent to her marriage to Francis Proctor in *c.* 1565 because her father told her she 'should never have a penny worthes of his goodes' if she did not.[189] Many of the children did so without comprehending the consequences of their parents' actions. Eleven-year-old Elizabeth Wofall was married by the compulsion and constraint of her father in 1552. When he died sometime after the wedding, she confided in a neighbour that she thought God had taken him so that she may have the freedom to marry when and whom she wanted.[190] Elizabeth's aversion to her arranged marriage was evident in her desire to be at liberty to choose her own husband. She did not realise that the death of her father, who had pressured her into saying the words, did not automatically guarantee her freedom from the marriage.

Depositions reveal an air of the inevitability of having to accept the wishes of parents and friends in relation to child marriage. Such was the case for twelve-year-old Peter Hope. Despite confiding in his foster father the night before his wedding that he would never take Alice Ellis for his wife, he went through with his marriage stating that 'biecause it was his mothers mynde, he durst not displease her'.[191] The situation of acceptance followed by apprehension or fear was played out many times in the depositions suggesting a conditioning of older early modern children that is not present today. Aristotle, whose writings greatly influenced medieval and Renaissance works, said of adolescents that 'they are shy, accepting the rules of society in which they have been trained, and not yet believing in any other standard of honour'.[192] For these children, parental authority was only to be challenged through their actions after the wedding, by refusing to accept their parents' choice of spouse.

One cannot always find descriptions in the depositions that can be classified specifically as sixteenth- or twenty-first-century emotions, but we can find descriptions of children 'weeping openly', which suggests unhappiness and fear.[193] Twelve-year-old John Bridge, who married *c.* 1558 to save his father from paying back a bond, had wept greatly to a neighbour on the day of his wedding. John was not only showing his unhappiness but confiding in the neighbour his fear of the marriage and of disobeying his father. He had then wept to go home with his father the night of his wedding but his father would not tolerate it. Instead, the father and the priest persuaded John to sleep in the same bed as his bride, although he spent the night with his back to her.[194] The depositions show that John's unhappiness was evident even before the wedding. For having lived in Elizabeth's house prior to marriage, a witness stated that Elizabeth was 'a bigge woman' and John 'but a child' and that 'she delt shrewdlie with hym'.[195] Clearly, Elizabeth was not happy either.

Similarly, the deep distress felt by ten-year-old Alice Hesketh of Rufford, Lancashire, after her marriage to Richard is apparent in the deposition given by her father in 1550. Moved by his daughter's unhappiness he separated her from Richard because she was 'dystressed with sekness after that tyme that the said Richard and Alice were married together and lyen together'.[196] Bartholomew Hesketh's compassion for Alice, however, did not alter his belief that Richard would be an asset to his family and promptly persuaded Richard to marry his younger daughter, Joan, by whom Richard eventually had seven children. Not all emotions are so readily observable in the depositions, with many implicit in the terminology used by the witnesses. Chief among these is the pairing that according to Aquinas occurred most often, love and hatred.

Many of the witnesses reported that children had confided in them that they could never love their spouse or consent to have them as husband or wife. Ellen Morris declared openly to her own friends and to those of her husband, John Ramsbottom, that she would never love him and that she would never have him as her husband and 'denied him flat'.[197] It is unsurprising that these children did not love each other as the boy and girl were not expected to be 'in love' at the time of the wedding, especially as in the case of Katherine Dutton and Robert Bushell, mentioned above, who were not even acquainted before the wedding. The marriage was to bring about affection and not vice versa.[198]

Particularly for the children discussed in this chapter, their young ages at the time of marriage made the development of affection between them unlikely. Witnesses were very definite about the fact that the children documented in this book did not love one another. Roger Massey who had been carried to the church at age seven to marry Jane Sommer in 1556, told the court that he had never loved Jane 'nor yet knows what Love means'.[199] The court official felt moved to add a post-script in Latin to Roger's comment which read 'as is evident by the look of his body' ('vt patet per aspectm eius corporis').[200] This was a boy who was both emotionally and physically immature for marriage even past the age of consent.

We can argue that the notion of love in the sixteenth century was far removed from our understanding of it today, instead being conditional upon achieving certain objectives. The frequency with which the witnesses referred to the word love conveys only a sense of liking. Moreover, it was even used with a prefix to imply dislike. Margerey Heydocke described to the court that since coming to lawful age 'dislove' had fallen between her and Peter Haworth, her husband.[201] Dislike occurs as a common emotion in the annulment petitions. Margaret Wall, who married her five-year-old step brother John Venables in 1562 when she was eleven, complained that she did not like him and of being married to 'suche a child'.[202] John Wright's reaction was more forceful to his marriage to Frances Stephenson in *c.* 1593 when he was thirteen. He was reported to 'dissent and dislike of her'.[203] He was so intent that Frances would not 'by anie means reape anie benefite by him or anie thing he had' that he sold all his land as soon as he was legally able to do so. Such extreme measures serve only to highlight John's dislike of Frances and his unhappiness of the situation.

The emotional reactions of children to their underage marriages were of unhappiness and discontent. Ecclesiastical marriage depositions by their nature record misery and unhappiness and there was no court to reveal the happy and contented marriage.[204] The testimonies themselves suggest that some of the children encountered extremes of emotions. Constance Good wavered between love and contempt for her husband, John, at times content to have him as her spouse and at other times not. Thomas Smith was vehement in his rejection of his wife Anne and yet, according to a witness, was still interested in making his marriage work by bribing her to come to bed with him. Other accounts portray pronounced distress like that of John Bridge, which may or may not have been a truthful interpretation of the emotions he felt at being married below the age of consent. He could well have felt the same emotions if he had been past lawful age. Yet the depositions provide the historian with a child's eye view of the experience of child marriage in the absence of any other accounts and allow us to read their emotional states. Elizabeth Rogerson's leaping from the bed would appear to demonstrate her lack of consent to her marriage, as did Constance Good's tearful declaration that she would not have John Bickerton as her husband.[205]

Perhaps the more telling aspect of the emotional distress of children upon their marriages is what this communicates more generally about childhood experiences. John Bridge's unhappiness was spawned by the fear of disappointing his parents and the knowledge that he had to acquiesce to the wishes of his father to protect his family. This need for compliance with, and obedience to, authority is a central thread running through all the depositions when discussing the children's reactions to their marriages. It was finding themselves at odds with authority that caused distress. Evidence of this can be witnessed by Elizabeth Wofall's belief that after the death of her father, who compelled her to marry against her wishes, she would be free to take a partner of her own choosing.[206] In obeying her father, she sacrificed her own happiness.

Conclusion

If we were to pose the question of how child marriage illuminates the larger topic of children and childrearing in sixteenth-century northern England, then we would have to suggest that the practice of child marriage emphasises the structures of families and society in particular geographical areas and within certain socioeconomic groups. This does not mean, however, that any findings will have limited application for childrearing practices in the period for the region, or indeed the country. As noted above, a systematic survey needs to be taken of ecclesiastical records at repositories around the country before we can emphatically conclude that child marriage is particular to a specific social class or geographical location. What we can conclude is that evidence indicates that parents and guardians married children under age in sixteenth-century northern England and that the community regarded it as an accepted practice, but we cannot assume that parents did so without regret. As one mother told the consistory court at York, she 'wold not have the mariedge to go forwarde yf it was in hir power but yet she could ill discharge hir conscience because she is sworn'.[207] Abiding by her agreement, the mother's conscience was directly linked in with the notion of family. By going ahead with the wedding she was seemingly neglecting her daughter's individual feelings but she was also redefining the notion of nurture to promote the interests of the entire family. All the members of the household were to put their own interests aside to work in unison for the good of the family and marriage was no exception. John Paston accentuated this need for family unity, telling his wife, Margaret:

> Also remembir yow in any howsold, felship, or company that will be of good rewle, purvyauns must be had that euery persone of it be helpyng and forthering aftir his discrecion and powyre, and he that woll not do so without he be kept of almes shuld be put out of the household or felachep.[208]

The importance of 'family' was far greater than individual happiness.

The whole process of marriage – including those contracted under age – in sixteenth-century northern England was a team effort that included not only the children and their parents but also family and friends. Complex negotiations were required to bring about a marriage, which Shannon McSheffrey believes resembled 'a choreographed dance' with numerous artists rather than 'a pas de deux'.[209] Those concerned did not accept any dissent towards these protracted negotiations lightly, as Elizabeth Savell found out to her cost. Had she agreed outright to marry John Clay, her kinsman Thomas Pek, who had to undertake 'so muche besines' on her behalf, would not have struck her in the face.[210] There was also a belief by family and friends that no matter how much the children were against the marriage they would eventually come around to the wisdom of such a union. The parents of John Bickerton and Constance Good certainly believed so, as did others surrounding the family. Alice Thompson deposed to the court at York in 1546 'that yn cowncell of their faders and moedre wold bringe them to gidre'.[211] The exercising of power over children in matters of marriage was intrinsic to the family organisation. Community also played its part in the process of child marriage. They signalled their acceptance of the practice by attending church services and wedding dinners. Banns were not challenged when read, or not read at all, and priests continued to marry children below the age of canonical consent regardless of directives given by the Church. Whatever the formal protocol of the Church, there existed a shared set of values and perceptions within the community that reinforced the notion that child marriage was an acceptable childrearing practice.

In marriage negotiations, nurturing was not a one-way process between the parent and child and involved agreement on the part of the child. The reasons behind child marriage may appear 'cruel' by modern-day standards, but by going through with the wedding children contributed to the financial security of their parents. On occasions this agreement kept a roof over the head of the family, as in the case of John Stevenson.[212] On other occasions it saved a family from financial ruin, as John Bridge admitted himself when he was forced to marry Elizabeth Ramsbottom.[213] Within this reciprocal, nurturing agreement, children acquiesced to their parent's wishes, although sometimes they did not fully understand the implications of the wedding ceremony as John Andrew told the Chester court in 1548. At the time of the marriage John reported that he and his wife, Ellen Dampart, 'knewe not what they did or els this respondent wold neuer have had her'.[214]

Promoting the interests of the whole family through the medium of child marriage did in some instances place children in homes other than their birth ones, but was this really a case of neglect? Blended and transitional families were not uncommon during the sixteenth century so the experience of children married under age may have differed little from that of other children.[215] For the most part the child spouse was treated like family in their new home. Thomas Nettleton told the consistory court at York in 1553 that he considered his wife, Margaret Clayton, to be a sister to his own sisters, often telling them to 'go call youre sister or bidde youre sister to do this or that'.[216] Overall, the children appear to have behaved towards each other as one child to another, as the case of Robert Randle jumping on the bed of his wife, Margaret, demonstrates.[217] The parents of these children had no doubt regarded the transfer of children from their own homes into that of the children's in-laws as beneficial to them in the long term. It allowed the children to foster emotional ties with other people in that household that may have been advantageous for the child in the future.[218] It could even have made the difference between a failed and a successful marriage.

Undoubtedly, the process of child marriage was difficult for a significant proportion of the children involved and the depositions give some insight into their emotional responses and reactions. It would be interesting to know if parents envisaged the emotional response their children would have to their marriages. But if we are to infer the emotions present between the parents and children using the depositions, then we must set them in the context of the sources and circumstances of the marriage. They will undoubtedly take unexpected appearances such as Bartholomew Hesketh's reaction to his daughter Alice's unhappiness. Similarly, Christian Hope, whose son Peter did not want to displease her by refusing to marry, had promised her son that she would extract him from his marriage should Peter and his wife not agree when they came to lawful age.[219] Christian was concerned enough for Peter's happiness to ensure that he did not have to stay in a loveless marriage, but only after a trial period with the hope that the union may actually work. After all, it had been the wish of Alice's father that the pair be married, setting out the terms in his will. We must regard such provision as an act of nurture rather than neglect as wills were often only made when the person was very sick. Knowing that death was near, making a will was part of the ritual preparation for death designed to comfort the soul and allow for the provision of the surviving family.[220]

Ultimately, child marriage did not diminish childhood experiences for those involved. Historians of childhood have argued that marriage was the primary escape from dependence on and subservience to parents identified in childhood.[221] This was not the case in child marriage. They continued with the activities expected of a child of their status: boys were sent to school or service, children continued to share beds with siblings and servants and youthful exuberance and familial affection could be detected in the manner in which they dealt with each other. No matter what the motive for the marriage had been, both the bride and groom were treated according to their place in the life-cycle and not as a spouse expected to fulfil the obligations of adult marriage in the sixteenth century.

Notes

1   D. Whitelock, M. Brett and C. N. L. Brooks (eds), *Councils & Synods with other Documents Relating to the English Church,* 2 parts, vol II (Oxford: Clarendon

Press, 1981), translation cited in C. N. L. Brooke, *The Medieval Idea of Marriage* (Oxford: Oxford University Press, 1989), p. 140.

2 *The Manchester Guardian*, 9 March 1885, p. 5.

3 Eleanor Rathbone, *Child Marriage; The Indian Minotaur an Object-Lesson From the Past to the Future* (London: Allen & Unwin, 1934); Nujood Ali with Delphine Minoui, *I Am Najood Ali, Age 10 and Divorced* (New York: Three Rivers Press, 2010).

4 Diana O'Hara, '"Ruled by my friends": Aspects of Marriage in the Diocese of Canterbury, *c.* 1540–1570', *Continuity and Change*, 6 (1991), 9–41 (p. 12).

5 O'Hara, '"Ruled by my friends"', p. 13; J. A. Sharpe, *Defamation and Sexual Slander in Early Modern England: The Church Courts at York* (York: Borthwick Papers, 1980), p. 3.

6 E. A. Wrigley and R.S. Schofield, *The Population History of England 1541–1871: A Reconstruction*, (Cambridge, Massachusetts: Harvard University Press, 1981), p. 423.

7 Richard Helmholz, *Marriage Litigation in Medieval England* (Cambridge: Cambridge University Press, 1974), pp. 98–100; Kathryn A. Taglia, 'Marriage's Original Purpose and First Good: Placing Children within the Medieval Church's Views on Marriage', in J. T. Rosenthal (ed.), *Essays on Medieval Childhood: Responses to Recent Debates* (Donington: Shaun Tyas, 2007), pp. 151–73.

8 Hugh Cunningham, *Children and Childhood in Western Society since 1500* (Harlow: Longman, 1995); Colin Heywood, *History of Childhood: Children and Childhood in the West from Medieval to Modern Times* (Cambridge: Polity, 2001); Shulamith Shahar, *Childhood in the Middle Ages* (London: Routledge, 1992); Nicholas Orme, *Medieval Children* (New Haven, CT: Yale University Press, 2001), pp. 334–47.

9 Frederick Furnivall (ed.), *Child Marriages, Divorces, and Ratifications in the Diocese of Chester, A.D. 1561–6* (New York: Kraus Reprint, 1973).

10 Ivy Pinchbeck and Margaret Hewitt, *Children in English Society*, 2 vols (London: Routledge & Kegan Paul, 1969–73), I (1969), 44–57.

11 Gary G. Gibbs, 'Child-Marriages in the Diocese of Chester, 1561–1565', *Journal of Regional and Local Studies*, 8 (1988), 32–42 (p. 32).

12 Gibbs, 'Child Marriages', p. 39.

13 Eric J. Carlson, *Marriage and the English Reformation* (Oxford: Blackwell, 1994), p. 96.

14 I am grateful to Professor Philippa Maddern for sharing this data with me.

15 Christopher Haigh, *Reformation and Resistance in Tudor Lancashire* (Cambridge: Cambridge University Press, 1975), pp. 48–49.

16 Peter Laslett, *The World We Have Lost* (London: Methuen, 1965), p. 86.

17 CALSS, EDC2/7/40–40ᵛ.

18 The cases presented here are not exhaustive of all child marriage cases in Chester and York for the dates of this study. Rather, they represent a selection of cases obtained through searching the relevant databases (where applicable) and the manual searching of depositions books as time allowed.

19 Alan MacFarlane, *Marriage and Love in England 1300–1840* (Oxford and New York: Basil Blackwell, 1986); Conor McCarthy, *Marriage in Medieval England: Law, Literature and Practice* (Woodbridge and Rochester: Boydell, 2004); Lawrence Stone, *The Family, Sex and Marriage* (New York: Harpers Torchbooks, 1977); Lawrence Stone,*Road to Divorce: England 1530–1987* (Oxford: Oxford University Press, 1990); Frederik Pedersen, *Marriage Disputes in Medieval England* (London and Ohio: Hambledon Press, 2000), pp. 153–5; pp. 162–6.

20 Carlson, *Marriage and the English Reformation*, p. 96; p. 21; pp. 107–8.

21 Shannon McSheffrey, *Marriage, Sex, and Civic Culture in Late Medieval London* (Philadelphia: University of Pennsylvania Press, 2006).

22   John Hajnal, 'European Marriage Patterns in Perspective', in D. V. Glass and D. E. C. Eversley (eds), *Population in History* (London: Edward Arnold, 1965), pp. 101–43.

23   Hajnal, 'European Marriage Patterns', p. 101.

24   Wrigley & Schofield, Population History, pp. 421–3.

25   TNA, Early Chancery Petitions, C1/635/35. There are instances where people married before they began their period of servanthood or apprenticeship. Apprentice Thomas Holgait was described as the son-in-law of Robert Herryson in a Chancery petition (1529–32) concerning Thomas's leaving his master without permission.

26   Helmholz, *Marriage Litigation*, pp. 98–9.

27   Henry Swinburne, *Treatise of Spousals or Matrimonial Contracts* (New York: Garland: 1985), p. 20.

28   Taglia, 'Marriage's Original Purpose', p. 155, n. 14.

29   DUSC, Visitation Book 1577–87, DDR/EV/VIS/1/1, fol. 4ᵛ.

30   Taglia, 'Marriage's Original Purpose', pp. 155–4 (esp. n. 16).

31   Taglia, 'Marriage's Original Purpose', p. 155, n. 14.

32   CALSS, EDC2/5/93ᵛ–94ᵛ.

33   Helmholz, *Marriage Litigation*, pp. 98–9.

34   Helmholz, *Marriage Litigation*, pp. 98–9.

35   BIA, CP.G.1167.

36   CALSS, EDC2/4/53.

37   BIA, CP.G.1808.

38   BIA, CP.G.575, Divorce petition of Margret Dickson and Michael Waterhouse, 1553.

39   BIA, CP.H.382.

40   LRO, DDTR/BOX29/10, Marriage Agreement between Edmund Trafford and John Booth.

41   CALSS, EDC2/2/159.

42   CALSS, EDC2/7/124.

43   CALSS, EDC2/9/81.

44   Michael M. Sheehan, 'Choice of Marriage Partner in the Middle Ages: Development and Mode of Application of a Theory of Marriage', *Studies in Medieval and Renaissance History*, 1 (1978), 3–33 (esp. p. 15).

45   O'Hara, '"Ruled by my friends"', p. 27.

46   CALSS, EDC2/9/640–645.

47   CALSS, EDC2/6/640–645.

48   CALSS, EDC2/7/252.

49   Brooke, *Medieval Idea of Marriage*, pp. 141–42.

50   DCA, Court Book of Prior's Official DCD off. bk 1487–98; DUSC, DDR/EJ/CCD/1/7, fols 200–202; DUSC, Bishop's Registers and Act Book, DDR/EA/ACT/1/2.

51   Haigh, *Tudor Lancashire*, p. 49.

52   Peter Rushton, 'Property, Power and Family Networks: The Problem of Disputed Marriage in Early Modern England',*Journal of Family History*, 11 (1986), 205–19 (p. 206).

53   Pinchbeck and Hewitt, *Children in English Society*, ɪ, 48–9.

54   Rushton, 'Property, Power and Family Networks', p. 208.

55   BIA, CP.G.347.

56   BIA, CP.G.347; CALSS, EDC2/4/2.

57   Philip Stubbes, *The Anatomie of Abuses* (ed.) M. J. Kidnie (Tempe, AZ: Renaissance English Text Society, 2002), p. 147.

58   Pinchbeck and Hewitt, *Children in English Society*, ɪ, 47.

59   O'Hara, '"Ruled by my friends"', p. 14.

60   CALSS, EDC2/3/88ᵛ.
61   CALSS, EDC2/5/84ᵛ.
62   CALSS, EDC2/6/242. (Court case, 1559).
63   CALSS, EDC2/2/534. (Court case, 1543).
64   BIA, CP.G.619. (Date of marriage, *c.* 1540).
65   CALSS, EDC2/8/114ᵛ.
66   CALSS, EDC2/7/119–120; 124–124ᵛ.
67   W. Fergusson Irvine (ed.), *A Collection of Lancashire and Cheshire Wills not now to be found in any probate registry 1302–1752* (London: Lancashire and Cheshire Record Society, 1896), p. 174.
68   BIA, CP.G.2322; CP.G.370.
69   CALSS, EDC2/8/266–266ᵛ.
70   CALSS, EDC2/7/79–80ᵛ.
71   CALSS, EDC2/7/11–12; EDC2/7/51–54.
72   CALSS, EDC2/7/19ᵛ.
73   This appears to be a common sum in relation to bonds for child marriage. See CALSS, EDC2/9/9–12: John Carter was married under age because his father was bound by the sum of £40 in an agreement where John was to be married to Joan Higginson by a certain day.
74   BIA, CP.G.294.
75   CALSS, EDC2/7/130ᵛ–131ᵛ.
76   CALSS, EDC2/6/640–645.
77   CALSS, EDC2/6/643.
78   CALSS, EDC2/7/12ᵛ–13ᵛ.
79   CALSS, EDC2/7/12ᵛ.
80   Rushton, 'Property, Power and Family Networks', p. 210.
81   CALSS, EDC2/7/205.
82   CALSS, EDC2/7/205.
83   CALSS, EDC2/7/73ᵛ–74 (Court case, 1562).
84   CALSS, EDC2/8/29–30. See also CALSS, EDC2/9/1–5: Robert Webster and Alice Rylannce were married because Robert had a good living and some goods had been left to him on his father's death.
85   CALSS, EDC2/9/80.
86   CALSS, EDC2/7/195.
87   CALSS, EDC2/7/195ᵛ.
88   BIA, CP.G.299.
89   CALSS, EDC2/4/314–317.
90   BIA, CP.G.3518.
91   BIA, CP.G.3518.
92   CALSS, EDC2/7/61–62.
93   CALSS, EDC2/7/62.
94   CALSS, EDC2/7/249.
95   CALSS, EDC2/7/249ᵛ.
96   CALSS, EDC2/7/253ᵛ.
97   CALSS, EDC2/7/253.
98   CALSS, EDC2/7/249ᵛ.
99   Elaine Clark, 'City Orphans and Custody Laws in Medieval England', *American Journal of Legal History*, 34 (1990), 168–87 (esp. p. 170).
100 Rupert H. Morris, *Chester in the Plantagenet and Tudor Reigns* (Chester, 1875), p. 547.
101 BIA, CP.G.404.
102 TNA, C1/659/40.
103 CALSS, EDC2/8/169.
104 CALSS, EDC2/9/26.

105   CALSS, EDC2/7/38.
106   CALSS, EDC2/7/38.
107   M. G. Smith, *Corporations and Society* (London: Duckworth, 1974), p. 8.
108   R. Trumbach, *The Rise of the Egalitarian Family: Aristocratic Kinship and Domestic Relations in Eighteenth-Century England* (London: Academic Press, 1978), p. 64.
109   Trumbach, *Rise of the Egalitarian Family*, p. 65.
110   Naomi Tadmor, *Family and Friends in Eighteenth-Century England: Household, Kinship, and Patronage* (Cambridge: Cambridge University Press, 2004), p. 171, n. 17.
111   Rushton, 'Property, Power and Family Networks', p. 211.
112   Rushton, 'Property, Power and Family Networks', p. 211.
113   BIA, CP.G.827.
114   CALSS, EDC2/7/3–4 (Court case, 1561).
115   CALSS, EDC2/7/3–3^v.
116   CALSS, EDC2/2/537.
117   CALSS, EDC2/4/53–57.
118   CALSS, EDC2/4/54.
119   CALSS, EDC2/7/156^v–157; 165–6.
120   CALSS, EDC2/7/195^v.
121   BIA, CP.G.299 (Date of marriage, *c.* 1526).
122   CALSS, EDC2/4/98.
123   CALSS, EDC2/2/202–203.
124   CALSS, EDC2/7/53^v.
125   CALSS, EDC2/3/15–15^v. (Date of marriage, *c.* 1532).
126   CALSS, EDC2/4/317. (Date of marriage, *c.* 1533).
127   BIA, CP.G.102.
128   Pinchbeck and Hewitt, *Children in English Society*, I, 48.
129   CALSS, EDC2/3/33^v. (Date of marriage, 1539).
130   CALSS, EDC2/4/165; EDC2/5/2; BIA, CP.G.803.
131   CALSS, EDC2/9/46.
132   CALSS, EDC2/7/157.
133   Michael M. Sheehan, 'The Formation and Stability of Marriage in Fourteenth-Century England: Evidence of an Ely Register', in J. K. Farge (ed.), *Marriage, Family and Law in Medieval Europe: Collected Studies* (Cardiff: University of Wales Press, 1996), pp. 38–76 (esp. p. 44).
134   CALSS, EDC2/5/85; EDC2/4/55 (Court case 1548).
135   BIA, CP.G.575; CALSS, EDC2/7/125^v.
136   BIA, CP.G.1341.
137   BIA, CP.G.2228; CP.G.1020.
138   BIA, CP.G.735.
139   John Myrc, *Instructions for Parish Priests*, (ed.) Edward Peacock (New York: Krauss Reprint, 1975), p. 7.
140   Wedding dinners are mentioned far more often by the witnesses in the York causes but would have been just as common for those marriages in Chester.
141   BIA, CP.G.1502; CP.G.3518.
142   BIA, CP.G.619; CP.G.1808.
143   CALSS, EDC2/7/74. (Court case, 1562).
144   See above p. 114, re: Andrew Haworth and Constance Entwisell.
145   Helmholz, *Marriage Litigation*, p. 161.
146   CALSS, EDC2/3/129–130.
147   CALSS, EDC2/4/5–7.
148   CALSS, EDC2/7/242^v–243^v.
149   CALSS, EDC2/7/251^v–253. (Date of marriage, *c.* 1560).
150   CALSS, EDC2/7/240–240^v(Date of marriage, *c.* 1558).
151   BIA, CP.G.735.

152 BIA, CP.G.299. (Date of marriage, *c.* 1526).
153 CALSS, EDC2/9/45.
154 CALSS, EDC2/7/117ᵛ–119.
155 Rushton, 'Property, Power and Family Networks', p. 206.
156 CALSS, EDC2/4/8–10.
157 CALSS, EDC2/6/131.
158 CALSS, 2/7/73–74.
159 BIA, CP.G.1103 (Court case, 1562); CALSS, EDC2/3/76 (Court case, 1545).
160 Philippa Maddern, 'Between Households: Children in Blended and Transitional Households in Late-Medieval England', *Journal of the History of Childhood and Youth*, 3 (2010), 65–86.
161 CALSS, EDC2/7/165–166.
162 John McLaughlin, 'Medieval Child Marriage: Abuse of Wardship?', Paper delivered at Conference on Medieval Studies, April 1997 at Plymouth state College, Plymouth, New Hampshire, unpaginated.
163 BIA, CP.G.556.
164 CALSS EDC2/7/79–80.
165 CALSS, EDC2/6/195ᵛ–196.
166 CALSS, EDC2/7/38.
167 CALSS, EDC2/2/161–162.
168 Rushton, 'Property, Power and Family Networks', p. 207.
169 CALSS, EDC2/9/28.
170 BIA, CP.G.404.
171 BIA, CP.G.3581.
172 CALSS, EDC2/8/74 (Date of marriage, *c.* 1526).
173 BIA, CP.G.299.
174 CALSS, EDC2/4/183–185.
175 CALSS, EDC2/4/54.
176 CALSS, EDC2/4/55.
177 Interview with Philippa Maddern, at the University of Western Australia (hereafter UWA) on 16 May 2011.
178 CALSS, EDC2/4/163–9.
179 Mary Garrison, 'The Study of Emotions in Early Medieval History: Some Starting Points', *Early Medieval Europe*, 10 (2001), 243–50 (esp. p. 244).
180 Garrison, 'Study of Emotions', p. 244.
181 Garrison, 'Study of Emotions', p. 245.
182 Robert Plutchik, 'The Nature of Emotions: Human emotions have deep evolutionary routes, a fact that may explain their complexity and provide tools for clinical practice', *American Scientist*, 89 (2001), 344–50 (p. 349).
183 Robert C. Roberts, 'Thomas Aquinas and the Morality of Emotions', *History of Philosophy Quarterly,* 9 (1992), 287–305 (p. 289).
184 Susan James, *Passion and Action: The Emotions in Seventeenth-Century Philosophy* (Oxford: Clarendon Press, 1999), p. 6.
185 Simo Knuuttila, *Emotions in Ancient and Medieval Philosophy* (Oxford: Oxford University Press, 2004), p. 245.
186 BIA, CP.G.347.
187 Cited in Knuuttila, *Emotions*, pp. 269–70.
188 CALSS, EDC2/4/1–4; BIA, CP.G.102.
189 BIA, CP.G.827
190 CALSS, EDC2/6/197.
191 CALSS, EDC2/7/120. (Date of marriage, 1547).
192 Aristotle, *Rhetoric*, Bk. II, Chaos. 12–14 (trans.) W. Rhys Roberts (Oxford, 1924), cited in J. A. Burrow, *The Ages of Man: A Study in Medieval Writing and Thought* (Oxford: Clarendon Press, 1986), pp. 191–4.

193   Maddern, Interview 16 May 2011.
194   CALSS, EDC 2/7/19–20.
195   CALSS, EDC 2/7/19–20.
196   CALSS, EDC 2/4/373.
197   CALSS, EDC2/9/508. (Date of marriage, 1563).
198   G. E. Mingay, *The Gentry: The Rise and Fall of a Ruling Class* (London and New York: Longman, 1976), p. 111.
199   CALSS, EDC2/7/146.
200   CALSS, EDC2/7/146.
201   CALSS, EDC2/7/59^v. (Date of marriage, 1544.)
202   CALSS, EDC2/9/80–83.
203   BIA, CP.H.382.
204   Pinchbeck and Hewitt, *Children in English Society*, I, 57.
205   CALSS, EDC2/4/54; BIA, CP.G.347.
206   CALSS, EDC2/6/197.
207   BIA, CP.H.3928. Divorce petition of Elizabeth White and William Brandesby, Yorkshire. (Dated between 1530–1600.)
208   Norman Davies (ed.), *Paston Letters and Papers of the Fifteenth Century*, Part I (Oxford: Clarendon Press, 1971), No. 72, pp. 126–31 (pp. 127–8).
209   Shannon McSheffrey, *Marriage, Sex, and Civic Culture in Late Medieval London* (Philadelphia: University of Pennsylvania Press, 2006), p. 78.
210   BIA, CP.G.102.
211   BIA, CP.G.347.
212   CALSS, EDC2/8/266–266^v.
213   CALSS, EDC2/7/19^v.
214   CALSS, EDC2/7/88.
215   See Maddern, 'Between Households'.
216   BIA, CP.G.3375.
217   CALSS, EDC2/9/13.
218   Susan Broomhall, 'Emotions in the Household', in Susan Broomhall (ed.), *Emotions in the Household, 1200–1900* (Basingstoke and New York: Palgrave Macmillan, 2008), pp. 1–37 (p. 3).
219   Furnivall (ed.), *Child Marriages*, p. 20.
220   Stephen Coppel, 'Willmaking on the Deathbed', *Local Population Studies*, 40 (1988), 37–45 (p. 37).
221   Elizabeth Foyster, 'Parenting Was for Life, not Just for Childhood: The Role of Parents in the Married Lives of their Children in Early Modern England', *History*, 86 (2001), 313–27 (p. 314).

4 Education

To you I am bound for life and education:
My life and education both do learn me
How to respect you; you are the lord of duty.[1]

Desdemona's loyal words to her father, Brabantio, embody the true sense of the word 'education'. For if we consider the accurate meaning of the Latin word '*educo*', to bring up a child physically and mentally,[2] then a child's education has to begin as soon as it takes its first breath. Extant records from ecclesiastical and secular courts bear witness to the fact that sixteenth-century parents thought of education in this way as opposed to our understanding of it today as instruction given in a school or formalised setting. Agnes Denton made an impassioned plea to the archbishop of York in 1570 so that the father of her illegitimate child, John Gowton, would take the child and 'educate and bring vp the same with meate drinke clothe and other necessaties'.[3] Around the same time, Jane Umfrey complained to the ecclesiastical courts in York that Thomas Peeres, the putative father of her child, had left the baby with a poor couple to care for it yet 'would gyve them nothing aforehand to educate the said childe'.[4] Other terminology that we presently associate with formal learning was used interchangeably with nurturing in the sixteenth century. John Thewenge was appointed 'tutor and curator' of Anne Lorimer's person and portion around 1585 because she was under twelve years of age. It is obvious that 'tutor' meant that Thewenge was Anne's guardian responsible for her welfare and not that the intention was for him to school her. Being in service himself, he immediately placed Anne with Robert Nettleton of Sledmere, Yorkshire as his servant.[5]

Taking into consideration these contemporary understandings of the term, it is necessary to locate within this sixteenth-century perspective on education, where the acquisition of literacy and book-based learning fits in. This study acknowledges that instruction of these skills can occur in a variety of contexts but is clearly evidenced in the setting of the grammar school. The aim of this chapter is to establish these contexts and to assess the availability of such educational opportunities for children from all status groups and both genders. Changes in the curriculum during the period will not be discussed as acquisition of literacy and book-based learning need only be considered in relation to learning opportunities within the community.[6] Taken in conjunction with the following chapter on apprenticeship, which discusses vocational skills acquired through manual work, this chapter is an attempt to explore the holistic nature of childhood education through the institutions and practices that have left us enough evidence to build a credible picture of educational provision.

In order to build this picture, we need to carefully address the evidence through the following questions, which will establish the educational experiences of all the children in this study. In what kinds of contexts could children acquire skills and some basic literacy? What sorts of schooling can be identified in sources for the north of England and are there indications that schooling became more widespread in the sixteenth century? Was there increasing professionalisation of teaching? Who participated in schooling – how available was it to the poor? To girls? What ages were the children? What were the children's lived experiences within the school?

As Joan Simon rightly observes, education is 'a key function of every human society from the most primitive age',[7] and yet historians of education have thus far treated education as synonymous with schooling. Simon has criticised historians for thinking of the early development of education in terms of present day institutions, and thus neglecting to establish what education meant to early English society and the forms of it that were generated by these beliefs. Instead, historians have narrowed their focus on to the formal provision of schooling at a time before society had even considered education in these terms.[8] The point Simon is making is that education had a more holistic application in pre-industrial England, but she does not differentiate between skills learnt, just that it is education in the home and in the local community that has taken the dominant part in human society.[9] When it comes to the acquisition of literacy and book-based learning, Simon's argument still holds true. As Anna Dronzek has identified, the formal setting of the classroom was only one of many places children were educated, and the schoolroom was an educational setting from which many children were excluded.[10] It is necessary then for this study to establish the contexts in which children were taught and which groups were engaged in each, bearing in mind there would have been a high level of interconnectedness between various contexts.

Schools, as Dronzek has mentioned, were just one of the many places children were taught, but they are the sole preoccupation for historians of education and, within the discussion, the focus is on institutions rather than the child. There could be various explanations for this state of affairs, not least the paucity of the available sources. But we cannot dismiss the fact that the research carried out thus far on schooling has concentrated on institutional histories to the detriment of the histories of children's experiences at these schools. What we do have in the historiography is a general description of the types of schools that existed in the sixteenth century. Jo Ann Hoeppner Moran discusses both elementary and grammar schooling in York up to the end of the first half of the sixteenth century,[11] while Lawrence Stone has categorised the types of schools, their clientele and what children might have expected from each establishment.[12]

Within this discussion on schooling, there has been much debate over the extent and timing of the expansion of the provision of schools in the north of England. A. F. Leach and Nicholas Orme have deliberated over the physical number of schools but there can never be a consensus on the actual total.[13] The improbability of obtaining the relevant records makes this task 'probably impossible',[14] particularly in view of the many schools which must have existed for such a short space of time that they left no trace in any records. It is equally impossible for historians to reach a comprehensive conclusion on why the rise in the number of schools may have occurred. Rosemary O'Day believes that a change in attitude towards children, in both the home and society at large, corresponded with this rise.[15] Alternatively, Stone is of the view that the educational revolution and the corresponding increase in the number of schools, is directly linked to the adoption of Protestantism and the increased need for lay administrators.[16] But evidence exists that the Reformation was not the catalyst for educational expansion, even though schools were subjected to political and social impetuses of their time that were not of their making.[17] Mrs J. R. Green, writing in the early twentieth century, believed that any 'revolution' was very much in evidence in the fifteenth century as the 'trading classes themselves' embraced education as a means of upward mobility by founding a number of free grammar schools for their local communities.[18]

There is perhaps some credence in Green's remarks. Wilbur Jordan cites the high number of schools endowed in Lancashire between 1480 and 1660 as 'the most persistent charitable interest of Lancastrians' during his period of study, which far exceeded the investment of any other county that he studied.[19] But, as with the physical number of schools, the amount of investment in schooling has been disputed by historians, leaving us no more informed on the causes of any possible educational revolution.[20] Jordan had his own ideas about why there had been so much investment during our period of study: the people of Lancashire aimed to address poverty and the lack of opportunity in the region by teaching children to be literate.[21] Such a utopian ideal may well have been in evidence in the endowments of the Lancashire schools but my records indicate that it was the children from fairly wealthy backgrounds or those whose father had a clerical position who attended them. As historians cannot definitively say if there was a rise in the number of schools and, if there was, what the impetus was for it, then we should concentrate on identifying the types of schools that can be recognised in the sources. At the same time, we should be observing if schooling was becoming more widespread across the north of England in the sixteenth century.

One way to observe if schooling was becoming more widespread is to identify the skills sixteenth-century society required in addition to the children likely to undertake the training. Colin Heywood argues that schooling was the preserve of those children where literacy and specific skills such as Latin were required to perform societal functions.[22] Contemporary commentators appear to have agreed with this outlook. John Aubrey, the seventeenth-century antiquary and biographer, discussing a certain John Hoskins, born in 1566, stated that 'in those dayes boyes were seldome taught to read that were not to be of some learned profession'.[23] Fathers, masters and priests would teach any other groups in society who required literacy or book-based learning.[24] Therefore, as David Cressy points out, while the level of illiteracy among certain social groups may reflect the lack of available schooling, it may also have much more to do with the level of literacy (and skills) required for specific occupations.[25] Furthermore, Cressy argues that despite grammar schools having been founded with the intention of providing access to learning for a proportion of the poor, admission records show that the wealthy were favoured over the less-prosperous majority.[26] There was good reason for this. Any expansion of educational opportunities was a threat to the social order[27] and this would include the admission of girls into schools primarily designed to educate boys. In consequence, historians have focused on grammar schools – because this is where the majority of the records are to be found – and the elite boys who attended them.[28] Very little scholarship has been directed towards the education of girls.

Regardless of evidence placing girls in schools, Moran argues that this suggests elementary learning as opposed to Latin grammar.[29] Caroline Barron too considers that it was unlikely that girls would have attended grammar schools,[30] which means that, with the spotlight of the historiography being firmly positioned on grammar schools, how girls actually acquired literacy and book-based learning is being overlooked in favour of the experiences of a very small percentage of the population. Even if, as Orme notes, opportunities for the schooling of girls were limited and that no woman had any incentive above learning to read and understand her native language and maybe read some Latin,[31] we are aware of a number of literate women in England during the period of this study.[32] So how did they become literate? Kim Phillips observes that the education of girls varied between social groups but that generally instruction was given orally.[33] It was just the sources used that differed according to social status. Their teachers could include mothers, priests and employers, as well as communities within and without the household.[34] Phillips is keen to point out that only for the privileged few were governesses, schools or nunneries an option, defining therefore that it was normative practice for girls to acquire literacy within informal contexts.

Due to the contexts in which girls were taught in the sixteenth century, we know very little about their experiences of learning. Any information in regards to children's experiences of learning that we do have comes courtesy of boys in grammar schools. In this respect, Keith Thomas notes that the learning process could not be separated from the social control aspect of schooling, where children were taken out of the household, segregated from the influences of others and trained to be obedient and civil.[35] While Thomas may be accurate in his observations on the benefits of formal education, it must be considered that these benefits were also obtained from children being placed into a household other than their birth family, for service or apprenticeship, or by interactions within the locality. For obedience and civility, qualities entrenched within the socialisation process of familial education, were crucial to all adult–child relationships regardless of the type of education the child received. Family, as Gouge noted, was 'a school wherein the first principles and grounds of government and subjection are learned'.[36] In other words, schooling cannot be distinguished in terms of its social function, since other types of education also performed similar functions. Nevertheless, it is important to examine children's lived experiences in schools as they reflect the social hierarchies and structures of contemporary society. The discussion should begin however, with identifying the contexts of learning that existed during the sixteenth century.

Contexts of learning

In what kinds of contexts could children learn skills and acquire some basic literacy? For modern-day society it is difficult to think of learning in any context other than schooling. But, for England, the mass schooling of the country's children has been a fairly recent phenomenon. Not until 1870 was there an act of Parliament to establish schools in areas where they were few or non-existent, and a further ten years before attendance was made compulsory between the ages of five and ten.[37] The availability of schooling in the north of England three or more centuries earlier, therefore, was circumscribed by wealth and geography. Compared to the south, the northern part of England was economically backward and less-densely populated and thus schooling was not as readily available.[38] Nevertheless, as the discussion below on the growth of schooling makes clear, the opportunities to partake in institutionalised education rose during the sixteenth century, with the costs of establishing schools, as well as the size, curriculum, fees and master's stipend, all conforming to a national rather than local model.[39] More importantly, we must also consider that schooling did not replace or diminish all other forms of education, which continued to provide instruction in literacy and skills other than those necessary for religious observance.[40]

For all children in the sixteenth century, education began as home-based activity, and it was here that children received an upbringing according to their station in life.[41] This was the way all social groups in sixteenth-century northern England would have initiated their children's education regardless of income. Instruction in any task was often given spontaneously and in an unstructured and casual manner,[42] and these were forms of education that could be much more influential on a child's future than any school. The farmer's son learnt about agriculture by working on the family's land, the craftsman's son about business in his father's workshop before apprenticeship and the nobleman's son in the traditions of the family ahead of instruction in another noble household.[43] Familial education then continued outside the home when children were placed with other families to start their working lives.

For elite and gentry boys, the importance of patronage and social networking as preparation for adult life was the key to their placement in other households. Around 1536, Randulph Ewer was placed in service with Lord Ewer at Barwick-in-Elmet, Yorkshire, at approximately fourteen years of age.[44] Although records indicate that Randulph went to school, his placement into Lord Ewer's household was to be his main educative experience. Schooling, in theory at least, was not the education that youths from the upper echelons required for their station in life. A gentleman's son should learn to 'blow the horn nicely, to hunt skilfully, and elegantly carry and train a hawk'. Schooling and its associated studying 'should be left to the sons of rustics'.[45]

This rather satirical view on education did hold true to some extent. A son was brought up in the profession of his father, which meant in effect a system of specialised education, and, as preparation for this role, the son had to participate in the work of the household.[46] Accompanying a father around an estate meant the child would understand their personal role in protecting the interests of the family as well as acquiring the family's values.[47] This did not mean that children who remained at home or were placed in noble households did not learn subjects taught in schools. William Westby, who was married to Anne Sothworth at Samlesbury in Lancashire in *c*. 1558, had been said by one witness at their divorce hearings in the ecclesiastical court at Chester for the 'most part ben at his owne fathers howse vnder a scholemaster'.[48] But, as noted by Frederick Furnivall, the ability to perform manly exercises and carve, the acquisition of manners and a strong sense of order of rank in society were valued as an education far more than Latin and philosophy.[49] This form of education was as much a social institution as any school.[50] Nevertheless, it is apparent that sons of gentry did in fact enjoy some formal schooling in addition to the familial education offered in their own and the noble households they were placed in, and as such offer us irrefutable evidence that schooling worked side by side with other learning contexts. For instance, William Stanley, who was married to Anne Dutton at the age of twelve in 1560 at Hatton, Cheshire, was said to 'for the most parte bene sins the said mariage, bene at Lathom, at schole there, and in service with therle of Derby'.[51] Hence, there appears to have been increasing investment in formal learning by the gentry and an acknowledgement of it as a complement to the skills learnt within the household.

For daughters from elite households, the main learning environment was within the home and consisted of reading, writing, needlework and sometimes French: an education common for girls for whom social and moral attainments were more desirable than academic ones.[52] Jane Prestall who had married around six or seven years of age in Manchester in 1481, must have been educated in much the same way. A witness in an ecclesiastical court case concerning her inheritance stated that Jane had been requested to go to the House of Lady Brereton to make things for her, 'the said Jane beying a silke woma[n]'.[53] Alongside needlework, literacy was evident. Lady Grace Mildmay, a Tudor gentlewoman who was governed by her father's niece, Mistress Hamblyn, told how she was 'set to cipher with my pen and to cast up and prove great sums and accounts' as well as being set the task of writing letters.[54] It was not uncommon for girls from wealthy backgrounds to be governed by their female relatives, as Grace Mildmay was. In addition, many elite women established small reading schools in their own homes, or offered hourly tutoring purposefully for the daughters of friends and relatives.[55]

Female literacy, however, varied considerably and so did the learning contexts in which they learnt it. Women from artisan households may not have had the benefit of a governess as Grace Mildmay did, or exposure to the small reading schools run by wealthy relatives, but they too demonstrated a valuable level of literacy. Elizabeth Wallington, the daughter of a skinner born *c.* 1562, and the mother of the seventeenth-century turner and diarist, Nehemiah Wallington, was said by her son to be able to recite the stories of the martyrs (probably from John Foxe's book), as well as knowing secular history from *The English Chronicles.*[56] It is not clear whether Elizabeth could actually read the texts but both were considered morally improving reading for all women regardless of status.

For the children of both sexes from more modest backgrounds, who either remained in their own homes indefinitely, or before they were sent into service or apprenticeship, the community offered a number of learning contexts where skills and basic literacy would be taught. Education was seen not only as the responsibility of the family. The parish community and the parish priest were responsible, alongside parents, for training the children to become upstanding members of society.[57] In 1577, the Bishop of Durham ordered that any priests not licensed to preach, were to 'dully, paynefully, and frely teache the children of their severall parishes and cures to reade and write etc'.[58] This was in addition to the Catechism, which they were to teach the children in the hour before evening prayer on Sundays.[59] Alongside their ordained colleagues, parish clerks who assisted the clergy to celebrate Mass and on occasions perform marriages and baptisms, contributed to this communal education. Orme notes that priests were required by canon law to have a clerk to assist with the singing, read the epistle and take school.[60] There is nothing to indicate whether this instruction was to be given in an institution or was to be an informal gathering in the church porch at ad hoc times, but the main purpose of this school was to teach boys the sung part of the liturgy so they could help out at the parish service.[61] Some reading would have been taught as part of this process but as the texts were in Latin it is debatable whether the instruction would have been of any constructive use to the boys. There appears to be no contingency plans should the parish not have a clerk or priest with the necessary skills to teach the children. But as priests were required to be literate to become ordained it might be reasonably supposed that they could pass on such skills to the local children regardless of the setting.

In towns, children from poorer homes could still receive an education of sorts despite the lack of institutions dedicated to their needs. Anne Bucke, who was described as a widow and 'souster',[62] was said to 'teatcheth children' in the 1570 Norwich census of the poor.[63] She was likely to have become one of the 'Select Women' specified by the 1571 Orders for the Poor, who were to teach children and young people skills in an attempt to stop them from begging.[64] Similar evidence is lacking for the north, but this example illuminates the contexts of elementary teaching possible in sixteenth-century England.

Opportunities to acquire literacy and book-based learning skills existed in a number of contexts both within the household and the wider community provided by a diverse range of people. Even if there was no organised instruction in literacy, there was a probability that children in better-off households would be exposed to books, although, like Elizabeth Wallington, there is no evidence to suggest they actually learnt to read them.[65] Where the acquisition of literacy and skills is clearly evidenced is in the setting of the grammar school and there are also assumptions of literacy acquisition at elementary institutions. How available both types of schooling were in sixteenth-century northern England is to some extent reflected in the sources which show not only that the children featured in this study attended them, but also the expansion of such educational opportunities throughout the area.

Types of available schooling

What sorts of schooling can be identified in sources for the north of England and are there indications that schooling became more widespread in the sixteenth century? Stone identified three types of overlapping schooling available during this period. First, there was the 'petty' school, which taught basic literacy and where the parish priest usually doubled as the schoolmaster. Next came the institutions which prepared children for apprenticeships, having an emphasis on English, practical mathematics and accounting. This, Stone argues, could be delivered in the lower forms of grammar schools or in free schools where the curriculum was dedicated solely to these subjects. At the top of Stone's rankings came grammar schools, whose function was to prepare the sons of gentry for university or the Inns of Court.[66] This is the institution that has attracted the majority of historians' attention because it is far more difficult to prove the existence of the smaller elementary schools than the endowed grammar schools. In spite of this, there are indications that elementary schools were valued as a foundation for grammar schooling and apprenticeship. Richard Mulcaster, a famous sixteenth-century headmaster and pedagogic writer, warned parents not to remove their children from the elementary school prematurely as 'insufficienceie skipping from thence to soone, makes a very weake sequele'.[67] However, many of the small schools in the parishes depended upon a single schoolmaster who would keep 'school' in his house. Once the schoolmaster left the parish or passed away, the school ceased to operate.[68] The paucity of evidence for elementary schools means that we can neither estimate the number of schools that would have been operating in any period nor speculate on the number of new schools that may have emerged.[69] That said, over twenty references have been found relating to charity schools in sixteenth-century Cheshire and this would not include the many short-lived small schools for which no references exist.[70]

From my own sources, the only institutions that can be positively identified are grammar schools and the children from the community who attended these schools fit the profile sketched out by Stone. Randulph Ewer, who went to serve his kinsman in 1536, was sent to school in Malton, Yorkshire, before going into service, while Henry Wittacres was sent to school in a number of places, 'being tabled at Donham and somtyme at Padiam' in Lancashire.[71] It is unclear to which institution Randulph Ewer was sent. Malton Grammar School was not founded until 1546 by Robert Holgate, the Archbishop of York, who also endowed two others in the area around the same time, namely Hemsworth Grammar School near Wakefield and Bishop Holgate's School in York. Evidence from the courts indicates that other schools existed in Yorkshire at this time. Sometime between 1500 and 1515, the prioress of Sinningthwaite Priory in Bilton-in-Ainsty lodged a petition with the Chancery court to recoup the amount of 40s. from the executors of John Exilbe that she had paid to James Scheffyld, schoolmaster of the High School, York, for the board and learning of Exilbe's son.[72] The evidence given here only represents the tip of the iceberg of the schooling available.

County Durham did not appear to be as well endowed with schools as its southern neighbour but this in part must be the lack of extant records and not the fact that schools did not exist.[73] A novices' school and an almonry school were noted by the writer of the Rites of Durham, written in the 1540s thus acknowledging their existence prior to this date.[74] The former housed six pupils (sometimes one more or one less), with novices attending this school for the space of seven years. They were provided with meat, drink and clothes for the duration. The Almonry School was founded by the priors of the Abbey Church at Durham in the fourteenth century and provided for thirty poor scholars who received instruction from a school as well as meat and drink. However, the food that the almonry boys received was the leftovers from the novices and their masters.[75] Bishop Langley endowed a public grammar school at Durham in 1414 and a grammar school existed in Darlington around this time.

Cheshire was well served with endowed grammar schools. Acton, Audlem, Bunbury, Chester, Macclesfield, Malpas, Nantwich, Northwich, Sandbach, Stockport and Wallasey all had schools either existing before or established during the sixteenth century.[76] Across the border in Lancashire, a county that supposedly endowed more schools during our period of study than any other, there existed a number of grammar schools especially in the major towns and urban areas. Lancaster, Liverpool, Preston, Wigan and Warrington had schools that could all be traced back to before the Reformation and many more were established as the century progressed, especially outside the major towns. Clitheroe, Penwortham and Winwick were areas where schooling was a priority for the community.[77]

While records suggest that there was a steady increase in the number of schools in sixteenth-century northern England, they were to be found in urban areas rather than rural ones. Vickerstaff argues that rural schools, like those established at Barnard Castle and Darlington in County Durham, attracted only children from local farming communities because where roads did exist they were impassable in inclement weather.[78] Many schools were thus established in the major towns and cities of the counties, but market towns also accounted for a considerable number having the advantages of communication, facilities and abundant lodging opportunities for pupils from the country-side.[79] These were important factors to consider because even for a distance of a few miles it could have been necessary for children to board with a family near to their school, as Henry Wittacres and John Exilbe's son did. The founders of grammar schools acknowledged such a system would exist, as the original order for the foundation of Bishop Holgate's York school indicates. It was established 'towardes thencrease of lerninge & bringing vppe of youthe in virtuous exercise in this his graces Realme of Englande and other his graces Domynyons', an admission that schools would be established in one city, but that children might be sent there from neighbouring ones or further afield.[80] As the number of schools increased in these urban areas and the cohort of pupils rose – although still only a small percentage of the population of children in the local communities – the demand for schoolmasters intensified and the idea of teaching as a vocation began to emerge.

Professionalisation of teaching

Was there increasing professionalisation of teaching? The subject of suitably qualified teachers was a concern to both authorities and contemporary writers in the sixteenth century. Roger Ascham, tutor to Elizabeth I and a proponent of theories of education, derided parents as neglectful for taking little care in finding an adequate schoolmaster for their children when 'commonly more care is had, yea, and that amongst very wise men to find out rather a cunning man for their horse than a cunning man for their children'.[81] Provision of an appropriate role model then, was of great importance when considering a schoolmaster. The English author and philosopher Thomas Elyot highlighted, in his translation of Plutarch's *The Education or Bringinge up of Children*, that parents 'muste diligently prouyde for youre children, schole maysters whose lyues be not despoiled to vice, ne of reprocheable maners or conditions, and whiche haue good experience and fourme of teachynge'.[82] These requirements were essential to nurture any child engaged in formal education. Elyot was of the opinion that 'many good and clene wittes of children be nowe a dayes perisshed by ignorant schole maisters'.[83]

Teaching thus assumed a much more important purpose once there was an increase in the number of laymen attending grammar schools or universities.

The success of the humanist and Protestant curriculum was their responsibility[84] and without suitably qualified teachers no educational expansion could flourish. Education in the Middle Ages had resided under the care of the Church and remained so during the dates of this study and long afterwards.[85] The clergy therefore took an active part in this expansion and, as Stone has pointed out, priests were not limited to teaching reading and writing in the parishes. It was the increased educational levels of priests that allowed for the expansion of formal educational opportunities in all parts of England in the sixteenth century, including the north of the country. A university education, in addition to those with ability to read and write Latin, allowed priests to train boys up to university level.[86] However, the level of education among priests appears to have been influenced by geography. By 1601, only 31 per cent of priests were graduates in the diocese of York, compared to 67 per cent in the diocese of Ely.[87]

The paucity of university-educated priests in the diocese of York is echoed in the examination of priests wishing to become licensed schoolmasters. In 1563 Henry Langdayle, a vicar at Scarborough and a Cambridge graduate, was considered to be fluent in the Hebrew and Latin tongue and thus suitable to teach boys their catechism and grammar. The next year, however, fellow clergyman Richard Collie, curate of Bagby, was banned from teaching grammar to all young students, while Thomas Standeven, a curate from Cooley, was found to neither read nor understand Latin well. Thomas was only admitted to teach boys the catechism in the vernacular.[88] The amount of Latin grammar required to administer the duties of a priest was insufficient when it came to teaching boys grammar.

The examination of priests was no different to that of their secular contemporaries. All teachers had to be licensed by the Church and the ecclesiastical authorities took great care to maintain professional standards in the schools of the diocese. Lay teachers who were discovered to be deficient in certain areas of the curriculum – like John Thompson of Wakefield, who in 1563 was found to be only 'moderately skilled' in Latin – were prohibited from the teaching of grammar.[89] When a suitable candidate was identified, this was noted in the examination record. Richard Michill of Heponstall, Yorkshire, was thought by the authorities to be 'a very well read young man of good ability'.[90] The authorities considered a university education a distinct advantage for schoolmasters and necessary to the nurturing of the scholars. George Sanders of Newart-upon-Trent had attended Cambridge for a number of years and his examiners thought his studies there had borne fruit or that he had prospered there.[91] The York examination of schoolmasters, occurring as they did in the 1560s, suggests that after the Reformation there was concern to monitor and enforce professional standards that perhaps did not exist in the fifteenth century. Accordingly, Orme suggests that although English bishops up to the Reformation were interested enough in education to protect the rights and privileges of schools they greatly ignored the curriculum and who was teaching it.[92]

The move towards professionalisation continued throughout the sixteenth century. Liverpool, which from its establishment in 1517 employed unqualified schoolmasters, sometimes related to its founder, John Crosse, began to take local subscriptions in 1565 to pay for a university-educated schoolmaster. John Ore, 'being a lernyd man', was hired in London on the 'prove and gud lykng' of the Liverpool authorities and was paid £10 per annum,[93] an amount that was common among most of the free grammar schools during the sixteenth century.[94] Unfortunately, Ore did not last long, as records indicate that the Bishop of Chester admitted John Rile to the position of schoolmaster thirteen months later and there appears to have been another schoolmaster in between the two. An entry in the Liverpool Town Books for September 1569 notes that the Duchy of Lancaster was refusing to pay the Crown stipend of John Rile until the town had paid the arrears of the previous teacher, Ralph Higynson.[95] Nurture had thus evolved to include a university-educated teacher for the boys who attended the school. This community involvement in schooling in Liverpool cost the local residents anything between 2d. and 12d. with the mayor paying the highest subscription of 4s.

The move towards university-educated schoolmasters at Liverpool indicates that the schools in northern England did their best to maintain high standards of teaching even though at times this proved to be difficult. At Ripon School, Yorkshire, in 1570, the establishment was obliged to retain John Nettleton – a schoolmaster who had been discharged from his duties due to being unsuitable – until a new master could be found 'lest the yowthe be neglected and untaughte'.[96] Clearly, the definition of neglect here rests upon the absence of a schoolmaster as opposed to being taught by an unsuitable one and links to Thomas's observation of schooling being an instrument of social control. The nurturing principal of governance and obedience, taught within the family and crucial to children's socialisation, was reinforced within the structures of the school environment.

Nurturing of children by a suitable schoolmaster was also a consideration for the endowers of schools during this period. The 1515 indenture detailing the provisions for Manchester Grammar School noted:

> that grace, virtue, and wisdom should grow, flower, and take root in youths during their boyhood, especially in boys of the county of Lancashire, who for a long time through the default of teaching and instruction had wanted such grace, virtue and wisdom.[97]

Echoing Elyot's sentiments above, a second deed from Manchester states that the children of the locality for lack of a suitable schoolmaster 'having pregnant wittis have been most parte brought up rudely and idely and not in vertue, cunnyng, eruducion, literature, and in good maners'.[98] It would appear that the men responsible for establishing these new schools were heavily influenced by humanist educators such as Elyot who assiduously recommended parents to choose wisely the people responsible for any part of their children's care. Any vices present in the carer would soon manifest themselves within the child.

The professionalisation of teachers was an inevitable consequence of the rise in formal schooling. Equally, without an increase in suitable teachers, the expansion of formal education could not have taken place. There was a deliberate 'weeding out' of unqualified teachers by authorities as well as a realisation that a university-educated teacher required to be paid considerably more than a non-university-educated one. The £10 salary given to the first 'lernyd man' employed at Liverpool Grammar School, John Ore, was £4 6s. 9d. more than his predecessors, who received £5 13s. 3d. Elyot felt that at times 'abundant salaries mought be required' so that the teachers were 'righte sufficient and able to induce their berers to excellent lernynge'.[99] Those teachers with only a 'sponefull of latine' for a small salary 'sette a false colour of lernyng on propre wittes wyll be washed away with one shoure of raine'.[100] It was therefore a false economy to employ an under-qualified teacher as all they would do was to encourage surface-learning, which would be easily forgotten by the pupils once outside the confines of the classroom.

Participants in formal education

Who participated in schooling – how available was it to the poor? To girls? What ages were the children? As noted above, the people responsible for establishing new schools adopted a humanistic approach to education that encouraged the widening of social groups engaging in formal education. Contemporary educators of the time such as Richard Mulcaster believed that change was due. Mulcaster wrote a manual for the education of children in English rather than Latin, stating that 'I meane good to the vnlearned, which vnderstand but English'.[101] There is a suggestion of the possibility of social mobility through education in Mulcaster's comments. He admits that the prevalence of Latin renders education 'mysteries to the multitude', a secret garden that can only be entered by the use of English, saying of it that 'the thing it selfe must be presented in her owne colours'.[102] If Mulcaster's sentiments heralded both a shift in the thinking on education and the social widening of participation in formal schooling by sixteenth-century children, then we must ask: for whom was this expansion intended?

Wills from the sixteenth century reflect individuals' wishes for children, both boys and girls, to attend school. Unfortunately, none of them mentions a particular school by name and therefore we cannot identify the types of schools to which members of the community were sending their children, but we may surmise the level of education a child was destined to receive from information contained within these sources. In 1513, George Atherton left 40s. per annum for fourteen years towards the schooling of his illegitimate brother's son John.[103] George is described as an esquire and able to afford the £28 in total he left to John. He had also left £40 for John's sister's marriage, and we may assume that John was destined for a grammar school. Similarly, in 1579 William Massey left twenty nobles, which was just over £7 6s., to his grandson, William Trafford, to be put towards keeping him at school.[104] The length of the term of George Atherton's bequest suggests that John had not started school at the time the will was written, whereas William Trafford's circumstances are more ambiguous. He may have already started school and the money was needed to allow him to continue, or he may have been yet to start.

There was awareness by the people who left money for the education of a child that any sources of income had to provide for a number of years of schooling. Sir Richard Sutton of Sutton, Cheshire, left lands in Cheshire to his nephew and heirs in 1524 on the understanding that they would not sell them but would use the profit to keep their children at school.[105] Sutton considered schooling to be of the utmost importance in the nurturing of a child and his stipulation reflected that his nephew might not have had the same dedication towards education. This was an unsurprising request from a man who had had the benefit of a grammar school education himself, probably attending Macclesfield Grammar School before going on to study at the Inns of Court. A life-long interest in education saw Sutton co-found Brasenose College, Oxford, along with William Smith, Bishop of Lincoln, in 1512 in addition to providing for a priest to be employed in teaching girls who intended to enter the nunnery at Syon Abbey in Middlesex.[106] Nor did he forget the local school in his will, leaving the grammar school master 8d. to ensure that all the children said diriges for his soul. The children were to receive 2d. yearly to perform the service.[107]

Some parents did not mention school at all but placed their emphasis on education and learning that might occur in a number of other contexts. In 1568, Henry Bedford of Liverpool requested that his wife should ensure that their children 'mainteyne ther learninge' and listed a number of men who could assist her, suggesting that he intended them to have formal schooling.[108] There is also evidence that schooling was intended to precede a period of industrial training as the sixteenth century progressed. Adam Bank of Wigan left money to his eldest son, Humfrey, in 1563 so that his younger son, Thomas, may 'be set to learning in his childhood to the schole & then to his occupacon of the Pewterers Crafte'.[109] In Liverpool in 1574, Rauff Alyn, an orphan, was apprenticed to Thomas Gaskill, and Brian Charlis, who stood surety for him, had paid the sum of 7s. for Rauff's education before the commencement of the apprenticeship.[110] Unfortunately, Rauff neither signed nor marked the indenture so there is no way of knowing if the money was well spent. On the other side of the Pennines, Richard Smythe, apprenticed to Peter Wilkinson, a York haberdasher, in 1591, is described in his indenture as a scholar.[111] This evidence suggests that practices in the north of England were similar to those in the south, where boys were increasingly required to be literate before commencing an apprenticeship.

That schooling preceded apprenticeship demonstrates many of the contexts of learning coexisted together even if we cannot determine how many children were educated this way. There are some indications that this situation was more common than records reveal. Margaret Spufford, who studied autobiographies of tradesmen and merchants to assess seventeenth-century literacy levels, concluded that the main use of formal education at the time was to prepare boys for apprenticeship. Once they had reached a suitable level of competency in their studies, boys were removed from school and apprenticed.[112] Furthermore, this scenario must have been a regular occurrence in the sixteenth century for in 1531 Thomas Elyot complained about parents who removed from schools 'theyr aptist and moste propre scholers, after they be well instructed in speaking latine' and are then 'bounden prentises'.[113] As there was no system for recording the schooling of apprentices, it is not surprising that records mentioning such a practice are few in sixteenth-century northern England. Nevertheless, we should not be surprised by the increasing interest in schooling by those classes who worked for a living. Popular rhymes reveal both their wish to learn and the advantages of schooling to their lives:

> Son, if thou wist what thing it were,
> Connynge to learn and with thee to bear,
> Thou would not mis-spend one hour,
> For of all treasure connynge is the flower:
> If thou wilt live in peace and rest
> Hear and see and say the best.[114]

Historians have suggested that as the number of schools increased the ability of children from the lower classes to take advantage of the opportunities afforded to them by such an expansion also increased. Jordan asserted that by the time of the Restoration 'a widespread and well-endowed system of education has been created within the reach of any poor boy and able boy who thirsted for knowledge and who aspired to escape the grip of poverty'.[115] There is some evidence that Jordan may be correct in his conclusion. The eldest children of Robert Clerk, Richard Peper and William Thaxter all attended school despite being described as 'veri pore' in the 1570 Norwich census of the poor[116] and contemporary writers embraced such ideals. Richard Mulcaster, who dedicated his education manual *Positions* to Elizabeth I and tailored the advice to the needs of the state, believed that education should be available to all regardless of wealth or gender, although he was concerned with the education of boys. By commenting that 'if all poore be restrained, the[n] will towardnesse repine', he acknowledges that barring poor children from formal schooling would breed discontent.[117] He also recognised that everyone desired to have their child educated as 'learning hath some strength to shore vp the person'.[118] It is interesting to note that Mulcaster did apply certain caveats to his views and that not all children should be sent to school. Only those with natural wit and parents or friends able to support them should attend school, which contradicts his vision of a commonwealth where all members are entitled to an education.[119] Fortunately, some members of the community facilitated the learning of children within their number whose parents were unable to pay for their education.

As Helen Jewell contends, the gratis provision of education to poor children was a 'pious act' but providing it at a cost to wealthier families was 'morally unremarkable'.[120] Yet it is through the statutes of the many chantry and endowed schools, in addition to the terms of benefactor's wills, that we can see the value people involved placed upon an education for all children, rich or poor. Liverpool Grammar School, which was established alongside a chantry under the will of John Crosse, late of Crosse Hall, Liverpool, charged those students able to pay but not 'the children whose namez be Crosse and poore children that have no socur'.[121] This was not an unusual measure for schools in sixteenth-century northern England. Lancaster, the earliest recorded grammar school in Lancashire, was endowed by John Gardyner in 1469 and was financed with the profits of a water mill in Newton so that 'the scole maister, being a profund grammarion keping a Fre Scole, teching and informing the children unto their most profitte nothing taking therefor'.[122] All children at Stockport school, residents and strangers alike, paid no fees until the 1570s[123] and its alumni included sons of gentlemen and husbandmen.

Some terminology was more precise about the type of children who were to be taught in these schools. The statute of the King's School in Chester, which was founded within the diocese in 1541, stated that there should be a master and an usher to instruct twenty-four 'poor and friendless boys' in the subjects of Latin and Greek.[124] Another King's School, the grammar school at Durham re-founded in 1541 and re-endowed by Henry VIII in the same year, made provision for 'eighteen boys, poor and destitute of the help of friends, to be nourished on the goods of the church'.[125] Before its re-endowment it took 'the poor indeed freely for the love of God, if they or their parents have humbly asked for this'.[126] The better-off students were expected to pay the 'moderate' fees charged at other grammar schools.

Poverty is of course relative and it is doubtful that the twenty-four poor boys at Chester King's School or the eighteen at Durham came from the lowest echelons of the community but, nonetheless, they may have been precluded from formal schooling due to the cost of attending. Subsequently, it appears that the dean and chapter of Chester Cathedral King's School did not adhere to the stipulation that the boys had to be poor and friendless, for in 1632 the Bishop of Chester had to remind them that children from wealthy homes were not to be made King's scholars,[127] an abuse of the founding ethos that must have happened in many schools as they became established. Regardless of these abuses, other free schools in Cheshire existed during the period of this study, including Malpas, which was free for all pupils regardless of where they lived, and Acton, whose existence was first mentioned in the will of Richard Wilbraham, who left £6 13s. 4d. per year, indefinitely, to employ a priest to teach the children and youth of the parish free of charge.[128]

A clear distinction must be drawn here between a school that used the term 'free school' to mean they offered a liberal education or that such a school was free from ecclesiastical authority, from one where no fees were charged. Sir John Percival, a member of the London Merchant Taylors and a former Lord Mayor of London, established Macclesfield School, Cheshire, as a free grammar school in 1502. The schoolmaster there was to teach 'gentlemen's sons and other good men's children of the town and country thereabouts'.[129] Undoubtedly, considering the social status of the pupils to be taught, the 'free' in the description of the school does not refer to the lack of fees. Those schools where 'free' did mean the absence of fees usually clarified this in their statutes or documents relating to the endowment. When the grammar school at Penwortham, Lancashire, was endowed in 1552, Christopher Walton stated that the profits of the lands he granted to maintain the school should be used to instruct the poor children of the parish of Penwortham, the younger children in their ABCs, catechism, primer and accidence, and the older children in grammar, without charge.[130] Failure by the priest or master to observe this proviso for the gratis education of the local children was treated with censure. In 1526, the mayor and other burgesses of Preston, Lancashire, forcibly evicted the chantry priest, Roger Lewyns, because he had not kept a free school for the children of the inhabitants and this amounted to a dereliction of part of his duties.[131]

How many 'poore children that have no socur' or 'poor and friendless boys' took advantage of the free instruction in the schools of sixteenth-century northern England is debatable. Stone argues that entry into grammar school was inaccessible to children of unskilled men or those without property.[132] Even if parents desired their children to be educated, it was a costly alternative to sending them out to work or employing them in the home, and would provide little compensation to the family economy. In addition to fees, costs associated with schooling made the prospect of poor children attending grammar schools extremely slight. Some schools charged admission fees while others charged to enter the names of pupils into the register in addition to the cost of books and board and lodging.[133] There might also have been a charge for fires, candles and birches.[134] Schools did, however, try to mitigate the costs for poorer pupils, like Bunbury in Cheshire, which reduced the admission fees from 12d. to 4d.,[135] but even reduced rates could act as a barrier to children attending school.

Closer inspection of the statutes of some schools exposes the flaws in an apparently inclusive admissions policy. Manchester School stated that all children were accepted, and that 'no scoller ne infaunt of what cuntrey or schire so ever he be of, being manchilde, be refused', with the exception of those that had 'some horryble or contagious infirmite infectyf'.[136] Sick or infected children therefore were not welcome and the use of the word 'manchilde' indicates that girls were also excluded. Laurent Joubert, the sixteenth-century French physician, acknowledged that boys and girls were treated differently in all things: 'not only in dress but also in food and education'[137] so it is unsurprising that girls were conspicuously absent from most statutes and admission policies. Moran argues any mention of girls attending a school usually referred to elementary rather than Latin learning, adding that girls were little referred to in any records on schooling.[138] The Reformation had centralised the state, the monarch was at the helm and highly educated civil servants were required to administrate the commonwealth: grammar schools were created precisely to educate boys for this life.[139]

Despite the emerging theories of Christian humanists in the sixteenth century that instruction of both boys and girls was desirable, there was no change in common opinion as to the form the education of girls should take.[140] Female education was useful only to produce learned mothers and wives.[141] Even Vives's *Instruction of a Christian Woman*, highly regarded as an epitome of female educational instruction for girls, was based upon the texts of the Christian Fathers, who recommended gendered curricula. Boys were to receive a classical education while girls were taught modesty and obedience, with reading as a morally improving hobby.[142] Reading was an infinitely more necessary skill than writing for girls, in order that they may know the perils of their souls and the route to salvation.[143]

Thomas Becon believed that young women should be taught 'to be sober-minded, to love their husbands, to love their children, to be discreet, chaste, housewifely, good, [and] obedient to their husbands'.[144] To do this, Becon advocated that schools should be set up with 'learned matrons' at the helm to instruct girls in their Christian duties.[145] Nunneries, as Becon comments, were just such schools but Henry VIII's dissolution of the religious houses of England removed this avenue of opportunity for girls. Eileen Power's study of medieval English nunneries identified them as the pre-Reformation institution most likely attended by daughters of the elite, although she is scornful of the type of education the girls received there. Power argues that sending girls to nunneries was not a long-term investment for parents as sending boys to grammar schools was. The education provided was basic and they were sent there for only short periods of time.[146] Any instruction the girls received was defined by the abilities of the nuns themselves, the subjects reflecting more the curriculum set out by Becon than one underpinned by books.[147]

The expansion of educational opportunities that continued after the Reformation did little to redress the imbalance between the sexes. Mulcaster recommended 'set not yong maidens to publike grammer scholes', but that they should be educated 'with distinction in degrees, with difference of their calling'.[148] Grammar schools were for boys as, 'the *male* is more worthy, and politikely he is more employed, and therefore that side claimeth this learned education'.[149] Girls, therefore, were either prohibited from attending grammar schools at all or required to leave once they reached a certain age. At Bunbury School, girls could start at the school alongside their male peers but had to leave either once they turned nine or could read English.[150] What this does suggest, though, is that schooling was more inclusive the younger the pupils, becoming segregated only around ten years of age, when they started to be taught the subjects that would direct them to their place in society. The main subject in grammar schools was Latin, required for boys to undertake clerical careers, so there was no need for girls to attend them. But a proportion of the school-age population of girls in the sixteenth century must have enjoyed some sort of formal schooling.

As Barron has noted, it is difficult to find anything more than incidental references to the education of girls in the fifteenth century[151] and this appears to have continued in sixteenth-century northern England. Evidence of educating girls is scant in archival sources but occasionally provision for the education of girls can be glimpsed. William Hockenhall of Prenton, Cheshire, left provision in his will in 1563 stating that his wife should bring up their daughters 'in good nurture & education'.[152] This request does not necessarily relate to formal schooling and may refer both to caring for his daughters and to an education experienced by Lady Grace Mildmay mentioned above. However, we do know that girls from wealthier homes were educated formally at this time. Katherine Dee, the eight-year-old daughter of the sixteenth-century mathematician and astronomer John Dee, was sent to a schoolmaster alongside her brothers in March 1590, although this arrangement was short lived. Two months later she was put to school at Mistress Brayce's, with whom she no doubt boarded.[153]

Smaller schools where girls would have been educated in reading and writing existed but have left no legacy due to their size. Licences from the bishop were not required for those persons teaching elementary subjects to up to six pupils (own family excepted), those that did not teach boys past the age of ten and those that did not use pupils to help teach. By keeping within these guidelines, schoolmistresses were considered to be running 'domestic schools' and therefore a task of the extended family. No trace, therefore, has been left in any administration.[154] Furthermore, schools or schoolmistresses that have been identified from indirect references in secular and ecclesiastical sources are surely just a fraction of those that existed. Jay Anglin has identified forty-seven schoolmistresses in twenty-eight London parishes between 1560 and 1603, which suggests that many small schools educating girls must have existed throughout the country.[155]

The age at which the children started school varied and, according to Orme, did not become a topic for discussion among the writers of the northern Renaissance until the sixteenth century.[156] Contemporary commentators like Mulcaster did not specify a set age for entry into school, suggesting rather that it depended upon the physical and mental attributes of the individual child. Children should have 'a body able to beare the trauell, which belongs vnto learning' but the age at which they should start school varied from child to child as they did not all mature at one specific age.[157] At Northwich School in Cheshire, pupils had to be at least six years old, while at Blackburn, Lancashire, they could start at age five, but older pupils rather than the schoolmaster instructed them.[158] This age stipulation would have been the minimum age and in reality children would have been much older when sent away to school. Henry Wittacres, William Westby and William Stanley, mentioned below and above, were all over ten when they were sent to school according to witnesses in their divorce cases and this concurs with the historiography on the subject. Orme concludes that children would be sent to school between nine and twelve years of age, but this depended upon the circumstances of the child, his abilities and the economic circumstances of the parents.[159]

Formal education in sixteenth-century northern England was not socially or gender inclusive. The expansion of educational opportunity that took place throughout the period of this study was intended for wealthy boys who required a classical education to enter the Church or Inns of Court on their way to serve the state. Bright, poorer boys were encouraged to attend school through the philanthropy of wealthy patrons but it is extremely unlikely that these would have been from the lowest echelons of society as schooling was still a costly business despite the lack of fees. People frequently bequeathed money to their families in order to meet these costs. Girls' participation in formal education was limited by both opportunity and opinion. The dissolution of the nunneries under Henry VIII may have reduced the number of institutions dedicated to girls' schooling, but this only affected a limited number of wealthy pupils. Most girls from elite families continued to be educated in the home whilst the majority of sixteenth-century schoolgirls remained firmly out of sight of the historian, all but absent in any available records on schooling.

Children's lived experiences at school

What were the lived experiences of children attending schools in sixteenth-century northern England? As with the acquisition of literacy and book-based learning, the experiences of children – predominately boys – is most clearly evidenced in grammar schools. The experiences for which any evidence is available are most likely to be those of wealthy boys attending grammar schools to the exclusion of all other social classes including all girls. Yet it is still valuable to examine their experiences as many of them have shaped present-day schools for pupils of all social classes and gender.

Regardless of whether parents had paid fees for their children to attend a school or not, or the age at which they started, the day-to-day experience was the same for all pupils. In the absence of school registers and personal accounts of the pupils, statutes provide some insight in to the lived experience of the schoolchildren. At Lancaster, the pupils' day began at 'sex of the clocke', continuing until 8 a.m. when they would break until 10 a.m., presumably for breakfast.[160] Lunchtime was at 12 p.m. for two hours, after which they worked until 6 p.m. when they would recite *de profundis*[161] for the souls of the founder, John Gardyner, and his wife, Isabell.[162] These hours were similar to those of other schools in the north of England. At Durham, a 'chief monyter' was appointed to note down the names of the boys who were late, reporting the perpetrators to the schoolmaster every Friday.[163]

Numbers of pupils taught by one schoolmaster varied from moderate to very large and were usually limited only by the size of the schoolroom. John Colet, the master of St Paul's school in London in the early sixteenth century expected to teach approximately 153 pupils 'acordyng to the noumber of the Setys in the scole'.[164] The cohort would have been smaller at provincial schools but numbers are hard to estimate unless admission criteria were set out in the statutes. At Rivington Grammar School in Lancashire, founded in 1566, the statutes instructed the master and the usher to divide the pupils into forms of ten or twelve. Each man was permitted to teach three forms, which would make the maximum number of pupils anything between sixty and seventy-two.[165] The briefs for other schools' intakes of pupils were less precise. The master at Rochdale School, Lancashire, was permitted to enrol no fewer than fifty boys up to a maximum of 150 to be taught by him and the usher.[166]

School terms were comparable to those observed in English schools today. In Durham, the year began on 7 January and continued until the Wednesday before Easter. After a break until Low Sunday, the first Sunday after Easter, the school recommenced until the Wednesday before Whitsunday, with the final term of the year ending on Christmas Eve.[167] But boys at Durham did not always enjoy a carefree holiday from school. There existed the equivalent of a summer school for those boys who needed to 'repeate such thinges as the schoolemaister shall think profitable for their better proceding'.[168] They were required to report to the school twice every day for an hour. This is a good indication that the boys were local and could in fact make the journey twice a day.

Subjects taught at grammar schools followed a predictable curriculum. Masters at Northwich School, Cheshire, originally known as Witton School, were to teach their pupils Latin and Greek literature, the catechism, Henry VIII's accidence and grammar, Erasmus's *Institutum, Christiani Hominis, Copia*, and *Colloquia*, Ovid's *Metamorphoses*, and the works of Terence, Cicero, Horace, Sallust and Virgil.[169] Latin was prioritised over French or English in schools for an extremely important reason. It was the language of the Christian Church and all the texts and ecclesiastical laws were written in Latin, as were the principal textbooks of the arts and sciences.[170] Indeed, practically all the scholarship at this date and all teaching and learning at university were done in Latin. The secular courts recorded their proceedings in Latin, with a few exceptions, such as witness depositions. If boys were going to be wise servants of the state, it was imperative that they had a firm grasp of the language. Teaching Latin in schools was no doubt a mechanism to keep the administration of the country firmly in the hands of the wealthy and, if the endowments of the grammar schools were followed, the able few. For, as discussed above, Mulcaster identified the sole use of Latin in schools as making education a mystery to the majority of the population in the sixteenth century.[171]

Boys who did not work diligently or were slow in their learning, were dealt with quite differently in each school. At Durham, the master was to report any boy to the dean as soon as possible so 'that he may not like a drone consume the bees honey'.[172] The slow learners were thus expelled, demonstrating that schools were academically driven in the north in the sixteenth century and high standards were expected of each boy. At Rivington the treatment was much harsher. If the boy were under sixteen, then he would be shown the error of his ways by use of the rod or by some penance that was designed to make him open to ridicule by the rest of the school, such as being on display to the rest of his peers, who could 'finger and point at him'.[173] Actions such as these made all boys complicit in their peers' learning and subliminally transmitted the message that there was a collective responsibility in keeping up high standards. It also meant that all boys participated in the government of the school by playing a part in the disciplinary procedures.

Humanist writers advocated corporal punishment as an integral part of school life. Mulcaster was of the belief that children should be punished if they were lazy and neglected their studies because 'the ende of our schooles is learning: if it faile by negligence, punish negligence'.[174] One parent who agreed with Mulcaster's advice was Agnes Paston, the matriarch of the Paston family, who wrote to the teacher of her fifteen-year-old son to say that if he 'had not done well, nor will not amend' his master was to 'truly belash him till he will amend'.[175]

Discipline, however, was not always physical. If the scholar were over sixteen (and above correcting with the rod), other methods were used. At Rivington, the boy had first to admit his faults in English to the whole assembled school before writing them down in Latin. If he were too proud to accept these punishments, then he was to be expelled.[176] There is an admission within the punishment meted out at Rivington that the rod was ineffective or seen to be inappropriate after a certain age. Medieval theorists believed that a child had to be beaten to make them learn as they had not yet attained full reason so could not be rationally convinced of their faults.[177] Once the child became morally and rationally responsible as an adult, then shame and repentance would have been possible. So, it was much more valuable to use shame than pain as a method of making boys accept their faults once they were older. Tardy schoolwork was not the only behaviour that could result in banishment from the school. Older scholars at Manchester who refused to teach the younger students their ABCs were 'to be banished the same scole for ever', demonstrating that all in the school community had a responsibility for each other's learning.[178]

The culture of the children can be discerned from the rules stipulated in the statutes. Similar to the expected behaviour outlined in apprentice indentures, the children were to refrain from unlawful games like cock fights or other displays of unseemly behaviour like 'ryddyngs aboute for victours or other disputes had in this parties'.[179] The pupils at Manchester had to play only honest games 'convenyent for youthe' which included all pupils in the one location. They were to converse only in Latin when they were playing.[180] This stipulation was not unusual as the pupils at Durham were required to 'use the Latin tongue in and about the schoole'.[181] It must also have been common for boys to wear a dagger or a weapon in everyday life, for many schools prohibited these items, stating that pupils were allowed only a penknife for their meat. Rivington School went further, prohibiting pupils from attending the 'fencing school', saying 'their chief pastime shall be shooting' and then only with honest people, targeting small game and not making a profit from it.[182] Fighting among the pupils was to be deterred as much in sixteenth-century schools as it is today.

Other peculiarities of the scholars' culture concerned the process of barring-out, where boys refused to admit their schoolmaster to the classroom unless the boys' demands were met. The situation was out of control at Durham in 1595, where the ceremony was thought to be 'a seditious and perillous example of other elder folkes'. Any scholar found barring-out the master was to be expelled as 'seditious and unfitt'.[183] The ritual was not frowned upon by all schools and even allowed in places. At Witton School, pupils were encouraged 'according to the old custom' to 'bar and keep forth of the school the schoolmaster, in such sort as other scholars do in great schools'.[184]

If we examine the culture of these schoolboys it informs us just as much about the purposes of formal schooling in the sixteenth century as looking at the subjects taught within the classroom. There existed, just as it still exists today, a 'hidden curriculum', or the non-official learning that takes place in schools. That is, the messages implied by the school rituals, learning how to be obedient, the 'unofficial' learning that can occur between pupils and all the social exchanges that happen within the institution.[185] The informal curriculum sent social messages that encouraged elitist characteristics like using a bow and arrow even though it was often a dangerous pastime. The boys absorbed these messages, both subliminal and explicit. Often, beatings were a subject dealt with in translation exercises confirming them to be an integral part of the curriculum. The vulgarias of John Standbridge and Robert Whittinton frequently refer to beatings in their translation exercises: 'I was beten this morning. The mayster hath bete me. The mayster gaue me a blowe on the cheke. I fere the mayster.'[186] By accepting their own beatings and those given to boys who had digressed from their work or by joining in the humiliation of a fellow peer the boys were learning to be obedient and contributing to the unofficial learning that occurred between pupils.

Within this hidden curriculum, there is evidence that the boys were expected to form a fraternity by undertaking communal action: playing only in one location, speaking Latin and barring-out ceremonies. And, although obedience was expected, opposition was encouraged with some of the rituals as it prepared the boys for independence. These were all cohesive factors that marked the pupils out as a unique community that would extend beyond the boundaries of the school. On further examination of the school rituals, one could argue that the schools used them as a defining process. Elite ideals were being reinforced through this curriculum and, even if the fees had been removed for poorer pupils, there were still other structures that separated the wealthy pupils from the poor ones. All boys would own a knife, but poorer boys might not have owned a bow and arrow.

Conclusion

Education will always be a fluid construct, one which addresses the needs and purposes of particular groups within a specific time and place. In pre-industrial northern England, education was no less important in the preparation for adult life than it is today, but the process was very different. Within this process there were many contexts in which children learnt to become literate but there were also many levels of literacy that accorded to particular positions in life. It could include contrasting knowledge of French, Latin and English, being able to identify and read aloud the words on a page, being able to read in one or more language, skill in both reading and writing, or simply committing to memory large sections of popular books.[187] It is not helpful to narrow literacy down to one definition as every variation counted as literacy.[188] The poor child who learnt some basic literacy alongside the skills of knitting in a local woman's house could be termed literate just as much as a wealthy schoolboy who was schooled in Latin in a grammar school.

It is with formal schooling that we see a narrowing of both the contexts and the curriculum in addition to restrictions on the participants. While the availability of schooling rose in the north of England during the sixteenth century, without exception schools recorded by means of statutes or otherwise were intended to train wealthier boys for a clerical life, a sphere from which poorer boys and all girls were mainly excluded. But this does not mean that poorer boys and girls did not receive an education, just that the education they received was not considered important enough to be recorded in any official documents, and in many instances would be termed 'informal'. There is, however, nothing within the sources relating to informal education of any kind that suggests what contemporaries thought constituted 'good nurture'. Therefore, we must conclude on educational good nurture for formal education only, restricted as it is to boys of a particular social standing.

It is apparent that sending a boy to school constituted an element of good nurture that, according to Mulcaster, all parents wanted for their children. 'They that cannot, will wish it, they that can, will haue it, with small charge if they may, if they may not with some coste, and very carefully comme[n]d the silly poore boy at his first entry, to his maisters charge.'[189] More important than the subjects taught was that the education the boys received was an agent of secondary socialisation, which reinforced the beliefs the child received in the family home. Education was a channel through which shared moral values, traditions and ideals of the ruling minority were transmitted to the next generation by means of the hidden curriculum. Boys were expected to follow school rules and embrace school rituals that would define them as an adult. This hidden curriculum, or 'internal workings' of the school, as Thomas rightly notes, conveys inherent contemporary beliefs concerning authority.[190] The government of a school reflected the government of society at large,[191] and the virtues of obedience and deference to those in authority were of most concern to parents and commentators alike. The most effective way to achieve these virtues was through discipline in the form of punishment and great significance was put upon its role.

Failure to punish was neglectful in schools and, as many contemporary proverbs testify, the rod was a necessary part of school life: 'a whip for a fool and a rod for a school are always in good season.'[192] Mulcaster advocated that the rod 'may no more be spared in schooles, then the sworde may be in the princes hand'.[193] As was apparent at Rivington, the schoolmaster did not work alone and all boys were complicit in the disciplining of others. The perils of not allowing the master to punish a child were only to be observed in later life. An excerpt from a fifteenth-century schoolbook tells the cautionary tale of a boy whose mother complained to her husband after the schoolmaster had beaten her son and she refused to let him be punished any more. The writer of the prose concludes that due to the lack of discipline when younger, the boy and those like him 'waxe bolde to do all myschevousnes, settynge litell to do the greatest shame that can be' and when punished for their errant ways 'curse the fathers and mothers and other that hade rule of them in ther youghe'.[194] Punishment was a normative part of school life and considered to be essential for the good nurture of boys. It was the 'fundamental sanction'[195] that was essential to produce upstanding members of society.

Obedience and deference could only flourish under the guidance of a suitable role model who was to be well qualified and those who failed to make the mark were quickly removed from their office. Other considerations were important such as having impeccable manners and lives free from vice. John Lacye, who in 1570 was the master at Bradford Grammar School, was discharged from the post due to being 'insuffyciente bothe for his learning and otherwise'.[196] But the most important function of the master as we have observed with John Nettleton at Ripon School, was one of control and discipline. Bad teaching was preferable to having no teacher as even an unsuitable master could provide a moral education in order to socialise the pupils. In this respect, the good nurture provided by formal education in sixteenth-century northern England was no different to that produced from informal education. Socialisation, not particular knowledge, was the aim of education regardless of the context within which it was taught.

Notes

1 William Shakespeare, *The Tragedy of Othello the Moor of Venice* (ed.) Christopher Bentley (Sydney: Sydney University Press, 1982), Act I, Scene 3, line 181.
2 William Smith and John Lockwood, *Chambers Murray Latin–English Dictionary* (Edinburgh: Chambers; London: J. Murray, 1976), p. 223.
3 BIA, HC.CP.ND.2.
4 BIA, CP.G.1521.
5 BIA, DC.CP.1590/4.
6 J. J. Vickerstaff, *A Great Revolutionary Deluge? Education and the Reformation in County Durham*, (Teeside Paper in North Eastern History, No. 2, 1992), p. 5.
7 Joan Simon, *The Social Origins of English Education* (London: Routledge & Paul, 1970), p. 4.

8   Simon, *Social Origins*, pp. ix–x.
9   Simon, *Social Origins*, p. 5.
10 Anna Dronzek, 'Gendered Theories of Education in Fifteenth-Century Conduct Books', in Kathleen Ashley and Robert L. A. Clark (eds), *Medieval Conduct* (Minneapolis: University of Minnesota Press 2001), pp. 135–59 (p. 135).
11 Jo Ann Hoeppner Moran, *The Growth of English Schooling, 1340–1548* (Princeton: Princeton University Press, 1985).
12 Lawrence Stone, 'The Educational Revolution in England, 1560–1640', *Past & Present*, 28 (1964), 41–80 (p. 42–4).
13 Arthur F. Leach, *English Schools at the Reformation 1546–8* (New York: Russell & Russell, 1896); Nicholas Orme, *English Schools in the Middle Ages* (London and New York: Methuen, 1973), p. 6.
14 A. Monroe Stowe, *English Grammar Schools in the Reign of Queen Elizabeth* (New York: Teachers College, Columbia University, 1908), p. 9.
15 Rosemary O'Day, *Education and Society, 1500–1800: The Social Foundations of Education in Early Modern Britain* (London and New York: Longman, 1982), p. 1.
16 Stone, 'Educational Revolution', p. 70.
17 Nicholas Orme, *Education and Society in Medieval and Renaissance England* (London and Ronceverte: Hambledon, 1989), p. 21.
18 Mrs J. R. Green, *Town Life in the Fifteenth Century*, vol. 2 (London and New York: Macmillan, 1907), p. 13.
19 Wilbur K. Jordan, *The Social Institutions of Lancashire: A Study of the Changing Patterns of Aspirations in Lancashire, 1480–1660* (Manchester: Chetham Society, 1962), pp. 29–75 (p. 29).
20 Helen M. Jewell, 'The Bringing up of Children in Good Learning and Manners: A Survey of Secular Education Provision in the North of England, c. 1350–1550', *Northern History*, 18 (1982), 1–25 (p. 18).
21 Jordan, *Social Institutions*, p. 29.
22 Colin Heywood, *A History of Childhood: Children and Childhood in the West from Medieval to Modern Times* (Cambridge: Polity, 2001), p. 161.
23 John Aubrey, *'Brief Lives', chiefly of Contemporaries, set down by John Aubrey, between the years 1669 & 1696, vol. 1* (ed.) Andrew Clark (Oxford: Clarendon Press, 1898), p. 416.
24 O'Day, *Education and Society*, p. 25.
25 David Cressy, 'Educational Opportunity in Tudor and Stuart England', *History of Education Quarterly*, 16 (1976), 301–20 (pp. 314–15).
26 Cressy, 'Educational Opportunity', pp. 313–14.
27 Cressy, 'Educational Opportunity', p. 304.
28 See Orme, *English Schools*.
29 Moran, *Growth of English Schooling*, p. 69.
30 Caroline Barron, 'The Education and Training of Girls in Fifteenth-Century London', in Diana E. S. Dunn (ed.), *Courts, Counties and the Capital in the later Middle Ages* (New York: St Martin's Press, 1996), pp. 139–53 (p. 141).
31 Orme, *English Schools*, pp. 52–5.
32 For example, the Paston women: Norman Davies (ed.), *The Paston Letters: A Selection in Modern Spelling* (London: Oxford University Press, 1963); and Grace Mildmay: Linda Pollock, *With Faith and Physic: The Life of a Tudor Gentlewoman Lady Grace Mildmay 1552–1620* (London: Collins & Brown, 1993).
33 Kim M. Phillips, *Medieval Maidens: Young Women and Gender in England, 1270–1540* (Manchester: Manchester University Press, 2003), p. 62.
34 Phillips, *Medieval Maidens*, pp. 62–3.
35 Keith Thomas, *Rule and Misrule in the Schools of Early Modern England* (Reading: University of Reading, 1976), p. 5.

36 William Gouge, *Of Domesticall Duties Eight Treatises* (London, 1622), p. 17.
37 UK Parliament, The 1870 Education Act, available at www.parliament.uk/about/living-heritage/transformingsociety/livinglearning/school/overview/1870educationact.
38 Jewell, 'Bringing up of Children', p. 18.
39 Jewell, 'Bringing up of Children', p. 20.
40 Simon, *Social Origins*, p. 50.
41 Joan Simon, *Education and Society in Tudor England* (Cambridge: Cambridge University Press, 1966), p. 48.
42 Sheila McIsaac Cooper, 'Servants as Educators in Early-Modern England', *Paedagogica Historica*, 43 (2007), 547–63 (p. 551).
43 Simon, *Education and Society*, p. 48.
44 BIA, CP.G.249.
45 Pace, *De Fructu*, cited in Beatrice White, 'Introduction', *John Stanbridge, The Vulgaria of John Stanbridge and the Vulgaria of Robert Whittinton* (ed.) Beatrice White (Oxford: Early English Text Society, 1971), p. xii.
46 Michael Mitterauer and Reinhard Sieder, *The European Family: Patriarchy to Partnership from the Middle Ages to the Present* (Oxford: Basil Blackwell, 1982), p. 88.
47 Anthony Fletcher, *Growing up in England: The Experience of Childhood 1600–1914* (New Haven, CT: Yale University Press, 2008), p. 293.
48 CALSS, EDC 2/7/240.
49 Frederick J. Furnivall (ed.), *The babees book: Aristotle's A B C. Urbanitatis. Stans puer ad mensam. The lytille childrenes lytil boke. The bokes of nurture of Hugh Rhodes and John Russell. Wynkyn de Worde's Boke of keruynge. The booke of demeanor. The boke of curtasye. Seager's Schoole of vertue, &c. &c. with some French & Latin poems on like subjects, and some forewords on education in early England* (New York: Greenwood Press, 1969), p. iv.
50 Simon, *Social Origins*, p. 50.
51 CALSS, EDC2/7/248–249; 251–2.
52 Pollock, *With Faith and Physic*, p. 6.
53 CALSS, EDC2/6/198–203. The case also appears in the cause: EDC1/15/98–98ᵛ; 100–101ᵛ.
54 Pollock, *With Faith and Physic*, p. 26.
55 Cooper, 'Servants as Educators', p. 561
56 Paul S. Seaver, *Wallington's World: A Puritan Artisan in Seventeenth-Century London* (London: Methuen, 1985), p. 74.
57 Shulamith Shahar, *Childhood in the Middle Ages* (London: Routledge, 1992), p. 242.
58 DUSC, DDR/EV/VIS/1/1, fol. 4.
59 DUSC, DDR/EV/VIS/1/1, fol. 3–3ᵛ.
60 Cited in Orme, *English Schools*, p. 67.
61 John Lawson and Harold Silver, *A Social History of Education in England* (London: Methuen, 1973), p. 68.
62 A seamstress or someone who sews.
63 John F. Pound (ed.), *The Norwich Census of the Poor, 1570* (Norwich: Norfolk Record Society, 1971), p. 43.
64 R. H. Tawney and Eileen Power (eds), *Tudor Economic Documents, being select documents illustrating the economic and social history of Tudor England*, 3 vols (London: Longman, 1924), II, 324–6.
65 Phillips, *Medieval Maidens*, p. 67.
66 Lawrence Stone, 'The Educational Revolution in England, 1560–1640', Past & Present, 28 (1964), 41–80 (p. 42–44).
67 Richard Mulcaster, *Positions Wherin Those Primitive Circvmstances Be Examined, Which Are Necessarie For The Training vp of Children, either for skill in their booke, or health in their bodie* (London, 1581; Amsterdam: Theatrum Orbis Terrarum, 1971), p. 5.

68   O'Day, *Education and Society*, p. 29.
69   B. E. Harris (ed.), *The Victoria History of the Counties of England: A History of Cheshire, vol.III* (London: Institute of Historical Research/Oxford University Press, 1980) (hereafter *VCH Cheshire*), p. 201.
70   *VCH Cheshire*, p. 201.
71   BIA, CP.G.249; Frederick. J. Furnivall, *Child Marriages, Divorces, and Ratifications in the Diocese of Chester, A.D. 1561–6* (New York: Kraus Reprint, 1973), p. 29.
72   TNA, C1/356/27.
73   William Page (ed.), *The Victoria History of the Counties of England: A History of Durham, vol.I* (London: Archibald Constable, 1905) (hereafter *VCH Durham*), p. 365.
74   Rites of Durham (Surtees Society), 84, cited in *VCH Durham*, pp. 367–8.
75   *VCH Durham*, p. 368.
76   *VCH Cheshire*, pp. 223–54.
77   William Farrer and J. Brownbill (eds), *The Victoria History of the County of Lancashire, vol. II* (London: Archibald Constable, 1908) (hereafter *VCH Lancashire*), p. 605; p. 603.
78   Vickerstaff, *Revolutionary Deluge*, pp. 8–9.
79   O'Day, *Education and Society*, p. 30.
80   EYLA, Archbishop Holgate's Free Grammar School York, Class E Book 21K, fol. 2.
81   Roger Ascham, *The Scholemaster: Or plaine and perfite way of teaching children, to vnerstand, write, and speake, the Latin tong, but specially purposed for the private bringing vp of youth in Intlemen and Noble mens houses, and comm. Also for all such, as haue forgot the Latin tongue etc* (London, 1570), pp. 26–7.
82   Plutarch, *The Bringinge Vp of Children*, (trans.) Thomas Elyot (Amsterdam: Theatrum Orbis, 1969), chap. 4.
83   Sir Thomas Elyot, *The Boke Named the Governour* (1531; Menston: Scolar Press, 1970), fol. 59^v.
84   O'Day, *Education and Society*, p. 166.
85   Orme, *English Schools*, p. 142.
86   Stone, 'Educational Revolution', p. 46.
87   Stone, 'Educational Revolution', p. 47.
88   J. S. Purvis (ed.), *Tudor Parish Documents* (Cambridge: Cambridge University Press, 1948), p. 106.
89   Purvis (ed.), *Tudor Parish Documents*, p. 105.
90   Purvis (ed.), *Tudor Parish Documents*, p. 106: 'bene multum versatum juvenem bone indolis'.
91   Purvis (ed.), *Tudor Parish Documents*, p. 107: 'non sine fruge bona'.
92   Orme, *English Schools*, pp. 142–3.
93   J. A. Twemlow (ed.), *Liverpool Town Books: Proceedings of Assemblies, Common Councils, Portmoot Courts, etc., 1550–1862*, 2 vols (Liverpool: University of Liverpool, 1918–), I: 1550–1571 (1918), 300.
94   Orme, *English Schools*, p. 158.
95   Twemlow (ed.), *Liverpool Town Books*, I, 374–5.
96   Purvis (ed.), *Tudor Parish Documents*, p. 108.
97   *VCH Lancashire*, p. 581.
98   *VCH Lancashire*, p. 583.
99   Elyot, *The Boke Named the Governour*, fols 60^v–61.
100   Elyot, *The Boke Named the Governour*, fol. 61.
101   Mulcaster, *Positions*, p. 2.
102   Mulcaster, *Positions*, p. 3.
103   W. Ferguson-Irvine (ed.), *A Collection of Lancashire and Cheshire Wills not now to be found in any probate registry 1302–1752* (London: Lancashire and Cheshire Record Society, 1896), p. 29; p. 197.
104   A noble was worth 6s. 8d.

105 Ferguson-Irvine (ed.), *Lancashire and Cheshire Wills*, p. 44.
106 James C. Clark, 'Sutton, Sir Richard (*c.* 1460–1524)', *DNB*.
107 Ferguson-Irvine (ed.), *Lancashire and Cheshire Wills*, p. 43.
108 Ferguson-Irvine (ed.), *Lancashire and Cheshire Wills*, p. 194.
109 Ferguson-Irvine (ed.),*Lancashire and Cheshire Wills*, p. 183.
110 LVRO, 352 MIN/COU I, B2, fol. 40.
111 EYLA, D12, fol. 5.
112 Margaret Spufford, 'First Steps in Literacy: The Reading and Writing Experiences of the Humblest Seventeenth-Century Spiritual Autobiographers', in Harvey J. Graff (ed.), *Literacy and Social Development in the West: A Reader* (Cambridge: Cambridge University Press, 1981), pp. 125–50 (p. 144).
113 Elyot, *The Boke Named the Governour*, fols 59ᵛ–60.
114 Cited in Green, *Town Life*, p. 12.
115 Wilbur K. Jordan, *The Charities of Rural England, 1480–1660* (London: Allen & Unwin, 1961), p. 165.
116 Pound (ed.),*Norwich Census*, p. 48; p. 85. There is a possibility that the schools mentioned in the census were in fact the houses of adults where the children were taught technical skills such as knitting so, although they were receiving instruction, they were not learning to read and write.
117 Mulcaster, *Positions*, p. 138.
118 Mulcaster, *Positions*, p. 141.
119 Mulcaster, *Positions*, pp. 140–1.
120 Jewell, 'Bringing up of Children', p. 6.
121 Cited in Jordan, *Social Institutions*, p. 37.
122 *VCH Lancashire*, pp. 562–3.
123 *VCH Cheshire*, p. 250.
124 *VCH Cheshire*, p. 230.
125 *VCH Durham*, p. 374.
126 *VCH Durham*, p. 372.
127 *VCH Cheshire*, p. 230.
128 *VCH Cheshire*, p. 240; p. 223.
129 *VCH Cheshire*, p. 237.
130 *VCH Lancashire*, p. 605.
131 *VCH Lancashire*, p. 570.
132 Stone, 'Educational Revolution', p. 45.
133 Cressy, 'Educational Opportunity', p. 307.
134 *VCH Lancashire*, p. 584.
135 *VCH Cheshire*, p. 227.
136 *VCH Lancashire*, p. 584.
137 Laurent Joubert, *Popular Errors* (trans. and annotated) Gregory David de Rocher (Tuscaloosa: University of Alabama Press, 1989), p. 241.
138 Moran,*Growth of English Schooling*, p. 69.
139 Kate Aughterson (ed.), *Renaissance Woman: A Sources Book, Constructions of Femininity in England* (London and New York: Routledge, 1995), p. 165.
140 Dorothy Gardiner, *English Girlhood at School: A Study of Women's Education through Twelve Centuries* (Oxford: Oxford University Press, 1929), p. 189.
141 Retha M. Warnicke, *Women of the English Renaissance and Reformation* (Westport and London: Greenwood Press, 1983), p. 3.
142 Aughterson (ed.), *Renaissance Woman*, p. 166.
143 Phillips, *Medieval Maidens*, p. 70.
144 Becon, *Catechism*, p. 376.
145 Becon, *Catechism*, p. 376.
146 Eileen Power, *Medieval English Nunneries c. 1275 to 1535* (Cambridge: Cambridge University Press), pp. 278–9.

147   Power, *Medieval English Nunneries*, pp. 261–2.
148   Mulcaster, *Positions*, pp. 167–8.
149   Mulcaster, *Positions*, p. 132.
150   *VCH Cheshire*, p. 227.
151   Barron, 'Education and Training of Girls', p. 148.
152   Ferguson-Irvine (ed.),*Lancashire and Cheshire Wills*, p. 191.
153   James Orchard Halliwell (ed.), *The Private Diary of John Dee, and The Catalogue of his Library of Manuscripts, from the original manuscripts* (New York: Johnson Reprint Corporation, 1842), pp. 33–4.
154   Jay P. Anglin, *The Third University: A Survey of Schools and Schoolmasters in the Elizabethan Diocese of London* (Norwood, PA: Norwood Editions, 1985), p. 86.
155   Anglin, *The Third University*, p. 86.
156   Orme, *English Schools*, p. 116.
157   Mulcaster, *Positions*, pp. 18–19.
158   *VCH Cheshire*, p. 245; *VCH Lancashire*, p. 591.
159   Orme, *English Schools*, p. 117.
160   *VCH Lancashire*, p. 564.
161   Psalm sung at evening prayers in commemoration of the dead.
162   *VCH Lancashire*, p. 564.
163   *VCH Durham*, p. 377.
164   Joseph H. Lupton, *A Life of John Colet, D. D., Dean of St. Paul's, and Founder of St. Paul's School* (New York: B. Franklin, 1974), p. 277.
165   *VCH Lancashire*, p. 607.
166   *VCH Lancashire*, p. 606.
167   *VCH Durham*, p. 378.
168   *VCH Durham*, p. 378.
169   *VCH Cheshire*, p. 245.
170   Orme, *English Schools*, pp. 87–8.
171   Mulcaster, *Positions*, p. 3.
172   *VCH Durham*, p. 374.
173   *VCH Lancashire*, p. 606.
174   Mulcaster, *Positions*, p. 278.
175   Davies (ed.), *Paston Letters*, p. 46.
176   *VCH Lancashire*, p. 607.
177   Shahar, *Childhood in the Middle Ages*, pp. 172–3.
178   *VCH Lancashire*, p. 584.
179   *VCH Lancashire*, p. 584.
180   *VCH Lancashire*, p. 584.
181   *VCH Durham*, p. 378.
182   *VCH Lancashire*, p. 607.
183   *VCH Durham*, p. 378.
184   *Witton Grammar School: The Original Statutes*, (ed.) John Weston (Northwich, 1885), cited in Thomas, *Rule and Misrule*, p. 21.
185   Steve Bartlet, Diana Burton and Nick Peim, *Introduction to Education Studies* (London: Paul Chapman Publishing, 2001), p. 73.
186   White, 'Introduction', in *John Stanbridge Vulgaria*, p. xix.
187   Phillips, *Medieval Maidens*, p. 63.
188   Phillips, *Medieval Maidens*, p. 63.
189   Mulcaster,*Positions*, pp. 16–17.
190   Thomas, *Rule and Misrule*, p. 4.
191   Thomas, *Rule and Misrule*, p. 5.
192   Morris P. Tilley (ed.), *A Dictionary of the Proverbs in England in the Sixteenth and Seventeenth Centuries* (Ann Arbor: University of Michigan Press, 1950), p. 720, W305.

193 Mulcaster, *Positions*, p. 277.
194 William Nelson (ed.), *A Fifteenth Century School Book from a manuscript in the British Museum (MS Arundel 249)* (Oxford: Clarendon Press, 1956), p. 13, no. 52.
195 Thomas, *Rule and Misrule*, p. 12.
196 Purvis (ed.), *Tudor Parish Documents*, p. 108.

5   Apprenticeship

'Byndyth hym well truelie & faythfullye to serve & obaye his sayd master in all articlis poyntes feattes and all other mistriis'.[1]

Having initiated a discussion on the holistic provision of education in regards to learning contexts and schooling in the previous chapter, it will be continued in this chapter with the institution of apprenticeship. As an educational practice, apprenticeship was unique, and to describe it purely as a mode of learning fails to adequately convey the complexities of a system that incorporated surrogate parenting, tuition, professional organisations, civic administration and government intervention. Traditional apprenticeship should not be confused with the system of pauper apprenticeship, implemented through the Elizabethan Poor Laws of 1597 and 1601, which forcibly apprenticed poor children at the expense of the parish.[2] Rather, traditional apprenticeship developed as a system of technical training in English towns around the thirteenth century and continued in the same form for many centuries afterwards.[3] It was regulated by guilds within each municipality and, according to the traditional view, it was an institution that invested in the health, moral well-being and technical education of each apprentice by means of an accountable framework consisting of guild, master and apprentice.[4] In addition, it inculcated the need for the apprentice to serve the state through his or her endeavours in a particular trade within the boundaries of a specific town.

The significance of apprenticeship is related to the notion of good nurture being one of the benefits the system could provide for the child. Parents maintained strong beliefs that an apprenticeship was a passage to a secure future for their children, with many leaving bequests in their wills 'wherbie he may be able to get his lyvinge with all'.[5] For some, it represented an opportunity for social mobility for their children and many fathers with lowly occupations gathered the resources necessary to put their sons to a trade. These include Edward Dunfield, a labourer from York, who placed his son Christopher with John Gell, an upholsterer, in 1583.[6] Support for the institution was to be found in the Church, whose priests were instructed to encourage all parents to put their children to learn husbandry 'or other good craftes'.[7] Businessmen, too, extolled the virtues of the system, with one London haberdasher leaving a £500 legacy for the benefit of apprentices in the City of Chester. His executors were not forthcoming with the money, however, and the mayor and citizens of Chester had to bring a case in the Chancery court in 1596 to force the money to be released.[8]

Apprenticeship was the primary avenue for recruitment of the urban population into work, ensuring that traditional values were passed on from generation to generation.[9] Towns became magnets for apprentices from the countryside, who faced considerably better prospects than their local peers destined for a life of rural labouring.[10] Records examined for this study indicate that parents and guardians consistently sent children great distances to be indentured. York in particular attracted apprentices from not only towns and villages in Yorkshire, but also neighbouring counties and from as far afield as Northamptonshire and Worcestershire. Mosey Stevenson from Horton, Northamptonshire, was apprenticed to Thomas Pottes, a linen weaver, in 1600 whilst James Norris from Branborough, Worcester, was apprenticed to John Gell, a carpenter, in 1597.[11] Some journeys even involved a sea passage for some apprentices. Robert Davie from the Isle of Man crossed the Irish Sea to take up an apprenticeship with Edward Wilson, a Liverpool slater, in 1566.[12] Family and friends played a pivotal role in deciding where to send a child to be apprenticed, as in the case of Robert Monkhouse, who was apprenticed to Christopher Mason, a York linen weaver, in 1579. Despite living in Castle Sowerby, Cumberland, 12 miles from Carlisle, he made the 110-mile journey to York to begin his apprenticeship.[13]

The sources used in this chapter are predominately apprentice indentures registered in the municipal books of Liverpool and York. Of the 263 indentures recorded in these books, only ninety describe the provisions and terms of the indenture. The remainder are short, Latin entries that state only the date, name of the apprentice and father, name and profession of the master and the term of the indenture. In addition, apprentices appear in six local court cases, six Chancery petitions and one private agreement in relation to a fee, from various parts of the region. Considering the importance of traditional apprenticeship to the pre-modern community, it is the aim of this chapter to analyse these sources for the defining features of apprenticeship in relation to the care and nurturing of the child, and, where possible, adopting a child-centred view. In particular, it seeks to establish if the child was protected should there be a breakdown within the system and how effectively children were inducted into the community of the guild and the town. How did the system of apprenticeship work? For whom was apprenticeship available – boys, girls, rich, poor – and at what ages? What was the relationship between apprentice and master? What were the consequences if the relationship between the apprentice and master deteriorated or was curtailed? What happened to the apprentice once they had finished their term?

Historically, apprenticeship has been approached from different perspectives depending on the interests of the historians. Studies like those of Jocelyn Dunlop and Ephraim Lipson highlight apprenticeship's role in child labour in both the pre-industrial and industrial world.[14] The economic impetus of a system, which addresses the vocational education of young people, still has resonance today.[15] Studies like Dunlop's and Lipson's, whose main source of evidence was guild records, inevitably produce a somewhat limited view of apprenticeship, one that I would argue does little to identify the experiences of the child.

The fact that apprentices were just children is a detail often overlooked in the scholarship. As Margaret Pelling insists, children who were of an age between infants and young adults were still vulnerable despite having a certain amount of independence from their parents.[16] It is the system of interdependence that Pelling has identified in relation to apprentices and the 'moral economy' of masters, children, families, relatives, servants, neighbours and even civic administrations that were all concerned in moving the child through the system of apprenticeship. I would suggest that the term 'moral guardians' would be more appropriate, especially when we examine the welfare of the child within the system. Ilana Krausman Ben-Amos has identified that where the parents or guardians were still alive they continued to support the child through their apprenticeship by sending money, clothes, shoes and even books, while providing a refuge for those children who became ill or lost their job.[17] Regardless of the continued involvement of parents, it was masters who had the greatest control over the lives of the apprentice and, as Paul Griffiths notes, it was the conceptions of social order within the master's household that had a direct effect upon the welfare of the apprentice. This included the management of any disputes that may have arisen.[18] Griffiths warns against assuming that order was the normative situation inside the master's household as it depended upon the attitude of the master towards his apprentice and it was not necessarily the way set out in the indenture. He could just as easily regard his apprentice as a nuisance as much as an employee.[19] It was not surprising that where children were routinely settled away from home – as was the system of life-cycle service that prevailed in northern Europe – that conflict should arise.[20] The age at which the child was sent away from home was the time at which the child would start to claim their independence from their parents.[21] However, if things did go wrong there was a means of redress.

Studies have shown that the official nature of apprenticeship meant that the relationship between the apprentice and master was governed by statutes, which afforded the intervention of the law in cases of conflict.[22] In his study of the north-east of England between 1600 and 1800, Peter Rushton found that apprentices brought far more cases than did the masters. This could have been due to the masters being able to utilise the disciplinary procedures of the guilds whereas the apprentices had to appeal to local justice.[23] Rushton's findings for the seventeenth and eighteenth centuries are not reflected in my records for the sixteenth century and Griffiths sounds a note of caution in relation to this matter. Apprentices' complaints of mistreatment can be abundant in some local courts but sparse in others. Lack of evidence was not a sign that abuse or misuse of the apprentice did not happen.[24] The silence in itself is meaningful according to Griffiths and there would have been other structures that prevented the apprentices from resolving their grievances in the courts. But, where evidence of disputes survives, it is an opportunity for the historian to identify how the apprentice interpreted the relationship. Their response to mistreatment allows us to view the apprentice experience from the perspective of the child.

Historians have examined motives for parents and guardians apprenticing their children. The most important factors in deciding a child's career remained unchanged across social status and chronological period according to Joan Lane. Long-term employment prospects and wages, as well as the status accorded to a profession, were always important considerations when apprenticing a child.[25] Having networks of support in the town in which the child was apprenticed was equally important as they offered assistance not only during the period of indenture, but also once it was finished.[26] Apprenticeship was a definite career strategy for boys from middle-class families, according to Christopher Brooks, and a means by which the urban structure was replicated.[27] In spite of this, Lane has commented that the vast majority of apprentices were bound to less-profitable trades such as plumber, mason or turner.[28] These were, nonetheless, still regarded as respectable trades and many of the indentures in this study fall into this category. Below this level were the trades such as shoemaker that were reserved for the poorest child, orphan or parish apprentices.

The compulsory apprenticing of poor children at the end of the sixteenth century altered the focus of apprenticeship. Pauper apprenticeship did not really establish itself until after the dates of this study, but we can certainly see the initiative taking shape by the end of the period. Steve Hindle has highlighted the social engineering factors of compulsory pauper apprenticeship, whereby the forced indenturing of pauper children was supposed to inculcate a strong work ethic into the child. At the same time, expenses were redistributed from poorer homes and the parish to the wealthier inhabitants.[29] Historians like Margaret Davies believe this push for economic redistribution led to the decline of traditional apprenticeship itself as it undermined the principles of the institution,[30] yet pauper apprenticeship was a long-enduring enterprise with benefits for both the parish and the child. Keith Snell has found that pauper apprenticeship was significant to the parish economy. If local youth were not trained, skilled workers had to be brought in from outside the village at higher prices, while the youth had to be supported by the parish rates. With the possibility of the skills base being lost to the village, pauper apprenticeship was enforced as much to protect that base as to relieve pressure on the rates.[31] Pauper apprenticeship was also of benefit to the apprentice. Ann Minister's study of apprentices in south Derbyshire identified that pauper apprenticeship offered hitherto unavailable opportunities for poor children to acquire skills.[32] Regardless of these opportunities, historians generally agree that there was a stigma attached to pauper apprenticeship. However, paupers were not the only marginalised group when it came to apprenticeship.

The place of girls within the apprenticeship system was firmly subordinated to their male peers. Girls were apprenticed but, as Brooks comments, indenturing of girls is a difficult topic to study due to their absence in the documents produced by male-controlled guilds and civic administrations[33] and in this respect apprenticeship was no different from other forms of learning. Nonetheless, there are a number of studies of female apprenticeship, including those of Caroline Barron, Ben-Amos, Richard Goddard and Lane, which describe both the limited options available to girls and the exceptions to this.[34] Female occupations were, on the whole, distinct from the professions followed by boys, with many being indentured into the textile industry as weavers and seamstresses.[35] This conclusion is certainly validated by Stephanie Hovland's study of apprenticeship in later medieval London, which found that the majority of girls were indentured into the textile trades as silkwomen, embroiderers and shepsters.[36] Textile trades were the destination for only two of the nine female apprentices featured in this study, the majority of whom were indentured to housewifery. As Lane argues, housewifery, was the occupation that most consistently attracted the highest number of girls in all periods, although her study does not begin until 1600.[37] We could still, however, make a comparison here between the north and London. Given a choice, parents would have apprenticed their daughters to trades like silk-weaving rather than housewifery and therefore the options available for girls decreased as you moved away from the capital. In this respect, the north of England was no different to the rest of the country.

Scholars agree that once the apprentice was removed from their term, either by completion of the agreed time or by other circumstances, there were a number of opportunities open to them. Lane has identified several of these options, which included marrying the master's daughter or his widow, as well as inheriting his master's business.[38] True, masters may take their apprentice into partnership or apprentices may succeed their fathers in their craft, but not all apprentices were this fortunate at the end of their term. The earning capacity of a tradesman was directly linked to the costs of setting up once a master and, as Graham Mayhew has identified, those apprentices who did not come from a wealthy background remained poor after the end of their term.[39] Many apprentices did not have the capital to become a master and, as such, Mrs J. R. Green argues, apprenticeship did not deliver the social inclusivity or stability believed to exist within the system. Instead it created a source of unskilled labour, an underclass that remained outside the protection of the guilds,[40] in addition to the skilled journeymen who were paid by the day. Apprenticeship may have been a method of passing down skills from generation to generation, but how these skills were valued at the end of the term differed for each apprentice.

The historiography to date has by and large been influenced by guild records including indentures, which has placed an emphasis on the authority of the master rather than the apprentice as a child. This chapter will consider the type of nurture given to the apprentice within the system of apprenticeship and the effect of that nurture on the apprentice's experiences. As much of the existing scholarship has been centred on the south of England, this study aims to give a sense of apprenticeship in the north as compared to elsewhere in the country, taking into consideration shifting attitudes created by social policy that saw the medieval system of apprenticeship become synonymous with forced indenturing by the seventeenth century.

System of apprenticeship

How did the system of apprenticeship work? Apprenticeship during the sixteenth century is not to be confused with service, which is often considered in the same context. Philippe Ariès commented that it would be unwise to differentiate between the two, as modern day distinctions are 'anachronistic'.[41] Despite Ariès's opinion, sixteenth-century understandings were quite clear about distinctions. Masters were paid by parents and guardians of apprentices to train and lodge their children, whereas the servant was paid by their master. In addition, the master and apprentice were bound by a written contract of several years' duration but servants and masters were bound by much shorter verbal contracts of usually no more than a year.[42] The main purpose of the agreement was for the master to teach the child the necessary skills of a particular craft, so, while there were strong structural similarities in regards to authority and obedience, the framework of mutual obligations in apprenticeship was more complicated.[43]

It was customary to place one's child into the home of another for the purposes of apprenticeship, a practice commented upon by a noble Venetian visitor to England in about 1500. He observed that the English sent their children away at seven or nine years old to the houses of other people to do 'hard service', leaving them there for another seven or nine years.[44] It does appear strange that craftsmen were sending out their children from their own homes while at the same time welcoming somebody else's children, even when they lived in the same city. Robert Sanghate was apprenticed to Thomas Dorecham, a York carpenter, in 1592, despite his father practising the same craft in the city.[45] The Venetian noble visitor also commented upon this habit, concluding that the householders thought themselves better served by strangers than their own children, and there was a good reason for this.[46] There was a belief and acceptance within pre-modern English society that a stranger was able to train a child more efficiently than the parents, who would encounter parent–child clashes.[47] We must also consider that sending a child to another master was not the choice for every craftsman and that there was a diversity of practice. Sons were sometimes apprenticed to their own fathers, although this was rare. In a study of 651 sixteenth-century Bristol apprentices whose fathers were freemen of the city, only fifty-seven were apprenticed to their own fathers or widowed mothers.[48] We know that William Long, a York tailor, apprenticed his son Thomas to himself in 1573,[49] and this may not have been uncommon in businesses able to accommodate more than one son. Indenturing a son was also a means to safeguard an established family business from dying out.[50] This was of great importance in trades where the father had died. Robert Catherall was apprenticed to his mother, Julia, in 1597, who was left to run the family business after the death of her webster husband, Evans.[51] However, for those children who left the natal home, it marked a separation from their childhood, and their parents did not expect them to return home.[52]

The indenturing of a child could be positioned within the system of patriarchy: the master–servant relationship was intended to replicate the parent–child relationship.[53] The master replaced the father as the authority figure, if indeed the apprentice's father were still alive. Out of forty-four apprentices indentured in Liverpool between 1563 and 1603, twenty-one of them were fatherless.[54] York displayed the same steep mortality rate for fathers of those apprenticed in the city, with sixty-three out of 214 children fatherless at the time of their indenturing.[55] The high statistic is borne out by other studies, which indicate the scale of parent mortality within households.[56] Mayhew's study of apprenticeship in Rye, Sussex, found that from his sample of 287 families the father had died when all his children were under fourteen in 111 of the cases and apprenticeship was thus inextricably linked to orphanhood.[57] For children like these and indeed migrants to a new town, apprenticeship offered security that was synonymous with present-day adoption.[58] For all apprentices, the influence of the master and his family became increasingly greater as the term of the indenture wore on.[59]

Masters belonged to a formal association of specialised artisans called craft guilds, which regulated both the masters' trades and their apprentices, although apprentices did not enjoy any membership rights.[60] Some crafts did operate independently from the guilds. For instance, in London, basket-weaving was usually undertaken by men with no allegiance to any guild, while female apprentices were indentured into housewifery skills, for which there was no craft guild.[61] But what the guilds did do for apprenticeship was to categorically place it within a social hierarchy with an attached economic significance that, in theory at least, marked the first step of a career for the apprentice.[62] The guilds were political in their nature and were actively encouraged by the towns to exercise control over workers and to maintain standards within a trade.[63] Guilds did not have autonomous authority and were subservient to civic authorities that amended guild rules to suit their purposes.[64] They did, however, have significant input into the terms of apprentice indentures.

The indenture was a binding contract that stated what was expected of both apprentice and master. They were customarily enrolled in the books of the guild but in towns where only a small number of trades were organised as guilds it was routine to enrol the indentures in the town's books. This had the added advantage of the apprentice's particulars being already recorded for when he had finished his term and would take up the freedom of the borough.[65] Enrolment of indentures in town books occurred in both Liverpool and York. In York, the authorities made it compulsory for all masters to register every indenture within three months of the apprentice being bound or they would have to pay 3s. 4d. as a forfeit,[66] although this does not seem to have been adhered to all the time. Some indentures were not recorded in the municipal records until two years after they were made and one can only speculate as to whether the requisite fine was paid.[67] Such directives emphasise not only the control the town authorities wielded over the system of apprenticeship, but also the recognition by the authorities of future members of the community.

The term of the indenture was established by the guilds in an attempt to ensure that no apprentice could set up in business without having mastered his trade, with seven years being the usual term. This term was usual for York, with trades such as tailoring being the most consistent. Liverpool apprentices, on the other hand, experienced a wide variety of terms even amongst the same trade and sometimes the same masters. In 1584, Edward Walker was apprenticed to mariner Edward Nicholson for seven years, while John Hughson was apprenticed to Nicholson for thirteen years.[68] The same year, Thomas Bavande, a merchant and alderman, apprenticed Rauffe Vernmam for nine years and Austin Twisse for seven years. The next year Bavande apprenticed Edward Dicconson for five years.[69] No reason is apparent for these inconsistencies but it could be that the term was a flexible benchmark dependent upon the ability of the apprentice as indentures frequently refer to the 'indolence and capacitie' of the apprentice to learn.[70] Another theory is the social status of the child, with the poorest serving the longer terms for the lowest premiums.[71] Often these children were local orphans, placed very soon after their parents' deaths, in the same occupation as their father and with families of similar social standing.[72] Robert Taylor, the son of a cutler of York, was placed in the same occupation of his dead father for a term of ten years in 1579.[73]

A more probable reason for the variations in terms is the introduction of the Statute of Artificers, passed in 1563, which stated that for all crafts a seven-year term would be obligatory.[74] The statute was not concerned with ensuring the apprentice was adequately trained as the guilds had been. Rather, this measure was about social policy and not releasing the apprentice before the age of twenty-one anywhere in England, or twenty-four in corporate towns like Chester, Durham, Liverpool and York.[75] This was in all probability to address the rise of poor families and mirrored measures taken by London in 1556, where 'the ouer hastie mariages and ouer soone setting vpp of howsholdes of and by the youthe youge folkes of the said cytye' was believed to be the cause of an increase of poverty in the city.[76] Hence, the statute added a further dimension to traditional apprenticeship, encouraging social order and economic stability alongside the transferral of skills and social mores down through the generations.

On a practical note, the time the apprentice served would be dependent on the age at which the apprenticeship commenced. This was usually between the ages of twelve and seventeen, with the majority being between fourteen and sixteen.[77] Where the age is mentioned on the indentures and documents studied for this chapter, it varied between ten and nineteen and there is the possibility that some apprentices may have been even younger or older. Henry Sawer, an orphan, was placed with a York carpenter in 1591 for fourteen years despite the usual term of seven to eight years for other carpentry apprentices, and, although his age is not mentioned, he must have been about ten or younger for such a long term to be undertaken.[78] Rauffe Crosbie, who at nineteen is the oldest of the apprentices in this study, was apprenticed for only three years to a Liverpool merchant in 1580.[79] Rules regarding the age at the termination of the apprenticeship, therefore, were open to negotiation depending upon the master. A boy in Chester was apprenticed to a tailor for eight years at the age of thirteen in 1575, while Alexander Rymmer (age unknown) was apprenticed for only four years in 1579.[80] Variation from the statutory term was purely due to local application.

Once the apprentice was under his tutelage, the master (or in some instances the mistress) was personally responsible for the physical, moral and training requirements of the apprentice.[81] According to the indenture, the master provided his apprentice with 'meat, drink, clothes, woollen hose, shoes bedding, all things needed to keep his health'.[82] Sometimes other services were mentioned like bedding or 'washinge of his shirtes'.[83] This must have been a welcome relief to families with a number of children, for not only would it take care of the expense but it would augment the survival chances of any that remained within the household by decreasing the demand on available resources.[84] Occasionally parents supplied these things so that the master 'shall not be charged with the same nor any parte therof'.[85] Even children apprenticed to their own fathers, like Thomas Long of York, mentioned above, had these requirements articulated in their indentures. Providing the requisite care for the apprentice was important but it was the master's workshop as a learning context that defined the system.

The master was responsible for the transmission of technical skills that parents hoped would enable their child to become financially independent at the end of the term. The apprentice was 'informed tawght and exercised in all thing and thynges lawfull and honest belongyng to his sayd [master's] occupacion tractes'.[86] Training was to be delivered throughout the whole term of the indenture and masters were warned not to leave instruction until the later years of the term. Robert Bainton, a York saddler, was told in 1580 to instruct his apprentice James Wetherall in 'the best manner he can without anie fraud delay or layvinge thereof'.[87] Lack of instruction was a common grievance between apprentices and masters and occurred for a number of reasons including imprisonment of masters for debt, as well as personal hostility and the exploitation of the apprentice as cheap labour.[88] There is no evidence that James complained about Bainton, but as the teaching of skills underpinned the system of apprenticeship it was imperative that the apprentice received adequate instruction, delivered consistently throughout the years of the term.

Caveats in indentures inferred not only to the technological skills necessary to carry on a trade but also the tacit skills such as the art of negotiation with other artisans and competitive techniques.[89] The expectation that apprentices would absorb hidden skills is evident within some indentures. In 1577, the York saddler Ainsbrasse Cooke was to teach his apprentice Philip Bylleye

(Bailey) in 'the best manner that he cane or may heare after maye learne and knowe without annie lavinge therof'.[90] Edward Johnson, a York tanner, implied that tacit skills would be part of the bargain to his apprentice Robert Malton in 1579. Edward promised to 'instruct him as well in buying and selling of hides and leather as in the artificial working and dressing' of the hides.[91] A period abroad was also part of the bargain for apprentices like Thomas Johnson of Liverpool, whose master promised to send him to France for one year to 'learne the language of that countrie' in 1582.[92] There appears to have been something of an exchange programme between English and French masters, for Thomas's indenture states that his father was to provide food and lodging for any French boy that Thomas's master, William Kelly, should bring over from France to learn English. Kelly was obviously an enlightened man, for a further clause stipulated that if Thomas did not like the sea after his first and second voyage, then he was allowed to leave William's service.

The system of apprenticeship determined both the nurture and instruction the child were to receive during the period of the contract. The placing of the child into another household meant that the master replaced the father – if he were alive – as an authority figure, with the master's family exerting increasing influence over the apprentice as the term progressed. However, there were obligations on both sides: apprentice and master entered into a relationship defined by the indenture, not unlike a marriage contract, which included a duty for the master to look after the apprentice in sickness and health.[93]

Relationship between apprentice and master

What was the relationship between apprentice and master? The relationship between the apprentice and master was one based on the authority of the household. As noted in Chapter 2, under the Roman family law principle of *patria potestas* the father exercised control over all of his children and those brought into the household such as servants or apprentices. In this respect, apprenticeship was not just about the transmission of technical skills. The moral education, important for all children in the household regardless of their affiliation to the family, underpinned the relationship between apprentice and master. Moral instruction was one of the most important aspects of the apprentice–master relationship and ostensibly the most challenging of the requirements of the agreement. The apprentice was placed with the master at an age when conflict between parents and the child would have occurred and this tension was then transferred to an unrelated person.[94]

Contemporaries believed that the age of adolescence was one of ignorance combined with indiscipline and bad behaviour.[95] Explicit codes of behaviour were thus incorporated into the indenture to endorse correct moral instruction. Apprentices were warned to avoid 'all unlawfull gammes, hores, harlottes, wyne taverns, ale howsies, evyll and nowghtie disposyed and suspiciouse companie',[96] in addition to not fornicating or committing adultery in the master's house.[97] Transgression from the rules was sternly dealt with. Richard

Madock, a Liverpool apprentice, was summoned before the mayor in 1575 and ordered to refrain from all 'kynd of vnlawfull games prohibited by the statutes parliament'.[98] He was committed to reappear before the mayor in three months' time and in the interim not to depart the city without the permission of the mayor or else the sum of £20 would be levied against his body and his goods. There was a need for restraint concerning these 'diversions' as plenty of 'suspicious company' existed who could part the apprentice from his or his master's money and goods. Richard Dobbie, Robert Crosbie and Edward Whyete found themselves before the magistrates in Liverpool in 1567 for waylaying apprentices and 'sufferyng them to pley at dice, cardes and unlawfull gammes and tymes' while in 1581 Welsh Alice was accused of enticing apprentices to buy unlawful items such as salt.[99] Such evidence testifies to the belief that apprentices' behaviour and their choice of acquaintances required careful monitoring in order to protect their moral well-being.

Control over the apprentice's moral compass extended to marriage and apprentices were forbidden to contract marriage with any woman or have the contract made for him without the 'speciall licence of his sayd master'.[100] This measure was more likely in place to prevent the disruption of the master's household that the apprentice's spouse and any potential children might cause.[101] Marriage of an apprentice would also blur the lines of authority within the household. The apprentice would have authority over his wife, but be subservient to the master.[102] Neither was the apprentice to absent himself from the master's house by day or night unless it was on his master's business. Should any apprentice go against these rules and not 'serve and obeye at all tyme and tymes in all thinge and thinges lawfull and honeste'[103] then the master could discipline them with 'reasonable and lawfull castigacion as occasion shall require'.[104] Towards the end of the period of this study, the strong Protestant ethos of the family as a breeding ground for both Church and state can be detected within the indentures. Edward Johnson, who was careful to imply the teaching of tacit skills of his trade to Robert Malton, stated that he would discipline Robert 'with necessary correction' and 'teach him to feare God and reverence his betters according to humanitie'.[105] Another of Edward's apprentices, Thomas Robinson, was in 1577 expected to behave towards his master in words and deeds 'both lowlie and reverentlie'.[106] Deference to authority comprised a major part of the moral education the apprentice received.

The moral instruction explicit in the indenture did not alter over time, as a verse outlining its contents penned at the beginning of the nineteenth century demonstrates. The organisation of industry had changed dramatically, but the nineteenth-century apprentice was to behave exactly the same as his sixteenth-century counterpart.

Each young Apprentice, when he's bounde to Trade,
This solemn vow to God and Man has made,
To do with joy his master's *just* commands,

Nor trust his secrets into other hands.
He must no damage to his substance do,
And see that others do not wrong him too.
His master's goods he shall not waste or lend,
But all his property with care defend.
He shall not buy or sell without his leave,
Nor lie, nor injure, nor all deceive.
Taverns and Ale-houses he shall not haunt,
Those snares to Youth, those scenes of vice and want.
At cards and Dice he shall not dare to play,
But fly from such temptations far way.
O Youth! remember thou art to this art bound,
See that no breach of this in thebe found.[107]

The relationship of apprentice and master was one of authority and obedience: the master exercised authority over the apprentice and the apprentice was deferential towards the master. This particular notion of authority was, as Griffiths argues, defined by certain rhetoric and a structure of 'place'.[108] So, although the apprentice learnt skills by instruction from the master, he was socialised into the mores of working life through the operations of the household.[109] The moral instruction that underlined the relationship was at times the most challenging aspect of it and could cause serious disagreement between the apprentice and master. Roger Edgeworth, the sixteenth-century theologian and preacher, warned apprentices that whether their masters 'be good, virtuous and honest' or 'crabbed, croked, and cumberous', the apprentice should always 'do youre duety and true service vnto them'.[110] At times, circumstances dictated that it be otherwise.

Conflicts and concerns between apprentice and master

What were the consequences if the relationship between the apprentice and master deteriorated or was curtailed? As noted above, the relationship between apprentice and master was a complex one. There was always going to be conflict because of the age structure of subordination and the domestic nature of apprenticeship.[111] Additionally, sixteenth-century adults considered male apprentices to be immature and reckless in their behaviour[112] and there are a number of examples in the legal sources that confirm this impression. Richard Mosse was imprisoned in 1566 at the mayor of Liverpool's command for 'raylyng upon Henrie Mason', a street cleaner, while Richard Bekensall of Chester, who was sent 'into the partues beyond the see' by his master in 1522 to trade, wasted his master's money.[113] So, although both the apprentice and the master signed a binding contract, this did not mean that the relationship would survive intact until the end of the term. This could occur for a number of reasons, and not necessarily to do with conflict. The most common reason was the death of the master.

A significant number of apprentices experienced the death of their master during the term of their indenture. Custom dictated that a replacement should be found and the duty of care for the apprentice transferred to them.[114] Often, this person was the widow of the master. Robert Harrison was 'set over' in 1576 to the widow of his late master, William Walker, a mariner, four years after his initial indenture. If the widow were to re-marry a mariner, then Robert was to serve them both. If she re-married a non-mariner then she was to 'put over the said Robert to some honest man, a mariner, as will not onlie instruct and teache him in the arte of navigacion, but also to performe all other covenauntes aforesaid'.[115] An understanding of the mutual obligations of all members of the apprenticeship fraternity existed: the apprentice was to continue contributing to the business of his late master, the widow to fulfil all the covenants of the original indenture and, should she remarry a non-mariner, thereby abandoning her late husband's craft, there was an obligation on her part to ensure that the apprentice completed his training. Such was the case for John Croswhale of York, who had served Alice Crostwhale, the widow of a York plumber, until she remarried in 1584. Upon the marriage, John was re-apprenticed to Richard Fairbank to serve out the remainder of his term.[116] Records do not indicate whether apprentices were either consulted about, or concurred with, any decisions in regards to being 'put over'. Rather, it was expected practice on the death of a master.

Other reasons for the termination of the contract included the master changing his craft, a lack of funds to maintain the apprentice or parental intervention. Thomas Utie was apprenticed to George Greathead, a joiner, in 1592 and within two years was set over to another joiner, Thomas Lasenbye.[117] The death of George Greathead is not mentioned nor is a widow, and the responsibility for re-apprenticing appears to have been taken by Thomas's father. Conversely, Thomas Jackson, a sawyer, appeared before the mayor of York in 1581 to 'put over Robert Wood his apprentice vnto Richard Hawkins', also a sawyer, for the remainder of the term of the original indenture.[118] No fee is mentioned but costs could be considerable and it was not a transaction that a master would take willingly.[119] The reason for Robert's re-apprenticing to Richard Hawkins must be left to conjecture, but taken alongside the movement of apprentices due to their masters' deaths it does highlight the transient nature of apprenticeship for many children in sixteenth-century northern England as elsewhere in the country.

The indenture was political in intent, with the wording articulating the mutual obligations, setting forth the ideal image of both apprentice and master.[120] It also meant that there were avenues for redress should there be a complaint from either party. Rushton found that in the north-east of England, while the guilds themselves had the ability to intervene in disputes between masters and their apprentices, these measures were of benefit to the masters rather than the apprentices. Apprentices had to engage the mediation of the local courts.[121] This was in contrast to London, where many of the elite guilds had their own courts to which apprentices could appeal.[122] What is revealing from my study is that cases brought before the local justices for contravening indentures are few: two to be precise. But, just because there is no recorded evidence of disagreements between masters and apprentices, this should not be interpreted as an absence of conflict in the artisanal households of sixteenth-century northern England.[123] What the evidence does suggest is that disputes were resolved before they reached the courtroom.

If we widen our search to include documents from courts outside those of the local authorities, deterioration of relationships between apprentices and their masters is apparent. These instances may have been exceptional cases and any analysis would be hampered by the lack of discernible evidence of disputes as well as an ignorance of the circumstances that surrounded the complaint.[124] However, they do give a good indication that the apprentices were not as well provided for or as protected as the indentures might otherwise show. Additionally, the testimony from such disputes demonstrates the imposition of authority upon the child from a group of moral guardians that encompassed the guild, master, parents, families, kin, neighbours and sources of local justice within the town.[125] This group intervened to ensure that the apprentice received his or her entitlement, but its behaviour displayed an unequivocal allegiance to the apprenticeship system that worked to keep the children within its structures, regardless of the outcome for the child.

The examination of disputes can expose how the magisterial relationship between apprentice and master appeared to the apprentice. Tales of dissatisfaction, unhappiness and resistance of the apprentice unravel in the testimony of the petitioners. Agency also played a part in the apprentice's outrage at his treatment, with some instigating proceedings themselves. John Birch took his grievance for lack of instruction by his master, Robert Rodley, to the Lancashire Quarter Sessions in 1601.[126] Rodley was ordered by the court to either teach his apprentice or repay him £4. Rodley evidently did not honour his part of the bargain as an entry from the following Quarter Sessions notes that Rodley was to pay John 20s. each session until the £4 was repaid.[127] If a breakdown in the relationship between apprentice and master resulted in the indenture being terminated, and if it were the fault of the master, then part of the premium paid at the beginning of the term was repayable to the apprentice,[128] which is what has transpired in this case. John Birch must have been sure of his rights to take the case to court.

Even if an apprentice exercised agency and complained about his master, they may not always have received justice. In 1492, Thomas Godfrey complained about his master, Robert Archer, for not feeding him properly, chastising him unduly and not sending him to school – contrary to Thomas's indenture. The Court of the Merchant Taylor's Guild dismissed Thomas's complaints twice before they ordered Archer to 'sette over' his apprentice.[129] Thomas was described as being of 'tendre age' as well as 'faderles and moderles',[130] revealing just how vulnerable he was. Nonetheless, he exercised his right to challenge the authority of the master in order to contest an abuse of his indenture, showing considerable persistence in the process. Orphans like Thomas could expect little help from family, but vulnerable apprentices did turn to family or friends for help to challenge the authority of the magisterial relationship.

In 1575, Katherine Preston petitioned the Quarter Sessions in Chester on behalf of her son. She stated that he had never even been taught his trade as a tailor 'the space of one wholle weeke' during the first two and a half years of an eight-year apprenticeship. Instead he 'hathe dayly gone vnto the collpytt for colles'.[131] Katherine was concerned that her son 'dothe dayly lose hys tyme' and urged the magistrate to enforce the master, Robert Thornley, to 'sett hym vnto hys ocupacon'.[132] As her son was sixteen at the time of the petition, Katherine was worried he would not be able to earn his keep once his apprenticeship came to an end, telling the mayor that 'ether now ys the tyme to lorne hys occupacion or never'.[133] Katherine was keen to let the mayor know that she had kept her side of the bargain, giving her son a new, brass pot and supplying his shirts throughout the term so far. She was now expecting the local courts to compel the master to honour his contractual obligations.

There may have been a presumption that because apprenticeship was meant to duplicate the parent–child relationship the child would be cared for in a similar manner to one of the family.[134] This did not always happen, and at times parents and guardians took measures to ensure the health and moral welfare of their child, despite having relinquished the day-to-day care to another family. In Newcastle upon Tyne in 1563 a mother alerted to the fact that John Atkinson was beating her son went to his shop and upbraided him about his treatment of the boy. The mother, Mrs Hewbanks, was said by witnesses to be 'something in anger & grief concerning hir child', and clearly felt that Atkinson's disciplining of her son transcended the 'lawful castigacion' permitted by the indenture.[135] It is possible that mediation and not local justice dealt with this matter of over-zealous disciplining because no record exists of a dispute in regards to the abuse. We are only aware of young Hewbank's predicament because his mother brought a case for defamation against Atkinson, for calling her a priest's whore, in the church courts. Incidents like this give weight to Griffith's argument that very few cases of abuse and misuse of apprentices can actually be found in the extant records of the local courts. Nonetheless, the grievances were still being recorded, but as incidental information in other courts.

The Chancery court was one of equity, and so was a popular place for disputes concerning the non-payment of apprenticeship bonds. For once the master or bondsman had brought an action of debt there was no redress from the common law until the debt had been paid. It is in the annals of this court that we learn the fate of many apprentices. In around 1483, John Feweler was put out of the service of John Pegham, a York merchant, within a year 'without any cause resonable'.[136] Another John Pegham, a priest, appears in the records between 1485 and 1500 complaining that his nephew William was being held against his will by his master, John Harper, until the bond had been paid for the apprentice. Pegham complained that Harper had taken out an action of debt against him for £100, and 'neyther wold lerne his said prentice as he shuld do ne fynd hym'.[137] Debt may have been the reason we are aware of the mistreatment of apprentices, but the testimony highlights the measures taken by family and friends to ensure the fulfilment of the indenture. William Tosilton was refused entry back into his master Thomas Dawson's house in York, sometime between 1500 and 1515, after sickness delayed him on a sanctioned trip home. His stepfather, John Woode, aware of the wording of the indenture, especially that William should not absent himself from his master, personally brought William back.[138] The mayor of York then ordered Dawson to take William back – which he did not do – before the dispute finished up as an action for debt. These actions suggest that moral guardians were keen to maintain the status quo and have the apprentice finish the term regardless of the circumstances.

Evidence given in Chancery can characterise a miserable and bleak existence for the apprentice at the hands of his master. Master Fonby, a York tailor, had beaten his apprentice Thomas Lincolne constantly with 'tonges off iron' and other 'vnreasonable wepons'.[139] Additionally, Fonby had not given Thomas any instruction or clothing after the first three years of his apprenticeship and Thomas was keen to leave his master. John Hewett, who had stood surety for Thomas, intervened and tried to persuade Fonby to take Thomas back and 'vse hym self reasonably' towards Thomas. The behaviour Hewett believed to be 'reasonable' is defined only in relation to its opposite, the 'unreasonable' weapons that Fonby used to beat Thomas with.[140] Hewett chose his words carefully using emotional terms that Griffiths argues came from notions of domestic order, which did much to bring into question the master's commitment to the moral aspect of the agreement.[141] The situation did not improve after Hewett's intervention and his master had Thomas put into prison, where he was 'almost famysshed' and had to be rescued by Hewett. Yet Hewett was *still* intent on returning Thomas to Fonby, who refused to take him back. As surety, Hewett would become financially liable during any dispute between the apprentice and the master and it would be for this reason that he tried to persuade Fonby to take Thomas back. Alternatively, perhaps it was the realisation that the courts acted merely as intermediaries between the master and apprentice and most cases of cruelty were concluded with the master being asked to 'use' his apprentice fittingly.[142] Courts, it seems, were reluctant to break the indenture regardless of the complaint.

The domestic nature of industry in the sixteenth century meant that the locus of power resided within the individual households, with the child dependent upon the goodwill of the head of the family unit. Apprentices were subordinated to their masters and the structures of the arrangement worked to keep the apprentice within this system when relationships between the apprentice and master broke down. There is, however, evidence to suggest that the apprentices themselves took an active part in their own welfare by challenging the authority of the master. Either through their own actions or by soliciting the help of family and friends, apprentices brought cases against their masters to ensure they were treated according to their indentures.

Resistance to authority could also be seen in the actions of the apprentices described in Chancery petitions. Thomas Holgait of York decided to leave the service of his master, Robert Grenwood, in 1528 without permission. Grenwood vigorously defended his right over his apprentice by stating all the clauses included in the indenture in his petition that Thomas was supposed to uphold.[143] There is little indication in the sources that apprentices were consulted as to their views or preferences in any matters, which is consistent with their subordinate position in the hierarchy of power relations. When evidence does show apprentices exercising agency, those cases are significant and are indicative of the exercise of agency on a wider scale. Even when formally subordinated to authority, apprentices proved they were capable of challenging that authority in regards to their own interests.[144]

Participants in apprenticeship

For whom was apprenticeship available – boys, girls, rich, poor – and at what ages? As Brooks has argued, the ability of parents to place children in a career that would enable them to set up and maintain a household depended upon three things: the gender of the child, the prosperity of the family and the profession of the family.[145] Husbandry and housewifery were the two most favoured indentured trades for poorer boys and girls respectively, especially for pauper children and orphans placed by the parish.[146] Apprentices from wealthier backgrounds were usually male, aged between thirteen and seventeen, with marriage the intended career for girls.[147] As skills were the 'the single most valuable asset' of traditional apprenticeship,[148] access to them was controlled by existing structures and unspoken rules of hierarchy, most overtly by the guilds.

The selection process for potential apprentices was one of political manoeuvring by the guilds to both define their community and protect their interests. Marginalisation of certain groups in society is critical to the definition of any such assembly,[149] and individual guilds held definite ideas about exactly the type of child who could be incorporated within their profession. Prohibitions were placed on children of illegitimate birth regardless of the ability of their parents to pay the necessary fee. This policy is evident in the Newcastle Merchants' rules of 1513, which stated that, despite having served a seven-year apprenticeship, the freedom of the city would not be granted to a person of illegitimate birth.[150] Despite such prohibitions, illegitimate children were still being indentured in sixteenth-century England. Thomas Garnet, the bastard son of Alexander Garnet, was apprenticed to Thomas Inglefeld, a Liverpool smith, in 1565.[151] The fact that Thomas's father was described as an alderman may demonstrate that the 'fraternal' aspect could extend beyond the guild itself or, more probably, that local government influence had currency within and without the guild community. There is a possibility that Thomas's apprenticeship was made possible by the 1563 Statute of Artificers, which stated that for many trades, including smiths, 'the sonne of any man could enter', but the statute would not alter access to the more lucrative professions.[152]

Internal policing by guild members turned informants assisted the marginalisation process as they reported any infringement of the rules, especially if they suspected that an apprentice had been born outside the jurisdiction of the sovereign. Thomas Conyngham was moved to bring a complaint against Alexander Richardson, a carpenter, in the Chancery court, *c*. 1467–85, because Richardson had accused Conyngham's apprentice of being Scottish.[153] Many guilds prohibited masters to take Scottish apprentices, but towns in the far north of the region attracted the sons of lowly farmers and tradesmen from over the border.[154] Apprentices from towns closer to home were treated in the same manner as their Scottish counterparts. Redesdale and Tynedale in Northumberland were regarded as even more treacherous than Scotland.[155] The term 'Scots', however, remained a local term of abuse.[156]

Outside the guild, economics regulated access to apprenticeship. The premium – an amount paid by the apprentice and their family to the master as an inducement and fee for teaching the child a trade – varied for each profession, its scale of operation and the social status of the master.[157] In theory, this was an optional amount, as it was not prescribed in law, and as part of a private contract between the individuals, was not mentioned in the indenture.[158] The profitable professions, which included mercers, merchants and goldsmiths, were highly regarded and attracted children from wealthier homes. In sixteenth-century London, premiums for these trades varied from hundreds of pounds up to £1,000 but premiums were lower in the regional towns and cities[159] Ben-Amos's study of Bristol apprentice premiums in the early seventeenth century found that fees were modest, the majority costing less than £10.[160]

There are only two references to premiums paid for apprentices in this study, both of whom were indentured to tailors. Christopher Webber was apprenticed to Robert Young in York in 1577 for the fee of 40s., paid for by the city's mayor and chamberlains, while in 1535 Thomas Baker paid 13s. 4d. to apprentice his cousin, Richard Willis, to William Prescotte in Kegworth, Leicestershire.[161] A few indentures mention bonds. Bonds were felt necessary to ensure the reasonable behaviour of both apprentice and master and were signed by both parties. The majority of apprentices that signed bonds were sons of fathers with modest occupations.[162] William Bolthill of Liverpool, the son of a mariner, signed a reciprocal bond with his master, Oliver Garnet, for £5 in 1565, and Edward Walker of Liverpool, whose father was dead, signed a bond for £10 in 1584.[163] For orphans like Edward Walker, somebody from outside the family would have stood surety but the bond added to the expense of indenturing a child for many families. Parents with very low wages or from trades where employment was inconsistent throughout the year would struggle to accumulate the money to apprentice one child, let alone two or more. Expense then could act as a significant barrier for the participation in apprenticeship by children from these families.[164] Moreover, trades that attracted the smallest premiums like husbandry, housewifery and shoemaking were seen to be impoverished with little or no career prospects once the apprenticeship term was finished. George Hulse described himself as a 'poore wastes man' after he had lost his living and was apprenticed to a shoemaker in Congleton, Cheshire, causing his wife, Elizabeth, to petition for divorce in 1561.[165] These trades became the destination of the poorest children and parish apprentices,[166] and by the end of the sixteenth century became a feature of Elizabethan legislation to set poor and vagrant children to work.[167]

Pauper apprenticeship

Pauper or enforced apprenticeship was a system that did not become established until the seventeenth century and so holds little relevance for this study. Yet, even though I only have one record that definitively suggests a pauper apprenticeship, the fact that this record exists is proof that pauper apprenticeship was a practice some children in sixteenth-century northern England were subjected to, and thereby deserves explanation.

The poor and vagrant child had always posed a problem for local and national government alike, particularly the practice of begging, which authorities and commentators believed was due to idleness and not need. Thomas Starkey, chaplain to Henry VIII, thought begging 'argueth no poverty, but rather much idleness and ill policy' and that it was through their own fault and negligence that people begged.[168] Starkey was also of the opinion that any man without a craft was idle and 'should be banished and driven out of the city'.[169] Extreme as Starkey's opinion may appear to present-day sentiment, the ethos behind his words is reflected in the early policies of the Tudor period, implemented in a bid to address the perceived social ills of the time. Enforced apprenticeship first appears on the statute book in 1536 as an act that authorised parishes to take any healthy child between the ages of five and fourteen found begging on their streets and apprentice them to masters in husbandry or other crafts. This measure was thought necessary for such children to acquire skills useful in maintaining themselves when they came of age.[170] Whether these measures were used or not, the problem of vagrants continued to grow and additional legislation was passed which strengthened the principle of enforced apprenticeship alongside schemes to set the idle poor to work. The Statute of Artificers, passed in 1563, gave parishes the authority to apprentice any unemployed person under the age of twenty-one. Further acts followed but it was the Poor Laws of 1597 and 1601 that allowed for forced apprenticeship on a larger and more consistent scale.

The first thing to note is that the acts themselves did not explicitly order that parents had to release their children, or that masters were obliged to take apprentices. These regulations were imposed after Elizabeth's death by the Stuart judiciary.[171] Second, unlike the terms of other legislation, these acts obliged churchwardens and the overseers of the poor to apprentice or find work for vagrant children, and for any children they deemed had parents unable to support them. All expenses incurred in the process were paid by the parish.[172] In so doing, the cost of raising these children was redistributed from poor families to wealthier families both inside and outside the parish.[173] So it was for Elizabeth Rymyngton of Melling, Lancashire, who in 1601 was so poor that she was awarded 2s. per month from the parish, but also had her sons apprenticed.[174] If Elizabeth refused to let her sons be apprenticed, then her poor relief would have been reduced or maybe even stopped altogether until she agreed to let them go. At best, the sons would have been denied relief and Elizabeth would have had to maintain them herself from her meagre allowance.

Elizabeth may have had fewer mouths to feed, but this redistribution of costs failed to consider the emotional upheaval for both mother and children. No age is mentioned for the boys but pauper apprentices could be indentured at an earlier age than traditional apprentices, from seven years old, and their terms were considerably longer. Nor did this legislation take into account the economic value of her sons to Elizabeth. Many households relied on contributions from all members of the family, including young children, to survive. Furthermore, as Pamela Sharpe has argued, children would be apprenticed at times of severe economic hardship such as bad harvests resulting in high wheat prices,[175] yet should the fortunes of the parents improve, there were no explicit reversal measures to return children to their parents. This was unlikely to be the case for Elizabeth, as no husband is mentioned and so presumably she had few means of improving her finances.

As a marginalised group, pauper apprentices would have been bound to a limited number of trades, which in turn deterred traditional apprentices from entering them. Additionally, the ease with which children could be bound left the system open to abuse, particularly with the advent of industrialisation, where pauper apprenticeship provided a plentiful and available workforce. For some historians, this abuse of pauper apprenticeship sounded the death knell for the institution of apprenticeship as a whole,[176] but then, due to its domestic origins, it was an institution that would have been severely challenged by industrialisation regardless. More importantly, there is little evidence as to the success of pauper apprenticeship in the traditional industries other than the number bound. Of 1,526 poor children apprenticed in 1619 in Hertfordshire, records indicate that many of them had absented themselves from their master, returned home and were unemployed by 1624.[177] Yet this was a social policy that was long lived and poor children did benefit from it. Ann Minister has shown that during certain periods and in particular places pauper apprenticeship was a significant opportunity for children of poor parents to acquire valuable work skills.[178] Unlike traditional apprenticeship, the cost was not a barrier to poor children obtaining a trade.

Tudor statutes may have formally classified pauper apprenticeship as an entity separate to that of traditional apprenticeship, but it is apparent that this categorisation existed long before the legislation was enacted. Wealth – or lack of it – filtered apprentices to specific trades within the institution. Poverty was not the only barrier preventing children from being indentured to certain crafts, with gender playing a significant part. Trades that attracted large numbers of girls were regarded as lowly professions.[179] Nonetheless, girls still featured in the economic structure of towns and villages in sixteenth-century northern England.

Female apprenticeship

As Ben-Amos noted in her work on female apprentices in early modern Bristol, the most prominent feature of female apprenticeship remarked upon by historians of early modern English society is the paucity of urban, female indenture records.[180] I am inclined to agree with this observation for the chronological period of this study, where number of the female indentures I have managed to locate does not even make double figures. Among the other concerns voiced by historians have been the barriers to certain trades for girls, a steadfast belief in the division of labour as envisaged by society in both public and domestic domains, and the fact that independent women craftspeople were generally widows.[181] All these concerns are reflected in the female indentures and the relevant male indentures that I have located. However, the lack of female apprenticeship indicates only that girls were not formally recognised as acquiring certain skills, not that they did not possess them.

Seven out of the nine girls featured in this study were indentured to housewifery, although the word 'housewifery' is not mentioned. Katherine Horobin, apprenticed to Robert Berry, a merchant-tailor, and Ellen, his wife, in 1594, was to 'well faithfullie & truelie serve, as an apprentice in the trade science or facultie which the said Ellen Berry her mistris usethe'.[182] Similarly vague descriptions of the skills to be taught are outlined in the other six indentures. Female apprentices were bound to both the master and the mistress and sometimes it is noted that the apprentice would serve both, like Anne Prescott, who was indentured to Robert Baker, a Liverpool yeoman, and his wife, Cicilie, in 1593. Both Robert and Cicilie promised to instruct Anne, but it is clear that the skills would be domestic in nature because of the ambiguous wording used. It was the trade or science that Cicilie 'nowe useth, or may happen to use or occupie herafter during the said terme' that Anne was to learn.[183] A further qualification was added to include any trade that Robert or Cicilie may use and that in the event of the death of one of them Anne was to continue serving the other.

Housewifery training was not well respected and so parents were reluctant to indenture their children to the craft.[184] There was the realisation that the long length of the indentures, fifteen years in some instances, represented nothing less than cheap labour. In addition, there existed the possibility of unwanted attention from the master or other male members of the household. The church court records testify to this attention foisted upon female servants in the form of maintenance cases, with claims by the servants that the masters were the fathers of their illegitimate babies.[185] Predictably, many of the female apprentices' fathers came from the lesser trades or, like their male equivalents, had fathers who were dead (see Table 5.1). It could be argued that female apprenticeship afforded orphans a home,[186] with housewifery providing skills that would ensure employment after the end of the contract in addition to being of use once married.[187]

Table 5.1 Female Apprentices Indentured in Liverpool 1577–1601[188]

Name	Age of apprentice	Father alive	Father's occupation if stated	Length of term in years	Place of origin
Dorothy Poolforde	12	Yes		10	Holt, north Wales
Dorethie Melling	14	Yes	Bricklayer	15	Ormskirk, Lancashire
Amie Hurdeson		No		12	Leeds
Margaret Griffith		No	Labourer	15	
Anne Prescott		No	Miller	7	Liverpool
Katherine Horobin		No	Sailor	10	Liverpool
Anne Corker		Yes	Glazier	5	Liverpool

Source: LVRO, MIN/COU I, Book 2.

After housewifery, the second most popular destination for female apprentices was the textile industry, usually knitting or sewing, and this is the craft to which the two remaining female apprentices were bound. Both Isabella Mansfield and Isabella Bulmer were apprenticed to Jane Anderson as knitters in York in May 1589.[189] Unfortunately, their Latin indentures are short in length, and give no more information than the date, their names, name of the mistress they were apprenticed to and the length of term they were to serve. Knitting was part of the upbringing of many girls and, although Ben-Amos comments that the skill was usually combined with domestic service, there is no evidence to indicate whether or not this was the case in York due to the brevity of the entries.[190] Solely the mistress of the house taught apprentices in these occupations, and usually it was only the mistress who went to register the indenture, as was the case with Jane Anderson. Jane is not described as a widow or as someone's wife in the indenture, and although her husband may have practised another craft within the household, her enterprise is evidence that not all independent women in sixteenth-century industry were widows who had inherited their business from their late husbands.

The lengthier indentures of the Liverpool female apprentices were very similar to those of the males: the apprentice promised to dwell with the master and mistress and to serve them fittingly; the master and mistress were to instruct the apprentice and provide board, lodging and clothes for the term. Unlike boys, girls were not warned off alehouses, unlawful games and suspicious company. Nor were they forbidden to make a contract of matrimony, while nothing is mentioned about keeping safe the mysteries of the trade – probably as there were no secrets to keep – causing damage or absconding. Possibly this was because girls were considered the more malleable of the sexes and unlikely to be affected by the excesses that caused male apprentices to be out of control and headstrong.[191] Fees for female apprentices were small compared to those of males, with most apprenticeships costing just a few pounds.[192]

Female apprentices were few in number and the crafts in which they were indentured so basic that the skills learnt warranted the lowest of wages. The dominance of boys in the highly skilled crafts ensured that transmission of knowledge, and therefore power, was firmly male oriented.[193] This does not take into account the large numbers of girls who were trained without a formal indenture and probably alongside indentured boys. Heather Swanson rightly comments that by the guilds ignoring one half of the workforce of a town, the system of apprenticeship is misleading in relation to the composition of workers in a town.[194] Female indentures may be few, but evidence of skilled work being performed by women can be found in wills that demonstrate the wide range of skills they possessed.[195] Swanson cites Agnes Hetche, who was left tools in her armourer father's will to enable her to make chain mail, proving that she was as much a part of the business as her brother, who was left instruments to make plate armour.[196] Furthermore, the lack of formal indentures for girls allowed them to compete favourably in the labour market, as they were not contracted to one master for a long term.[197] Girls may have been marginalised in traditional apprenticeship but they were prominent in industry alongside their male peers.

Apprenticeship was a system that would offer a place to all who wished to enter it, dependent upon gender, wealth and status of both the would-be apprentice and the trade itself. Pelling remarks that there was the possibility that apprenticeship offered a place for children who were less able intellectually, disabled or diseased.[198] There is some evidence within the indentures to support this argument. William Collton, a York goldsmith, apprenticed his son John to Edward Darke, a pin maker, in 1594.[199] As a member of one of the most affluent guilds it would be unlikely that William would apprentice his son to such a lowly trade as pin making were it not for the fact that John was not capable mentally of a more demanding craft. These arguments aside, there were structural barriers in place for the poorest boys and all girls regardless of status. Apprenticeship in high-status and respectable trades remained the preserve of the male apprentice, whose family or guardians were able to pay the required premium. Girls were generally confined to housewifery and the clothing industry while poor children of both sexes were relegated to the most demeaning and labour intensive of the trades. Traditionally, as many of a town's ruling elite came from the high-status guilds, apprenticeship orchestrated the reproduction of structures in society that kept wealthy men in positions of power and poorer men and female members subservient and dependent upon them.

Life after apprenticeship

What happened to the apprentice once they had finished their term? Apprenticeship was not necessarily the avenue to social mobility for the majority. Some did not complete their terms and it has been estimated that one-third to a half of London medieval apprentices finished their careers in this way.[200] This attrition rate would possibly not have been as high in the north of England, but it did occur as the court cases and Chancery petitions detailing disputes indicate. Aside from the disputes already mentioned, apprentices failed to complete their terms for a number of reasons: businesses failed, masters died and apprentices did not wish to serve their widows like Robert Harrison did, while others were unable to settle in their new environments and were drawn back to their own homes. Some left before the end of the term but were content with the skills that they had attained and therefore able to make a living.[201] Richard Gill contracted himself to Richard Smythe, a Liverpool ship's carpenter, in 1576 for four years with all the advantages of apprenticeship such as meat, drink, woollen hose and shoes.[202] The completion of an apprenticeship was not the only way to make a living.

Even for those apprentices who finished their terms, traditional apprenticeship may not have been the catalyst to the freedom of the city that some historians believe it to have been. Many did not take up the freedom of the city, but this may not necessarily be due to the cost of registration fees. These were not excessive and often the master had agreed to cover the cost at the binding of the apprentice. Hugh Radbrucke, who was admitted to the freedom of Liverpool in 1576 for the sum of 6s. 8d., agreed to pay all costs for his own apprentice, William ab Raath ab Griffith of Ruthin, north Wales, to 'bryng the sayd William … to be frie burges of this towne after custome [here after he has] truelie served his sayd master as apprentice duryng the said terme of x yeres'.[203] It is therefore apparent that other structures prevented apprentices from becoming freemen.

One argument for the low take-up of freedom of the town was the need for capital to enable apprentices to trade on their own. Indentures show that at times masters did help their apprentices towards independence. A number of apprentices received wages throughout their term, like Henry Watson, indentured to William Challener for eight years in 1582. He received 6d. for the first seven years and 13s. 4d. in the last year.[204] Capital and goods were also routinely given at the end of the term to the apprentice. Thomas Hughson of Liverpool was to receive 13s. 4d., two sets of clothes and 'every kinde of toole belonging to the saide science' from his master, William Gallaway, a ship's carpenter, when his term came to an end in 1592.[205] This benevolence was not uniform across the system and Mayhew has argued that those apprentices who had begun with little capital behind them never prospered. Only those who came from well-heeled families went on to be wealthy citizens of the town.[206] This argument has been challenged by Ben-Amos in her study of Bristol apprentices, which found that social class of the apprentice did not influence the take up of freedom of the town.[207] She also found that family networks were of more importance, offering not only support by way of lodging or employment but also information on local opportunities that would enable the setting up of a business.[208] Such help may not have been available to the

high percentage of orphans identified in this study. Without capital or the
support of family, many were forced to become journeymen, working on a
daily basis, a far cry from the envisaged premiums of life as a freeman. It is
possible that agency had more to do with the lack of apprentices becoming
freemen. Just as apprentices migrated to the town to be trained, they migrated
back home again or to other places once they had acquired useful skills.[209]

Like many of their male contemporaries, once female apprentices finished
their term they were unlikely to become free of the city. Despite Ben-Amos
identifying female apprentices being promised money towards obtaining the
freedom of Bristol in the 1530s and 1540s, the incomplete records for the
sixteenth century have made it difficult to establish whether or not they did
indeed became burgesses of the city. Seventeenth-century records show that
there are no women listed in the Burgess Books, nor is there any mention of
money being obtained towards freedom.[210] Not taking up the freedom of the
town did not preclude women from taking apprentices, as we are aware from
Jane Anderson and her knitters. Alongside the widows who continued to
employ apprentices to help them run their late husband's businesses, mis-
tresses allowed for women to be substantially represented in a town, with the
distribution of crafts not dissimilar to that of the craftsmen[211] and thereby
not confined to housewifery and the textile industry.

The system of apprenticeship in sixteenth-century northern England did
not necessarily induct children into the community of the guild, nor did it
provide for the child in the larger, urban community. Apprentices frequently
did not finish their term, becoming a source of unskilled, cheap labour without
protection from the guilds or the law, a position that has been argued to swell
the numbers of paupers on the streets of towns.[212] Apprentices that did complete their term were not always assured of the freedom of the city, or of
having the capital to set up on their own. Due to the domestic nature of the
system, there is nothing to suggest that apprentices in the rest of the country
were treated any differently. Nevertheless, it was entrenched in the wider
urban values necessary to educate the next generation[213] and, in this way,
enabled children to acquire skills regardless of whether they completed the term
of their indenture or not. Skills survived in the community in which the
children were trained as well as in the community in which the apprentice
chose to practise.

Conclusion

Apprenticeship was one of many learning contexts in which sixteenth-century
children could acquire skills. As opposed to schooling, where children's learning was book-based, apprentices learnt vocational skills through participation
in manual work, and it was assumed that they had much to learn. Masters
pledged to teach their charges all they knew about their crafts, promising that
they would teach them with 'just and uncoloured instruccions and tokyne as
belongyth to an apprentice'.[214] In respect of good nurture, it was the benefits

that these skills could provide for their child that motivated parents and guardians to gather the resources necessary to pay for an apprenticeship.

Parents wished to expand their children's educational opportunities while allowing for stricter discipline of their child than could be achieved in the natal home.[215] In this respect, apprenticeship was no different to sending children away to school. Ideas of good nurture in the sixteenth century were consistently framed in terms designed to instil obedience and deference to authority in the child, with both schools and the master's household acting as institutions of secondary socialisation. But, whereas schooling was very definite in the benefits it could offer a child – usually as training for university or the priesthood – apprenticeship hinted at social mobility and a meritocracy that would allow the child of lowly parents to move beyond the world of his father. Children apprenticed in towns other than their birthplace were less likely to be placed into the same trade as their father.[216] 'Betterment migration'[217] appealed to parents who sent their children to towns that on occasion were so far away from their homes that they must hardly have seen their children after they were apprenticed. Sir Martin Bowes was sent to London from York as an apprentice when he was thirteen in 1511. He recalled that he was 'younge and with small substaunce'.[218] After his apprenticeship he became a successful businessman and in 1549 he presented the City of York with a silver and gilt ceremonial sword as an acknowledgement to the place that he was 'brought uppe and nourished' when he was young. It was probable that Sir Martin's parents had contacts in London, one of the many considerations of parents when deciding where to send their children.

Friends and family played a large part in betterment migration, with parents choosing places where they had relatives in order to offer support to their child if needed.[219] With networks of support in place, children had a good chance of succeeding in a foreign town.[220] Apprentices turned to this network when they were in trouble, particularly when there was a problem during the term of the indenture. It is sometimes through the testimony of these family and friends that we can gauge how the apprentice felt about their relationship with their master. Often they were frustrated by the lack of instruction by their master, like Katherine Preston's son. At other times, they were miserable and unhappy in their relationship, like Thomas Lincolne, and just wanted help to leave the master. Some even managed to show their resistance to authority by taking action themselves. What all the examples discussed above demonstrate is that apprentices were able to challenge authority in a number of ways when it came to their own welfare.

What we should consider is that the majority of relationships between apprentice and master were positive and cases of mistreatment few.[221] Parents and guardians placed children with masters in the understanding that they would nurture the children according to the terms of the indenture and apprentices were more often than not treated as part of the family. Apprentices developed close emotional ties with their masters and it was not unheard of for the master to bequeath the apprentice his tools and equipment,[222] or for the apprentice to name his eldest son after his master.[223] In addition to the master's promise to nurture the child correctly, guilds sometimes advised the masters on the correct care of the apprentice. An early regulation by the Newcastle Merchant Adventurers specified the maximum number of times per week an apprentice could be served salmon from the Tyne. It was so plentiful that it was given little merit as an appropriate food to serve to a growing child.[224]

Apprenticeship may be regarded as a technical education, but it was also a period of intense socialisation. Children were placed in the master's household and expected to become part of the family. Edgeworth cautioned apprentices to 'lyke as you were your masters child, reuerently fearing to offend or displease their father'. They should also have a 'louinge feare' not to do anything that might displease the master.[225] It was through the discipline of the household that the master tamed the excesses of youth and integrated the child into the adult world.

Notes

1   LVRO, 352 MIN/COU I, B1, fol. 130, apprenticeship indenture of Thomas Garnet of Liverpool (1565).
2   Pauper apprenticeship will be discussed below on pp. 264–7. Pauper apprenticeship is also referred to as parish or forced apprenticeship in the scholarship.
3   O. Jocelyn Dunlop and Richard D. Denman, *English Apprenticeship & Child Labour: A History with a Supplementary Section on the Modern Problem of Juvenile Labour* (London: Macmillan, 1912), p. 18.
4   Dunlop and Denman, *English Apprenticeship*, p. 16.
5   W. Ferguson-Irvine (ed.), *A Collection of Lancashire and Cheshire Wills Not Now to Be Found in Any Probate Registry 1302–1752* (London: Lancashire and Cheshire Record Society, 1896), p. 183.
6   EYLA, D12, fol. Q.
7   DUSC, Visitation Book 1577–87, DDR/EV/VIS/1/1, fol. 4.
8   TNA, Chancery Petitions, C2/Eliz./C23/42.
9   Anne Yarborough, 'Apprentices as Adolescents in Sixteenth-Century Bristol', *Journal of Social History*, 13 (1979), 67–81 (p. 67).
10 Peter Rushton, 'The Matter in Variance: Adolescents and Domestic Conflict in the Pre-Industrial Economy of Northeast England, 1600–1800', *Journal of Social History*, 25 (1991), 87–107 (p. 90).
11 EYLA, D12, fol. 13; EYLA, D12, fol. 11v.
12 LVRO, 352 MIN/COU I, B1, fol. 150^v.
13 EYLA, D12, fol. L^v.
14 Dunlop and Denman, *English Apprenticeship*; Ephraim Lipson, *The Economic History of England*, 9th edn, vol. 1 (London: Adam and Charles Black, 1947), pp. 308–439.
15 Keith D. M. Snell, 'The Apprenticeship System in British History: The Fragmentation of a Cultural Institution', *History of Education*, 25 (1996), 303–21.
16 Margaret Pelling, 'Apprenticeship, Health and Social Cohesion in Early Modern London', *History Workshop Journal*, 37 (1994), 33–56 (p. 33).
17 Ilana Krausman Ben-Amos, 'Reciprocal Bonding: Parents and Their Offspring in Early Modern England', *Journal of Family History*, 25 (2000), 291–312 (p. 294).
18 Paul Griffiths, *Youth and Authority: Formative Experiences in England 1560–164* (Oxford: Clarendon Press, 1996), pp. 313–24.

19 Griffiths, *Youth and Authority*, p. 320.
20 Rushton, 'Matter in Variance', p. 89.
21 Yarborough, 'Apprentices as Adolescents', p. 69.
22 Rushton, 'Matter in Variance', p. 89.
23 Rushton, 'Matter in Variance', p. 92.
24 Griffiths, *Youth and Authority*, pp. 313–14.
25 Joan Lane, *Apprenticeship in England 1600–1914* (London: UCL Press, 1996), pp. 33–63.
26 Ilana Krausman Ben-Amos, 'Failure to Become Freemen: Urban Apprenticeship in Early Modern England', *Social History*, 16 (1991), 155–72 (p. 165).
27 Christopher Brooks, 'Apprenticeship, Social Mobility and the Middling Sort, 1550–1800', in Jonathan Barry and Christopher Brooks (eds), *The Middling Sort: Culture, Society and Politics in England, 1550–1800* (Basingstoke: Palgrave Macmillan, 1994), pp. 52–83 (pp. 53–4).
28 Lane, *Apprenticeship in England*, p. 38.
29 Steve Hindle, '"Waste" Children? Pauper Apprenticeship under the Elizabethan Poor Laws, *c.* 1598–1697', in Penelope Lane, Neil Raven and K. D. M. Snell (eds), *Women, Work and Wages in England, 1600–1850* (Woodbridge and Rochester: Boydell, 2004), pp. 15–46.
30 Margaret G. Davies, *The Enforcement of English Apprenticeship: A Study in Applied Mercantilism, 1563–1642* (Cambridge, MA: Harvard University Press, 1956), p. 13.
31 Snell, 'Apprenticeship System', pp. 311–2.
32 Ann Minister, 'Pauper Apprenticeship in South Derbyshire: A Positive Experience?', in Anne M. Scott (ed.), *Experiences of Poverty in Late Medieval and Early Modern England and France* (Farnham: Ashgate, 2012), pp. 64–84.
33 Brooks, 'Apprenticeship, Social Mobility', p. 53.
34 Caroline Barron, 'The Education and Training of Girls in Fifteenth-Century London', Diana E. S. Dunn (ed.), *Courts, Counties and the Capital in the later Middle Ages* (New York: St Martin's Press, 1996), pp. 139–53; Ilana Krausman Ben-Amos, 'Women Apprentices in the Trades and Crafts of Early Modern Bristol', *Continuity and Change*, 6 (1991), 227–52; Richard Goddard, 'Female Apprenticeship in the West Midlands in the Later Middle Ages', *Midland History*, 27 (2002), 165–81; Lane, *Apprenticeship in England*, pp. 38–42.
35 Brooks, 'Apprenticeship, Social Mobility', p. 53.
36 Stephanie Hovland, 'Apprenticeship in Later Medieval London (*c.* 1300–*c.* 1530)' (unpublished Ph.D. thesis, Royal Holloway, University of London, 2006), p. 283.
37 Lane, *Apprenticeship in England*, p. 39.
38 Lane (*Apprenticeship in England*, pp. 229–39) discusses post-apprenticeship opportunities in a positive light.
39 Graham Mayhew, 'Life-Cycle Service and the Family Unit in Early Modern Rye', *Continuity and Change*, 2 (1991), 201–26.
40 Mrs J. R. Green, *Town Life in the Fifteenth Century*, 2 vols (London: Macmillan, 1907), ii, 86–109.
41 Philippe Ariès, *Centuries of Childhood* (London: Jonathan Cape, 1962), pp. 365–6.
42 Ann Kussmaul, *Servants in Husbandry in Early Modern England* (Cambridge: Cambridge University Press, 1981), p. 4.
43 Pelling, 'Apprenticeship, Health and Social Cohesion', p. 36.
44 Charlotte A. Sneyd (ed. and trans.), *A relation or rather a true account of the island of England; with sundry particulars of the custom* (London: Camden Society, 1847), p. 24.
45 EYLA, D12, fol. 5^v.
46 Sneyd (ed.), *A relation*, p. 25.

47   Shulamith Shahar, *Childhood in the Middle Ages* (London: Routledge, 1992), p. 237.
48   Anne Yarborough, 'Bristol Apprentices in the Sixteenth Century: the Cultural and Regional Mobility of an Age Group' (unpublished Ph.D. dissertation, Catholic University of America, 1977), pp. 121, 156–97, cited in Yarborough, 'Apprentices as Adolescents', p. 68.
49   EYLA, D12, fol. A.
50   Mayhew, 'Life-Cycle Service', pp. 212–21.
51   EYLA, D12, fol. 12^{v}.
52   Pelling, 'Apprenticeship, Health and Social Cohesion', p. 42.
53   Pelling, 'Apprenticeship, Health and Social Cohesion', p. 41.
54   A total of forty-six indentures were examined but two children appear twice, having been re-apprenticed to different masters. Of the fatherless children, two were brothers.
55   A total of 217 indentures were examined between 1573 and 1603 but four children appear twice having been re-apprenticed to different masters.
56   Philippa Maddern, 'Between Households: Children in Transitional and Blended Households in Late Medieval England', *Journal of the History of Childhood and Youth*, 3 (2010), 65–86; Ben-Amos, 'Women Apprentices', p. 233.
57   Mayhew, 'Life-Cycle Service', p. 205.
58   Mayhew, 'Life-Cycle Service', p. 222.
59   Pelling, 'Apprenticeship, Health and Social Cohesion', p. 41.
60   S. R. Epstein, 'Craft Guilds, Apprenticeship and Technological Change in Pre-Industrial Europe', in S. R. Epstein and Maarten Prak (eds), *Guilds, Innovation and the European Economy, 1400–1800* (Cambridge: Cambridge University Press, 2008), pp. 52–80 (p. 53).
61   Sylvia L. Thrupp, *The Merchant Class of Medieval London, 1300–1500* (Chicago: Chicago University Press, 1948), p. 3; LVRO, 352 MIN/COU I, B2, fol. 201, indenture of Amie Hurdeson. The indenture states she was to obey her master and mistress 'in the manner of a woman or maide apprentice'.
62   Heather Swanson, *Medieval British Towns* (Basingstoke: Macmillan, 1999), p. 52.
63   Lipson, *Economic History of England*, p. 384.
64   Lipson, *Economic History of England*, p. 384.
65   See J. A. Twemlow (ed.), *Liverpool Town Books: Proceedings of Assemblies, Common Councils, Portmoot Courts, etc., 1550–1862*, 2 vols (Liverpool: University of Liverpool, 1918–), I: 1550–1571 (1918), p. 522, n. 1.
66   EYLA, B12, fol. 31.
67   See EYLA, D12, fol. 4^{v}. Christopher Dightryn's indenture with Anthony Risscharte, a York linen weaver was made in 1589 but not recorded until 1591.
68   LVRO, 352 MIN/COU I, B2, fol. 138^{v}; 139^{v}.
69   LVRO, 352 MIN/COU I, B2, fol. 152; 152^{v}; 154^{v}.
70   See LVRO, 352 MIN/COU I, B2, fol. 53. The indenture of George Fisher stated that he was to be 'instructid, in all thyng & thynges accordyng to his indolence and capacitie'.
71   Lane, *Apprenticeship in England*, p. 17.
72   Mayhew, 'Life-Cycle Service', p. 219.
73   EYLA, D12, fol J-J^{v}.
74   S. T. Bindoff, 'The Making of the Statute of Artificers', in S. T. Bindoff, J. Hurtsfield and C. H. Williams (eds), *Elizabethan Government and Society: Essays Presented to Sir John Neale* (London: Athlone Press, 1961), pp. 56–94 (p. 62).
75   Davies, *Enforcement of English Apprenticeship*, p. 2.
76   E. Arber (ed.), *A transcript of the Registers of the Company of Stationers of London, 1554–1640 A.D.*, 5 vols (London, 1875–94), I, xli.

77 Yarborough, 'Apprentices as Adolescents', p. 68.
78 EYLA, D12, fol. 7.
79 LVRO, 352 MIN/COU I, B2, fol. 102.
80 CALSS, Quarter Session Petitions, QSPT/7; LVRO, MIN/COU I, B2, fol. 83^v.
81 Dunlop and Denman, *English Apprenticeship*, p. 16.
82 EYLA, D12, fol. A, indenture of Thomas Long (1573).
83 LVRO, 352 MIN/COU I, B2, fol. 179, indenture of William Radbrucke (1590).
84 Goddard, 'Female Apprenticeship', p. 172.
85 LVRO, 352 MIN/COU I, B2, fol. 300, indenture of Thomas Potter (1603).
86 LVRO, 352 MIN/COU I, B1, fol. 130, indenture of Thomas Garnett (1565).
87 EYLA, D12, fol. K.
88 Rushton, 'Matter in Variance', p. 95.
89 Emma Rothschild, 'Adam Smith, Apprenticeship and Insecurity', Centre for History and Economics Working Paper, King's College, Cambridge, July 1994, pp. 13–15, cited in Epstein, 'Apprenticeships and Technological Changes', p. 57, n. 13.
90 EYLA, D12, fol. G.
91 EYLA, D12, fol. O.
92 LVRO, 352 MIN/COU I, B2, fol. 125; J. W. Horrocks, *Assembly Books of Southampton*, vol. II (Oxford: Oxford University Press, 1920), p. xix. This was not uncommon in trades such as mariner to which Thomas was apprenticed, or merchant. In Southampton an apprentice was sent to Spain for two years of his term to learn the language and to 'make him free of the merchants'.
93 Pelling, 'Apprenticeship, Health and Social Cohesion', p. 42; LVRO, MIN/COU I, B1, fols 138^v–139. The indenture of William Bolthill, for example, states that his master Oliver Garnet, was to 'ordre governe and use, sicke and holle, in honest and lawfull maner', his apprentice.
94 Yarborough, 'Apprentices as Adolescents', p. 69.
95 Susan Brigden, 'Youth and the English Reformation', *Past & Present*, 95 (1982), 37–67 (p. 38, n. 6).
96 LVRO, 352 MIN/COU I, B1, fol. 130, indenture of Thomas Garnet (1565).
97 LVRO, 352 MIN/COU I, B1, fol. 138^v–139, indenture of William Bolthill (1565).
98 LVRO, 352 MIN/COU I, B2, fol. 60.
99 Twemlow (ed.), *Liverpool Town Books*, I, 347; LVRO, 352 MIN/COU I, B2, fol. 114.
100 This was a common prerequisite in all indentures. See LVRO, 352 MIN/COU I, B1, fols 138^v–139; EYLA, D12, fol. A^v, indenture of Reynold Huton.
101 Goddard, 'Female Apprenticeship', p. 168.
102 Philippa Maddern, '"In myn own house": The Troubled Connections between Servant Marriages, Late-Medieval Household Communities and Early Modern Historiography', in Stephanie Tarbin and Susan Broomhall (eds), *Women, Identities and Communities in Early Modern Europe* (Aldershot: Ashgate, 2008), pp. 45–59 (p. 46).
103 LVRO, 352 MIN/COU I, B2, fol. 74, indenture of Dorothie Poolforde (1577).
104 LVRO, 352 MIN/COU I, B2, fol. 53, indenture of George Fisher (1575).
105 EYLA, D12, fol. O.
106 EYLA, D12, fol. M^v.
107 Hannah More, *Path to Riches and Happiness. To which are added, The Apprentice's Monitor or Indentures in Verse: and, the Market Woman; or Honesty id the Best Policy, a True Tale* (Dublin: William Watson, 1810), p. 18.
108 Griffiths, *Youth and Authority*, p. 64.
109 Yarborough, 'Apprentices as Adolescents', p. 60.
110 Roger Edgeworth, *Sermons very fruitfull, godly, and learned, preached and sette foorth by Maister Roger Edgeworth, doctoure of diuinitie, canon of the cathedrall churches of Sarisburie, Welles and Bristow, residentiary in the cathedrall churche of Welles, and chauncellour of the same churche: with a repertorie or table,*

directinge to many notable matters expressed in the same sermons(London, 1557), fols clxxxiiiD–clxxxiiiiA.

111   Rushton, 'Matter in Variance', p. 101.
112   Yarborough, 'Apprentices as Adolescents', p. 67.
113   Twemlow (ed.),*Liverpool Town Books*, I, 301; TNA, Early Chancery Petitions, C1/516/23.
114   Pelling, 'Apprenticeship, Health and Social Cohesion', p. 42.
115   LVRO, 352 MIN/COU I, B2, fol. 65^v.
116   EYLA, D12, fol. Q.
117   EYLA, D12, fols 6, 7^v.
118   EYLA, D12, fol. K^v.
119   Rushton, 'Matters in Variance', p. 93. At the beginning of the eighteenth century in the northeast of England, transfer fees could be as high as £25.
120   Griffiths, *Youth and Authority*, p. 299.
121   Rushton, 'Matters in Variance', p. 92.
122   See Matthew Davies (ed.), *The Merchant Taylors' Company of London: Court Minutes 1486–1493* (Stamford: Paul Watkins, 2000), pp. 31–38.
123   Griffiths (*Youth and Authority*, p. 313) makes the point that the paucity of the cases varies from court to court and that such cases can be absent from the records for many years.
124   Rushton, 'Matter in Variance', p. 92.
125   Pelling, 'Apprenticeship, Health and Social Cohesion', p. 33.
126   LRO, QSR 4/19.
127   LRO, QSR 4/49.
128   Hovland, 'Apprenticeship', p. 80.
129   Davies, *Merchant Taylors' Company*, pp. 197–8.
130   Davies, *Merchant Taylors' Company*, p. 198.
131   CALSS, Quarter Session Petitions, QSPT/7.
132   CALSS, Quarter Session Petitions, QSPT/7.
133   CALSS, Quarter Session Petitions, QSPT/7.
134   Pelling, 'Apprenticeship, Health and Social Cohesion', p. 41.
135   DUSC, DDR/EJ/CCA/3/2, fols 30^v–31.
136   TNA, C1/67/31.
137   TNA, C1/106/8.
138   TNA, C1/375/53.
139   TNA, C1/324/12. (Petition 1500–1515.)
140   Griffiths (*Youth and Authority*, p. 315) argues that an idea of reasonable and lawful correction was only articulated in opposites.
141   Griffiths, *Youth and Authority*, p. 315.
142   Griffiths, *Youth and Authority*, p. 322.
143   TNA, C1/635/35.
144   Rushton, 'Matter in Variance', p. 94.
145   Brooks, 'Apprenticeship, Social Mobility', p. 52.
146   Brooks, 'Apprenticeship, Social Mobility', p. 53.
147   Brooks, 'Apprenticeship, Social Mobility', p. 53.
148   Ben-Amos, 'Failure to Become Freemen', p. 170.
149   Barbara Hanawalt, *Of Good and Ill Repute: Gender and Social Control in Medieval England* (Oxford: Oxford University Press, 1998), p. 31.
150   J. R. Boyle and F. W. Dendy (eds), *Extracts from the Records of the Merchant Adventurers of Newcastle-upon-Tyne*, vol. I (Durham: Surtees Society, 1895), p. 15.
151   LVRO, 352 MIN/COU I, B1, fol. 130.
152   R. H. Tawney and Eileen Power (eds), *Tudor Economic Document: Being Select Documents Illustrating the Economic and Social History of Tudor England*, 3 vols (London: Longman, 1924), I, 346–7.

153 TNA, C1/61/347.

154 Rushton, 'Matter in Variance', p. 91.

155 Geoff Nicholson, 'Tracing Your Family History in Northumberland and Durham: Apprenticeships', *Journal of the Northumberland and Durham Family History Society*, 26 (2001), 43–5 (p. 44).

156 Rushton, 'Matter in Variance', p. 91.

157 Ilana Krausman Ben-Amos, *Adolescence and Youth in Early Modern England* (New Haven, CT: Yale University Press, 1994), p. 87.

158 Hovland, 'Apprenticeship', pp. 78–9.

159 Ben-Amos, *Adolescence and Youth*, p. 87.

160 Ben-Amos, *Adolescence and Youth*, p. 91.

161 'EYLA, D12, fol. Gv; Indenture of an Apprentice, 1535', *Transactions of the Historic Society of Lancashire and Cheshire*, 91 (1939), p. 218. The latter indenture was found amongst deeds belonging to a house in Lathom, Lancashire suggesting that either Richard or his cousin came from the area. It is also possible that due to his surname, the master originated from Prescott, which is only thirteen miles from Lathom.

162 Ben-Amos, *Adolescence and Youth*, p. 88.

163 LVRO, 352 MIN/COU I, B1, fols 138^{v}–139; B2, fol. 138^{v}.

164 Ben-Amos, *Adolescence and Youth*, p. 91.

165 CALSS, EDC2/7/12^{v}. See also Chapter 3, p. 131.

166 Lane, *Apprenticeship in England*, p. 38.

167 Hindle, '"Waste" Children', p. 17.

168 Thomas Starkey, *A Dialogue between Reginald Pole & Thomas Lupset*, (ed.) Kathleen M. Burton, (preface) E. M. W. Tillyard (London: Chatto & Windus, 1948), p. 89.

169 Starkey, *Dialogue*, p. 142.

170 27 Henry VIII c 25, *An Act for Punishment of Sturdy vagabonds and Beggars*, in John Raithby (ed.), *The Statutes at Large of England and of Great Britain: From the Magna Carta to the Union of the Kingdoms of Great Britain and Ireland*, vol. iii (London: Eyre and Strahan, 1811), p. 243.

171 Hindle, '"Waste" Children', p. 17.

172 39 Elizabeth I c 3 1597 states that overseers of the poor were to be appointed who, along with the Justices of the Peace, will be charged with 'settinge to worke of the Children of all such whose Parentes shall not by the saide persons be thought able to kepe and maytaine their Children'. See Tawney and Power (eds), *Tudor Economic Documents*, I, 346–54.

173 Hindle, '"Waste" Children', p. 19.

174 LRO, QSR 4/39d. Entry does not state how many sons Elizabeth had.

175 Pamela Sharpe, 'Poor Children as Apprentices in Colyton, 1598–1830', *Continuity and Change*, 6 (1991), pp. 253–70 (p. 254), p. 260.

176 Davis, *Enforcement of Apprenticeship*, p. 13.

177 J. S. Cockburn (ed.),*Calendar of Assize Records, Hertfordshire Indictments, James I* (London: H. M. S. O., 1975), p. 275, number 1369.

178 Minister, 'Pauper Apprenticeship in South Derbyshire', pp. 64–84 (p. 84).

179 Lane, *Apprenticeship in England*, p. 38.

180 Ben-Amos, 'Women Apprentices', p. 227.

181 Ben-Amos, 'Women Apprentices', pp. 227–8.

182 LVRO, 352 MIN/COU I, B2, fol. 228.

183 LVRO, 352 MIN/COU I, B2, fol. 227.

184 Lane, *Apprenticeship in England*, p. 39.

185 See BIA, CP.G.1544. Alice Frankland of Glaisdale, Yorkshire became pregnant by her master's grandson, Robert Thompson, who lived in the same house; DUSC, DDR/EJ/CCD/1/2. Margaret Moreland of Sedgefield, County Durham,

gave birth to an illegitimate child in 1541 fathered by Raphe Davidson, her master, a married man.

186 Mayhew, 'Life-Cycle Service', p. 220.
187 Lane, *Apprenticeship in England*, p. 39.
188 No female apprentices were indentured during the dates of Book 1, 1550–71.
189 EYLA, D12, fol. 2^v.
190 Ben-Amos, 'Women Apprentices', p. 236.
191 Brigden, 'Youth and the English Reformation', p. 38.
192 Ben-Amos, 'Women Apprentices', p. 234.
193 Goddard, 'Female Apprenticeship', p. 169.
194 Heather Swanson, 'The Illusion of Economic Structure: Craft Guilds in Late Medieval English Towns', *Past & Present*, 121 (1988), 29–48 (p. 39). See also Ben-Amos, 'Women Apprentices'. Ben-Amos argues that women acquired skills as daughters, servants and wives.
195 Swanson, 'Illusion of Economic Structure', p. 39.
196 BIA, probate register 3, fol. 102^v, cited in Swanson, 'Illusion of Economic Structure', p. 39.
197 Goddard, 'Female Apprenticeship', pp. 169–70.
198 Pelling, 'Apprenticeship, Health and Social Cohesion', p. 49.
199 EYLA, D12, fol. 8^v.
200 Hovland, 'Apprenticeship', p. 207.
201 Hovland, 'Apprenticeship', pp. 208–10.
202 Twemlow (ed.), *Liverpool Town Books*, II: 1571–1603 (1935), 930–1.
203 LVRO, 352 MIN/COU I, B1, fol. 164.
204 EYLA, D12, fol. M.
205 LVRO, 352 MIN/COU I, B2, fol. 140^v.
206 Mayhew, 'Life-Cycle Service', p. 211.
207 Ben-Amos, 'Failure to Become Freemen', p. 159.
208 Ben-Amos, 'Failure to Become Freemen', p. 165.
209 Ben-Amos, 'Failure to Become Freemen', p. 166.
210 Brigden, 'Youth and the English Reformation', p. 238. Ben-Amos, 'Women Apprentices', pp. 237–8.
211 Ben-Amos, 'Women Apprentices', p. 238.
212 Green, *Town Life*, II, 103–9.
213 Brooks, 'Apprenticeship, Social Mobility', p. 75.
214 LVRO, MIN/COU I, B1, fol. 126, indenture of Giles Radclif.
215 Mayhew, 'Life-Cycle Service', p. 202.
216 Mayhew, 'Life-Cycle Service', p. 219.
217 See Peter Clark, 'The Migrant in Kentish Towns 1580–1640', in Peter Clark and Paul Slack (eds), *Crisis and Order in English Towns: Essays in Urban History* (London: Routledge & Kegan Paul, 1972), pp. 117–63 (pp. 134–8).
218 EYLA, 'City of York Catalogue of the Charters, House Books, Freeman's Rolls, Chamberlain's etc., Accounts and other Books, Deeds and Old Documents, belonging to The Corporation of York; together with Report on their Renovation', complied by William Giles, Deputy Town Clerk (1908).
219 Clark, 'The Migrant in Kentish Towns', p. 135.
220 Clark, 'The Migrant in Kentish Towns', p. 135.
221 Mayhew, 'Life-Cycle Service', pp. 220–1.
222 Marjorie. K. McIntosh, 'Servants in the Household in an Elizabethan English Community', *Journal of Family History*, 9 (1984), 3–10 (p. 13, n. 10).
223 Mayhew, 'Life-Cycle Service', p. 221.
224 Nicholson, 'Tracing Your Family', p. 44.
225 Edgeworth, *Sermons very fruitfull, godly, and learned*, fol. clxxxiiiiA.

6   Parental deprivation

'She this examinat was brought to this citie but by whom by reason she was
then of verie tender Age saithe she knoweth not and was heere lefte behynde in
this citie where she hath remained ever sithence'.[1]

Parental deprivation, a phrase borrowed from Peter Laslett, refers to children
in pre-industrial England who were without parents, either through orphanhood
or illegitimacy. But what place does parental deprivation have in a study on
nurture and neglect? The answer lies in the fact that there were substantial
numbers of children in late fifteenth- and sixteenth-century England who were
left without one or both of their parents due to illegitimacy, death or enforced
separation through practices such as abandonment or fostering. This in turn
influenced the quality and type of nurture they received. It is these children
who are discussed in this chapter. Who was to provide the nurture for such
children and how were they to do it? Furthermore, to what extent were they
neglected?

Many of the themes in this chapter build upon those mentioned in preceding
chapters. The common acceptance of placing a child into an authoritative
household where nurture was given by adults other than the parents, routinely
done in cases of child marriage and apprenticeship, continued to constitute
the care of a significant number of children who had lost a parent. Implicit
too is the importance of the family, evidenced in all chapters, as the best
environment through which to dispense moral counsel; to give practical
advice including how to teach a child to know its place within the family; and
to instruct them to place the wishes of the family above the child's own. This
is brought to the fore in this chapter by the homes into which parentally
deprived children were placed by the municipal authorities and private
individuals, as well as the expectation that poorer children were required to
work so as to contribute to the family economy and thereby, their own
nurture. There is also the juxtaposition of nurture and neglect as female
traits articulated through the writings of ecclesiastical authors discussed in
Chapter 2, which can be detected in the treatment by ecclesiastical and
secular authorities of women who had illegitimate babies or had abandoned
their children.

Nurture of these parentally deprived children consisted of a number of requirements. There was the provision of material support such as food, clothing and housing; the provision of training and education; and the provision of emotional and social bonds. Sixteenth-century thinking reflects that at least the first requirement should have been available to all children regardless of the income of parents. Court records detailing maintenance awards state that whoever was to have custody of the child should provide it with meat, drink, clothes and lodging.[2] The provision of training and education was usually only for those children who came from wealthier backgrounds, evidenced by bequests in wills or appeals to chancery to recoup costs. Of the third requirement, there is very little evidence of specific attempts to provide emotional and social nurturing. This may have been because nurturing of this type was taken for granted and therefore never talked about explicitly, or that the emotional and social needs were subjugated to material needs.

Fundamental assumptions about the basic necessities of nurture require addressing in this chapter. Modern children are viewed as being 'economically "worthless" but emotionally "priceless"'.[3] They do not contribute monetarily to the household but create an emotional attachment for their parents to the extent that the value we put on a child today has become almost overwhelmingly sentimental. Conversely, sources indicate that contemporary attitudes accepted the need for children from poorer families to provide for their own maintenance at some stage in their childhood. This was particularly pertinent in the case of parentally deprived children. The 1570 census of the poor in Norwich records many instances where children as young as five from single-parent families were set to work.[4] However, also noted are children from two-parent families, where both parents were employed and the children did not have to work. Harry Palliner, a tanner whose wife spun and sewed, had three children of eight, four and three who 'do nothing'.[5] This example serves to illustrate that, although children lived in what were termed 'poor households', they had variable experiences depending upon the physical make-up of their family and the employment opportunities of the adults within them.

Chronologically, childhood as discussed in this chapter refers to the ages between birth and twelve years. I have been directed to this particular upper limit of childhood through the maintenance sums awarded by the courts to illegitimate children, the payment of which is generally allocated until the age of twelve. Thereafter, the child was supposed to be put to work. A contemporary comment from the period reinforces this fact in the course of discussing employment for fatherless children: the writer states that 'hee is very idle that is past twelve yeares of age and cannot doe so much'.[6] There is the possibility that I have used records for children above this age where the age of the child is not stated.

The sources used in this chapter come from secular and ecclesiastical courts. Evidence has been gathered using depositions, Act Books, Early Chancery petitions, church court records, Quarter Session records, House Books and wills. We cannot be certain that this sample of cases is typical, but as there appears to have been no particular choice in the survival of records to exclude or favour certain groups it is not unreasonable to assume that definite trends of expectation and behaviour within the sample do at least reflect the nurture (or neglect) of parentally deprived children during the period. We still do, however, need to examine why these records exist. Although what survives appears to be fundamentally different types of evidence, without exception all the records concern the maintenance of children in one form or another and who had the responsibility for nurturing them. Furthermore, the sources reveal that parish officials took responsibility for children when there were no family or friends willing or able to do so.

What the sources succinctly establish is the disparity of the wealth (as well as the means of obtaining it) that the families involved in this study experienced. Hence the type of nurture available to these children was dependent upon the income and ability of the family to survive. Take for example the maintenance awards from the Church and secular courts. The 1576 statute 18 Elizabeth I, c 3 was the first legislation to address illegitimacy, but it was not concerned with the welfare of the child, only with minimising the amount of parish relief paid for such children and the public admonishment of their parents.[7] Certainly, directions in court records chronicle the punishment given to, and the maintenance to be paid by, the parents. Lancashire Quarter Sessions ordered James Meyall and Isabel Crompton to be set in the stocks at Bolton, Lancashire, in 1601 with papers on their heads indicating that they were both adulterers. At the same sitting, Isabel was ordered to keep their daughter for two years, with James paying her 20s. per year until such time as it was otherwise ordered by the justices of the peace.[8] Illegitimate children of wealthier parents are rarely to be found in maintenance disputes in the courts but feature predominately in wills and Chancery petitions. Monetary values discussed are predictably higher than those determined by the courts and the parents' behaviour is never brought into question. Wealth at least protected parents of illegitimate children from the humiliation of having to petition the secular and ecclesiastical courts.

Despite the evidence in the sources, scholarship on parental deprivation is a complex subject to access. This in part must be because so much energy has been invested in recent years by historians of childhood into the Philippe Ariès-fuelled debate concerning parent–child relationships that more tangible and equally important facets of childrearing have been overlooked. In continuing with this same anachronistic view of childhood, historians are ignoring (or missing) the fact that nurture does not hinge solely on parental affection. Often nurture was delegated to others and as it embraced the need for parents to supply children with the basic requirements of life, at some point in their childhoods, this could include sending them out to work or to beg on the streets. Thus we find little has been written about parental deprivation as a standalone topic, which is surprising considering the known high death rate amongst adults in pre-industrial England. The discussion on orphaned apprentices in the previous chapter bears witness to this fact.[9] As it stands, the historiography of parental deprivation is a heterogeneous mix of topics that includes orphans and illegitimate children discussed most often in relation to poverty and poor relief, with references to associated practices such as abandonment.

Peter Laslett has considered parental deprivation as an entity, although his definition does not include forced separation other than death and illegitimacy, with orphans being his primary focus. His hypothesis is confined to the actual number of parentally deprived children in pre-industrial England and thereby Laslett's work ignores the complex mix of familial situations that contributed to the deprivation and its effect upon the lives of the children involved.[10] Lawrence Stone's interpretation of parental deprivation is far removed from either Laslett's or this chapter's. Stone's concern is the 'deprivation syndrome' experienced by children whose parents used wet nurses and nannies to bring up their children and practices such as swaddling which Stone believes amounted to 'sensory deprivation'.[11] This psychological analysis of deprivation adopts Lloyd deMause's psychogenic theory of the liberal history of childcare, which is based on completely anachronistic notions of childrearing.[12] As such, it fails to observe the material and emotional deprivation associated with children who have lost a parent for whatever reason. Stone's work does, however, address the need to be clear as to what the term deprivation means in regards to children with absent parents. So often the term deprivation in relation to children is taken to mean solely that they are poor and destitute, as Pinchbeck and Hewitt do in their discussion on the 'Succourless poor child'.[13] While this may be so for many of the children featured in this present chapter who had endured great hardships and misery, this was not true in all the cases. It is therefore necessary for this chapter to look towards studies on orphans, illegitimacy and abandonment in an attempt to place the scholarship being undertaken within an historical framework.

Too often, as Laslett has demonstrated in his work on parental deprivation, the discussion on orphans is subsumed within statistics with little enlightenment on lived experiences. He does, however, argue that poorer orphaned children within the English peasantry were brought up with all the other children of the community, 'attended to by a knot of other mothers and other adults'.[14] Similarly, Nicholas Orme contends that losing parents may mean that children were sent away to live with relatives.[15] The truth is that we do not know if either situation was normative for orphaned children in the sixteenth century but it does not appear to be so from the sources used in this chapter. Certainly there are examples of family and unrelated adults providing a home for parentless children, but there are plenty of other illustrations of similar children being exploited by members of their own family as well as members of the community.

The biggest difficulty in accessing the scholarship of poor orphaned children is the historians' practice of treating all poor children as a homogeneous group. Orphans appear in the context of studies of poor children but have not necessarily been treated as a category of analysis in their own right. It is then necessary to 'sift through' the information to locate evidence that may have set the orphans apart from any other group in their struggle for survival. Often, as Steve Hindle and Patricia Crawford have done, this may be by the amount or type of relief widows with children received from the parish authorities.[16] Other discussions, like Stephanie Tarbin's, consider the physical places poor orphans were cared for in pre-industrial times or how wealthier families provided a home for their poorer orphaned kin.[17] But, on the whole, poor orphans are indistinguishable as a definite group from all poor children in the historiography. Moreover, it is only in relation to wealth that orphans are presented as a distinctive entity in the scholarship.

Children who lost their fathers at an early age and were left money and land were considered in need of municipal intervention and protection from the civic courts. The legislation and documentation that have accompanied such intervention have provided historians, including Charles Carlton, Elaine Clark, and Pinchbeck and Hewitt, with evidence to recreate the experiences of a very small percentage of the total number of fatherless children in pre-industrial England.[18] As Clark argues, the children's legacies drew attention to their wealth and subjected their lives to constant civic regulation.[19] It is indeed these interventions, featuring in disputes in Chancery petitions, that reveal the circumstances of a wealthier orphan.

When we consider the treatment of illegitimate children in the historiography, both wealthy and poor illegitimate children are readily visible but not necessarily side by side. Shulamith Shahar details how the illegitimate children from both noble and prosperous European urban families were sent to monasteries or the Church.[20] Likewise, Orme is more concerned about the illegitimate children of noblemen than those from the lower orders, but then noble bastards were more visible than ones from poorer families whose legal status was not always apparent.[21] The majority of the scholarship on illegitimacy is supplied courtesy of the poorer classes, particularly after the 1576 statute due to the increased quantity and quality of the Poor Law records. In addition, Alan MacFarlane believes, illegitimacy was more visible in both secular and ecclesiastical records than any other offence.[22] Intercourse leading to illegitimacy was more likely to be recorded and it is this data that is valuable to demographic historians like Laslett and Richard Wall when reconstructing families.[23]

As it is the case that much of the available data in relation to illegitimacy in the sixteenth century revolves around the court records, the discussion leans towards the mechanisms of illegitimacy itself. This is true of Laslett's observation of a 'bastardy-prone sub-society' and Richard Adair's study on illegitimacy, both of which focus on the numbers rather than the outcomes for children of such unions.[24] It is not surprising, therefore, that there is little evidence of the day-to-day experiences of these children. Additionally, like orphans, much of the historiography on illegitimate children is subsumed within scholarship on poverty. This is not unexpected considering the distinct correlation between poverty and illegitimacy and the types of sources in which illegitimate children appear. Crawford's *Parents of Poor Children* has resonance with the parenting of illegitimate children and how material circumstances affected their ability to nurture their children.[25] Additionally, Dave Postles contends, unmarried mothers were the most vulnerable women in the community, both immediately before they gave birth and after the delivery. Postle argues that this had direct consequences for the nurture of their children due to the actions of the men involved, as well as deep-rooted societal values that shaped their treatment by those who came into contact with them.[26] Cases for maintenance of illegitimate children brought before both the ecclesiastical and secular courts by unmarried women testify to this fact. As Goldberg rightly concludes, the fate of the mothers does have implications for the childrearing practices they employed with their children, and so historians have mostly been concerned with the outcomes for the mother and not the child.[27]

Turning to the historiography of abandonment, both Shahar and John Boswell consider it to have been practised in the main by parents of unwanted, illegitimate children[28] and, as Hugh Cunningham notes, any increase of abandonment mirrored an increase in illegitimacy.[29] In fact, Colin Heywood remarks that infanticide would have been more common in past centuries if it had not been so easy to abandon a child.[30] Stephanie Tarbin's research uncovered that many infants were abandoned at institutions like Christ's Hospital in London, founded in 1552. Although not established as a foundling hospital, it cared for babies abandoned by their parents at its door.[31] Ruth McClure's work establishes that England was without such institutions until 1741, when the London Foundling Hospital was founded.[32] It appears likely that parents who abandoned their babies at institutions like the Christ's were, according to Alysa Levene, driven by excessive poverty.[33] There was the possibility that unmarried mothers used the institutions to protect their reputations as well as employment prospects. Also apparent was a direct correlation between any rise in abandonments in general and severe economic conditions, a fact commented upon by both Heywood and Valerie Fildes.[34] And, as Fildes notes, abandoned children were not necessarily unwanted by their parents as many were reclaimed when the mother remarried or was employed and thus able to keep the child.[35] Fildes's study of children abandoned in London and Westminster between 1550 and 1800 also found that the place and the season chosen to abandon a baby were significant to the child's survival. Children abandoned in a public place were likely to be found quickly and cared for, whereas those abandoned in a privy or a backstreet where the mother had delivered were intended to die.[36]

The historiography of parental deprivation leaves more questions than it provides answers for, particularly in respect to the quality and nature of the nurture the children received, as well as the intimate details of who were the caregivers. By the very nature of the arrangements that had to be made for such children, cost was an important consideration and yet we are uninformed as to the microeconomics of parental deprivation. Additionally, we are ignorant about many of the measures taken by the parties involved to ensure survival for these children. What we need is more detailed knowledge of these aspects of parental deprivation. What were the main causes of parental deprivation in sixteenth-century northern England and how did the causes affect the child's expectation of nurture? Can we establish how much it cost to raise a parentally deprived child in sixteenth-century northern England? To what extent could parents and guardians make provision for children to meet the costs of bringing up a child in the event of separation? Where were the children placed in cases of disputed authority or absence of both parents? What survival expedients were employed by parents and guardians in relation to parentally deprived children? What part did the children themselves play in the provision of their own nurture?

Types of parental deprivation

What were the main causes of parental deprivation in sixteenth-century northern England and how did the causes affect the child's expectation of nurture? This is an important question to consider at the start of the discussion because the type of parental deprivation significantly predisposed the kind of upbringing a child would experience. This in turn influenced the variety of sources that survive for historical enquiry today, providing evidence for assumptions of nurture. Poorer children are overrepresented within these sources, suggesting that a high proportion of parentally deprived children survived on the margins of society. What we do know is that, unlike today, the breakdown of a marriage in the sixteenth century was not a major factor in parental deprivation. Michael Anderson found that, even as late as the nineteenth century, the number of marriages ended by the death of a partner was equal to those ended through death and divorce combined in 1983.[37] Divorce rates have continued to rise in the thirty-two years since Anderson's report, but so too have the number of births outside of marriage, making illegitimacy a consistent feature of parental deprivation over time.

In sixteenth-century northern England, rates of illegitimacy were markedly higher than the rest of the country.[38] Laslett and Karla Oosterveen found that in certain parishes in Lancashire and Cheshire during the reign of Elizabeth I illegitimacy rates were as high as 9 or 10 per cent over whole decades,[39] and this had consequences for both the parents and the children.[40] Illegitimacy was seen to challenge not only the family unit as a domestic group but also the unity of society.[41] It was a moral offence punishable by the Church but also penalised by secular laws in relation to inheritance, which excluded illegitimate children from automatically inheriting property or titles from their parents. Yet the causes of illegitimacy were manifold and a complex interaction of various factors and circumstances.[42] In spite of this, two main arguments are promoted in the historiography to explain the incidences of illegitimacy in the sixteenth century.

The first argument centres on the fact that a proportion of the mothers of illegitimate children were victims in the breakdown of the marriage process.

Sixteenth-century marriages were not always formal contracts solemnised in the church. Rather, they could be informal, improperly witnessed affairs that were liable to be broken if one or other of the couple had misgivings about the union.[43] Even using words of present consent in their exchange of vows, which were considered to be immediately binding, did not induce all people who spoke the words to honour the contract. Despite contracting words of present consent sometime in 1567 with Jane Umfrey, Thomas Peeres of Stainton, Yorkshire, refused to accept Jane as his wife. The child she had with him in 1569 was determined to be illegitimate and Jane was then forced to petition the Archdeacon of Cleveland to validate the marriage and for maintenance of the child.[44] As to the second argument, this considers many of the unwed mothers to be found in the sources were female servants living away from home. The position female servants held in the household made them both physically and economically vulnerable, which in turn allowed them to be easily sexually compromised by any resident or visiting males.[45] Frequently these servants were very young – between fifteen and twenty-four years old – and, without a family to support them, were sent away to have their babies or dismissed from service.[46] It seems unlikely that there were more young women living away from home as servants in the north of England than the south so this would not explain the greater incidences of illegitimacy in the north. This arrangement, however, would certainly have been a factor in a percentage of illegitimate births.

Not all female servants conformed to the accepted stereotypical characteristics of the pregnant female servant. Janet Spence was thirty-five when she became pregnant with the child of her master, Robert Ward of Hurwoth-on-Tees, near Darlington around 1575. Consistory court depositions betray her precarious position within the household. When Ward's wife discovered Janet was pregnant and claiming Robert to be the father, the wife sent her away, saying that had her husband realised Janet was pregnant he 'wold have had hir to have goon to the brand wyffes off Darlington to have had adrink to dystroy her child'.[47] Janet was then obliged to seek relief from the neighbours around Hurwoth. When the time came for her baby to be born, Janet was found at Ward's door, 'lyinge in the streit … crying pyttifully'. Witnesses said that Janet was 'like to be lost for womenes help' and was then taken into a poor woman's house to give birth. Robert refused to acknowledge that the baby was his but offered Janet 12d. 'to go hir way'.[48] No information is available as to how Janet looked after the child before she petitioned the church court, but perhaps the same neighbours who relieved her after she was dismissed from Ward's service and then helped her at the time of her delivery continued to provide her and the child with support.

Despite the fact that illegitimacy features so strongly in the sources used for this study, this was not the foremost cause of parental deprivation in the sixteenth century. Laslett has argued that this was because although there were a great number of children born outside marriage, many of them died soon after birth or were saved from the ignominy of bastardy by the marriage of their parents.[49] Death of a parent emerges as the primary cause of parental deprivation, especially of the father, as his death was more likely to break up the family. This resulted in the children being cared for by adults other than the surviving parent.

The meaning of the word 'orphan' in the sixteenth century had a different connotation than it does today. Children, who had lost only one parent, as well as those who had lost both, were considered to be orphans, and, as Laslett observes, those children who had lost a parent outnumbered children who were born out of wedlock.[50] In the village of Claythorpe in 1688 (a little later than the dates of this study) a census conducted by the rector found that 35.5 per cent of dependent children in the parish had lost their fathers.[51] Carlton concludes from this that there were proportionally ten times as many orphans in Tudor and Stuart England than there are today, with one child in three losing a father before they became an adult. Accordingly, the children's inheritance was smaller than it might have been if the father had lived, assuming, that is, the father had not squandered it. Furthermore, the family sometimes lacked the influence or acquaintances to help their children to find employment.[52]

For children who had lost a parent, particularly a father, life was considerably altered. They could find themselves further along the life-cycle than their contemporaries from two-parent families, being compelled to enter the workforce at an earlier age than had been anticipated. As discussed in Chapter 5, for those children without the benefit of an inheritance apprenticeship was inextricably linked to orphanhood. Many children were indentured at a younger age than was expected to ameliorate the costs of bringing up the child and provide the orphan with a home and surrogate family. Children left an inheritance encountered different problems to those without but were equally vulnerable, although in different ways. Discussion in Chapter 3 highlights how unscrupulous kin or associates of the child's family could abduct and forcibly marry the child under age to gain control of child's lands and its profits. In this respect, orphaned children became a commodity to their guardians, and the child itself was not the author of its own destiny.[53]

Wards of court in theory had the protection of the law in regards to their inheritance and the profit on their lands. As early as the twelfth and thirteenth centuries, custumals existed in all parts of England that provided for the wardships of children who had lost a father.[54] In the cities and larger towns, the mayor or chamberlain was appointed to act as special guardian to the orphaned children of the freemen of these towns to safeguard the property and ensure the welfare of the children.[55] Authority to act for these children often came from the sovereign with the municipal authorities tasked with providing for 'the safety, defence, and government of orphans and infants' within its boundaries.[56] The intervention of the authorities reflected the thinking of the time that the family was the foundation for political and social organisation. Just as the king was the father to his subjects, the father was king of his household.[57] The gender assumptions of the legal system were prominent, with the father maintaining authority over his wife and children and the role as arbiter of godly authority in his household.[58] With guardianship, that exercise of power over children passed from natural parents to surrogate ones appointed by the courts.

At times, this exercise of power allowed abuse of the child's assets by the guardian. Christopher Vascour was obliged to petition Chancery to obtain the profits of his lands in Sickinghall, North Yorkshire, that were amassed during his wardship by the men who had the use of them.[59] Even the mayor of London was not exempt from being accused of profiting from the orphans under his care. Elizabeth Rawlings from Croston, Lancashire, sued the mayor for the rest of her legacy left to her by her father, William Dalton, a skinner, payable upon her marriage in 1522. Not only was this against the last will and testament of her father but also 'contrarie to all justice right and good conscience and contrairie to the laudable custome of the said citie' of London, according to the petition.[60] The legal body charged with protecting an orphan's interests at times could be just as manipulative as the guardians.

In a number of cities, measures were in place to protect the orphan should their surviving parent remarry. Usually, a stepfather had to give a recognisance to protect his stepchildren's portions. In 1559 Gilbert Martyn of Liverpool entered into such an agreement upon his marriage to the widow Elizabeth Abrams. He promised to deliver to each of her three children the money and goods left to them by their father.[61] At times, the agreement took the form of a bond to guarantee the children would be treated fairly and we can again look to Gilbert Martyn as an example of this practice. In 1565, an undertaking by Gilbert was entered into the Liverpool Town Books which stated that Gilbert would 'kepe governe and bring uppe … Alice Abram … upon his costs and charges untill suche tyme as the sayd Alice shalbe and come to the age of fourtyne yeres'.[62] The reason for this agreement was the death of Elizabeth and, as Alice was the only child mentioned, it presupposes that the other children were passed the age of fourteen or dead. Similar arrangements were made in a marriage agreement for the children of Anne Chamber of Barrow-in-Furness, Cumbria[63] when she married Thomas Wilson of Kendal, Cumbria, in 1588. Both Anne and Thomas were charged to 'bring up, maintain and educate' Anne's children for a fifteen-year term. If Anne Chamber were to die during the term and Thomas neglected the children, he was to pay supervisors £13 6s. 8d. per annum for the remainder of the term.[64] This reflects the monies required to pay for adequate nurture of the children.

The Abrams and Chamber children came from families that appeared to be comfortably well off and their mothers quickly remarried men of similar status and wealth to their husbands, but not all orphans were that fortunate. Widows were a particularly vulnerable group and censuses of the population of towns in early modern Europe reflect that disproportionately large numbers of them were to be found in the category of inhabitants registered as 'poor'.[65] The loss of a husband affected both the status and the material wealth of many widows, radically altering the care options available to them for their children. Some widows were forced to co-reside with other women and their families in the cheapest tenements or cottages.[66] Widow Johnes, along with her two children, lived with the wife of a certain Arthur and four children in an ill-maintained cottage in Trinitie Lane, Chester, in 1599. The owner, Richard Treneld, was fined 2s. for allowing the cottage to fall into disrepair.[67] In all probability, the authorities were not concerned about the conditions the women and children lived in. They were exercising their civic duty to ensure that all buildings were kept in good order.

When we consider forced separation of children and parents through means other than illegitimacy and orphanhood, the practice of abandonment would have been familiar to sixteenth-century Christian parents. Canon law dictated that priests should excommunicate those guilty of the crime,[68] while the Bible contained an example of the most famous abandoned child: Moses. Placed in a basket of bulrushes daubed with slime and pitch, Moses was set adrift on the River Nile to safeguard him from being killed by the Egyptians.[69] But Moses was not unwanted. He was abandoned to give him the best possible chance of survival and, in a miraculous twist, his own mother was hired to be his wet nurse by the Pharaoh's daughter, who found him. The story of Moses' abandonment is just that: a story. The reality of abandonment in sixteenth-century northern England was far more complex and the extent of the practice at the time difficult to estimate.

It has been argued that the abandonment of a child was a viable alternative to infanticide.[70] There are indeed similarities between the two practices: both could be used for the disposal of unwanted, and mostly illegitimate, babies, and both were anonymous acts by the parents or other adults. Elizabeth Kyrke, an unmarried woman from Chester, was suspected of being pregnant by a neighbour, Elizabeth Hudson, in 1566. In previous weeks Hudson had witnessed Elizabeth's 'great belly' but when Hudson found Elizabeth outside her house one night, she appeared to be 'not then as she had before'. On examination, Elizabeth admitted to burying her baby – which she claimed was born dead – in the sands near the River Dee.[71] Similar stories emerge of those women who abandoned their child.

For parents who abandoned their children, it was commonly a measure of desperation. Anne Smyth of York, who like Elizabeth Kyrke was probably unmarried as no husband is mentioned, took the option of abandonment to dispose of her new born baby. The York House Books record that in 1577 'latly begotten with child contrary to the lawe, and also unmotherly and unnaturally', Anne had left the child in Coney Street in the city and further-more 'will not kepe hir said child'.[72] We do not know what happened to Anne's child but undoubtedly it was sent to a wet nurse at the expense of the parish. What would push a mother to leave her child to an uncertain fate? Fildes argues that a mother would not have abandoned her child unless her personal circumstances were so dire that her only choice was between infan-ticide and abandonment.[73] At no stage did contemporary commentators view abandonment as a survival expedient by poor parents, particularly mothers, to ensure that their child would be fed and cared for. The York authorities' opinion of the act, however, was that it was unnatural and unmotherly, suggesting that Anne was a callous mother who did not care about the fate of her child. No such condemnation was visited on the father, whoever he was. Stereotypical gender assumptions were present in the words of the local magistrates, with Anne's actions not conforming to their idea of normal maternal behaviour. William Gouge, an English clergyman and author, compared the actions of 'vnnaturall women' who abandon their babies to the Virgin Mary who, 'though she were very poore', nurtured her son as soon as he was born. Mothers who abandoned their babies 'oft lay their children forth in publike places, for others to shew that mercy, which they themselues have not'.[74]

Anne had abandoned her child in a busy thoroughfare in York where it would be quickly found and thus cared for. Evidence suggests that mothers (and sometimes fathers) did as Anne Smyth did and left their children in well-frequented locations so that they could be found quickly and in some cases be assured of the required care.[75] As Laura Gowing suggests, a great deal of thought went into where to abandon a child to ensure it was well looked after.[76] Was this the mother's reasoning when she left her baby at the door of Alexandra Tweddell? Alexandra told the Archdeacon of Durham in 1574 'that the harlot childe was lefft' at her door and that she 'toke & succerd her'.[77] Clearly, the mother of the baby knew that Alexandra had recently fed her own or other people's babies and would be able to suckle an infant. It was also possible that the child was Alexandra's own and she was trying to avoid a conviction for fornication.

While it has been argued that instances of children abandoned over the age of one were rare,[78] sources from the north of England reveal that it was not exceptional. Nor was abandonment solely an urban phenomenon. Lola Valverde suggests that in the early modern Basque Country members of the rural population specifically travelled to the city in order to abandon their children.[79] The same situation prevailed in sixteenth-century northern England and became particularly acute at times of bad harvests and the resultant high prices, as happened in 1594–97. The case of Maud Preece, discussed below, illustrates both that older children were abandoned and that abandonment was exercised by parents from outside the city.[80]

Despite the paucity of recorded abandonment in this study, it was arguably a reality for some parents within communities in sixteenth-century northern England, with the act itself being in the best interests of the family as a whole. It can be argued that once free of the child the mother was able to return to the workforce and contribute to the family economy, thereby increasing the chance of survival for the remaining children.[81] It is, however, important to remember that the decision to abandon a child was not usually taken lightly. Unless the child was abandoned as soon as it was born, the mother would have formed a maternal bond with the child strengthened by the act of breastfeeding. Leaving the child would be distressing and only undertaken if the mother felt she had no alternative to ensure the child's survival.[82] Furthermore, abandoning a child in a public place, as Anne Smyth did, was a recognised way of providing surrogate parents.[83] With the parents came an authoritative household by which the child would learn obedience and come to know its place in the world, while the new parents would take responsibility for the child.

Costs of raising a parentally deprived child

Can we establish how much it cost to raise a parentally deprived child? The experience of parental deprivation was not the same for all children in sixteenth-century northern England. The resources available to the families of these children differed according to economic and social status, and the type of nurture would vary correspondingly. The only similarity was that these families had to provide for their children the best way they could, but how much money was required to ensure adequate nurture?

Patricia Crawford has commented that it is practically impossible to estimate the annual cost of bringing up a child.[84] This does not mean we cannot at least make an attempt to estimate what that cost may have been. Today, there is a plethora of available data that defines how much a child will cost to maintain. In 2014, Liverpool Victoria, the UK's biggest friendly society, estimated that it would cost parents £216,846 to raise a child from birth to twenty-one years in Yorkshire, an area covered in this study.[85] This equates to almost £10,326 per annum, with the greatest outlay being on childcare. Of course, the majority of indicators used in contemporary surveys, including the upper age limit, are not valid for the early modern child, whose requirements were far more humble.

Recreating the financial outlay of families becomes less complicated for historians as the early modern period continued into the seventeenth century. Probate records concerning labourers as well as wealthier farmers analysed by Amy Erikson revealed that the median cost of keeping a child amounted to £5 per annum, with no identifiable increase for the higher status child or any differentiation between boys and girls.[86] Further down the social scale, additions to the Poor Laws, which appointed overseers of the poor in each parish entrusting them to pay appropriate amounts of money to people unable to work through illness or misfortune,[87] have informed other studies. Keith Wrightson and David Levine have used the accounts of the overseers in the village of Terling, Essex, to estimate the budget of poor families. A pauper child at the end of the seventeenth century cost the parish £1 10s. per annum.[88] Erikson, who examined the same accounts, has challenged this figure, arguing that a pauper child would have cost £4 per annum or 1s. 6d. per week.[89] A century later than my study, and at the other end of the country, Wrightson and Levine's findings, in addition to Erikson's re-calculations, do give an indication of what authorities and individuals believed the cost of bringing up a child to be.

Regional variations should also be considered when estimating the cost of a child. While Erikson had estimated that the medium cost was £5 per annum, the autobiographer William Stout, sent to a school near Ambleside, Cumbria, in 1678, was boarded out with Jennet Hynd for £4 per annum. Here he was 'plentifully provided for and diligently taught'.[90] No such detailed mechanisms as Poor Law accounts are available for this study, but we do have indications of how much authorities and individuals believed a parentally deprived child would cost to maintain. Not surprisingly, the type of record used to recreate these costs reflects the status of the child and its family. Implicit in the amounts stated are the assumptions of what type of support families would provide for the child: wealthier families provided a high level of valuable support, poorer families provided the absolute basics. It is therefore wise to recreate the costs in relation to the status of the child, beginning with the poorest children recorded in the sources.

Gowing observes that illegitimacy had 'immediate consequences' for both the parents and their communities in relation to the maintenance and care of illegitimate children.[91] Hence, we find the greatest number of records relating to poor children, indicating that costs were generated by maintenance orders being brought against putative fathers of illegitimate children in the ecclesiastical and secular courts. The financial responsibility for these children was laid firmly at the door of both parents. As the early modern period progressed, Quarter Session maintenance records indicate that it was common practice for one of three outcomes to occur: the father was to keep the child at his own expense; the father was to keep the child but be paid maintenance by the mother; or a third party was to keep the child with both parents, where possible, contributing towards its board and lodging.[92] The mother keeping the child and being paid maintenance was also an outcome, although the practice of a child remaining with its mother in early modern England was not as commonplace as it is today. As the child became older, it could work alongside its father with the father receiving the child's wage in addition to his own.[93] Poorer children who were not illegitimate but whose care was compromised by the lack of a parent also feature within these records.

Mothers of illegitimate children using the courts as means of redress to care for their children were particularly vulnerable. Philippa Maddern makes the point that this group of mothers was inevitably dependent on the fathers of their children having the income as well as the desire to offer them support.[94] Those without resources of their own or the support of a family were left to take desperate measures. Dionisia Wheldrake of Healaugh, Yorkshire, who was described in 1570 as 'a very pore woman not worth xijd.', was fortunate enough to have a brother who 'for conscience sake hath releved her' prior to and during the case she brought against Richard Dobson, the father of her illegitimate child.[95] Jane Pringle of Wistow, Yorkshire, was not so fortunate. She was forced to sell all her clothes to pay for the upkeep of her illegitimate child, her ex-master Henry Sawgeld claimed in 1578 that Jane 'haithe bene driven to greate extermities by bringinge vpp the said childe of hir chargies'.[96] The dire situation of the mother was made all the more poignant as Ralph Bilborough, the father of the child, had the resources to pay for maintenance by way of lands in Wistow for which Henry Sawgeld was prepared to pay £20.

Before the 1576 statute, which directed Justices of the Peace in each town to establish protocols for maintaining illegitimate children, the majority of maintenance suits were heard in the ecclesiastical courts. In 1533, Hugh Whitacre of Padiham in Lancashire was ordered to pay to the chaplain of Padiham 6s. 8d. twice a year for the maintenance of the child he had with Katherine Botheman until the child was ten.[97] At 13s. 4d. per annum this amounts to less than ½d. per day and this was not adequate for survival. Using diet sheets from Bridewell Hospital in London, Ian Archer has estimated that in the 1580s the minimum amount of money needed for food and drink was 1¼d.[98] This amount was slightly less than the 1½d. per day the York authorities thought necessary for survival in 1587, 'under wiche some a poore creator cannot lyve'.[99] Even taking into account the fifty years' time difference and the geographical location, the court at Whalley Abbey where the Padiham case was heard, this grossly underestimated the costs that Katherine Botheman would incur in relation to her illegitimate child, especially as the amount would not alter over the proceeding ten years. The meagre amount awarded to Katherine Botheman was not unusual in the ecclesiastical courts. Maddern has found that church courts systematically underestimated the amounts necessary to support a child. Amounts were low, the duration of the award short and there was little opportunity for them to increase over the allotted period.[100]

Awards from the Quarter Sessions do appear to be higher than those from the church courts although they still underestimate the cost of nurturing a child. David Briggs, who was charged with looking after the illegitimate daughter of Margaret Haworth and Abraham Nuttall in between sittings of the Quarter Sessions in Manchester in 1601, was paid 10s. for the quarter by Nuttall.[101] This amounts to just over the 1¼d. estimated by Archer for dietary requirements alone, and it would be difficult for carers to make any profit from these sums. This brings into question the care the children received. Unscrupulous minders could reduce the amount of food given in order to benefit monetarily from their charges.

Margaret Haworth it seems was a common name, for another Margaret Haworth appeared before magistrates at Ormskirk, Lancashire, the same year swearing that Robert Seddon was the father of her son Thomas. Robert had disappeared and the inhabitants of Prescott were to pay Margaret 20s. a year until he reappeared.[102] Per annum, this was half of what Abraham Nuttall was to pay to David Briggs, which could illustrate that illegitimate children maintained out of the parish purse fared far worse than those maintained by their supposed fathers, or rather that the status of the father had a direct bearing on the sums of maintenance awarded. Abraham Nuttall was described in the court papers as a yeoman and his father, who was to stand surety for him, as a gentleman. Arguably, the court decided that Abraham could afford to pay a more realistic price for fathering a child.

Awards from the parish fund were not consistent across authorities or even the same court (see Table 6.1). The Lancashire Quarter Session court at

Table 6.1 Selection of Maintenance Awards from Lancashire Quarter Session Records
1588–1603

Amount of Maintenance per annum	Number of times awarded	Total over 12 years
6s (and a cow)	1	£3 12s
6s 8d	2	£4
10s	3	£6
13s 4d	5	£8
14s	1	£8 8s
16s	1	£9 12s
17s 4d	2	£10 8s
£1	8	£12
£1 6s 8d	5	£16
£1 10s	2	£18
£1 14s 7d	1	£20 15s
£1 19s	1	£23 8s
£2	3	£24
£2 6s 8d	1	£28
£2 12s	3	£31 4s
Average per annum	£1 4s 9¾d	
Average over 12 years	£14 17s 9d	

Source: LRO, Quarter Session Records, QSR1, 4–6.

Ormskirk that granted Margaret Haworth 20s. per annum, amounting to just
over 4½d. per week, the following year awarded Margaret Toppinge 8d. per
week (34s. 7d. per annum) for her illegitimate daughter and 9d. per week
(39s. per annum) towards the maintenance of Richard Stopford, whose father
was dead and whose mother had absconded.[103] Both amounts suggest that
children maintained by the parish did not always fare worse than those
maintained by their parents. Rates therefore varied, and it is doubtful that the
authorities considered their awards definitive costs of bringing up a child as is
indicated by their terminology in the sources. In 1577, the Mayor of York
gave Thomas and Mary Waite, whose father was in prison, 4d. per week
towards their relief while the parishioners of Huyton had to pay 26s. 8d. per
annum towards the maintenance of Ellen Spencer, the illegitimate daughter of
Robert Spencer, in 1603.[104] It was expected that mothers were to supplement
maintenance through their own labours or funding from family or a third
party.[105] Moreover, the allocation of funds directly to poor children was not
unusual as authorities attempted to address the ongoing affects of poverty.[106]
Courts also acknowledged the precariousness of the lives of these children.

Edward Powle of Pyllin, Lancashire, was ordered in 1601 to pay Agnes Champney 13s. 4d. per annum to maintain his illegitimate daughter Jane until she was twelve, but only if 'the saide Jane soe longe shall lyve'.[107] The death of a child must have cut short many a maintenance order.

In order to calculate the amount it would cost to keep a poor parentally deprived child it is necessary to regard all the awards together. If we discount the award given to Katherine Botheman as excessively small but consider all the maintenance records awarded by the Lancashire Quarter Sessions included in this study, then the average per annum would be £1 4s. 9¾d (see Table 6.1). This is below Erikson's estimate of £4 per annum for a pauper child and even below Wrightson and Levine's estimate of £1 10s. So, what sort of nurture did the court expect to be provided for such low premiums? For Wrightson and Levine, their estimate included food and drink only and it is more than likely that these basics were all that were budgeted for by the Lancashire Quarter Sessions. The parent awarded custody and maintenance of the child was expected to keep the child in 'meate drinke cloath and lodginge' but there is no indication that provision was made for anything else such as learning.[108] As the Quarter Sessions were not even giving the minimum identified for food and drink by Wrightson and Levine, it is probable that the awards were made on the basis that they covered only the absolute basics of food and drink, and that other people were expected to contribute to the upkeep of the child.

Table 6.1 confirms the average amount a poorer, and in the main illegitimate, child was thought to cost by the secular authorities, although in some cases the courts enforced only a contribution. Despite the average of the monies awarded being £1 4s. 9¾d., the amount most often awarded by the courts was just £1. This was approximately ⅔d. per day, much less than the 1½d. the York authorities thought a 'pore creator' needed to survive. The story is the same for the highest second most frequently awarded amount and, although higher at £1 6s. 8d., still works out to less than 1d. per day. Even the highest award of £2 12s. only just limps past the York estimate. But, as this table only represents poorer children, can we assume that as the status of the child increased there was also a discernible increase in the amount of money paid for that child?

Parentally deprived children were often cared for by way of private agreements but this did not necessarily mean that the children and families involved were what could be termed wealthy. If for any reason these arrangements broke down, parties from both sides of the agreement would turn to the courts to recoup their costs. Most often, squabbles over monies in regards to children were aired in the Chancery court. Unlike the Church and secular courts, disputes in the Chancery court concerned only the money that had been allegedly paid or withheld. It was not concerned about the nurture of the child or its living arrangements and any information on the same was unintentional information arising from the plaintiff's or defendant's statements.

Often, family or friends placed children in the homes of unrelated adults. Francis Bothe, who was described in a Chancery petition, *c.* 1550, as a child and a kinsman of John Bothe (probably an orphan or maybe even John Bothe's illegitimate son), was placed with John and Agnes Styles in Chester. For ten years or more Mr and Mrs Styles provided for Francis in sickness and health, supplying him with meat, drink and clothes. For this service, John Bothe had promised to pay John and Agnes and others 12d. weekly (£2 12s. per annum). At his death, John Bothe owed a debt of £26 to the Styles, which he had promised to deliver when he was alive but never did. The amount offered by John Bothe was higher than amounts most often offered by the courts and perhaps a more realistic reflection of the cost of keeping a child. However, although more than double the average payment awarded by the secular courts, this amount was still just over 1½d. a day and therefore similar to the basic amount required to survive estimated by the York authorities. The fact that the Styles agreed to look after Francis for this amount and then do so for ten years without actually receiving payment would appear to signal an emotional or economic attachment on their part in regards to the child. The ages of the couple were not recorded and it is feasible that they took in Francis as insurance in their old age to help with household chores and even to be set to work when he reached a useful age.[109]

Elsewhere in the Chancery petitions, pleadings indicate that family stepped in to offer homes to orphaned children, although the cost of care was sometimes a contentious issue. Eleanor Copydale lived with her brother Edmund near York for twelve years before her marriage. She must have been quite young when she arrived in Edmund's household and she did not appear to have any provision left for her upkeeping in a parent's or relative's will. Edmund maintained his sister 'uppon truste & promyse' that Eleanor would pay him back all the charges he had incurred on her behalf. Edmund claimed the sum of thirty pounds for her board and lodging from her husband for 'apperell and other charges'.[110] At £2 10s. per annum this was marginally less than promised for Francis Bothe. In reality, the cost of keeping Eleanor would have been greater than the amount claimed by her brother. Edmund said the debt was £30 or 'yerely iij li', which would make the total for twelve years actually £36, but often when family looked after children they absorbed some of the costs themselves.[111] Maybe this was the case for Francis Bothe as well, but it seems unlikely and it does appear that there was a sort of 'sliding scale' of the worth of a parentally deprived child dependent on its social status. The higher the social standing of the family, the higher the costs claimed for the child.

Care arrangements for orphaned children could sometime prove contentious. After the death of her parents when she was a baby *c*. 1530, Frances Aungell of Yorkshire was placed into the household of her maternal grandfather, William Hungat, esquire. For keeping Frances 'aswell in mete & drynke as clothes & other charges', William was promised the sum of £4 per annum from Roger Wilberforce, executor of Frances's father's will, and money for the 'advanncement of the mariage' of Frances. William kept Frances for six years but he did not receive any payment from Wilberforce and petitioned the Chancery court to recoup his costs.[112] The sum of £4 per year for her upkeep was £1 8s. more than the amount paid for Francis Bothe approximately ten years later. While we may look to the social standing of the family as an explanation of the difference in cost, the amount promised by Wilberforce still hovers beneath the £5 considered adequate to keep a child who was not a pauper. We could surmise that William absorbed costs in relation to Frances both because she was his granddaughter and because he knew he would make a profit from the money for her marriage. Even a child from a wealthy family who was not sent out to work could be economically attractive to their families or carers.

None of the monetary examples given above can be shown to definitively outline the cost of bringing up a parentally deprived child in sixteenth-century northern England. What they do allow us to do is to make an estimate of that basic cost. The average amount a poorer illegitimate child, was thought by the secular authorities to cost over twelve years was £14 17s. 9d. For the wealthier parentally deprived child, if we take the mid-range of provision claimed in the cases of Francis Bothe and Eleanor Copydale of approximately 12d. per week, then the total cost of maintaining a child of this status for twelve years would be £31 4s. This is equal to the highest award listed in the selection of maintenance awards from the Lancashire Quarter Sessions shown in Table 6.1, but much higher than the average of these awards. The discrepancy between £31 4s. and £14 17s. 9d., reflects the amount and type of support to be provided for each child in accordance with the wealth of its family. Privileged families like that of Frances Aungell provided greater support again and thus the average amount was higher still. As all the examples above demonstrate, funding the care of the parentally deprived child was at best complicated and at worst litigious.

Provisions made by parents

To what extent could parents and guardians make provision for children to meet the costs of bringing up a child in the event of separation? Realistically, this is a question that only applies to wealthier children but nonetheless, it is important to establish the ways and means families provided for their children's future nurturing, if they were able to do so.

Families who had been separated through the death of a parent nevertheless hoped their children would prosper in the same manner as those from two-parent families.[113] Notwithstanding this desire, parentless children were vulnerable to exploitation by those charged with their care. In 1486, the executors of William Ronsson's will took out a bond for misappropriation of money left for the upbringing of William's sons John and Nicholas by the appointed carers of the two boys.[114] Care arrangements appeared complicated, with each boy being cared for by a different person and all the executors of the will made accountable for the boys' upbringing. The carers do not appear to have been related to John and Nicholas but relatives are mentioned who are to 'remove hymm from the kepyng and fyndyng' of the carer when it pleased them.[115] This caveat ensured that the relatives could intervene had they considered William's sons not to be receiving adequate care. To pay for this care, the goods and chattels of William had been sold and each carer received £8 13s. 4d., the interest from which was to pay for the children's upkeep. If the child was removed from their carers or worse still died, the money was to be given 'to the next ffryndes and kynesfolk of the said childe'.[116] Although the interest would vary, the initial amount does not appear to be great enough to generate a suitable income for the care of the boys. The guardians of children were expected to invest the monies of the children they cared for, and it would seem that they expected a high interest rate in return.[117] The Court of Orphans in Medieval London used orphans' assets as a commercial loan fund for which they expected a return of 10 per cent.[118] Even at 10 per cent, the yearly interest on £8 13s. 4d. would amount to 17s. 4d., less than the yearly average awarded by the Lancashire Quarter Sessions. So, although not articulated in the wording of the bond, perhaps the sense of the arrangement was that the children were supported out of the profit of any lands. At least the executors had meticulously recorded the procedures to be followed by carers. Not all bequests were monitored so efficiently.

Orphaned children were often at the mercy of their guardians. Sometime before 1544, Richard Joyce of Shropshire left £10 in his will towards the care and marriage of his infant daughter Jane. It was entrusted to her brother John, with whom Jane lived alongside John's wife for the space of seven years. Unfortunately, the petition, lodged by Jane's other brothers, Thomas, Edward and Robert, gives few details of the care Jane received from John, except to say that 'by the meanes of misorder ... the said ynfant thereby was inforste to steale awaie and so dyed'.[119] Quite why a child of under seven would need to 'steale awaie' as in hide away or perhaps run away, which would ultimately lead to her death, we can never know and we should conclude that it is not concrete evidence of cause of death. Jane's treatment only comes to light because John had died and the brothers were trying to reclaim the £10 from his widow and her new husband. There is no suggestion that the brothers had been concerned for Jane's welfare while she had lived in John's household, but what this case does demonstrate is that, despite parents providing for their children in their will, it did not ensure the nurture and well-being of the child no matter how many concerned relatives the child had.

Provision specified in wills could be viewed as a reflection of the emotional attachment that parents felt for their children in addition to the realisation that 'care' had to ensure a child's future as well as immediate well-being. As discussed in Chapter 4, William Hockenhall of Prenton, Cheshire, left instructions for his wife to bring up his daughters 'in good norture & education'.[120] For this purpose he left his wife £3 6s. 8d. per annum. The education of children was of concern to parents particularly the informal agencies such as familial education and this was almost certainly the education that William Hockenhall's daughters would have received. Formal education was more limited but bequests in wills illustrate that some children benefitted from the educational opportunities of the period. In 1563 Adam Bank of Wigan left money for his younger son Thomas to go to school and thereafter be put 'to his occupacon of the Pewterers Crafte wherbie he may be able to get his lyvinge'.[121] Equipping a child for adult life was a costly business and one that required funds from parents whether they were alive or dead. The costs involved in bringing up a parentally deprived child in the period in question would thus vary depending upon the wealth and status of the parents, both alive and dead, or the adult giving the care.

It was not uncommon for illegitimate children to be provided for in their father's or a relative's will, a reminder that illegitimacy was not always associated with poverty. Notwithstanding, this was not an occurrence that was typical of the lives of the majority of illegitimate children whose mothers struggled to extract maintenance out of the fathers of their children when they were alive, let alone dead. In 1551, Richard Legh of Swinehead, Cheshire, left to his illegitimate daughter Joan an in-calf heifer that his wife was to deliver to her 'within two years next after the date thereof'.[122] Piers Daniell, who had five illegitimate children, left money and land to his illegitimate son John in 1522 but land only to his other illegitimate son and three daughters.[123] However, just because the provision has been made for illegitimate children, it did not necessarily follow that the children received the intended legacy. Alice Fetcher petitioned Chancery sometime between 1515 and 1529 to persuade the brother of John Pyke, the father of her children, to allocate them the money and goods John had left to his children in his will. Alice required the money and the profit from the goods to help her raise her children describing them as 'beyng but yong and tender of age not able to helpe theme selfe'.[124] Their father had clearly intended the children to be maintained in a similar manner to how they would have been cared for if he were alive.

Legacies left in wills for illegitimate children reflect the fathers' desires for their illegitimate children to have the same sort of family structure and opportunities that their legitimate families would have. A father, as one lawyer noted, would employ 'a faithful care and providence to advance everye of his children according to his Abilitie with some small porcion of lyvinge or substance'.[125] Just as Adam Bank wished his son to be apprenticed to enable him to make a living, Piers Daniell provided the means of a living to his illegitimate children by leaving them land. As Wrightson argues, the obligations of fathers to provide for their children extended even to those who were yet to be born,[126] and this included illegitimate offspring.

It was not always possible for fathers to provide for their unborn illegitimate children as they sometimes died before arrangements were made by them to include the children in their will. Roger Ticle of Prescott, Lancashire, had already made his last will and testament when he discovered that Katherine Forstar was carrying his child. He called on his kinsman Thomas Ticle to discuss the problem of the child. Roger became too sick to continue the discussion, telling Thomas that he would resume the conversation another time. Unfortunately, Roger died before he could do this and Katherine's child was not mentioned in the will. The brothers of Katherine Forstar subsequently asked Thomas Ticle to 'take the said childe … off the said Katerine and to norisshe it vpp off the goodis off the said Roger ticle'. The case came before the ecclesiastical courts in 1551 as Thomas refused to take the child because 'itt was not expressed in the will off the said Roger ticle that yt he shuld so do'.[127] Death did not free a parent from maintaining their illegitimate children, with executors sometimes having to manipulate deceased estates to provide funds for the care of the child.[128] Be that as it may, Thomas Ticle's reaction to Katherine Forstar's family's request for maintenance of her illegitimate child with Roger Ticle demonstrates the difficulties experienced by mothers of illegitimate children whose fathers had died. Those mothers without the means to challenge the will of the father of their child would always struggle to provide adequate maintenance for their families. Noticeably, provision in wills took into account that dependent children would have a home in accordance with the wishes of the testator or through the involvement of the executors. However, this was not the case for all parentally deprived children and, for a number of illegitimate children, their custody appears to have been a contentious issue.

Disputed authority

Where were children placed in cases of disputed authority or absence of both parents? Just as provision left in wills was primarily the preserve of wealthier parentally deprived children, then this question relates almost exclusively to illegitimate poorer parentally deprived children.

Care arrangements for poor illegitimate children were defined by the court alongside the amount of maintenance to be paid for them and by whom. When the child was very young it was often left with the mother. Alice Facett, a widow, was told by the judge at the ecclesiastical court at Whalley, Lancashire, in 1532 that she was to support her child until the father was known. Alice subsequently failed to purge herself of the charge by compurgation so the judge told Alice to 'to feed the child from her breast until better knowledge of the father had been obtained under penalty of law'.[129] At other times, custody was split between the parents, with the father receiving the child after it had been weaned. In 1601, Jane Southworth from Wrightington in Lancashire was ordered to keep her illegitimate daughter Alice for two years and then hand the care over to the father, who would keep the child until she was twelve.[130] The following year, Jenet Wyldman was ordered to keep her son John for a year, with the father receiving the child at Bentham Church, Lancashire, a year after that.[131] What these provisions amount to is that the mother was essentially paid to wet-nurse the child until it was weaned. Thereafter, she lost all rights and responsibility of custody. Nurture for these children, therefore, was considered to entail living with the parent who could best support the child economically regardless of their ability to physically care for the child.

Grandparents became carers of illegitimate children in cases of disputed authority, primarily because they may have allowed their own child to evade the responsibility and cost of parenthood.[132] Ellen Astley from Westleigh, Lancashire, who had left her illegitimate son John, 'to be kepte at the charges of the parish where yt was borne', was ordered to look after John in 1602 for one year, with the father, Roger Renakers, paying her 20s.[133] Thereafter, Richard Renakers, Roger's father, was to keep the child until he turned ten years old. Grandparents also became sureties for their children's illegitimate offspring, ensuring that the maintenance set by the courts would be paid regardless of the parent's ability to do so, as Richard Mawdesley found to his cost in 1601. He was obliged to pay 6s. 8d. arrears to the constable of Darwin, Lancashire, for the illegitimate child of his son who had failed to keep up the instalments of the 40s. per annum he was ordered to pay in maintenance by the courts.[134]

The underlying tenet of the court in regards to the child was establishing who should house and feed them. Financial accountability was paramount in the court's decision, and there does not appear to be any concern for the child's educational or emotional welfare. The authorities merely strove to curtail the number of people who required relief and, in so doing, ease the stain on parish budgets.[135] Notwithstanding, authorities recognised that mothers had to earn their own living, often as a servant, and employers were reluctant to support illegitimate children.[136] In this scenario, the authorities would see the need to remove the child from the mother or provide alternative support. However, just because a father was ordered by the courts to take the child, this did not mean that he would be the caregiver, although he was responsible for the costs.

Fathers often accepted the responsibility for a child but relinquished the care to other adults. Thomas Peeres was instructed to take the child he had supposedly fathered with Jane Umfrey by the Archdeacon of Cleveland when it was two months old at Whitsuntide 1569. Peeres first placed the child with a wet nurse, and after it was weaned gave it to Robert Johnson and his wife, who were to bring it up 'vntil yt Cam to the age that yt shoulde be hable to be put to an occupacion'.[137] This would probably be about the age of twelve, or younger if it were a poor child. For this service, Peeres was to pay the Johnsons £3, of which he stated that he had given them 9s. 6d. in part payment. According to Thomas Peeres, after about three weeks Jane Umfrey forcibly took the child from the Johnsons and had looked after it up to the date of the court case in 1571. Jane gave a different story, telling how Peeres did not pay the Johnsons – a couple so poor they lived off charity – the amount he stated to the court. She claimed that the Johnsons had brought the child to her mother's house and had begged Jane and her mother to keep it, adding that the child was dressed in rags and 'pittifully burnt vpon the breast'.[138] Jane said that she tried to persuade Johnson's wife to take back the child because her mother was 'so grevid at the leving of the chylde in her house'.[139]

The reaction of Jane's mother, Margaret Smithson, is significant in understanding the disputed authority in regards to the child. Jane came from a comfortable home which employed a number of servants and financially the family could have looked after the child. In this respect, Jane was an exception among the mothers of parentally deprived children who petitioned the courts for maintenance and care of their child. The shame and the social stigma attached to illegitimacy in the sixteenth century must have contributed to the decision to make the father responsible for the care of the child. Jane had obviously wanted to keep the child describing herself as being full of 'motherly pity'. She did manage to have her child for a time as the Johnsons refused to take it back despite being offered payment by Jane to do so, during which time Peeres was away from home fighting in the Rising of the North.[140] The reunion of mother and child was short lived for as soon as Peeres obtained his pardon Jane's brother Germayne demanded that Peeres take the child from Jane and her mother and compensate them for the costs incurred when looking after the child. The welfare of the child, in this case at least, appears secondary to that of the reputation of the family.

The amount paid by Peeres to the Johnsons was woefully inadequate to keep a child for ten years or more: £3 over ten years amounts to less than 1½d. per week. There was of course, no control over the amount paid by individuals in private maintenance transactions. Awards from the courts on the whole appear to have been inadequate, but we can infer from the records that the courts at least had a moral as well as practical duty to conform to a certain expectation of what a particular child was entitled to, and to place that child with suitable carers. The Johnsons were described as 'beggers' and the libel specifically asked if they were 'meete persons' to bring up the child 'seing the said child was so eyvell kept and they so vnable to keepe yt'.[141] It seems that both the authorities and Jane Umfrey recognised neglect as a phenomenon of childcare as the child was dressed in rags and badly burned. There may also have been a concern that the Johnsons were so poor they could not feed the child adequately. It would not be extreme to suggest that it was the child as a resource and not the payment that was attractive to the Johnsons. The ability of the child to contribute to the household economy as it grew older was essential to the survival of many poor families.[142]

Peeres at least took the child as he was ordered, even if his choice of carers was less than adequate for the child. Yet not all fathers were willing to comply with court orders that allocated them sole care for their illegitimate offspring with some going to extreme measures to avoid the responsibility. Despite a citation from the church courts ordering John Gowton to take his illegitimate child from the mother, Agnes Denton, he 'utterly refused' to do so, subsequently fleeing his home in Whorlton, Yorkshire.[143] When located in the service of a Mr Bowser at Beningborough, 36 miles away, John told Agnes that if she caused any more actions to be served upon him he would flee to London. Gowing describes this as the 'precariousness of paternity' whereby men were only too ready to deny their part in relation to the child, unable as they were to accept the household authority imposed upon them by the courts.[144] As a servant, John would not have had a house in which to place the child even if he did want to take it and, as with single mothers, employers were often reluctant to house illegitimate children of their servants. Agnes had to petition the Archbishop of York to enforce the order, telling him that she had tried many times to have John 'tayke the said childe and to educate and bring vp the same with meate drinke clothe and other necessaties'. In the meantime, she had looked after the child at her own cost, 'whereby she is vtterlie impoverisshed and like to be beggered'.[145]

Bringing a case before the courts was always a last resort and many mothers attempted to persuade the fathers of their illegitimate children to take the child without secular or ecclesiastical intervention. Around 1540, Margaret Moreland had given birth to an illegitimate child fathered by her master Raphe Davidson, a married man, and her father had initially refused to take her into his house at Sedgefield in the north-east of England. However, he must have relented because a witness stated that the baby lived at Sedgefield for a year, after which time 'it was carried in a shawl by Margaret and her brother Anthony Moreland to Raphe at Bewly Grange, and there Raphe brought him up as his bastard son'.[146] Although some historians argue that many men brought their illegitimate children home to their mothers or wives to be brought up alongside their own children, this argument is not upheld on the evidence of families featured in this study.[147] Raphe Davidson appears as an anomaly among the records and even the acceptance of Margaret's child was not without its problems. A witness told the church court that Raphe Davidson's wife would not suffer her husband's illegitimate child to be brought up in her house, which may explain the delay of a year before Raphe took the child.[148] Alternatively, perhaps the delay was due to the fact that the baby would have been weaned after a year or so and thus be less of an economic drain to the father and his marital household.

Of those men unwilling to take in their illegitimate child, some were still willing to pay for them, as Elena Mason testified to the church court in Durham. Elena, whose child was fathered by her master, John Eden, was sent to Robert Wright's house to have her child. When the child was born it was given to one of Wright's daughters to care for, with the costs being met by Eden.[149] Both Margaret Moreland and Elena Mason were fortunate in ensuring that their children would be looked after, but, for many children, adequate nurture was only obtained through many and varied interactions between agencies and individuals within the community.

Parental survival expedients

What survival expedients were employed by parents and guardians in relation to parentally deprived children? The effects of parental deprivation were not uniform and thus the choices families had to make to provide nurture for their children varied accordingly. As we have seen, wealthier parentally deprived children were insulated from the effects of losing a parent by provisions in wills, inheritance and the ability of a mother to remarry a man of similar wealth and status to that of her deceased husband. For poorer parentally deprived children, these strategies were not an option and so alongside every other poor household in sixteenth-century northern England they supplemented their income by a number of expedients.

Begging, as Steve Hindle argues, was the most established survival expedient available to the poor in early modern England.[150] Both secular and ecclesiastical authorities understood that begging was intrinsic to the survival of their poorer citizens and many towns attempted to control it through regulations. Chester assigned all needy and mendicant people to a specific ward within the town where they were to beg. Householders in these wards were given a bill with licensed beggars' names on it to identify to whom to give alms.[151] Measures like this, however, meant that begging was only tolerated and not accepted. Reference to begging in earlier Lancashire Quarter Sessions maintenance records, written in Latin, are unclear as to whether it is the mother or the child who is not to beg, stating only 'ita quod interim non mendicabit'. The message, however, is clear: the child is not to be sustained through begging.[152] Later entries written in English state that it is the child that is not to beg, but evidence from other parts of the country demonstrates the benefits of begging to single mothers. Grace Martyn, originally from Cornwall, was found begging in the streets of Salisbury in 1598 and was ordered to leave the city within a month and to take her three children with her, all of whom were under seven years old.[153] Without a support network of family and friends, begging offered Grace a realistic means of obtaining relief.

Begging at least allowed the mother to maintain the child in her own family, but at times the best way to provide care for a child was in the household of others. Margaret Pelling has highlighted the practice of fatherless children living with the elderly poor or infirm.[154] In this reciprocal arrangement the elderly provided lodgings for the child while the child was able to carry out tasks the elderly were unable to do. Often orphaned or illegitimate children were placed into the households of masters by the parish, with the cost of the care of the child being met by the master. The child would have the benefit of an authoritative household and the householder could set them to work and thereby profit from the labours of the child.[155] Agnes Harwood of Salisbury was only six years old when she was apprenticed to a knitter with 'her master to have the work'.[156] Evidence is lacking of parish officials placing children into homes for this study, but it is apparent that the poor made arrangements with other people of similar social standing to give support to children from outside their family.

Quarter Session petitions in Chester show that in many households adults were looking after children that were not their own. In 1590, John Johnson petitioned the mayor of Chester to be excused from paying the poor rate because he 'dothe kepe a fatherless child not vnknowne'.[157] This setting was repeated in other households. Laurence Robenson of Chester described himself in 1575 as a 'power mane' without a farm or tenement to enable him to pay the increase in the poor rate from 1d. to 2d. Despite his relative poverty, he had kept a fatherless child for the past six years to his 'great cost and charges' in addition to his own children and a 'litell wenche' of his brother's.[158] In the same year, a Chester butcher claimed that he could not pay the poor rate as he was 'burthenid with the kepinge of an infant' he had kept for the last three years, for whom he paid for 'meate drincke clothes, and also learnynge'. Apart from the boy, he also bore the great costs of his own children. He hoped that the mayor would discharge him from paying the rate in consideration of keeping the child, stating that if this was not to be, then 'it might please yowe to take the saied childe awaye' and the butcher would continue to pay his contributions each month.[159] There is no indication of whether the butcher's petition succeeded, but it must be concluded that the mayor and the municipal authorities had the better part of the bargain. If they had to remove the child from the butcher it would cost them considerably more to re-house the child with another family than it received from his poor rate contributions.

Formal poor relief had been established at varying rates across England in the sixteenth century. York had introduced the collection of poor rates by 1550 while Chester had established a similar system by 1567[160] and contemporary writers heralded the benefits of such a scheme. Robert Allen, the late sixteenth-century religious writer, believed prescribed poor relief to be necessary 'as well to set the poore to worke, as to contribute to their reliefe, so farre as they shall furthermore be found to stand in neede'.[161] When paid employment and strategies like begging were insufficient to provide the basics for parentally deprived families, appeals to the authorities for an allocation from the poor relief coffers were often the next resort.

Katherine Robenson, a widow who had lived in Chester for 'thre score yeares', her widowed daughter, Anne Matha, and Anne's three small children all lived in Katherine's house in Chester. In 1584, she petitioned the mayor in the hope 'that you of youre goodnessse will be good vnto vs'.[162] The family were, Katherine said, in 'grete nede' and unless the mayor could help them they were 'lyke to be famyshed for wante of fode'. Katherine was no doubt conversant with the existence of poor relief in Chester as she requested the mayor give her family 'sum parte or porcion of the charite gevin vnto the poore of this citie'. In York, Kathryn Pape, 'a poor wenshe whiche hath hir fete almost rotted of' received 12d. every week for five weeks in January 1579. The relief was paid from 5s. of fines received from those persons not attending church and was to continue until the amount was used up 'if she do not recover or die in the meane tyme'.[163]

Katherine Robenson's and Kathryn Pape's situations highlight the problem of life-cycle poverty. Many people were able to support themselves and their families for the most part, but at particular times in their lives had to rely on poor relief. As Tim Wales puts it, those who applied for poor relief were the 'victims of the breakdown of the household economy'.[164] Katherine Robenson was too old to work, her grandchildren too young and her daughter was either un- or under-employed. Kathryn Pape was young and possibly parentless with an infirmity that stopped her from providing for her own nurture.[165] Katherine Robenson's petition does not reveal how the family had managed financially up until the time of the petition, only stating about herself that 'beyenge aged' she was 'not abull to do ani towardes the gettinge of our lyvinge'. No doubt her daughter had worked when she could and it is possible the family were the recipients of neighbourly charity. Her application to the mayor suggests that Kathryn and her daughter did not receive regular relief from the city and that the relief, if granted, would be only one of a number of options taken by them to support themselves and the children including casual labour, charity hand-outs, neighbourly assistance and begging.[166] None of these strategies could be relied upon permanently and at times of extreme distress some single-parent families were unable physically or financially to care for their children. They adopted drastic measures by which they relinquished responsibility for the welfare of their children, ensuring that their survival was dependent on unrelated adults through practices such as abandonment.

Children's contributions to nurture

What part did the children themselves play in the provision of their own nurture? Mothers without a husband or a source of income and small children to support were hampered in their search for work by childcare costs. Women were limited in their choice of employment and few earned enough to pay for childcare.[167] In most cases, children became a source of income for these families, contributing to their own keep and thereby their own nurture, supplemented by the labours of their remaining parent and siblings. Children's capacity to earn money for their parents as they became older reduced the amount of relief or maintenance that child required. This fact could be offered as an explanation as to why maintenance awards from the ecclesiastical and secular courts remained static throughout their tenure.

Archer contends that children were rarely an economic asset to the family before they were ten years old.[168] Yet the Norwich census of the poor revealed that young children were often put to work to earn their keep. The widow Anne Bucke, who was described as 'veri pore', had two children aged five and nine who 'worke lace', while both children of Joan Burges, deserted by her husband, knitted, the eldest being only eight.[169] The 1625 employment survey of the poor for Salisbury confirmed similar arrangements for poorer children. Mary, the six-year-old daughter of Margaret Moodye, was set to bone-lace making for two years by the overseers of St Edmund's Parish, while her mother was to receive 6d. weekly in return.[170] Whilst records of young children engaging in paid work other than apprenticeship were not found for this study, the ability for the parentally deprived child to generate income through begging was apparent in many of the records.

Children sent out to beg were a common sight in sixteenth-century England and often it was the best option for income by people overburdened with children. In Newcastle upon Tyne, the widow of Gilbert Bulman not only had her own children to look after but also those of Edward Bulman (possibly her brother-in-law). Although she had remarried, her situation was such that all the children 'goeth begging', much to the dismay of the ecclesiastical authorities in 1565.[171] Secular authorities were also aware that children were sent out to beg. Those who had been awarded maintenance by the Lancashire Quarter Sessions were ordered not to beg and this stipulation was given without exception in all maintenance awards regardless of the age of the child. Apparent in this proviso is a dichotomy of the importance of begging to the family economy and the authorities' dislike of the act, emphasising the economic value of children within poor families.

Contemporary commentators were quick to condemn the practice of sending children out to beg. Many believed the majority of children to be illegitimate, with their parents purposefully disfiguring them to appeal to people's compassion.[172] Nevertheless, the profit of a parentally deprived child's labours through begging was not confined to the family in which the child lived. Parentless children – and certainly those who appeared to be without a caring adult to look after them – were attractive to certain adults who profited from the begging of these children. Civic authorities in sixteenth-century York moved to ban their poorer citizens from profiting in this way by stating that 'none of the said power folks shall take nor receyve any strange chyldren into ther houses to thent that any of them shall goe abowte within this Citie to begg'.[173] Those strange children already resident within poor families were to be turned out of the house within the next eight days or the householders would 'be avoyded this Citie'.[174]

Stories of children being found in the company of unrelated adults were a common occurrence in all parts of England in the sixteenth century. In 1602, the ten-year-old son of Joan Reynolds, John, was found to be in the company of one Simon Tucke and his wife in addition to a woman called Olive Hallame in Salisbury, Wiltshire. Parish officials ordered that he should return to Devizes, where his mother lived, a distance of 21 miles. Simon Tucke and his wife were ordered back to their hometown of Kingston, Dorset, while Olive Hallame was ordered back to Bristol, both places being 40 miles or more away from John's home town.[175] John's situation highlights the economy in the begging of children, not only to adults but also to the children themselves in providing for their own nurture. In addition, their peripatetic lifestyle suggests that a network of beggars operated around the country, picking up children along the way, supported by local people in the towns in which they begged. At Lancashire Quarter Sessions at Preston in 1603, Ralph Eives, a husbandman of Fishwick, Lancashire, was charged with entertaining 'pedlers, tyncklers, and wandring people'.[176]

There is also the possibility that John was not 'kidnapped' by the Tuckes, or given by his mother, but went of his own volition in an attempt to provide for himself and relieve the burden on his mother. However, while it was necessary for poor children to find some occupation that would supply them with bed and board, they would have had a narrow choice as to which one they adopted. That choice would always be influenced by an ongoing relationship with adults, and, like the strange children of York, not necessarily their parents. Any agency children may have had was constrained by this relationship with significant others. The York authorities were keen to emphasise that it was lawful to take in and give relief to any child that was born in the city, but unscrupulous adults could just as easily send local children out to beg alongside strange ones. Officials did not appear to be concerned about the whereabouts of the parents of the strange children or of their geographical origins except to know where to send them back to. Andrew Hogeson, a 'poore boye', was given 10s. by the York Chamberlains in 1585 to enable him to travel to his brother in Bamburgh, Northumberland, with the instructions 'not to retourne hither agayne'.[177]

Many children like Andrew Hogeson appeared to be alone in towns and villages without an appropriate adult to supervise them. In 1599, Maud Preece told a magistrate that she was 'of a verie tender age' when she was brought to Chester four or five years previously and was 'left behind'.[178] So young was Maud that she did not remember who had brought her to the city. We may therefore assume that at the time of the examination by the magistrate she would not have been more than about twelve years old. She was not an infant who required wet-nursing and so did not attract parish intervention and, being one of the 'strange' children that the York authorities had warned their poorer citizens about, did not evoke community spirit in the Cestrian families nearby. Instead Maud had to provide for herself in various ways. She survived by receiving alms from charitable people and living in a number of strange households, first in the house of John Morgan, second in the house of Elizabeth O'Bryne, who had since married John Taylor, most recently in the house of Margery Hancuckes (Hancock) and sometimes with Margret ap Shone Goughe at the latter's sister's house near the castle. Maud was exploited in at least one of these houses and used as petty thief. She explained to the magistrate that she had stolen the hat that was in her possession from John Morgan's house under the instructions of Margaret ap Shone, who did 'entyce and encoured her to doe the said deel'.[179] In fact, Margaret had told the girl to bring her all she could get and Maud admitted to taking things from the houses of two other men. In exchange for the ill-gotten gains, Maud believed that Margaret would relieve her from time to time, a story hotly disputed by Margaret, who said she knew Maud only by sight. The only thing that Maud had brought her, Margaret told the magistrate, was an iron hook that Maud had found on a midden.

What is obvious here is the mobility and uncertainty of Maud's living arrangements. It is not even clear that the person who brought her to Chester in the first place was a parent and it is possible that she had been abandoned outside the city and brought in by an adult to help them beg. Once there, she had to rely on the charity of people she did not know and move from house to house, each household varying in its residential make-up. We have no record of what happened to Maud after her examination by the magistrate and only her word for how she lived up until then. What we do know is that she remained under the radar of the authorities and there must have been many like Maud in Chester and other cities in sixteenth-century northern England. The underlying implication here is the perceptions of life stages that the authorities had of these children. Up until the age of four or five they needed to be cared for by the parish, but after that they could fend for themselves.

Materially, Maud had to provide for herself by stealing and foraging in return for 'relief'. Stealing, for poor children like Maud, was just another skill that would have been taught to her by adults and could be considered part of a child's informal education. It was how poor children survived in a world that would see them in a negative light.[180] It is obvious from her testimony that Maud was streetwise and exercised some agency in her situation. She moved from one house to the next, working out how to survive and forming relationships with adults along the way. However, the adults with whom Maud lived did not take her in out of charity: their interest lay in Maud's usefulness to them. Maud's situation was not unique in Tudor England, as is shown by the description given in Thomas Harman's rogue literature, *A Caveat for Common Cursitors*. Known as Dells, these young girls 'go abroad young, either by the death of their parents and nobody to look unto them, or else by some sharp mistress that they serve do run away out of service'.[181] They then come to the attention of 'the upright man', a con man who survives by exploiting others and criminal acts. John Morgan, in whose house Maud said she first lived, may have been an 'upright man', and we could surmise that the other households in which Maud lived were connected with the underworld. In reality though, there is scant evidence to suggest that crime was organised to such a degree in English cities during the sixteenth century.[182] The actions of Maud and her companions were part of a survival strategy that at other times included begging and working when the opportunity arose.

Conclusion

It is evident that parental deprivation affected a great number of children and families in sixteenth-century northern England, particularly their quality of life. The overriding concern of these families was the economics of caring for their children, with single mothers far more vulnerable and reliant on parish welfare than single fathers.[183] For both families and the authorities alike, there was the importance of placing a child in a surrogate household with its structure of authority. In evaluating the means by which these families supported themselves it is necessary to look past the family as a contained unit able to help themselves and examine what Laslett calls the 'nuclear hardship hypothesis', where death of a parent, sickness, lack of employment and old age require families to seek help from extended family and the community.[184] None of the households discussed in this chapter conforms to the idea of 'nuclear' – a household consisting of two parents and dependent children – but Laslett's underlying theory of hardship assistance can easily be applied.

For all of the children and families featured in this chapter had to rely on family or turn to the community by way of neighbourly assistance, alms, begging, maintenance payments or parish relief in attempts to meet the cost of maintaining a parentally deprived child.

We must acknowledge that, for the most part, any monetary amounts given in this chapter fell below the true cost of maintaining a child. Wealthier children were assured of material comfort by way of inheritance or maintenance from their families. Parents provided the child with the means to experience an upbringing as close as possible to that of being raised in a two-parent household. Poorer parents and carers, however, were compelled to adopt a number of expedients to provide adequate nurture for their children. Requests for poor relief buttressed meagre wages and other unreliable sources of income like begging while orphaned and illegitimate children were to be found living in surrogate households where unrelated adults provided nurture.

Mothers of illegitimate children were at times able to pass the responsibility of nurture on to the putative fathers of their children either through private negotiation or by the directive of the court. Others abandoned the care of their child to the parish. Both practices raise questions about the value emotionally and economically that these parents placed on their children.[185] In spite of this assumption, analysis of these parents' actions expose not uncaring, detached people, but ones in which complex considerations underlie their treatment of their children. Even in such a seemingly negligent act as abandoning a child, a dichotomy of nurture and neglect can be detected in approaches to childcare. Leaving a baby in a place where it would be easily found, as Anne Smyth did in York, was not 'unmotherley' but a caring option taken by a desperate mother. Nevertheless, practicable choices available to despairing parents that would give the child the best chance of survival were not always acceptable to society as a whole.

The children themselves had a part to play in providing for their own nurture depending upon the economic status of their families. For poorer children and their families, life-cycle poverty determined that they would be sent out to work or beg on the streets at an early age. A number of these children came to the attention of the authorities because they were separated from their families. Andrew Hogeson was found in York, over 80 miles away from his brother in Bamburgh, Cleveland, while Maud Preece was unable to remember how she came to be living by herself in Chester as she was so young when she was abandoned. This suggests that children were instrumental in providing for their own nurture even to the point of moving from one town to the next, either by themselves or in the company of unrelated adults, or soliciting relief from local people. In spite of this, we should not take the fact that children had to provide their own nurture as evidence of neglect. Relationships in the late medieval and early modern England were marked by expectations and obligations and not emotional attachment.[186] For poor parentally deprived children, these expectations included being active in providing for their own material needs, a necessity that set them apart from their wealthier counterparts.

The implications of all these arrangements in regards to the concepts of nurture and neglect as they appear in practice in this period are significant. First, predominant is the notion that 'nurture' was seen to comprise only physical care such the provision of food, clothing and housing. Occasionally learning is mentioned, although the context is unclear. At no time is there any reference to protecting or maintaining the emotional well-being of the child. Second, there are suggestions that individuals and authorities did recognise 'neglect', especially in terms of what they thought nurture to be. Where children, like Jane Umfrey's child, were not being fed, housed or clothed properly then this seems to have been read as neglect. Sometimes, recognition of neglect of children spurred the authorities to act in order that they would be 'nurtured', as in the case of Thomas and Mary Waite of York. Of course, some actions looked upon as neglect by authorities – abandonment, for instance – were not read this way by poor parents or carers. This means that the conceptualisation of nurture and neglect that sixteenth-century people had was directly related to wealth and social status. As a consequence, we could argue that there can be no definitive narrative as to what these notions might have been, and it is imperative that we are guided by the context in which the nurture or neglect occurred.

Notes

1   CALSS, QSE/5/123, Examination of Maude Preece in Chester (1599).
2   See LRO, QSR4/54. Agnes Champney was to keep her illegitimate daughter Jane in 'meate drincke cloath and lodging'.
3   Viviana A. Zelizer, *Pricing the Priceless Child: The Changing Social Value of Children* (New York: Basic Books, 1985), p. 3.
4   John F. Pound (ed.), *The Norwich Census of the Poor, 1570* (Norwich: Norfolk Record Society, 1971), p. 56. Widow Elizabeth Willington had a five-year-old child that spun wool.
5   Pound (ed.), *Norwich Census,* p. 56.
6   James Horn (ed.), *Captain John Smith: Writings with other narratives of … the first English Settlement of America* (New York: Library of America, 2007), p. 144.
7   Ivy Pinchbeck and Margaret Hewitt, *Children in English Society,* 2 vols (London: Routledge & Kegan Paul, 1969–73), I, 207.
8   LRO, QSR 4/35d–36.
9   See Chapter 5, p. 148.
10 Peter Laslett, *Family Life and Illicit Love in Earlier Generations* (Cambridge: Cambridge University Press, 1983), pp. 160–73.
11 Lawrence Stone, *The Family, Sex and Marriage in England 1500–1800* (London: Weidenfeld and Nicolson, 1977), pp. 99–102.
12 Lloyd deMause, *Foundations of Psychohistory* (New York: Creative Roots, 1982).
13 Pinchbeck and Hewitt, *Children in English Society,* I, 126–46.
14 Laslett, *Family life,* p. 166. Laslett does not refer to any particular sources here, just 'such evidence as has been surveyed'. He does state that these sources cannot definitely confirm his argument.
15 Nicholas Orme, *Medieval Children* (New Haven, CT: Yale University Press, 2001), pp. 317, 325–7.
16 Patricia Crawford, *Parents of Poor Children in England, 1580–1800* (Oxford: Oxford University Press, 2010), pp. 210–11; Steve Hindle, *On the Parish: The*

Micro-Politics of Poor Relief in Rural England c. 1550–1750 (Oxford: Clarendon Press, 2004), pp. 271–82.

17 Stephanie Tarbin, 'Caring for Poor and Fatherless Children in London, *c.* 1350–1550', *Journal of the History of Childhood and Youth*, 3 (2010), 391–410.

18 Charles Carlton, *The Court of Orphans* (Leicester: Leicester University Press, 1974); Elaine Clark, 'City Orphans and Custody Laws in Medieval England', *American Journal of Legal History*, 34 (1990), 168–87; Pinchbeck and Hewitt, *Children in English Society*, I, 75–90.

19 Clark, 'City Orphans', p. 172.

20 Shulamith Shahar, *Childhood in the Middle Ages* (London: Routledge, 1992), p. 184.

21 See Orme, *Medieval Children*.

22 Alan MacFarlane, 'Illegitimacy and Illegitimates in English history', in P. Laslett, K. Oosterveen and R. Smith (eds), *Bastardy and its Comparative History* (London: Edward Arnold, 1980), pp. 71–85.

23 Richard Wall, Jean Robin and Peter Laslett (eds), *Family Forms in Historic Europe* (Cambridge: Cambridge University Press, 1983).

24 Peter Laslett, 'The Bastardy-Prone Sub-Society', in P. Laslett, K. Oosterveen and R. Smith (eds), *Bastardy and its Comparative History* (London: Edward Arnold, 1980), pp. 217–46; Richard Adair, *Courtship, Illegitimacy and Marriage in Early Modern England* (Manchester: Manchester University Press, 1996), pp. 48–91.

25 Crawford, *Parents of Poor Children*, pp. 112–49.

26 Dave Postles, 'Surviving Lone Motherhood in Early-Modern England', *Seventeenth Century*, 21 (2006), 160–83 (pp. 161–2).

27 P. J. P. Goldberg, *Women, Work and Life Cycle in a Medieval Economy: Women in York and Yorkshire c. 1300–1520* (Oxford: Clarendon Press, 1992).

28 Shahar, *Childhood in the Middle Ages*, p. 121; John Boswell, *The Kindness of Strangers: The Abandonment of Children in Western Europe from Late Antiquity to the Renaissance* (New York: Pantheon, 1988), p. 19, n. 34.

29 Hugh Cunningham, *Children and Childhood in Western Society Since 1500* (London and New York: Longman, 1995), p. 93.

30 Colin Heywood, A *History of Childhood: Children and Childhood in the West from Medieval to Modern Times* (Cambridge: Polity, 2001), pp. 77–82.

31 Tarbin, 'Poor and Fatherless Children', pp. 392–3.

32 Ruth. K. McClure, *Coram's Children: The London Foundling Hospital in the Eighteenth Century* (New Haven, CT: Yale University Press, 1981), pp. 7–9.

33 Alysa Levene, *Childcare, Health and Mortality at the London Foundling Hospital 1741–1800; 'Left to the mercy of the world'* (Manchester: Manchester University Press, 2007), pp. 16–17.

34 Valerie Fildes, 'Maternal Feelings Re-Assessed: Child Abandonment and Neglect in London and Westminster, 1550–1800', in V. Fildes (ed.), *Women as Mothers in Pre-Industrial England* (London and New York: Routledge, 1990), pp. 139–78 (p. 155).

35 Fildes, 'Maternal Feelings', p. 158.

36 Fildes, 'Maternal Feelings', pp. 149–52.

37 Michael Anderson, 'What is New about the Modern Family: A Historical Perspective', in British Society for Population Studies, *The Family* (London, 1983), p. 4 and Fig. 2, p. 5.

38 Adair, *Courtship, Illegitimacy and Marriage*, pp. 48–64.

39 Peter Laslett and Karla Oosterveen, 'Long-term Trends in Bastardy in England: A Study of Illegitimacy Figures in the Parish Registers and in the Reports of the Registrar General, 1561–1960', *Population Studies*, 27 (1973), 255–86 (p. 255).

40 I am inclined to believe that this disparity between the north of England and the rest of the country can be attributed to errors in documentation rather than the actual rate of illegitimacy.

41 Peter Laslett, 'Introduction: Comparing Illegitimacy over Time and between Cultures', in P. Laslett, K. Oosterveen and R. Smith (eds), *Bastardy and its Comparative History* (London: Edward Arnold, 1980), pp. 1–68.

42 See Laslett (*Family Life*, pp. 108–109) for a detailed description of the circumstances that led to a child being classed as illegitimate.

43 P. J. P. Goldberg, 'Marriage, Migration, Servanthood and Life-Cycle in Yorkshire Towns of the Later Middle Ages: Some York Cause Paper Evidence', *Continuity and Change*, 1 (1986), 141–69 (p. 156).

44 BIA, CP.G.1521. This case is discussed in detail below pp. 282–4.

45 R. C. Richardson, *Household Servants in Early Modern England* (Manchester: Manchester University Press, 2010), p. 165.

46 Adair, *Courtship, Illegitimacy and Marriage*, p. 84.

47 DUSC, DDR/EJ/CCD/1/4, fol. 89.

48 DUSC, DDR/EJ/CCD/1/4, fols 91–92ᵛ.

49 Laslett, *Family Life*, p. 160.

50 Laslett, *Family Life*, p. 160.

51 Carlton, *Court of Orphans*, p. 66.

52 Carlton, *Court of Orphans*, pp. 80–1.

53 Jerome Kroll, 'The Concept of Childhood in the Middle Ages', *Journal of the History of the Behavioural Sciences*, 13 (1977), 384–93 (p. 387).

54 Clark, ' City Orphans', p. 168

55 Pinchbeck and Hewitt, *Children in English Society*, I, 75.

56 Rupert H. Morris, *Chester in Plantagenet and Tudor Reigns* (Chester, 1875), p. 547.

57 Susan Dwyer Amussen, *An Ordered Society: Gender and Class in Early Modern England* (New York: Columbia University Press, 1988), p. 1.

58 Crawford, *Parents of Poor Children*, p. 194.

59 TNA, C1/587/55.

60 TNA, C1/565/33.

61 J. A. Twemlow (ed.), *Liverpool Town Books: Proceedings of Assemblies, Common Councils, Portmoot Courts, etc., 1550–1862*, 2 vols (Liverpool: University of Liverpool, 1918–), I: 1550–1571 (1918), 486–7.

62 Twemlow (ed.), *Liverpool Town Books*, I, 488–9.

63 In the sixteenth century, Barrow was in the county of Lancashire.

64 Cumbria Record Office, Kendal, Marriage Settlement, 20 November 31 Elizabeth I WD U/Box/50/1/1.

65 Ariadne Schmidt, 'Survival Strategies of Widows and their Families in Early Modern Holland *c.* 1580–1750', *History of the Family*, 12.4 (2007), 268–81 (p. 270).

66 P. J. P. Goldberg, *Women, Work and Life Cycle in a Medieval Economy: Women in York and Yorkshire c. 1300–1520* (Oxford: Clarendon Press, 1992), p. 313.

67 CALSS, Mayor's Books, ZMB/28a, fol. 67. (Date 1599/1600).

68 Shahar, *Childhood in the Middle Ages*, p. 122.

69 Exodus 2, *The King James' Bible*, available online at www.kingjamesbibleonline.org.

70 Shahar, *Childhood in the Middle Ages*, p. 121.

71 CALSS, QSF/24, fol. 3.

72 EYLA, B27, fol. 27.

73 Fildes, 'Maternal Feelings' p. 153.

74 William Gouge, *Of Domesticall Dvties: Eight Treatises* (London, 1622), p. 507.

75 Fildes, 'Maternal Feelings', p. 153.

76 Laura Gowing, 'Giving Birth at the Magistrate's Gate: Single Mothers in the Early Modern City', in Stephanie Tarbin and Susan Broomhall (eds), *Women, Identities and Communities in Early Modern Europe* (Aldershot: Ashgate, 2008), pp. 137–50 (p. 144–5).

77 DUSC, DCD/D/SJA/1, fol. 73^v.
78 Fildes, *Maternal Feelings*, pp. 148–9.
79 Lola Valverde, 'Illegitimacy and the Abandonment of Children in the Basque Country, 1550–1800', in John Henderson and Richard Wall (eds), *Poor Women and Children in the European Past* (London and New York: Routledge, 1994), pp. 51–64 (p. 61).
80 See below pp. 204–05.
81 Cunningham, *Children and Childhood*, pp. 95–6.
82 Fildes, *Maternal Feelings*, pp. 152–3.
83 Crawford, *Parents of Poor Children*, p. 47.
84 Crawford, *Parents of Poor Children*, p. 126.
85 Liverpool Victoria, *Cost of a Child: From Cradle to College*, 2012 Report, PDF available online at www.lv.com/upload/lv-rebrand-2009/pdf/2014/Janurary/COAC-2014-report.pdf. Accessed 7 December 2015.
86 Amy L. Erikson, *Women and Property in Early Modern England* (London and New York: Routledge, 1993), pp. 50–1.
87 A. E. Bland, P. A. Brown and R. H. Tawney (eds), *English Economic History: Select Documents* (London: G. Bell & Sons, 1925), p. 380.
88 Keith Wrightson and David Levine, *Poverty and Piety in an English Village Terling, 1525–1700* (New York: Academic Press, 1979), p. 40.
89 Erikson, *Women and Property*, p. 51, n. 13.
90 William Stout, *The Autobiography of William Stout of Lancaster, Wholesale and Retail Grocer and Ironmonger, A Member of the Society of Friends AD1665–1752* (ed.) J. Harland (London: Simpkin, Marshall, & Co, 1851), p. 6.
91 Laura Gowing, *Common Bodies: Women, Touch and Power in Seventeenth-Century England* (New Haven, CT: Yale University Press, 2003), p. 193.
92 Walter J. King, 'Punishment for Bastardy in Early Seventeenth-Century England', *Albion*, 10 (1978), 130–51 (p. 131).
93 Snell and Millar, 'Lone-Parent Families', p. 394.
94 Philippa Maddern, '"Oppressed by Utter Poverty": Survival Strategies for Single Mothers and Their children in Late Medieval England', in Anne M. Scott (ed.), *Experiences of Poverty in Late Medieval and Early Modern England and France* (Farnham: Ashgate, 2012), pp. 41–62 (p. 44).
95 BIA, CP.G.1524.
96 BIA, DC.CP.1578/4.
97 Margaret Lynch and others (eds), *Life, Love and Death in North-East Lancashire: A Translation of the Act Book of the Ecclesiastical Court of Whalley* (London: Chetham Society, 2006), p. 203.
98 Ian W. Archer, *The Pursuit of Stability: Social Relations in Elizabethan London* (Cambridge: Cambridge University Press, 1991), pp. 190–1.
99 A. Raine (ed.), *York Civic Records VIII* (Yorkshire Archaeological Society Record Office, 1953), pp. 157–8.
100 Maddern, '"Oppressed by Utter Poverty"', pp. 53–5.
101 LRO, QSR 4/35d.
102 LRO, QSR 4/32.
103 LRO, QSR 5/31d.
104 EYLA, B27, fol. 62^v; LRO, QSR 6/34d.
105 Maddern, '"Oppressed by Utter Poverty"', pp. 56–59.
106 Marjorie K. McIntosh, 'Networks of Care in Elizabethan English Towns: The Example of Hadleigh, Suffolk', in Peregrine Horden and Richard M. Smith (eds), *The Locus of Care: Families, Communities, Institutions, and the Provision of Welfare Since Antiquity* (London and New York: Routledge, 1998), pp. 71–89 (p. 84).
107 LRO, QSR 4/54.

108 This is a common stipulation in the Lancashire Quarter Session Records. See LRO, QSR 4/35d–36, the case of James Meyall and Isabel Crompton.

109 See Margaret Pelling, 'Old Age, Poverty, and Disability in Early Modern Norwich: Work, Remarriage, and Other Expedients', in Margaret Pelling and Richard M. Smith (eds), *Life, Death and the Elderly: Historical Perspectives* (London and New York: Routledge, 1991), pp. 74–101 (esp. pp. 85–7).

110 TNA, C1/397/29. (Date 1515–1529).

111 Erikson, *Women and Property*, pp. 50–1.

112 TNA, C1/810/9.

113 Carlton, *Court of Orphans*, p. 67.

114 CALSS, ZMB/7a, fols 40d–41d.

115 CALSS, ZMB/7a, fol. 41.

116 CALSS, ZMB/7a, fol. 41.

117 Caroline M. Barron, *London in the Later Middle Ages: Government and People 1200–1500* (Oxford: Oxford University Press, 2004), p. 270.

118 Sylvia L. Thrupp, *The Merchant Class of Medieval London, 1300–1500* (Chicago: Chicago University Press, 1948), p. 107.

119 TNA, C1/1238/69.

120 William Ferguson-Irvine (ed.), *A Collection of Lancashire and Cheshire Wills not now to be found in any probate registry 1302–1752* (London: Lancashire and Cheshire Record Society, 1896), p. 191.

121 Ferguson-Irvine (ed.), *Lancashire and Cheshire Wills*, p. 183.

122 Ferguson-Irvine (ed.), *Lancashire and Cheshire Wills*, p. 89.

123 Ferguson-Irvine (ed.), *Lancashire and Cheshire Wills*, p. 201.

124 TNA, C1/408/3.

125 No reference given. Cited in Keith Wrightson, *Earthly Necessities: Economic Lives in Early Modern Britain* (New Haven, CT: Yale University Press, 2000), p. 63.

126 Wrightson, *Earthly Necessities*, p. 63.

127 CALSS, EDC2/5/21–22.

128 King, 'Punishment for Bastardy', p. 132.

129 Lynch and others (eds), *Life, Love and Death*, pp. 190, 192, 199–200.

130 LRO, QSR 4/32.

131 LRO, QSR 5/15.

132 King, 'Punishment for Bastardy', p. 132.

133 LRO, QSR5/22.

134 LRO, QSR 4/28.

135 King, 'Punishment for Bastardy', p. 139.

136 Maddern, '"Oppressed by Utter Poverty"', p. 58.

137 BIA, CP.G.1521.

138 BIA, CP.G.1521.

139 BIA, CP.G.1521.

140 The Rising of the North or The Earls' Rebellion, was a campaign headed by the Earls of Northumberland and Westmoreland in late 1569 to free the imprisoned Mary Queen of Scots and to restore Catholicism to England.

141 BIA, CP.G.1521.

142 Margaret Pelling, *The Common Lot: Sickness, Medical Occupations, and the Urban Poor in Early Modern England* (London and New York: Longman, 1998), pp. 110–1.

143 BIA, HC.CP.ND/2. (Dates of court case, 1570–76).

144 Gowing, *Common Bodies*, p. 182.

145 BIA, HC.CP.ND/2.

146 DUSC, DDR/EJ/CCD/1/2, fols 288, 288ᵛ.

147 Pinchbeck and Hewitt, *Children in English Society*, I, 201.

148 DUSC, DDR/EJ/CCD/1/2, fol. 288ᵛ.

149 DUSC, DDR/EJ/CCD/1/2, fol. 183ᵛ. (Dated between 1565 and 1573).

150   Hindle, *On the Parish*, p. 67.
151   Bland, Brown and Tawney (eds), *Select Documents*, p. 366.
152   See LRO, QSR 4/35d, for the case of Margaret Howarth from Manchester whose daughter was cared for by Daniell Briggs.
153   Paul Slack (ed.), *Poverty in Early-Stuart Salisbury* (Devizes: Wiltshire Record Society, 1975), p. 22.
154   Pelling, *Common Lot*, pp. 145–6.
155   Marjorie K. McInstosh, 'Local Responses to the Poor in Late Medieval and Tudor England', *Continuity and Change*, 3 (1988), 209–45 (p. 232).
156   Slack (ed.), *Poverty in Early-Stuart Salisbury*, p. 67.
157   CALSS, QSPT 20.
158   CALSS, QSF 27/89.
159   CALSS, QSF 35/58.
160   Paul Slack, 'Great and Good Towns 1540–1700', in Peter Clark (ed.), *The Cambridge Urban History of Britain, Vol. II 1540–1840* (Cambridge: Cambridge University Press, 2000), pp. 347–76 (p. 367).
161   Robert Allen, *A Treatise of Christian Beneficence and That Like Christian Thankefulnesse Which is Due to the Same* (London, 1600), p. 127.
162   CALSS, QSF 35/57.
163   EYLA, B27, fol. 133^v.
164   Tim Wales, 'Poverty, poor relief and life-cycle: Some evidence from seventeenth-century Norfolk', in Richard M. Smith (ed.), *Land, Kinship and Life-Cycle* (Cambridge: Cambridge University Press, 1984), pp. 351–404 (pp. 352–3).
165   York authorities often awarded the maintenance directly to the child, as in the case of Thomas and Mary Waite above, p. 190.
166   Wales, 'Poverty, poor relief and life-cycle', p. 352.
167   Crawford, *Parents of Poor Children*, pp. 52–9.
168   Archer, *Pursuit of Stability*, pp. 195–7.
169   Pound (ed.),*Norwich Census*, p. 43; p. 29.
170   Slack (ed.), *Poverty in Early-Stuart Salisbury*, p. 66.
171   DUSC, Northumberland Act Book, DDR/EJ/CCA/3/2, fol. 38^v.
172   Orme, *Medieval Children*, p. 91.
173   EYLA, B18, fol. 38^v. (Recorded between 1536 and 1548).
174   EYLA, B23, fol. 38^v.
175   Slack (ed.), *Poverty in Early-Stuart Salisbury*, pp. 30–1.
176   James Tait (ed.), *Lancashire Quarter Session Records, vol. 1: Quarter Session Rolls 1590–1606* (Chetham Society, 1917), p. 189.
177   EYLA, B29, fol. 20.
178   CALSS, QSE 5/123.
179   CALSS, QSE 5/123.
180   Crawford, *Parents of Poor Parents*, p. 136.
181   Cited in Arthur V. Judges (ed.), *The Elizabethan Underworld: A collection of Tudor and early Stuart tracts and ballads telling of the lives and misdoings of vagabonds, thieves, rogues and cozeners, and giving some account of the operation of the criminal law* (London: George Routledge & Sons, 1930), p. 107.
182   James A. Sharpe, *Crime in Early Modern England 1550–1750* (London and New York: Longman, 1999), pp. 141–50.
183   Snell and Millar, 'Lone-Parent Families', p. 397.
184   Peter Laslett, 'Family, Kinship and Collectivity as Systems of Support in Pre-industrial Europe: A Consideration of the "Nuclear Hardship" Hypothesis', *Continuity and Change*, 3 (1988), 153–75.
185   Hugh Cunningham, 'Histories of Childhood', *American Historical Review*, 103 (1998), 1195–208 (p. 1204).
186   Kroll, 'Concept of Childhood', p. 385.

Conclusion

This book has been concerned with analysing childrearing practices and their effects on children's life experiences in northern England during the period 1450–1603. It aimed to address four major issues and questions: how did pre-modern adults access and conceptualise what was good and bad nurture? What was the effect of these notions on children's experiences? What sort of family and household contexts were responsible for raising children? Did notions and practices of nurture and neglect change over the period of the Reformation?

As has been shown by this study, approaches to childcare in sixteenth-century northern England displayed a number of notable features in relation to the manner and the context in which the care was given. Nurturing a child did not just consist of feeding, clothing and sheltering, but included the socialisation of the child within the household, with a strong emphasis on moral education. Children were taught to know their place within the family by the inculcation of manners, particularly at the table, where children were taught to be respectful of the authority of their parents and other adults present. Further, adults considered the best environment in which to raise a child to be that of the authoritative, patriarchal household. The placement of a child into a household where care was given by others – routinely done in child marriage, apprenticeship, schooling and care arrangements for the parentally deprived child – demonstrates the importance sixteenth-century adults ascribed to the appropriate socialisation of children in an authoritative household – whether parental or not – as part of their nurture.

How did pre-modern adults access and conceptualise what was good and bad nurture? As Chapter 2 identifies, adults were able to access ideas of what was good and bad nurture in a number of ways. Both the Church and printed advice literature offered a theoretical ideal of childcare: the Church based its advice on ecclesiastical law while advice literature concentrated on the moral instruction of the child with an emphasis on religion, manners and discipline. Legal records provide evidence of the concepts of nurture and neglect as they appear in practice during the period. This study has shown that, unlike present-day understandings, which see expressions of love and affection of parents towards their children as nurture, sixteenth-century notions involved diverse connotations depending upon the source and context. They ranged from providing the basic support of food, clothing and housing to ensuring a child was soundly beaten in order that they learnt more effectively.

Advice on nurture differed according to the age of the child. Parents of children up to the age of seven years were counselled by the Church to protect their infants from the dangers of fire, water and overlaying. Supervision of children related only to these three hazards and thereby notions of good nurture in canonical advice revealed themselves through definitions of neglect. Supervision of children around dangers other than fire, water and overlaying were not discussed by canonical sources, although the reality was that there were many more dangers that we would consider 'neglect' today from which children needed protection. Unlike current notions of nurture where supervision of small children to protect them from danger is one of the criteria of 'good nurture', in the sixteenth century it was only the immobile, helpless infant who required constant looking after. Young, mobile children were expected to wander and play freely, relying on nothing more than obedience as a means to stop them doing what they should not.

For the older child, physical punishment comprised a significant part of nurture. Advice literature advocated that it was essential to instil obedience and deference into the child. Batty, Becon, Vaux and Whitford all advocated correction as an important part of nurture and, in some instances, as important as meat and drink. As Chapters 4 and 5 highlight, beatings were an essential part of nurture for schoolboys and apprentices alike. Parents and other adults responsible for the care of children were instructed to use the rod, which in turn ritualised and thereby normalised the process. Evidence in the legal records demonstrated that adults agreed beatings were an important part of nurture, but it can also be discerned when beatings were unjustified. The use of terms such as 'unmercifully' by witnesses in cases concerning the abuse of apprentices indicate that there was a reasonable degree of punishment that could be considered 'merciful' and thus punishment was expected in order to nurture the child. Beatings, therefore, were discipline, not violence.

The evidence from legal sources offers a different interpretation on the meaning of nurture. Maintenance orders from ecclesiastical and secular courts used in Chapter 6 reveal a predominant notion that nurture was to comprise only food, clothing and housing. The emotional well-being of the child – an essential consideration in the care of the modern-day child – was never considered by authorities. Poor parents and authorities had conflicting ideas about appropriate nurture and its goals. Authorities understood that children from poor families provided for their own nurture, most often by begging, but maintenance orders specifically forbade the child from begging while the order was in place, regardless of their age. As my cost analysis in Chapter 6 shows, the monetary amounts awarded by the courts were woefully inadequate to maintain a child. Parents and carers had to adopt a number of expedients, the most common of which was begging, to provide even the basic nurture the courts thought sufficient for the child. Like Gilbert Bulman's widow in

Newcastle, who 'stodd charged' with looking after her own and a relative's children, any adult that did not take their parenting duties seriously and allowed their children to beg were guilty of neglect. From the authorities' viewpoint, this showed a deep disrespect to authority and, worse still, children were not acquiring skills to be able to work for a living.

Not only did poor parents and authorities have conflicting ideals but they also had conflicting ideas about realistic possibilities given the circumstances. Authorities could not empathise that, when faced with being unable to afford to feed and clothe a child, parents turned to desperate measures in order to ensure their child was adequately looked after. For instance, abandonment of babies in busy, urban environments was one means to ensure the survival and nurturing of the child. This did not mean, however, that there was an absence of emotional attachment between parent and child, just that parents knew the child would be quickly found and was assured of care. Authorities viewed this act as 'unmotherly' and grossly negligent, publicly condemning any parents who did so. There were, however, occasions when a consensus of opinion between authorities and individuals can be detected. These same criteria of what basic nurture should be allowed both individuals and authorities to recognise neglect by identifying children who were not clothed or housed properly. In some instances, this recognition of neglect moved authorities to provide for the child so that its basic needs would be met.

The pluralities of interpretations of nurture and neglect adults held in the sixteenth century indicate that definitions of these concepts varied across social class. This 'social essentialism', whereby members of the same social categories share essential characteristics like values and attitudes, is formed by experience and interactions with other people from the same social group.[1] Therefore, whatever notions people held they had a significant effect upon the experiences of the children for whom they were responsible.

What was the effect of these notions on girls' and boys' experiences? There was a diverse experience of childcare in sixteenth-century northern England and the widest variation depended upon the social status of the child. In poorer families, ensuring even basic support for a child was sometimes beyond parents' ability. The life-cycle poverty they experienced meant that they were not always able to support the children within their households and parents frequently had to adopt several survival expedients in order to provide that nurture. Among the options were begging, reliance on charity and poor relief. When carers were unable to work, poor relief provided a means by which the family could be fed, without which these children could not survive. Katherine Robenson's grandchildren were likely to have starved for want of food if they did not receive money from the poor rates in Chester. But poor relief was only a temporary respite and there was also an understanding that children had a responsibility to provide for their own care.

Children were often sent out to work in order to earn money to supplement the wages of the adults in the household. In some instances, poorer children exercised agency in relation to the nurture they provided for themselves.

Many were found in the company of unrelated adults wandering and begging, despite having a living parent or relative in another town. Often, they made a deliberate choice as to which household they lived in as well as the means by which they supported themselves as is shown by the parentally deprived children discussed in Chapter 6. Maud Preece lived in no less than four strange households, relying on charity, begging and stealing in an attempt to provide for herself. The suggestion here is the exploitation of poor children by adults, but Maud chose to move around various situations as and when it suited her. Social status by itself, however, did not always determine children's experiences. The age of the child also played a part.

For the most part, younger children from poorer families were at greater risk from the belief that supervision was not necessary except in cases of fire, water and overlaying. Children of both sexes were allowed to play freely in the streets, where dangers of passing wagons, horses, being accosted by strangers and suchlike were ignored. Young children were also left unsupervised inside the home but it was only those dangers postulated as perilous by the Church that were prosecuted by ecclesiastical authorities should there have been an accident. Older children also had a considerable amount of freedom, often being allowed to bathe unsupervised near fast-flowing water, despite the dangers it entailed. We can never be certain of the actual total number of cases in which children went unsupervised in dangerous situations, for unless the practice resulted in a particularly bad accident or the death of a child it was unlikely to come to official notice. The most important point is that in almost none of the records is there any evidence that parents, or communities, thought that it was at all unusual or reprehensible that children should be allowed such precarious independence. In fact, authors of paediatric manuals recommended parents give their children plenty of freedom. John Jones thought parents who paid too much attention to their children 'unreasonable'. By 'coddling' them they stopped the child from becoming resilient and self-reliant. Freedom was desirable to condition the child to become independent.

Obedience and deference to authority were qualities initiated in domestic environments from an early age and were fundamental to all adult–child relationships. The socialisation process, for boys at least, was continued outside the home in the setting of the school and the master's household. Scholars were taught to be obedient under the supervision of the schoolmaster who enforced the school rules by means of control and discipline. For apprentices, their indentures contained specific clauses underlining the fact that they were to obey their masters at all times and behave towards them 'lowly and reverently'. For those scholars and apprentices who rebelled against authority, the most effective way for them to see the error of their ways was to discipline them through punishment. The use of the rod was a necessary part of school life and the equivalent must have existed for apprentices. Witnesses mentioned 'unreasonable' weapons in relation to the beatings of apprentices, which implies that they considered some weapons to be reasonable and therefore acceptable to use for disciplining purposes.

For wealthier girls, obedience was an equally, if not more, important part of their nurture. They were taught obedience alongside modesty at home and punishment was as forthcoming for girls as it was for boys if they did not respect the authority of the household. Mothers were commonly the disciplinarians for all girls in the household and could be just as forceful as men when it came to meting out punishment. Evidence is lacking of how poor girls were socialised, but we might assume that there was a tacit understanding of the behaviour expected of them and of the punishments should they not conform. For all children, regardless of status, knew their place within the family.

Teaching children to know their place in the family and to put the interests of the family before their own applied to all children regardless of status and gender. Poorer children were expected to work both inside and outside the household to contribute to the family economy, as the discussion in Chapter 6 emphasises. The expectation that children from wealthier families were to put their family before their own wishes is demonstrated most clearly in the practice of child marriage discussed in Chapter 3. Children went ahead with these unions despite their unhappiness at the prospect of the marriage because they understood the implications for their family if they did not. Often these marriages were arranged for economic reasons, and the financial security of the family rested upon the child agreeing to go to the church and exchange vows. At other times, the child did not wish to displease their parents by going against their wishes. Of course, many of the children married under age were too young even to question their parents' decisions but the majority of children understood that relationships were built upon expectations rather than emotional attachment. This was evident in the obedience and deference children showed towards their parents when acquiescing to their wishes. Children did, however, exercise agency after their marriages and demonstrated resistance to them. They often refused to be in the same household as their spouse, at times leaving to live with relatives. In extreme cases like that of Thomas Smith, his father was forced to send Thomas's wife, Anne, away to stay with friends because of Thomas's objections. The children in underage marriages may have gone through with the ceremony, conforming and obeying outwardly, but through their actions they ensured that the marriage would never be ratified.

What sort of family and household contexts were responsible for raising children? Children in sixteenth-century northern England received care in a number of contexts, many of which were outside of their biological households. This study has shown that children were resident in the homes of family members other than their parents, as well as in those of unrelated adults. Surrogate families were a common arrangement in the care of orphans, apprentices, boarding for schooling purposes, child marriage, illegitimate children and reciprocal arrangements between poorer households. Evidence suggests that, for the most part, these arrangements worked well and children were well cared for. Chapter 3 has shown how children married under age were one of the most mobile groups of the period. Once married, it was common for one of the children to relocate to the home of their father-in-law, moving from one authoritative, patriarchal household to another. This was generally the oldest irrespective of gender. The responsibility of nurturing the child was then transferred to the new family. The child, however, remained obedient to their own parents as well as being obedient to those of their spouse. In most instances, these children were treated as part of the family, often being referred to in affectionate terms by their spouse's family members. Furthermore, child marriage did not lessen childhood experiences. Children were not expected to behave as husband or wife and fulfil marital obligations as adults were. They were treated according to their place in the life-cycle and their status; boys were sent off to school, service and apprenticeship and all children continued with childhood arrangements such as sharing beds with servants and siblings.

Parentally deprived children lived in a variety of households. Orphaned children were frequently domiciled with the male authority figures of brothers, uncles and grandfathers but it was not uncommon for households to contain unrelated children as well. Imploring letters to civic authorities from householders often cited a 'fatherless child' or the 'kepinge of an infant' that was not their own as a reason they should be excused from payment of poor rates. Charity must have played a part here, as the cost of caring for the children was described as being met by the petitioners who provided the children with meat, drink, clothes and, at times, learning of some sort. On occasions, courts appointed an unrelated adult to care for illegitimate children, but this was a financial and short-lived arrangement, part of long-term provision, which saw the child return to one of its parents after the agreed term. Private arrangements existed for the care of illegitimate and otherwise parentally deprived children, but the evidence we have of their experiences within these contexts is not always positive, coming as it does from court cases highlighting the neglect children suffered at the hands of the adults charged with their care. The account of Jane Umfrey's illegitimate baby, who was dressed in rags and badly burnt by its carers, should leave the reader in no doubt that the child was poorly treated and cost played a major part in this neglect. Authorities recognised the minimum amount of money a poor person needed to be able to survive, and privately arranged surrogate care often involved amounts well below this benchmark. The lower the amount of maintenance paid for a child, the greater the risk of that child being neglected and not being provided with adequate nurture. Babies and small children were at the mercy of their carers, but older children could, at times, exercise agency when they were unhappy with the care they received from their surrogate parents.

Masters had a duty to look after their apprentices in sickness and in health. Indentures stated that masters were not only to provide instruction but also to attend to the apprentice's physical and moral needs. It has been shown that when masters failed to fulfil their obligations in regards to the care they should provide apprentices turned to the courts, family and friends to challenge the authority of the master in order to guarantee their own welfare. Existing research on apprenticeship shows that apprentices in the north of England were no different to those in the south in this respect. At times it was lack of instruction that comprised the neglect of care of the apprentice, as in the case of Katherine Preston's son, but at others the situation was more serious. The plight of Thomas Lincolne, who was not given any instruction or clothing by his master in addition to enduring excessive beatings and being thrown into prison, demonstrates one extreme of possible lack of care a child in a surrogate household could experience. While families did their best to ensure that the apprentice received justice, the courts were reluctant to break the indenture and thus challenge the magisterial relationship. Yet, even when formally subordinated to the authority of their masters, apprentices were capable of challenging that authority in regards to their own interests.

Did notions and practices of nurture and neglect change over the period of the Reformation? In all topics under discussion, this study has shown that it has been possible to observe continuity in adult attitudes towards children and childcare throughout the era. The socialisation of the child, particularly in regards to putting the needs of the family above those of the child and a stress on the obedience and deference of the child to authority remained defining characteristics in the nurture of all children from 1450 to 1603. The guidance offered by the Church remained constant throughout the period of this book mainly because the Reformation did not alter the central elements of ecclesiastical jurisdiction and so the teaching of the Church was not adjusted. The advice offered in the didactic literature also displays a remarkable resilience to change. Many of the childrearing ideas from the fifteenth century and earlier were reproduced throughout the sixteenth, suggesting that they remained pertinent. The advice was, however, revised and adapted over time to suit different audiences. These consistencies are also observable in practices employed by adults. Babies continued to be routinely wet-nursed and swaddled and to lie in cradles; the practices of child marriage, apprenticeship and schooling for boys continued unchanged for older children. Apples remained the bribe of choice for most parents and adults.

Where we see the greatest alteration in practice is in relation to poorer children, but the Reformation did not directly bring this about. Instead, increasing legislation generated by successive Tudor governments affected the ways in which children were managed and treated. The change in the record keeping – namely, the increased quantity and quality – that accompanied the statutes means that we are more aware of the experiences of poor children. For example, 18 Elizabeth I, c 3, passed in 1576, stipulated that the courts were responsible for establishing the maintenance of illegitimate children by their parents and for giving directives as to who was to care for them. The resultant entries in Quarter Session files have left us with written evidence of who was responsible for the nurture of a child in addition to how much money the primary carer of that child received to cover the expenses related to their upbringing. In 1597, 39 Elizabeth I, c 3 created Overseers of the Poor, who were given the task of setting to work all children whose parents the overseers thought were not able to keep them. Rates were levied upon all non-poor inhabitants of every parish in order to pay for these children to be apprenticed. Not only were children forcibly separated from their parents but also the parish had to pay for them to be so. These principles were reinforced by 43 Elizabeth I, c 2 in 1601. From all these statutes we can see attitudes towards children by authorities reflected in social policy. All agree that children should be provided for, but the responsibility for the care of the poor child ceased to be solely the responsibility of the parents or their connections and friends and moved to a collective responsibility shared by all the community.

Overall, the experiences of children in the north of England in the sixteenth century did not appear to differ greatly from those of children from the south of the country. Evidence offered in this study from Devizes, Norwich, London and Salisbury reflect similar experiences to those children from the north. There is one exception and that is what appears to be the frequent occurrence of child marriage in the north. But, as remarked upon in Chapter 3, this childhood experience cannot be assumed to be a particularly northern phenomenon due to the lack of research on the subject in other parts of the country. Further inquiry is required into child marriage in other regions of England to establish the extent of the practice across the country as a whole.

The analysis of childrearing practices and their effects on children's life experiences in this study has at times been challenging due to the paucity of the sources. However, this is a common problem in social history and one encountered for all subordinate groups. It has been necessary to piece together fragmentary evidence and read sources against the grain to discern the echo of children's voices. This study has proven that children were not a voiceless group in the sixteenth century but did frequently make themselves heard in the testimony of others. The same argument in regards to sources is relevant to the issue of children's agency. My evidence has established that children did exercise agency in their relationships with adults, frequently thinking and acting for themselves. There is, however, more work to be done by historians to uncover the voices and experiences of children, not only in the north but also in all regions of England, by widening the nature of the documents to be examined. If we narrow our sources to specific types of archives such as letters and diaries, then we are in danger of never being able to know the experiences of a significant proportion of the children in sixteenth-century England. By widening the type of sources analysed, we can then be assured of writing a more judicial history of children's experiences as well as understanding the reasoning behind them.

Note

1 Sandra R. Waxman, 'Social Categories are Shaped by Social Experience', *Trends in Cognitive Science*, 6 (2012), pp. 531–2.

Bibliography

Archival sources

Borthwick Institute for Archives

Cause Papers:
CP.G
CP.H
DC.CP
HC.CP, ND.2

Cheshire Archives and Local Studies Services

Consistory Court Depositions: EDC2/1–9
Quarter Session Examinations: QSE 5
Quarter Session Files: QSF 20, 24, 27, 35, 48
Quarter Session Petitions: QSPT 7, 20
Coroners' Inquests: QCI/6
Mayors Books: ZMB 7a, 28a

Cumbria Record Office, Kendal

Marriage Settlement, 20 November 31 Elizabeth I, WDU/Box/50/1/1

Durham Cathedral Archives

Court Book of the Prior's Official DCD off. bk, 1487–98

Durham University Special Collections

Archdeaconry Act Book: DCD/D/SJA/1
Bishop's Registers and Act Book: DDR/EA/ACT/1/2
Consistory Court Depositions: DDR/EJ/CCD/1/1, 2, 4, 7
Northumberland Act Book: DDR/CCA/3/2
Visitation Book 1577–1587: DDR/EV/VIS/1/1

Lancashire Record Office

Quarter Session Rolls: QSR 1, 4, 5, 6
Marriage Agreement between Edmund Trafford and John Booth: DDTR/BOX29/10

Liverpool Record Office

Liverpool Town Books 352 MIN/COU, Book 1
Liverpool Town Books 352 MIN/COU, Book 2

The National Archives, Kew

Early Chancery Petitions: C1
Petitions in the Time of Elizabeth I: C2/Eliz

Explore York Libraries and Archives

Archbishop Holgate's Free Grammar School York, Class E Book 21K
City of York Catalogue of the Charters, House Books, Freeman's Rolls, Chamberlain's
    etc., Accounts and other Books, Deeds and Old Documents, belonging to The
    Corporation of York; together with Report on their Renovation, compiled by William
    Giles, Deputy Town Clerk
Corporation House Books Class B: Books 2–30
Register of Apprentice Indentures Class D Book 12

Printed primary sources

Alcock, John, 'Sermon for a Boy Bishop, c. 1489–1491', in Mary C. Erler (ed.),
    Records of Early English Drama: Ecclesiastical London (London: British Library;
    Toronto: University of Toronto Press, 2008), pp. 238–47.
Allen, Robert, *A Treatise of Christian Beneficence and That Like Christian Thankefulnesse
    Which is Due to the Same* (London, 1600).
Anon., *A glasse for housholders, wherin that they may se, both howe to rule them selfes
    & ordre their housholde verye Godly and frutfull* (London: in officina Richard
    Graftoni, 1542).
Anon., 'Indenture of an Apprentice, 1535', *Transactions of the Historic Society of
    Lancashire and Cheshire*, 91(1939), 218.
Arber, E. (ed.), *A Transcript of the Registers of the Company of Stationers of London,
    1554–1640 A.D.*, 5 vols (London, 1875–94).
Ascham, Roger, *The Scholemaster: Or plaine and perfite way of teaching children, to
    vnerstand, write, and speake, the Latin tong, but specially purposed for the private
    bringing vp of youth in Intlemen and Noble mens houses, and comm. Also for all such,
    as haue forgot the Latin tongue etc.* (London, 1570).
Aubrey, John, *'Brief Lives', Chiefly of Contemporaries, set down by John Aubrey,
    between the years 1669 & 1696, vol. 1*, (ed.) Andrew Clark (Oxford: Clarendon
    Press, 1898).
Aughterson, Kate (ed.), *Renaissance Woman: A Sourcebook. Constructions of Femininity
    in England* (London and New York: Routledge, 1995).
Barnum, Priscilla Heath (ed.), *Dives and Pauper, vol. i, Part 1* (London: Oxford
    University Press for the Early English Text Society, 1976).
Bateson, M. (ed.), *Borough Customs, vol. ii* (London: Seldon Society, 1906).
Batty, Bartholomew, *The Christian's Man's Closet*, (trans.) William Lowth (London,
    1581).
Becon, Thomas, *The Catechism of Thomas Becon, S. T. P. Chaplain to Archbishop
    Cranmer, Prebendary of Canterbury, &c. With Other Pieces Written by Him in the*

Reign of King Edward the Sixth, (ed.) John Ayre, vol. II (Cambridge: Cambridge University Press, 1844).

Bennett, J. H. E. and J. C. Dewhurst (eds), *Quarter Session Records With Other Records of the Justices of the Peace for the County Palatinate of Chester, 1559–1760* (Manchester: Lancashire and Cheshire Record Society, 1940).

Bland, A. E., P. A. Brown and R. H. Tawney (eds), *English Economic History: Select Documents* (London: G. Bell & Sons, 1925).

Bond, Ronald B. (ed.), *Certain Sermons or Homilies (1547) and a Homily against Wilful Rebellion (1570): A Critical Edition* (Toronto: University of Toronto, 1987).

Boyle, J. R. and F. W. Dendy (eds), *Extracts from the Records of the Merchant Adventurers of Newcastle-upon-Tyne, vol. i* (Durham: Surtees Society, 1895).

Bullard, J. V. and H. Chalmer Bell (eds), *Lynwood's Provinciale: The text of the canons therein contained, reprinted from the translation made in 1534* (London: Faith Press, 1929).

Bullinger, Henry, *The Golden Book of Christian Matrimony* (trans.) Miles Coverdale (London, 1542).

Chambers, R. W. and M. Daunt (eds), *A Book of London English 1384–1425* (Oxford: Clarendon Press, 1931).

Cleaver, Robert, *A Godly Forme of Hovsholde Government: For The Ordering of Private Families, according to the direction of Gods word* (London, 1614).

Cockburn, J. S. (ed.), *Calendar of Assize Records, Hertfordshire Indictments, James I* (London: H. M. S. O., 1975).

Davies, Matthew (ed.), *The Merchant Taylors' Company of London: Court Minutes 1486–1493* (Stamford: Paul Watkins, 2000).

Davies, Norman (ed.), *The Paston Letters: A Selection in Modern Spelling* (London: Oxford University Press, 1963).

Davies, Norman (ed.), *Paston Letters and Papers of the Fifteenth Century, Part I* (Oxford: Clarendon Press, 1971).

Earwaker, E. J. (ed.), *An Index to the Wills and Inventories Now Preserved in the Court of Probate, Chester from A.D. 1545–1630* (Manchester: Lancashire and Cheshire Record Society, 1879).

Edgeworth, Roger, *Sermons very fruitfull, godly, and learned, preached and sette foorth by Maister Roger Edgeworth, doctoure of diuinitie, canon of the cathedrall churches of Sarisburie, Welles and Bristow, residentiary in the cathedrall churche of Welles, and chauncellour of the same churche: with a repertorie or table, directinge to many notable matters expressed in the same sermons* (London, 1557).

Elyot, Thomas, *The Boke Named the Governour* (1531; Menston: Scolar Press, 1970).

Erler, Mary C. (ed.), *Records of Early English Drama: Ecclesiastical London* (London: British Library; Toronto: University of Toronto Press, 2008).

Erasmus, Desiderius, *The ciuilitie of childehode with the discipline and instruction of children distributed in small and compe[n]dious chapters* (trans.) Thomas Paynell (London, 1560).

Ferguson-Irvine, William (ed.), *A Collection of Lancashire and Cheshire Wills not now to be found in any probate registry 1302–1752* (London: Lancashire and Cheshire Record Society, 1896).

Fishwick, H. (ed.), *A List of the Lancashire Wills Proved at the Archdeaconry of Richmond and not Preserved in Somerset House, London From A.D. 1457 to 1680 and of Abstracts of Lancashire Wills (Belonging to the Same Archdeaconry) in the*

British Museum from A.D. 1531 to 1652 (Manchester: Lancashire and Cheshire Record Society, 1884).

Fishwick, H. (ed.), *Pleadings and Depositions in the Duchy of Lancaster, Time of Edward VI and Philip and Mary* (Manchester: Lancashire and Cheshire Record Society, 1899).

Fitson, William, *The Schoole of good manners. Or, A new Schole of Vertue; teaching children & youth how they ought to behave themselues in all companies, times, and places* (London, 1595).

Forman, Simon, *The Autobiography and Personal Diary of Dr Simon Forman, 1552–1602*, (ed.) James Orchard Halliwell (London, 1849).

Foxe, John, *The Acts and Monuments of John Foxe* (ed.) Josiah Pratt (London: Religious Tract Society, 1877).

Furnivall, Frederick J., *Child Marriages, Divorces, and Ratifications in the Diocese of Chester, A.D. 1561–6* (New York: Kraus Reprint, 1973).

Furnivall, Frederick J. (ed.), *Tell-Trothes New-Years Gift etc.* (London, 1876).

Furnivall, Frederick J. (ed.), *The babees book: Aristotle's A B C. Urbanitatis. Stans puer ad mensam. The lytille childrenes lytil boke. The bokes of nurture of Hugh Rhodes and John Russell. Wynkyn de Worde's Boke of keruynge. The booke of demeanor. The boke of curtasye. Seager's Schoole of vertue, &c. &c. with some French & Latin poems on like subjects, and some forewords on education in early England* (New York: Greenwood Press, 1969).

Goldberg, P. J. P. (trans. and ed.), *Women in England c. 1275–1525: Documentary Sources* (Manchester: Manchester University Press, 1995).

Gouge, William, *Of Domesticall Duties Eight Treatises* (London, 1622).

Halliwell, James Orchard (ed.), *The Private Diary of John Dee, and The Catalogue of his Library of Manuscripts, from the original manuscripts* (New York: Johnson Reprint Corporation, 1842).

Hatt, Cecilia A. (ed.), *English Works of John Fischer, Bishop of Rochester (1469–1535): Sermons and Other Writings, 1520–1535* (Oxford: Oxford University Press, 2002).

Horn, J. (ed.), *Captain John Smith Writings with other Narratives of Roanoke, Jamestown, and the First English Settlement of America* (New York: Library of America, 2007).

Horrocks, J. W., *Assembly Books of Southampton, vol. II* (Oxford: Oxford University Press, 1920).

Houlbrooke, Ralph (ed.), *English Family Life 1576–1716: An Anthology from Diaries* (Oxford: Basil Blackwell, 1989).

Johnson, H. C., *Wiltshire County Records: Minutes of the proceedings in sessions 1563 and 1564 to 1592* (Devizes: Wiltshire Archaeological and Nat Hist Society, Records Branch, 1949).

Jones, John, *The Arte and Science of preseruing Bodie and Soule in al Health, Wisedome, and Catholike Religion: Phisically, Philosopically, and Diuinely deuised* (London, 1579).

Joubert, Laurent, *Popular Errors* (trans. and annotated) Gregory David De Rocher (Tuscaloosa: University of Alabama Press, 1989).

Judges, A. V. (ed.), *The Elizabethan Underworld: A collection of Tudor and early Stuart tracts and ballads telling of the lives and misdoings of vagabonds, thieves, rogues and cozeners, and giving some account of the operation of the criminal law* (London: George Routledge & Sons, 1930).

Kirby, Joan (ed.), *The Plumpton Letters and Papers* (London: Cambridge University Press for the Royal Historical Society, 1996).

Leslie, Shane and Ronald A. Knox (eds), *The Miracles of King Henry VI* (Cambridge: Cambridge University Press, 1923).

Lynch, Margaret *et al.* (ed.), *Life, Love and Death in North-East Lancashire: A translation of the Act Book of the Ecclesiastical Court of Whalley* (London: Chetham Society, 2006).

McNeil, John T., and Helena M. Gamer (eds), *Medieval Handbooks of Penance: A translation of the principal libri poenitentiales and selections from related documents* (New York: Columbia University Press, 1938, 1990).

More, Hannah, *Path to Riches and Happiness. To which are added, The Apprentice's Monitor or Indentures in Verse: and, the Market Woman; or Honesty is the Best Policy, a True Tale* (Dublin: William Watson, 1810).

Morey, Adrian, *Bartholomew of Exeter Bishop and Canonist: A Study in the Twelfth Century* (Cambridge: University Press, 1937).

Mulcaster, Richard, *Positions Wherin Those Primitive Circvmstances Be Examined, Which Are Necessarie For The Training vp of Children, either for skill in their booke, or health in their bodie* (London, 1581; New York: Da Capo Press, 1971).

Myrc, John, *Instructions For Parish Priests*, (ed.) Edward Peacock (New York: Kraus Reprint, 1975).

Nelson, William (ed.), *A Fifteenth Century School Book from a manuscript in the British Museum MS Arundel 249* (Oxford: Clarendon Press, 1956).

Phayer, Thomas, *The Regiment of life, whervnto is added a treatyse of the pestilence, with the booke of children newly corrected and enlarged* (London, 1545).

Phiston, William, *The Schoole of good manners or, a new Schoole of Vertue, teaching children & youth how they ought to behave themselues in all companies, times, and places* (trans.) W. F. Phiston (London, 1895).

Plutarch, *The education or bringinge vp of children* (trans.) Thomas Elyot (London, 1532).

Pound, John F. (ed.), *The Norwich Census of the Poor, 1570* (Norwich: Norfolk Record Society, 1971).

Purvis, J. S. (ed.), *Tudor Parish Documents* (Cambridge: Cambridge University Press, 1948).

Raine, Angelo (ed.), *York Civic Records VIII* (York: Yorkshire Archaeological Society, 1953).

Raine, J. (ed.), *Depositions and Other Ecclesiastical Proceedings from the Courts of Durham Extending from 1311 to the Reign of Elizabeth* (London: Surtees Society, 1845).

Raine, J. (ed.), *The Injunctions and other Ecclesiastical Proceedings of Richard Barnes, Bishop of Durham, from 1576 to 1587* (London: Surtees Society, 1850).

Raithby, John (ed.), *The Statutes at Large of England and of Great Britain: From the Magna Carta to the Union of the Kingdoms of Great Britain and Ireland, vol. III* (London, 1811).

Rhodes, Hugh, *The boke of Nurture, or Schoole of good maners: for men, Seruants, and children, with Stans puer ad mensam. Newly corrected, very necessary for all youth and children* (London, 1577).

Salter, Thomas, *A mirrhor mete for all mothers, matrons, and maidens, intituled the Mirrhor of Modestie no lesse profitable and pleasant, then necessarie to bee read and practiced* (London, 1579).

Sandys, Edwin, *The Sermons of Edwin Sandys, D.D., to which are added some miscellaneous pieces by the same author* (ed.) John Ayre (Cambridge: Cambridge University Press, 1842).

Shakespeare, William, *The Tragedy of Othello The Moor of Venice* (ed.) Christopher Bentley (Sydney: Sydney University Press, 1982).

Slack, Paul (ed.), *Poverty in Early-Stuart Salisbury* (Devizes: Wiltshire Record Society, 1975).

Smith, William and John Lockwood, *Chambers Murray Latin–English Dictionary* (Edinburgh: Chambers; London: J. Murray, 1976)

Sneyd, C. A. (ed.), *A relation or rather a true account of the island of England; with sundry particulars of the custom* (London: Camden Society, 1847).

Stanbridge, John, *The Vulgaria of John Stanbridge and the Vulgaria of Robert Whittinton* (ed.) Beatrice White (Oxford: Early English Text Society, 1971).

Starkey, Thomas, *A Dialogue between Reginald Pole & Thomas Lupset* (ed.) Kathleen M. Burton; (preface) E. M. W. Tillyard (London: Chatto & Windus, 1948).

Stubbes, Philip, *The Anatomie of Abuses* (ed.) J. M. Kidnie (London, 1538; Tempe, AZ: Arizona Center for Medieval and Renaissance Studies/ Renaissance Text Society, 2002).

Swinburne, Henry, *Treatise of Spousals or Matrimonial Contracts* (New York: Garland, 1985).

Taite, James (ed.), *Lancashire Quarter Session Records, Vol. 1: Quarter Session Rolls 1590–1606* (London: Chetham Society, 1917).

Tawney, R. H. and Eileen Power (eds), *Tudor Economic Documents, Being Select Documents Illustrating the Economic and Social History of Tudor England*, 3 vols (London: Longman, 1924).

Tilley, Morris P. (ed.), *A Dictionary of the Proverbs of England in the Sixteenth and Seventeenth Centuries: A Collection of the Proverbs Found in English Literature and the Dictionaries of the Period* (Ann Arbor: University of Michigan Press, 1950).

Thomas of Chobham, *Summa Confessorum* (ed.) Frederick Broomfield (Paris: Beatrice-Nauwelaerts, 1968).

Twemlow, J. A. (ed.), *Liverpool Town Books: Proceedings of Assemblies, Common Councils, Portmoot Courts, etc., 1550–1862*, 2 vols (Liverpool: University of Liverpool, 1918–)

Tyndale, William, *The Obedience of a Christian Man* (1528; Menston: Scolar Press, 1970).

Vaux, Laurence, *A catechisme or Christian doctrine necessarie for children and ignorante people, briefly compiled by Laurence Vaux ... with an other later addition of instruction of the laudable ceremonies vsed in the catholike churche. VVhereunto is adioyned a brief forme of confession* (Rouen: George Olyselet, 1583).

Vives, Juan Luis, *The Education of a Christian Woman: A Sixteenth-Century Manual* (ed. and trans.) Charles Fantazzi (Chicago: University of Chicago Press, 2000).

Whitford, Richard, *A werke for housholders/ or for them [that] have the gydynge or gouernaunce of any company* (London, 1533).

Newspapers

The Manchester Guardian, 9 March 1885.

Secondary sources

Adair, Richard, *Courtship, Illegitimacy and Marriage in Early Modern England* (Manchester: Manchester University Press, 1996).

Adler, Franz, 'The Value Concept in Sociology', *American Journal of Sociology*, 62 (1956), 272–9.

Alexandre-Bidon, Danièle and Didier Lerr, *Children in the Middle Ages* (trans.) Jody Gladding (Notre Dame, IN: University of Notre Dame Press, 1999).

Ali, Nujood with Delphine Minoui, *I Am Najood Ali, Age 10 and Divorced* (New York: Three Rivers, 2010).

Amussen, Susan Dwyer, *An Ordered Society: Gender and Class in Early Modern England* (New York: Columbia University Press, 1988).

Anglin, Jay P., *The Third University: A Survey of Schools and Schoolmasters in the Elizabethan Diocese of London* (Norwood, PA: Norwood Editions, 1985).

Archer, Ian, *The Pursuit of Stability: Social Relations in Elizabethan London* (Cambridge: Cambridge University Press, 1991).

Ariès, Philippe, *Centuries of Childhood* (London: Jonathan Cape, 1962).

Attreed, Lorraine C., *York House Books, 1461–1490, vol. 1* (Phoenix Mill: Alan Sutton, 1991).

Bailey, Merridee L., 'In Service and at Home: Didactic Texts for Children and Young People, c. 1400–1600', *Parergon*, 24(2007), 23–46.

Bailey, Merridee L., 'Between the Household and the School: Socialising the Child in England, c. 1400–1600' (unpublished Ph.D. thesis, Australian National University, 2008).

Bailey, Merridee L., *Socialising the Child in Late Medieval England c. 1400–1600* (York: York Medieval Press, 2012).

Baker, J. H., 'Introduction', in J. H. Baker (ed.), *Legal Records and the Historian: Paper Presented to the Cambridge Legal History Conference, 7–10 July 1975, and in Lincoln's Inn Old Hall on 3 July 1974* (London: Royal Historical Society, 1978), pp. 1–6.

Barron, Caroline, 'The Education and Training of Girls in Fifteenth-Century London', in Diana E. S. Dunn (ed.), *Courts, Counties and the Capital in the Later Middle Ages* (New York: St Martin's Press, 1996), pp. 139–53.

Barron, Caroline, 'The Education and Training of Girls in Fifteenth-Century London', in Caroline Barron (ed.), *London in the Later Middle Ages: Government and People 1200–1500* (Oxford: Oxford University Press, 2004).

Barry, Jonathan, 'Introduction', in Jonathan Barry and Christopher Brooks (eds), *The Middling Sort of People: Culture, Society and Politics in England, 1550–1800* (Basingstoke: Macmillan, 1994), pp. 1–27.

Bartlet, Steve, Diana Burton and Nick Peim, *Introduction to Education Studies* (London: Paul Chapman, 2001).

Beattie, Cordelia, 'Single Women, Work, and Family: The Chancery Dispute of Jane Wynde and Margaret Clerk', in Michael Goodich (ed.), *Voices from the Bench: The Narratives of Lesser Folk in Medieval Trials* (New York and Basingstoke: Palgrave Macmillan, 2006), pp. 177–202.

Beattie, Cordelia, 'Economy', in Sandra Cavallo and Silvia Evangelisti (eds), *A Cultural History of Childhood and Family in the Early Modern Age* (Oxford and New York: Berg, 2010), pp. 49–67.

Beddel, John, 'Memory and Proof of Age in England 1272–1327', *Past & Present*, 162 (1999), 3–27.

Ben-Amos, Ilana Krausman, 'Women Apprentices in the Trades and Crafts of Early Modern Bristol', *Continuity and Change*, 6(1991), 227–52.

Ben-Amos, Ilana Krausman, 'Failure to Become Freemen: Urban Apprenticeship in Early Modern England', *Social History*, 16(1991), 155–72.

Ben-Amos, Ilana Krausman, *Adolescence and Youth in Early Modern England* (New Haven, CT: Yale University Press, 1994).

Ben-Amos, Ilana Krausman, 'Reciprocal Bonding: Parents and Their Offspring in Early Modern England', *Journal of Family History*, 25(2000), 291–312.

Ben-Amos, Ilana Krausman, 'Community', in Sandra Cavallo and Silvia Evangelisti (eds), *A Cultural History of Childhood and Family in the Early Modern Age* (Oxford and New York: Berg, 2010), pp. 33–48.

Bindoff, Stephen T., 'The Making of the Statute of Artificers', in S. T. Bindoff, J. Hurstfield and C. H. Williams (eds), *Elizabethan Government and Society: Essays presented to Sir John Neale* (London: Athlone Press, 1961), pp. 56–94.

Black, Jeremy and Donald D. MacRaild, *Studying History* (Houndmills: Palgrave, 2000).

Boswell, John, *The Kindness of Strangers: The Abandonment of Children in Western Europe from Late Antiquity to the Renaissance* (New York: Pantheon, 1988).

Braddick, Michael J. and John Walter, 'Introduction: Grids of Power: Order, Hierarchy and Subordination in Early Modern Society', in Michael J. Braddick and John Walter (eds), *Negotiating Power in Early Modern Society: Hierarchy and Subordination in Britain and Ireland* (Cambridge: Cambridge University Press), pp. 1–42.

Brigden, Susan, 'Youth and the English Reformation', *Past & Present*, 95(1982), 37–67.

Brooke, Christopher N. L., *The Medieval Idea of Marriage* (Oxford: Oxford University Press, 1989).

Brooks, Christopher, 'Apprenticeship, Social Mobility and the Middling Sort, 1550–1800', in Jonathan Barry and Christopher Brooks (eds), *The Middling Sort of People: Culture, Society and Politics in England, 1550–1800* (Basingstoke: Macmillan, 1994), pp. 52–83.

Broomhall, Susan, 'Emotions in the Household', in Susan Broomhall (ed.), *Emotions in the Household, 1200–1900* (Basingstoke: Palgrave Macmillan, 2008), pp. 1–37.

Brundage, J. A., 'Legal Aid for the Poor and the Professionalization of the Law in the Middle Ages', *Journal of Legal History*, 9(1988), 169–79.

Burns, Edward, *The Chester Mystery Cycle: A New Staging Text* (Liverpool: Liverpool University Press, 1987).

Burns, Richard, *Ecclesiastical Law with Notes and References by Simon Fraser, Esq., vol. i* (London, 1809).

Burns, K. R., 'The Administrative System of the Ecclesiastical Courts in the Diocese and Province of York: The Medieval Courts' (unpublished paper, Borthwick Institute, 1952).

Burrow, J. A., *The Ages of Man: A Study in Medieval Writing and Thought* (Oxford: Clarendon Press, 1986).

Calvert, Karin, *Children in the House: The Material Culture of Early Childhood, 1600–1900* (Boston: Northeastern University Press, 1992).

Carlson, Eric J., *Marriage and the English Reformation* (Oxford: Blackwell, 1994).

Carlton, Charles, *The Court of Orphans* (Leicester: Leicester University Press, 1974).

Cavallo, Sandra, 'Family Relationships', in Sandra Cavallo and Silvia Evangelisti (eds), *A Cultural History of Childhood and Family in the Early Modern Age* (Oxford and New York: Berg, 2010), pp. 15–32.

Cavallo, Sandra, 'Introduction', in Sandra Cavallo and Silvia Evangelisti (eds), *A Cultural History of Childhood and Family in the Early Modern Age* (Oxford and New York: Berg, 2010), pp. 1–14.

Cambers, Andrew, *Godly Reading: Print, Manuscript and Puritanism in England, 1580–1720* (Cambridge: Cambridge University Press, 2011).

Coppel, Stephen, 'Willmaking on the Deathbed', *Local Population Studies*, 40(1988), 37–45.

Clark, Elaine, 'City Orphans and Custody Laws in Medieval England', *American Journal of Legal History*, 34(1990), 167–87.

Clark, Elaine, 'Mothers at Risk of Poverty in the Medieval Countryside', in John Henderson and Richard Wall (eds), *Poor Women and Children in the European Past* (London and New York: Routledge, 1994), pp. 139–59.

Collinson, Patrick, *The Birthpangs of Protestant England: Religious and Cultural Change in the Sixteenth and Seventeenth Centuries* (Basingstoke: Macmillan, 1988).

Clark, Peter, 'The Migrant in Kentish Towns 1580–1640', in Peter Clark and Paul Slack (eds), *Crisis and Order in English Towns: Essays in Urban History* (London: Routledge & Kegan Paul, 1972), pp. 117–163.

Crawford, Patricia, 'The Construction and Experience of Maternity in Seventeenth-Century England', in Valerie Fildes (ed.), *Women as Mothers in Pre-Industrial England* (London and New York: Routledge, 1990), pp. 3–38.

Crawford, Patricia, *Parents of Poor Children in England, 1580–1800* (Oxford: Oxford University Press, 2010).

Cressy, David, 'Educational Opportunity in Tudor and Stuart England', *History of Education Quarterly*, 16(1976), 301–20.

Cunningham, Hugh, *Children and Childhood in Western Society Since 1500* (Harlow: Longman, 1995).

Cunningham, Hugh, 'Histories of Childhood', *American Historical Review*, 103(1998), 1195–204.

Darnton, Robert, *The Great Cat Massacre and Other Episodes in French Cultural History* (New York: Vintage Books, 1985).

Davies, Kathleen M., 'The Sacred Condition of Equality: How Original Were Puritan Doctrines of Marriage?' *Social History*, 2(1977), 563–80.

Davies, Margaret G., *The Enforcement of English Apprenticeship: A Study in Applied Mercantilism, 1563–1642* (Cambridge, MA: Harvard University Press, 1956).

Davis, Natalie Zemon, *Fiction in the Archives: Pardon Tales and their Tellers in Sixteenth-century France* (Stanford: Stanford University Press, 1987).

Deal, L. K., 'Widows and Reputation in the Diocese of Chester, England, 1550–1650', *Journal of Family History*, 23(1998), 382–92.

Demaitre, Luke, 'The Idea of Childhood and Child Care in Medical Writings of the Middle Ages', *Journal of Psychohistory*, 4(1977), 461–90.

DeMause, Lloyd, 'The Evolution of Childhood', in Lloyd deMause (ed.), *The History of Childhood* (New York: Harper & Row, 1975).

DeMause, Lloyd, *Foundations of Psychohistory* (New York: Creative Roots, 1982).

Dent, K. S. (ed.), *Informal Agencies of Education: Proceedings of the 1977 Annual Conference of the History of Education of Great Britain* (Leicester: History of Education Society, 1979).

Dodd, Gwylim, 'The Rise of English, the Decline of French: Supplications to the English Crown, c. 1420–1450', *Speculum*, 86(2011), 117–50.

Dodd, Gwylim, 'Trilingualism in the Medieval English Bureaucracy: The Use – and Disuse – of Languages in the Fifteenth-Century Privy Seal Office', *Journal of British Studies*, 51(2012), 253–83.

Donahue Charles, Jr., 'Proof by Witness in the Church Courts of Medieval England: An imperfect Reception of the Learned Law', in M. S. Arnold, T. A. Green, S. Scully and S. D. White (eds), *On the Laws and Customs of England: Essays in*

Honor of Samuel E. Thorne (Chapel Hill: University of North Carolina Press, 1981), pp. 127–58.

Donahue Charles, Jr., 'Female Plaintiffs in Marriage Cases in the Court of York in the Later Middle Ages: What Can We Learn form the Numbers?', in S. Sheridan (ed.), *Wife and Widow in Medieval England* (Ann Arbor: University of Michigan Press, 1993), pp. 183–213.

Donahue Charles, Jr., *The Records of the Medieval Ecclesiastical Courts: Reports of the Working Group on Church Court Records, II: England* (Berlin: Dunker & Humblot, 1994).

Dronzek, Anna, 'Gendered Theories of Education in Fifteenth-Century Conduct Books', in Kathleen Ashley and Robert L. A. Clark (eds), *Medieval Conduct* (Minneapolis: University of Minnesota Press, 2001), pp. 135–59.

Dunlop, Jocelyn O. and Denman, Richard D., *English Apprenticeship and Child Labour: A History with A Supplementary Section on the Modern Problem of Juvenile Labour* (London: Fisher Unwin, 1912).

Emmison, F. G. and Irvine, Gray, *County Records (Quarter Sessions, Petty Sessions, Clerk of the Peace and Lieutenancy)* (London: Historical Association, 1961).

Epstein, S. R., 'Apprenticeships and Technological Change in Pre-Industrial Europe', in S. R. Epstein and Maarten Prak (eds), *Guilds, Innovation and the European Economy, 1400–1800* (Cambridge: Cambridge University Press, 2008), pp. 52–80.

Erickson, Amy L., *Women and Property in Early Modern England* (London and New York: Routledge, 1993).

Farrer, William and J. Brownbill (eds), *The Victoria History of the County of Lancashire, vol. ii* (London: Archibald Constable, 1908).

Fentress, James and Chris Wickham, *Social Memory* (Oxford and Cambridge, MA: Blackwell, 1992).

Fildes, Valerie, 'Maternal Feelings Re-assessed: Child Abandonment and Neglect in London and Westminster, 1550–1800', in Valerie Fildes (ed.), *Women as Mothers in Pre-Industrial England* (London and New York: Routledge, 1990), pp. 139–78.

Finacune, Ronald C., 'The Toddler in the Ditch: A Case of Parental Neglect?' in Michael Goodich (ed.), *Voices from the Bench: The Narratives of Lesser Folk in Medieval Trials* (New York and Basingstoke: Palgrave Macmillan, 2006), pp. 128–48.

Fletcher, Anthony, *Growing up in England: The Experience of Childhood 1600–1914* (New Haven, CT: Yale University Press, 2008).

Fowler, R. C., 'Legal Proofs of Age', *English Historical Review*, 22(1907), 101–3.

Foyster, Elizabeth A.,'Silent Witness? Children and the Breakdown of Domestic and Social Order in Early Modern England', in A. Fletcher and S. Hussey (eds), *Childhood in Question: Children, Parents and the State* (Manchester: Manchester University Press, 1990), pp. 57–73.

Foyster, Elizabeth A., 'Parenting Was for Life, Not Just for Childhood: The Role of Parents in the Married Lives of their Children in Early Modern England', *History*, 86(2001), 313–327.

Fox, Adam, *Oral Literature Culture in England 1500–1700* (Oxford: Oxford University Press, 2000).

Fulbrook, Mary, *Historical Theory* (London and New York: Routledge, 2002).

Garrison, Mary, 'The Study of Emotions: Some Starting Points', *Early Medieval Europe*, 10. 2(2001), 243–250.

Gelles, Richard J., 'What to Learn from Cross-Cultural and Historical Research on Child Abuse and Neglect: An Overview', in Richard J. Gelles and Jane B. Lancaster (eds), *Child Abuse and Neglect: Biosocial Dimensions* (New York: Aldine de Gruyter, 1987), pp. 15–55.

Geertz, Clifford, *The Interpretations of Cultures: Selected Essays* (London: Fontana, 1993).

Gibbs, Gary G., 'Child-Marriages in the Diocese of Chester, 1561–1565', *Journal of Regional and Local Studies*, 8(1988), 32–42.

Glaisyer, Natasha and Sara Pennell, 'Introduction', in Natasha Glaisyer and Sara Pennell (eds), *Didactic Literature in England 1500–1800: Expertise Constructed* (Aldershot: Ashgate, 2003), pp. 1–18.

Goddard, Richard, 'Female Apprentices in the West Midlands in the Later Middle Ages', *Midland History*, 27(2002), 165–81.

Goldberg, P. J. P., 'Marriage, Migration, Servanthood and Life-Cycle in Yorkshire Towns of the later Middle Ages: Some York Cause Paper Evidence', *Continuity and Change*, 1(1986), 141–69.

Goldberg, P., *Women, Work and Life Cycle in a Medieval Economy: Women in York and Yorkshire c. 1300–1520* (Oxford: Clarendon Press, 1992).

Goldberg, P., 'Girls Growing up in Later Medieval England', *History Today*, 45(1995), 25–32.

Goldberg, P., 'Fiction in the Archives: The York Cause Papers as a Source for Later Medieval Social History', *Continuity and Change*, 12(1997), 425–45.

Goldberg, P., 'Migration, Youth and Gender in Later Medieval England', in P. J. P. Goldberg and F. Riddy (eds), *Youth in the Middle Ages* (York: York Medieval Press, 2004) pp. 85–99.

Goldberg, P., 'Childhood and Gender in Later Medieval England', *Viator*, 39(2008), 249–62.

Goldberg, P., *Communal Discord, Child Abduction and Rape in Later Middle Ages* (New York and Basingstoke: Palgrave Macmillan, 2008).

Goody, Jack, *The Development of the Family and Marriage in Europe* (Cambridge: Cambridge University Press, 1983).

Gordon, E. C., 'Accidents Among Medieval Children as Seen from the Miracles of Six English Saints and Martyrs', *Medical History*, 35.2(1991), 145–63.

Gowing, Laura, *Domestic Dangers: Women, Words, and Sex in Early Modern London* (Oxford: Clarendon Press, 1996).

Gowing, Laura, *Common Bodies: Women, Touch and Power in Seventeenth-Century England* (New Haven, CT: Yale University Press, 2003).

Gowing, Laura, 'Giving Birth at the Magistrate's Gate: Single Mothers in the Early Modern City', in Stephanie Tarbin and Susan Broomhall (eds), *Women, Identities and Communities in Early Modern Europe* (Aldershot: Ashgate, 2008), pp. 137–50.

Green, J. R., Mrs, *Town Life in the Fifteenth Century, vol. ii* (New York and London: Macmillan and Co., 1907).

Griffiths, Paul, *Youth and Authority: Formative Experiences in England 1560–1640* (Oxford: Clarendon Press, 1996).

Haigh, Christopher, *Reformation and Resistance in Tudor Lancashire* (Cambridge: Cambridge University Press, 1975).

Haigh, Christopher, 'Slander and the Church Courts in the Sixteenth Century', *Transactions of the Lancashire and Cheshire Antiquarian Society*, 78(1975), 1–13.

Hajnal, John, 'Two Kinds of Pre-Industrial Household Formation', in Richard Wall, Jean Robin and Peter Laslett (eds), *Family Forms in Historic Europe* (Cambridge: Cambridge University Press, 1983), pp. 65–104.

Hajnal, John, 'European Marriage Patterns in Perspective', in D. V. Glass and E. C. Eversley (eds), *Population in History* (London: Edward Arnold, 1965), pp. 101–43.

Hanawalt, Barbara, 'Childrearing among the Lower Classes of Late Medieval England', *Journal of Interdisciplinary History*, 8(1977), 1–22.

Hanawalt, Barbara, *The Ties that Bound: Peasant Families in Medieval England* (New York: Oxford University Press, 1986).

Hanawalt, Barbara, *Growing up in Medieval London* (New York: Oxford University Press, 1993).

Hanawalt, Barbara, *Of Good and Ill Repute: Gender and Social Control in Medieval England* (Oxford: Oxford University Press, 1998).

Hanawalt, Barbara, 'Medievalists and the Study of Childhood', *Speculum*, 77(2002), 440–60.

Harris, B. E. (ed.), *The Victoria History of the Counties of England: A History of Cheshire, vol. iii* (London: Institute of Historical Research/ Oxford University Press, 1980).

Haskett, Timothy S., 'The Presentation of Cases in Medieval Chancery Bills', in W. M. Gordon and D. Fergus (eds), *Legal History in the Making: Proceedings of the Ninth British Legal History Conference Glasgow 1989* (London and Rio Grande: Hambledon Press, 1991), pp. 11–21.

Haskett, Timothy S., 'Country Lawyers', in Peter Birks (ed.), *The Life and the Law: Proceedings of the Tenth British Legal History Conference Oxford 1991* (London and Rio Grande: Hambledon Press, 1993).

Hendrick, H., 'The History of Childhood and Youth', *Social History*, 9(1984), 87–96.

Helmholz, R. H., *Marriage Litigation in Medieval England* (Cambridge: Cambridge University Press, 1974).

Helmholz, R., 'Infanticide in the Province of Canterbury During the Fifteenth Century', *History of Childhood Quarterly*, 75(1974–75), 379–90.

Herrstein Smith, Barbara, 'Narrative Versions, Narrative Theories', in W. J. T. Mitchell (ed.), *On Narrative* (Chicago: University of Chicago Press, 1981).

Herrup, Cynthia, *A House in Gross Disorder: Sex, Law and the 2nd Earl of Castlehaven* (New York and Oxford: Oxford University Press, 1999).

Heywood, Colin, *A History of Childhood: Children and Childhood in the West from Medieval to Modern Times* (Cambridge: Polity, 2001).

Hill, Christopher, *Society and Puritanism in Pre-Revolutionary England* (London: Secker & Warburg, 1964).

Hilton, R. H., 'Review of Calendar of Inquisitions Post Mortem, XV, 1–7 Richard II (1970)', *English Historical Review*, 88(1973), 170–1.

Hindle, Steve, *On The Parish? The Micro-Politics of Poor Relief in Rural England c. 1550–1750* (Oxford: Clarendon Press, 2004).

Hindle, Steve, *On The Parish? The Micro-Politics of Poor Relief in Rural England c. 1550-1750* (Oxford: Clarendon Press, 2004).

Hindle, Steve, '"Waste" Children? Pauper Apprenticeship under the Elizabethan Poor Laws, c. 1598–1697', in Penelope Lane, Neil Raven and K. D. M. Snell (eds), *Women, Work and Wages in England, 1600–1850* (Woodbridge and Rochester: Boydell, 2004), pp. 15–46.

Hockaday, F. S., 'The Consistory Court of the Diocese of Gloucester', *Transactions of the Bristol and Gloucestershire Archaeological Society*, 46(1924), 195–287.

Houlbrooke, Ralph A., *The English Family 1450–1700* (London: Longman, 1984).

Houlbrooke, Ralph A., *Church Courts and the People During the English Reformation* (Oxford: Oxford University Press, 1979).

Houlbrooke, Ralph A., 'The Decline of Ecclesiastical Jurisdiction under the Tudors', in Rosemary O'Day and Felicity Heal (eds), *Continuity and Change: Personnel and Administration of the Church of England 1500–1642* (Leicester: Leicester University Press, 1976), pp. 239–57.

Hovland, Stephanie, 'Apprenticeship in Later Medieval London (c. 1300–c. 1530)' (unpublished Ph.D. thesis, Royal Holloway, University of London, 2006).

Hudson, Pat, *History by Numbers: An Introduction to Quantitative Approaches* (London: Arnold, 2000).

Hull, Suzanne W., *Chaste Silent and Obedient: English Books for Women 1475–1640* (San Marino: Huntingdon Library, 1982).

Hunnisett, R. F., 'The Reliability of Inquisitions as Historical Evidence', in D. A. Bullough and R. L. Storey (eds), *The Study of Medieval Records: Essays in honour of Kathleen Major* (Oxford: Clarendon Press, 1971), pp. 206–35.

Hunt, D., *Parents and Children in History: The Psychology of Family Life in Early Modern France* (New York and London: Basic, 1970).

Hurnard, Naomi D., *The King's Pardon for Homicide before 1307 A.D.* (Oxford: Clarendon Press, 1969).

Ingram, Martin, *Church Courts, Sex and Marriage in England, 1570–1640* (Cambridge: Cambridge University Press, 1987).

Ingram, Martin, 'Child Sexual Abuse in Early Modern England', in Michael J. Braddick and John Walter (eds), *Negotiating Power in Early Modern Society: Order, Hierarchy and Subordination in Britain and Ireland* (Cambridge: Cambridge University Press, 2001), pp. 63–84.

James, E., 'Childhood and Youth in the Early Middle Ages', in P. J. P. Goldberg and Felicity Riddy (eds), *Youth in the Middle Ages* (York: York Medieval Press, 2004) pp. 11–23.

James, Susan, *Passion and Action: The Emotions in Seventeenth-Century Philosophy* (Oxford: Clarendon Press, 1999).

Jarman, Emerlinda K. M., 'An Edition of the Depositions from EDC 2/6, Deposition Book of the Consistory Court of Chester, September 1558–March 1558–9' (unpublished Master's thesis, University of Liverpool, 2010).

Jewell, Helen M., 'The Bringing up of Children in Good Learning and Manners: A Survey of Secular Education provision in the North of England, c. 1350–1550', *Northern History*, 18(1982), 1–25.

Johansson, Sheila R., 'Neglect, Abuse, and Avoidable Death: Parental Investment and the Mortality of Infants and Children in the European Tradition', in Richard J. Gelles and Jane B. Lancaster (eds), *Child Abuse and Neglect: Biosocial Dimensions* (New York: Aldine de Gruyter, 1987), pp. 57–93.

Jones, W. J., *The Elizabethan Court of Chancery* (Oxford: Clarendon Press, 1967).

Jordan, Wilbur K., *Philanthropy in England 1480–1660* (London: Allen & Unwin, 1959).

Jordan, Wilbur K., *The Charities of Rural England, 1480–1660* (London: Allen & Unwin, 1961).

Jordanova, Ludmilla, 'Children in History: Concepts of Nature and Society', in G. Scarre (ed.), *Children, Parents and Politics* (Cambridge: Cambridge University Press, 1989), pp. 3–24.

Jordanova, Ludmilla, 'New Worlds for Children in the Eighteenth Century: Problems of Historical Interpretation', *History of the Human Sciences*, 3(1990), 69–83.

Jordanova, Ludmilla, *History in Practice* (London: Arnold, 2000).

Kellum, Barbara, 'Infanticide in England in the Middle Ages', *History of Childhood Quarterly*, 1(1974), 367–388.

Kemp, Eric, 'Review of Arthur J. Willis (ed.), *Winchester Consistory Court Depositions, 1561–1602* (1960)', *Journal of Ecclesiastical History*, 14(1965), 266.

King, Walter J., 'Punishment for Bastardy in Early Seventeenth-Century England', *Albion*, 10.2(1978), 130–151.

Knuuttila, Simo, *Emotions in Ancient and Medieval Philosophy* (Oxford: Oxford University Press, 2004).

Kroll, Jerome, 'The Concept of Childhood in the Middle Ages', *Journal of the History of Behavioural Sciences*, 13(1977), 393–4.

Kussmaul, Ann, *Servants in Husbandry in Early Modern England* (Cambridge: Cambridge University Press, 1981).

Lane, Joan, *Apprenticeship in England 1600–1914* (London: UCL Press, 1996).

Langer, William L., 'Foreword', in Lloyd deMause (ed.), *The History of Childhood* (New York: Harper & Row, 1975), pp. vii–viii.

Laslett, Peter, *The World We Have Lost* (London: Methuen, 1965).

Laslett, Peter, 'The Comparative History of Household and Family', *Journal of Social History*, 4(1970), 75–87.

Laslett, Peter, 'Introduction: Comparing Illegitimacy over time and between cultures', in P. Laslett, K. Oosterveen and R. Smith (eds), *Bastardy and its Comparative History* (London: Edward Arnold, 1980), pp. 1–68.

Laslett, Peter, 'The Bastardy-Prone Sub-Society', in P. Laslett, K. Oosterveen and R. Smith (eds) *Bastardy and its Comparative History* (London: Edward Arnold, 1980), pp. 217–46.

Laslett, Peter, *Family Life and Illicit Love in Earlier Generations* (Cambridge: Cambridge University Press, 1983).

Laslett, Peter, 'Family, Kinship and Collectivity as Systems of Support in Pre-Industrial Europe: A Consideration of the "Nuclear Hardship" Hypothesis', *Continuity and Change*, 3(1988), 153–75.

Laslett, Peter, and Karla Oosterveen, 'Long-term Trends in Bastardy in England: A Study of Illegitimacy Figures in the Parish Registers and in the Reports of the Registrar General, 1561–1960', *Population Studies*, 27(1973), 255–86.

Laughton, Jane, *Life in a Late Medieval City: Chester 1275–1520* (Oxford: Windgather, 2008).

Lawson, John and Harold Silver, *A Social History of Education in England* (London: Methuen, 1973).

Leach, Arthur F., *English Schools at the Reformation 1546–8* (New York: Russell & Russell, 1896).

Levene, Alysa, *Childcare, Health and Mortality at the London Foundling Hospital 1741–1800: 'left to the mercy of the world'* (Manchester: Manchester University Press, 2007).

Lipson, Ephraim, *The Economic History of England, vol. I*, 9th edn (London: Adam and Charles Black, 1947).

Loar, Carol, 'Medical Knowledge and the Early Modern English Coroner's Inquest', *Social History of Medicine*, 23(2010), 475–91.

McCarthy, Conor, *Marriage in Medieval England: Law, Literature and Practice* (Woodbridge and Rochester: Boydell, 2004).

McClure, Ruth K., *Coram's Children: The London Foundling Hospital in the Eighteenth Century* (New Haven, CT: Yale University Press, 1981).

MacFarlane, Alan, 'Review of The Family, Sex and Marriage in England 1500–1800 by Lawrence Stone', *History and Theory*, 18(1979), 103–26.

MacFarlane, Alan, 'Illegitimacy and Illegitimates in English History', in P. Laslett, K. Oosterveen and R. Smith (eds), *Bastardy and its Comparative History* (London: Edward Arnold, 1980), pp. 71–85.

MacFarlane, Alan, *Marriage and Love in England: Modes of Reproduction 1300–1840* (Oxford and New York: Blackwell, 1986).

McIntosh, Marjorie K., 'Local Responses to the Poor in Late Medieval and Tudor England', *Continuity and Change*, 3(1988), 209–45.

McIntosh, Marjorie K., 'Servants and the Household in an Elizabethan Community', *Journal of Family History*, 9(1984), 3–23.

McIntosh, Marjorie K., 'Networks of Care in Elizabethan English Towns: The Example of Hadleigh, Suffolk', in Peregrine Horden and Richard Smith (eds), *The Locus of Care: Families, Communities, Institutions and the Provision of Welfare Since Antiquity* (London and New York: Routledge, 1998), pp. 71–89.

McIsaac Cooper, Sheila, 'Servants as Educators in Early-Modern England', *Paedagogica Historica*, 43(2007), 547–63.

McLaughlin, J., 'Medieval Child Marriage: Abuse of Wardship?', Paper delivered at Conference on Medieval Studies, April 1997 at Plymouth State College, Plymouth, New Hampshire.

McLaughlin, Mary M., 'Survivors and Surrogates: Children and Parents from the Ninth to the Thirteenth Centuries', in Lloyd deMause (ed.), *The History of Childhood* (New York: Harper & Row, 1975), pp. 101–81.

McLaughlin, R. Emmet, 'Truth, Tradition and History: The Historiography of High/ Late Medieval and Early Modern Penance', in Abigail Firey (ed.), *A New History of Penance*, (Leiden, Boston: Brill, 2008), pp. 19–71

McSheffrey, Shannon, *Love and Marriage in Late Medieval London* (Kalamazoo, MI: TEAMS, 1995).

McSheffrey, Shannon, *Marriage, Sex, and Civic Culture in Late Medieval London* (Philadelphia: University of Pennsylvania Press, 2006).

Maddern, Philippa C., 'In myn own house: The Troubled Connections between Servant Marriages, Late-Medieval English Household Communities and Early Modern Historiography', in Susan Broomhall and Stephanie Tarbin (eds), *Identities and Communities in Early Modern Europe* (Aldershot: Ashgate, 2008), pp. 41–59.

Maddern, Philippa C., 'Between Households: Children in Blended and Transitional Households in Late-Medieval England', *Journal of History of Youth and Childhood*, 3(2010), 65–86.

Maddern, Philippa C., '"Oppressed by Utter Poverty": Survival Strategies for Single Mothers and their Children in Late Medieval England', in Anne M. Scott (ed.), *Experiences of Poverty in Late Medieval and Early Modern England and France* (Farnham: Ashgate, 2012), pp. 41–62.

Maddern, Philippa C. and Stephanie Tarbin, 'Life Cycle', in Sandra Cavallo and Silvia Evangelisti (eds), *A Cultural History of Childhood and Family in the Early Modern Age* (Oxford and New York: Berg, 2010), pp. 440–60.

Mayhew, Graham, 'Life-Cycle Service and the Family Unit in Early Modern Rye', *Continuity and Change*, 6(1991), 201–26.

Mechling, Jay, 'Advice to Historians on Advice to Mothers', *Journal of Social History*, 9(1975), 44–63.

Merritt, Julia, 'The Social Context of the Church in Early Modern Westminster', *Urban History*, 18(1991), 20–31.

Mingay, G. E., *The Gentry: The Rise and Fall of a Ruling Class* (London and New York: Longman, 1976).

Minister, Ann, 'Pauper Apprenticeship in South Derbyshire: A Positive Experience?', in Anne M. Scott (ed.), *Experiences of Poverty in Late Medieval and Early Modern England and France* (Farnham: Ashgate, 2012), pp. 64–84.

Mitchell, L. E., *Family Life in the Middle Ages* (Connecticut and New York: Greenwood, 2007).

Mitterauer, Michael and Reinhard Sieder, *The European Family: Patriarchy to Partnership from the Middle Ages to the Present* (Oxford: Basil Blackwell, 1982).

Moir, Esther, *The Justice of the Peace* (Harmondsworth: Penguin, 1969).

Moran, Jo Ann Hoeppner, *The Growth of English Schooling, 1340–1548* (Princeton: Princeton University Press, 1985).

Morris, Rupert H., *Chester in the Plantagenet and Tudor Reigns* (Chester, 1875).

Morris, Colin, 'A Consistory Court in the Middle Ages', *Journal of Ecclesiastical History*, 14(1963), 150–9.

Newall, Fiona, 'Wet Nursing and Child care in Aldenham, Hertfordshire, 1595–1726: Some Evidence on the Circumstances and Effects of Seventeenth-Century Child Rearing Practices', in V. Fildes (ed.), *Women as Mothers in Pre-Industrial England* (London and New York: Routledge, 1990), pp. 122–38.

Nicholson, Geoff, 'Tracing Your Family History in Northumberland and Durham: Apprenticeships', *Journal of the Northumberland and Durham Family History Society*, 26(2001), 43–5.

O'Day, Rosemary, *Education and Society 1500–1800: The Social Functions of Education in Early Modern Britain* (London and New York: Longman, 1982).

O'Day, Rosemary, *The Family and Family Relationships, 1500–1900: England, France and the United States of America* (Basingstoke: Macmillan, 1994).

O'Hara, Diana, 'Ruled by my Friends: Aspects of Marriage in the Diocese of Canterbury, c. 1540–1570', *Continuity and Change*, 6(1991), 9–41.

Orme, Nicholas, *English Schools in the Middle Ages* (London and New York: Methuen, 1973).

Orme, Nicholas, *Early British Swimming 55BC–AD1719: With the First Swimming Treatise in English, 1595* (Exeter: University of Exeter, 1983).

Orme, Nicholas, *Education and Society in Medieval and Renaissance England* (London and Ronceverte: Hambledon Press, 1989).

Orme, Nicholas, 'The Culture of Children in Medieval England', *Past & Present*, 148 (1995), 48–88.

Orme, Nicholas, *Medieval Children* (New Haven, CT: Yale University Press, 2001).

Osborne, Bertram, *Justice of the Peace 1361–1848: A History of the Justices of the Peace for the Counties of England* (Shaftesbury: Sedgehill, 1960).

Owen, Dorothy, 'Ecclesiastical Jurisdiction in England 1300–1550: The Records and their Interpretation', in Derek Baker (ed.), *The Material Sources and Methods of Ecclesiastical History: Papers Read at the Twelfth Summer Meeting and the Thirteenth Winter Meeting of the Ecclesiastical Society* (Oxford: Basil Blackwell, 1975), pp. 199–221.

Ozment, Steven, *When Fathers Rules: Family Life in Reformation Europe* (Cambridge, MA: Harvard University Press, 1983).

Page, William (ed.), *The Victoria History of the Counties of England: A History of Durham, vol. i* (London: Archibald Constable, 1905).

Payne, G. H., *The Child in Human Progress* (New York and London: G. P. Putnam's Sons: 1916).

Pedersen, Frederik, *Marriage Disputes in Medieval England* (London and Ohio: Hambledon Press, 2000).

Pedersen, Frederik, 'Demography in the Archives: Social and Geographical Factors in Fourteenth-Century York Cause Paper Marriage Litigation', *Continuity and Change*, 10(1995), 405–36.

Pelling, Margaret, *The Common Lot: Sickness, Medical Occupations and the Urban Poor in Early Modern England* (London and New York: Longman, 1998).

Pelling, Margaret, 'Apprenticeship, Health and Social Cohesion in Early Modern London', *History Workshop Journal*, 37(1994), 33–56.

Pelling, Margaret, 'Old Age, Poverty, and Disability in Early Modern Norwich: Work, Remarriage and other Expedients', in Margaret Pelling and Richard Smith (eds), *Life, Death and the Elderly: Historical Perspectives* (London and New York: Routledge, 1991), pp. 74–101.

Pfister, Ulrich, 'Craft Guilds, the Theory of the Firm, and Early Modern Proto-industry', in S. R. Epstein and Maarten Prak (eds), *Guilds, Innovation and the European Economy, 1400–1800* (Cambridge: Cambridge University Press, 2008), pp. 25–51.

Pilgrim Trust, *Survey of Ecclesiastical Archives: Report of the Committee appointed by the Pilgrim Trustees in 1946 to carry out a survey of the provincial, archidiaconal and capitular archives of the Church of England* (London:Pilgrim Trust, 1952).

Plutchik, Robert, 'The Nature of Emotions: Human emotions have deep evolutionary routes, a fact that may explain their complexity and provide tools for clinical practice', *American Scientist*, 89(2001), 344–350.

Pollock, Linda A., *Forgotten Children: Parent–Child Relations from 1500–1900* (Cambridge: Cambridge University Press, 1983).

Pollock, Linda A., *With Faith and Physic: The Life of a Tudor Gentlewoman Lady Grace Mildmay 1552–1620* (London: Collins & Brown, 1993).

Poos, L. R., *A Rural Society after the Black Death: Essex 1350–1525* (Cambridge: Cambridge University Press, 1991).

Poos, L., 'Sex, Lies and the Church Courts of Pre-Reformation England', *Journal of Interdisciplinary History*, 25(1995), 585–607.

Postles, Dave, 'Surviving Lone Motherhood in Early-Modern England', *Seventeenth Century*, 21(2006), 160–183.

Phillips, Kim M., *Medieval Maidens: Young Women and Gender in England, 1270–1540* (Manchester: Manchester University Press, 2003).

Pinchbeck, Ivy and Margaret Hewitt, *Children in English Society*, 2 vols (London: Routledge & Kegan Paul, 1969–73).

Powell, Colin L., *English Domestic Relations 1487–1653: A Study of Matrimony and Family Life in Theory and Practice as Revealed by the Literature, Law, and History of the Period* (New York: Russell & Russell, 1917).

Power, Eileen, *Medieval English Nunneries c. 1275 to 1535* (Cambridge: Cambridge University Press, 1922).

Premo, Bianca, *Children of the Father King: Youth, Authority, and Legal Minority in Colonial Lima* (Chapel Hill: University of North Carolina Press, 2005).

Purvis, J. S., *An Introduction to Ecclesiastical Records* (London: St Anthony's Press, 1953).

Pythian-Adams, Charles, *The Desolation of a City: Coventry and the Urban Crisis of the Late Middle Ages* (Cambridge: Cambridge University Press, 1979).

Rathbone, Eleanor, *Child Marriage; The Indian Minotaur an Object-Lesson From the Past to the Future* (London: George & Unwin, 1934).

Richardson, R. C., *Household Servants in Early Modern England* (Manchester: Manchester University Press, 2010).

Riddy, Felicity, 'Mother KnowsBest: Reading Social Change in a Courtesy Text', *Speculum*, 71(1996), 66–86.

Rigby, Stephen H., *English Society in the Later Middle Ages: Class, Status and Gender* (Basingstoke: Macmillan, 1995).

Ritchie, C. J. A., *The Ecclesiastical Courts at York* (Arbroath: Herald Press, 1957).

Roberts, Robert C., 'Thomas Aquinas and the Morality of Emotions', *History of Philosophy Quarterly*, 9(1992), 287–305.

Robertson, D. W., 'Frequency of Preaching in Thirteenth-Century England', *Speculum*, 24(1949), 376–88.

Roper, Lyndal, *Oedipus and the Devil: Witchcraft, Sexuality and Religion in Early Modern Europe* (London and New York: Routledge, 1994).

Rosenthal, Joel T. (ed.), *Essays on Medieval Childhood: Responses to Recent Debates* (Donington: Shaun Tyas, 2007).

Rushton, Peter, 'Property, Power and Family Networks: The Problem with Disputed Marriage in Early Modern England', *Journal of Family History*, 11(1986), pp. 205–19.

Rushton, Peter, 'The Matter in Variance: Adolescents and Domestic Conflict in the Pre-Industrial Economy of Northeast England, 1600–1800', *Journal of Social History*, 25(1991), 87–107.

Ruys, Juanita Feros, 'Introduction: Approaches to Didactic Literature – Meaning, Intent, Audience, Social Effect', in Juanita Feros Ruys (ed.), *What Nature Does not Teach: Didactic Literature in the Medieval and Early-Modern Periods* (Turnhout: Brepols, 2008), pp. 1–38.

Schmidt, Ariadne, 'Survival Strategies of Widows and their Families in Early Modern Holland c. 1580–1750', *History of the Family*, 12(2007), 268–81.

Seaver, Paul S., *Wallington's World: A Puritan Artisan in Seventeenth-Century London* (London: Methuen, 1985).

Shahar, Shulamith, *Childhood in the Middle Ages* (London: Routledge, 1992).

Sharpe, James A., *Defamation and Sexual Slander in Early Modern England: The Church Courts at York* (York: Borthwick Papers, 1980).

Sharpe, James A. *Crime in Early Modern England 1559–1750* (London and New York: Longman, 1999).

Sharpe, Pamela, 'Poor Children as Apprentices in Colyton, 1598–1830', *Continuity and Change*, 6(1991), 253–70.

Sheehan, Michael M., 'The Formation and Stability of Marriage in Fourteenth-Century England: Evidence of an Ely Register', *Mediaeval Studies*, 33(1971), pp. 228–63.

Sheehan, Michael M., 'Choice of Marriage Partner in the Middle Ages: Development and Mode of Application of a Theory of Marriage', *Studies in Medieval and Renaissance History*, 1(1978), 3–33.

Sheehan, Michael M., 'The Formation and Stability of Marriage in Fourteenth-Century England: Evidence of an Ely Register', in J. K. Farge (ed.), *Marriage, Family and Law in Medieval Europe: Collected Studies* (Cardiff: University of Wales Press, 1996), pp. 38–76.

Shorter, Edward, *The Making of the Modern Family* (New York: Basic Books, 1975).

Simon, Joan, *Education and Society in Tudor England* (Cambridge: Cambridge University Press, 1966).

Simon, Joan, *The Social Origins of English Education* (London: Routledge & Paul, 1970).

Simon, Joan, 'Childhood in Earlier Seventeenth-Century England', in K. Dent (ed.), *Informal Agencies of Education: Proceedings of the 1977 Annual Conference of the History of Education of Great Britain* (Leicester: History of Education Society, 1979), pp. 1–27.

Slack, Paul, *Poverty and Policy in Tudor and Stuart England* (London and New York: Longman, 1988).

Slack, Paul, *From Reformation to Improvement: Public Welfare in Early Modern England* (Oxford: Clarendon Press, 1999).

Slack, Paul, 'Great and Good Towns 1540–1700', in Peter Clark (ed.), *The Cambridge Urban History of Britain, Vol. II 1540–1840* (Cambridge: Cambridge University Press, 2000), pp. 347–376.

Smith, C., 'Medieval Coroners' Rolls: Legal Fiction or Historical Fact?', in E. S. Dunn (ed.), *Courts, Counties and the Capital in the later Middle Ages* (New York: St Martin's Press, 1996), pp. 93–115.

Smith, M. G., *Corporations and Society* (London: Duckworth, 1974).

Snell, Keith D. M., 'The Apprenticeship System in British History: The Fragmentation of a Cultural Institution', *History of Education*, 25(1996), 303–12.

Snell, Keith D. and J. Millar, 'Lone-Parent Families and the Welfare State: Past and Present', *Continuity and Change*, 2(1987), 387–422.

Sommerville, C. John, *The Discovery of Childhood in Puritan England* (Athens: University of Georgia Press, 1992).

Spufford, Margaret, 'First Steps in Literacy: The Reading and Writing Experiences of the Humblest Seventeenth-Century Spiritual Autobiographers', in Harvey J. Graff (ed.), *Literacy and Social Development in the West: A Reader* (Cambridge: Cambridge University Press, 1981), pp. 125–50.

Stone, Lawrence, 'The Educational Revolution in England, 1560–1640', *Past & Present*, 28(1964), 41–80.

Stone, Lawrence, *The Family, Sex and Marriage in England, 1500–1800* (New York: Harper & Row, 1977).

Stone, Lawrence, *Road to Divorce: England 1530–1987* (Oxford: Oxford University Press, 1990).

Storey, R. L., 'Ecclesiastical Causes in Chancery', in D. A. Bullough and R. L. Storey (eds), *The Study of Medieval Records: Essays in Honour of Kathleen Major* (Oxford: Clarendon Press, 1971), pp. 236–59.

Stowe, A. Monroe, *English Grammar Schools in the Reign of Queen Elizabeth* (New York: Teachers College, Columbia University, 1908).

Swanson, Heather, 'The Illusion of Economic Structure: Craft Guilds in Late Medieval English Towns', *Past & Present*, 121(1988), 29–48.

Swanson, Jenny, 'Childhood and Childrearing in ad status sermons by later thirteenth century friars', *Journal of Medieval History*, 16(1990), 309–31.

Tadmor, Naomi, *Family and Friends in Eighteenth-Century England: Household, Kinship, and Patronage* (Cambridge: Cambridge University Press, 2004).

Taliga, Kathryn A., 'Marriage's Original Purpose and First Good: Placing Children Within the Medieval Church's Views on Marriage', in J. T. Rosenthal (ed.), *Essays on Medieval Childhood: Responses to Recent Debates* (Donington: Shaun Tyas, 2007), pp. 151–73.

Tarbin, Stephanie, 'Caring for Poor and Fatherless Children in London c. 1350–1550', *Journal of the History of Childhood and Youth*, 3(2010), 391–410.

Tarver, Anne, *Church Court Records: An Introduction for Family and Local Historians* (Chichester: Phillimore, 1995).

Thomas, Keith, *Rule and Misrule in the Schools of Early Modern England* (Reading: University of Reading, 1976).

Thomas, Keith, *History and Literature* (Swansea: University of Swansea, 1988).

Thomas, Keith, 'Children in Early Modern England', in G. Avery and J. Briggs (eds), *Children and their Books* (Oxford: Clarendon Press, 1989), pp. 35–77.

Todd, Margo, 'Humanists, Puritans and The Spiritualized Households', *Church History*, 49(1980), 18–34.

Tosh, John, *The Pursuit of History: Aims, Methods and New Directions in the Study of Modern History*, 5th edn (Harlow and New York: Longman, 2010).

Trankell, Arne, *Reliability of Evidence: Methods for Analysing and Assessing Witness Statements* (Stockholm: Beckmans, 1972).

Trexlor, Richard C., 'Infanticide in Florence: New Sources and First Results', *History of Childhood Quarterly*, 1(1972), 98–116.

Trumbach, R., *The Rise of the Egalitarian Family: Aristocratic Kinship and Domestic Relations In Eighteenth-Century England* (London: Academic Press, 1978).

Thrupp, Sylvia L., *The Merchant Class of Medieval London, 1300–1500* (Chicago: Chicago University Press, 1948).

Tucker, M. J., 'The Child as Beginning and End: Fifteenth and Sixteenth Century English Childhood', in Lloyd deMause (ed.), *The History of Childhood* (New York: Harper & Row, 1975).

Valverde, Lola, 'Illegitimacy and the Abandonment of Children in the Basque Country, 1550–1800', in John Henderson and Richard Wall (eds), *Poor Women and Children in the European Past* (London and New York: Routledge, 1994), pp. 51–64.

Wales, Tim, 'Poverty, Poor Relief and Life-Cycle: Some Evidence from Seventeenth-Century Norfolk', in Richard M. Smith (ed.), *Land, Kinship and Life-Cycle* (Cambridge: Cambridge University Press, 1984), pp. 351–404.

Wall, Richard, 'The Age of Leaving Home', *Journal of Family History*, 3(1978), 181–202.

Wall, Richard, Jean Robin and Peter Laslett (eds), *Family Forms in Historic Europe* (Cambridge: Cambridge University Press, 1983).

Warnicke, Retha M., *Women of the English Renaissance and Reformation* (Westport and London: Greenwood, 1983).

Waxman, Sandra R., 'Social Categories are Shaped by Social Experience', *Trends in Cognitive Science*, 6(2012), 531–2.

White, Hayden, 'The Value of Narrativity in the Representation of Reality', in W. J. T. Mitchell (ed.), *On Narrative* (Chicago: University of Chicago, 1981), pp. 1–23.

Wilson, Adrian, 'The History of the History of Childhood: An Appraisal of Philippe Ariès', *History and Theory*, 19(1980), 132–54.

Wrightson, Keith, 'Infanticide in Earlier Seventeenth-Century England', *Local Population Studies*, 15(1975), 10–22.

Wrightson, Keith, 'Sorts of People in Tudor and Stuart England', in Jonathan Barry and Christopher Brooks (eds), *The Middling Sort of People: Culture, Society and Politics in England, 1550–1800* (Basingstoke: Macmillan, 1994), pp. 28–51.

Wrightson, Keith, *Earthly Necessities: Lives in Early Modern Britain* (New Haven, CT: Yale University Press, 2000).

Wrightson, Keith, and David Levine, *Poverty and Piety in an English Village Terling, 1525–1700* (New York: Academic Press, 1979).

Wrigley, E. A., 'Family Limitation in Pre-Industrial England', *Economic History Review*, 19(1966), 82–109.

Wrigley, E. and Schofield, R. S., *The Population History of England 1541–1871* (Cambridge, Massachusetts: Harvard University Press, 1981).

Yarborough, Anne, 'Apprentices as Adolescents in Sixteenth Century Bristol', *Journal of Social History*, 13(1979), 67–81.

Zelizer, V. A., *Pricing the Priceless Child: The Changing Social Value of Children* (New York: Basic Books, 1985).

Online resources

Dictionary of National Biography: www.oxforddnb.com
King James Bible: www.kingjamesbibleonline.org
Liverpool Victoria: www.lv.com
The National Archives: www.nationalarchives.co.uk
UK Parliament: www.parliament.uk

Index

Page numbers in **bold** refer to tables.